FOUNDATIONS OF MARKETING SERIES

MARKETING IN THE CANADIAN ENVIRONMENT

BRUCE E. MALLEN
Sir George Williams University

in association with
V. KIRPALANI (on Chapters 4, 5 and 12)
and **G. LANE** (on Chapter 11)

P
h
PRENTICE-HALL ♣ OF CANADA LTD.

Scarborough, Ontario

FOUNDATIONS OF MARKETING SERIES

MARKETING IN THE CANADIAN ENVIRONMENT
BRUCE E. MALLEN, V. KIRPALANI and G. LANE

© 1973 by Prentice-Hall of Canada Ltd.
Scarborough, Ontario

Printed in Canada

Library of Congress
Catalog No. 72-7834

0-13-557223-1 (cl.)
0-13-557215-0 (pa.)

1 2 3 4 5   77 76 75 74 73

PRENTICE-HALL, INC., *Englewood Cliffs, New Jersey*
PRENTICE-HALL INTERNATIONAL, INC., *London*
PRENTICE-HALL OF AUSTRALIA, PTY., LTD., *Sidney*
PRENTICE-HALL OF INDIA PVT., LTD., *New Delhi*
PRENTICE-HALL OF JAPAN, INC., *Tokyo*

FOUNDATIONS OF MARKETING SERIES

The Foundations of Marketing is a series of authoritative and concise books prepared to serve the need for teaching materials incorporating the results of recent research and developments in the study and practice of marketing. The structure of the series—its flexibility within unity of purpose—enables the teacher to construct a complete basic marketing course, adjustable to a level of rigor of the teacher's choosing. Certain or all books can be combined to accomplish individual course objectives. Individual books are self-contained, reasonably complete treatments of the fundamental changes taking place in their areas. Students have the benefits of being introduced to the managerial approach to the field and to the socioeconomic process of marketing by authorities actively engaged in study and research in each field.

An overview of the series and of the managerial approach to marketing is provided by

Marketing Planning and Competitive Strategy

Four books treat important aspects of scientific methodology and decision making in marketing.

Consumer Behavior
Marketing Management and the Behavioral Environment
Men, Motives, and Markets
Quantitative Methods in Marketing

Key policy areas of marketing are covered in

Pricing Decisions in Marketing Policy
Product Policy and Strategy
Promotion: A Behavioral View
Sales Management
Channel Management
Marketing Logistics
Organizational Buying Behavior

Important environmental areas in marketing are emphasized in

> *International Marketing, 2nd ed.*
> *Marketing and Public Policy*
> *Marketing in the Canadian Environment*

All books may profitably use as supplements

> *Cases in Marketing Management*
> *Advanced Cases in Marketing Management*
> *History of Marketing*

It is hoped that the series will stimulate independent and intelligent thought about the central issues of marketing analysis and policy and that readers will find the books useful guides to a creative and disciplined approach to meeting complex and changing marketing problems.

EUGENE J. KELLEY, *Editor*

I am indebted to my two associates, Dr. V. Kirpalani and Dr. G. Lane, who have made significant contributions to this book. I am also indebted to Editor Eugene Kelley and Dr. I. A. Litvak of Carleton University for their encouragement and help since the inception of this project some seven years ago. Finally, I would like to express my sincere appreciation to Helen Yeomans of Prentice-Hall, for her editorial assistance.

Bruce Mallen
December, 1972

CONTENTS

PART TWO   THE INTERNAL ENVIRONMENT:
MARKETING PROBLEMS, PRACTICES AND INSTITUTIONS

FOREWORD

Canadian marketing is being influenced by many of the developments affecting marketing policies and strategies in the United States and other countries. One such development is the increased use of more sophisticated measuring techniques; another is the more frequent use made by marketers of behavioral concepts. Marketing is also broadening its concerns. It is acquiring a "social conscience," demonstrated by its increasing sensitivity to social values and responsibilities. MARKETING IN THE CANADIAN ENVIRONMENT provides background for the examination of such developments as they operate in the Canadian context.

Professor Mallen presents a detailed analysis, segment by segment, of the Canadian market as well as furnishing a unique compilation of statistical material. These features make this book useful to the professional marketer as well as to the student. The author has used a comparative analysis throughout, examining the interregional as well as the international aspects of Canadian marketing. Consequently the book will also be useful to students of comparative marketing. Furthermore, MARKETING IN THE CANADIAN ENVIRONMENT, with its emphasis on environmental understanding will also be useful to those students of marketing management and general marketing who want to know more about marketing in one of the world's ten largest economies.

It is not a simple task to describe the complex external and internal environments which influence marketing in Canada, particularly when a comparative approach is used. However, Professor Mallen provides a helpful analytical framework, evolved through the comparative analysis of Canadian markets and institutions with those of the United States and, to a lesser extent, with those of Europe and Japan. Descriptive material from this book and from other sources can be readily integrated into this framework. Background materials are also provided to aid in analyzing many subjects of current interest in Canadian marketing: consumerism, the features of the French-Canadian market, and the costs of marketing and distribution in Canada.

It is a privilege to present this book as an addition to the FOUNDATION OF MARKETING SERIES.

Eugene J. Kelley

1

Introduction

OBJECTIVES

In writing this book the author's objective has been to develop the first comprehensive work devoted entirely to the differences and peculiarities of marketing in Canada; particularly the differences vis-à-vis the U.S.A. Stemming from this basic objective are two sub-objectives:

1.   To avoid the superficiality of simply regurgitating the American textbooks, adding a sprinkling of Canadian statistics, slapping the word "Canadian" in the title — and offering (lo and behold!) a "Canadian" creation.

2.   To present a thorough description of the Canadian situation; and to do so not simply by listing raw data or cataloguing facts but by accomplishing the following:

> a) screening and selecting the most important and relevant facts from the extremely wide existing universe of data, and whenever possible, making use of future-oriented or forecasted data;
>
> b) reminding the reader, without going into great depth — (because it is assumed a basic marketing text has been used, or will be used alongside this book) — why such facts are relevant; and
>
> c) analysing the data in order to explain, where possible, why a given factor is different, what the prognosis is, and what the implications are for Canadian marketing as a whole.

As noted above, a basic assumption is that the student taking his first course in marketing will be reading or will have read a basic principles book in marketing (probably American, perhaps from the *Foundations of Marketing* series). Such a book will provide him with the analytical and managerial tools and insights required to make best use of the environmental understanding which he can gain from *Marketing in the Canadian Environment*. Thus, the screening process mentioned above attempts, as one of its criteria, to identify variables and particular facts for the Canadian scene, that one normally finds identified in a principles book, for the U.S. scene.

Though the book is basically to be used as a supplement by students in Canada who are taking their first course in marketing, it can be used independently by students who have already had a marketing course, or by marketing executives and others interested in Canadian marketing management.

It is hoped that this book will help anybody, be he student or businessman, to answer the question, "What is different about marketing in Canada?" As described and defined below, that difference lies in the environment — hence *Marketing in the Canadian Environment*.

THE ENVIRONMENT

A marketer operating in any given market does so within a framework of constraints, to which he must adapt if he is to survive and profit. The word "adapt" must be emphasized, as few, if any, individual marketers (firms) can alter any of these constraints. The marketer, not the constraints, must adjust. To adjust, the marketer must have a thorough understanding of the entire framework of constraints on his marketing system. These constraints have been referred to in differing contexts as: exogenous factors, external factors, frames of reference, and the environment. The latter term seems best suited to the purposes of this book.

One can denote several external environmental factors within which the marketer must operate. These include the political-legal-governmental environment, the physical-geographical-climatic environment, the demographic-economic-financial environment and the ethical-sociological-philosophical environment.

In addition to the external environmental factors, basic marketing textbooks usually divide the managerial portions of their discussion into three broad categories: (1) the variables dealing with channel and physical distribution management; (2) the variables dealing with pricing and product (goods and service) management; and (3) the variables dealing with information, advertising and personal selling. The total is often referred to as the marketing management mix, to suggest the idea that this is the universe of variables which the marketing manager must manipulate in order to achieve his objectives. The outcome of programming these variables is the manager's marketing strategy.

This book uses the above two concepts — environment and marketing mix — in developing its structure. However, the first concept is further defined as the "external environment" and forms Part I of the book, to distinguish it from the "internal environment" which forms Part II. The external environment is defined as the exogenous forces on the marketing system, while the internal environment is defined as part of the marketing system itself — its problems, practices and institutions. Though it deals with the same variables, a discussion of the internal environment should not be confused with a discussion of managerial marketing techniques. Rather, Part II is limited to the general problems, practices and existing marketing institutions which affect the marketing manager's decisions.

The chapters cover the environmental topics as follows:

Chapter No.	Chapter Title	Environmental Factors Covered

PART ONE — The External Environment

Chapter	2	The Demographic and Economic Dimensions of the Canadian Consumer Market	Demographic, Economic Financial, Geographic
	3	The Cultural and Comparative Dimensions of the Canadian Consumer Market	Ethical, Sociological Philosophical International
	4	The Economic Dimension of the Canadian Industrial Market	Economic, Financial Geographic
	5	The International Dimension of Canadian Marketing	International, Governmental, Economic Geographic
	6	The Governmental and Legal Dimension of Marketing in Canada	Political, Legal Governmental, Ethical

PART TWO — The Internal Environment

Chapter	7	Distribution in Canada	Channels, Physical Institutions Practices
	8	Retailing in Canada	Institutions, Problems Practices, Geographic
	9	Wholesaling in Canada	Institutions, Problems Practices, Geographic
	10	Pricing and Product Management in Canada	Problems, Practices Climactic
	11	Promotion in Canada	Problems, Practices Institutions
	12	Marketing Research in Canada	Problems, Practices

The table on the following pages lists the corresponding chapters in twenty-one basic marketing textbooks published between 1968 and 1972 inclusive, which provide the basic analytical framework and/or U.S. data for the twelve chapters of *Marketing in the Canadian Environment*. Also included in the second line are the other books from the *Foundations of Marketing* series which correspond to the chapters in this book.

RECENTLY PUBLISHED BASIC MARKETING TEXTS —

Marketing in the *Canadian Environment,* Chapter:	*1*	*2*	*3*	*4*
E. J. Kelley, Editor *Foundations of Marketing* Series* Prentice-Hall	Kelley	Alderson & Halbert	Bliss; Kassarjian & Bennett	Webster & Wind
Bell *Marketing Concepts and Strategy* 2nd ed., Houghton Mifflin, 1972	1-3, 5,29	6	7,8,9	
Boyd, Massy *Marketing Management* Harcourt Brace & World, 1972	1,2	4	3,5	
Buskirk *Principles of Marketing,* 3rd ed., Holt Rinehart & Winston, 1970	1	4,6	7	
Buzzell, Nourse, Matthews, Levitt *Marketing: Contemporary Analysis* 2nd ed., McGraw-Hill, 1972	1,2	3-5	6,7	8,9
Cundiff, Still *Basic Marketing* 2nd ed., Prentice-Hall, 1971	1,2	5,6	7	
Gist *Marketing & Society* Holt, Rinehart & Winston, 1971	1-3	7,8	9	
Holloway, Hancock *Marketing in a Changing Environment* John Wiley, 1968	1-3	4-6	4-6	
Kerby *Essentials of Marketing* South-Western Publishing, 1970	1	8	6	
Kotler *Marketing Management* 2nd ed., Prentice-Hall, 1972	1,2, 3,6	4		5
Lazer *Marketing Management* John Wiley, 1971	1-6	16,17	18-20	

*See back cover for titles of these works.

KEY TO CHAPTERS

5	6	7	8	9	10	11	12
Fayer-weather	Grether	Cox & Schutte; LaLonde			Palda; Luck	Thompson; Boyd & Levy	Frank & Green
	10,11	4,23, 24			12, 20-22, 28	25-27	13-19
		14,15, 20			11-13	16-19	6-10, 22
26	25	12,15, 16	13	14	9-11, 17,18	19-21	2,3, 5,22
24	27	18,19	10,11	12	14-17	20-22	25,26
	23	14,15	13	12	8-11, 19-21	16-18	22
	6	14-17			20-23	18,19	10,11
20,21	10,11	17			15,16	18,19	9,12, 13
	24	13-16			10-12 21-23	17-20	2,3, 9
23	22	15,16			12-14	17-19	7,10 20,21
24	23	12,13			10	14,15	7-9

RECENTLY PUBLISHED BASIC MARKETING TEXTS —

Marketing in the Canadian Environment, Chapter:	*1*	*2*	*3*	*4*
Lipson & Darling *Introduction to Marketing* John Wiley, 1971	1-3	7-11	7	12
McCarthy *Basic Marketing* 4th ed., Irwin, 1971	1-3	6	8	9
Phelps, Westing *Marketing Management* 3rd ed., Irwin, 1968	1			
Phillips, Duncan *Marketing: Principles & Methods* 6th ed., Irwin, 1968	1	3-5		17-21
Rathmell *Managing the Marketing Function* John Wiley, 1969	1			
Rewoldt, et al. *Introduction to Marketing Management* Irwin, 1969	1		2,3	3
Stanton *Fundamentals of Marketing* 3rd ed., McGraw-Hill, 1971	1,2	4	5-7	8
Sturdivant, et al. *Managerial Analysis in Marketing* Scott Foresman, 1970	1		4,5	
Taylor, Shaw *Marketing,* 2nd ed., South-Western Publishing, 1969	1	3	4,5	12
Zober *Principles of Marketing* Allyn & Bacon, 1971	1	4,5	6	20-21

KEY TO CHAPTERS (Concluded)

5	6	7	8	9	10	11	12
14	8,13		4,5	4,5	20,21	23	24
7	27	15,18, 19,30	16	17	10-14 23-26	20-22	4,5
	13,19	20			3-11	22-32	17
	32	2,24, 26	6-11	12-16	23, 29-31	27,28	22
17	15,16	12			9,10	5-7, 11	4
		7,9			5,6, 13,14	10-12	4
26	29,30	12,15- 17	13	14	9-11, 18-21	22-24	3, 28
	3	11-13			7,9	8	10, 14,15
26, 27	15	14,24	6-9	11	19-22	23	16-18
30	19	7,23	8-14	15-18	27,28	29	24

Part One

THE EXTERNAL ENVIRONMENT:

Markets and Laws

2

The Demographic and Economic Dimensions of the Canadian Consumer Market

This chapter presents a demographic and economic "profile" of the Canadian consumer market. There are three sections. The first explores the demographic aspects — population and its distribution, age, occupation, ethnic origin, and so on — in order to give some idea of the shape and character of the consumer market. In the second section, the economic and financial condition of the Canadian consumer is examined, and an analysis is made of the effect of income and asset holdings on consumer expenditures. Finally, there is a special section devoted to Canada's urban markets and the megalopolis; because of the uniqueness of the latter area and its importance to marketers, it is well worth a separate look.

THE DEMOGRAPHIC DIMENSION

Population

The consumer market in Canada contains approximately 21½ million persons. About 10 percent of this market is located in the four Atlantic provinces, which are composed of Newfoundland and the Maritime provinces of Prince Edward Island, Nova Scotia and New Brunswick. Slightly under 28 percent is to be found in Quebec, 36 percent in Ontario, and slightly over 26 percent in the four western provinces — British Columbia and the Prairie provinces of Manitoba, Saskatchewan and Alberta.

Table 2-1 presents population data by province. The heavy concentration of population in the central provinces of Quebec and Ontario should be noted. An elaboration of this market concentration will be discussed in the section entitled "Canada's Megalopolis." There, it will be noted that the high proportion of Canada's population in these two provinces is further concentrated into a 750-mile long and 100-mile wide strip which runs through southwestern Quebec and continues into southeastern Ontario. In this very narrow band of land over half of the consumer population resides; as well, it is where over half of Canada's consumer expenditures and incomes are made. However, note that the fastest-growing province in recent years (1966–70), is the far western one of British Columbia, which is considered to be the most attractive by migrants from other provinces. Still, Ontario has been growing faster in recent years than the national average, and had the second highest rate of growth over the ten-year period.

The population of Canada itself doubled in the 36-year period 1935–71. It is important for the marketer to bear in mind, of course, that the growth rate is by no means uniform. Table 2-1 shows the ten-year growth rate ranging from −6 percent for Saskatchewan to 38 percent for British Columbia, in comparison to Canada's 17 percent.

TABLE 2-1 Population Distribution and Growth Rate by Province, 1971

Province	Population (Thousands)	% of Total Population	% Change 66/71	% Change 61/71	Households (Thousands)
Newfoundland	523	2.4	6	13	104
Prince Edward Island	111	.5	2	5	28
Nova Scotia	770	3.6	2	4	191
New Brunswick	629	2.9	2	4	148
Quebec	6,030	27.9	4	9	1,493
Ontario	7,795	36.0	12	26	2,143
Manitoba	985	4.6	2	5	272
Saskatchewan	927	4.3	−3	−6	258
Alberta	1,628	7.5	11	24	447
British Columbia	2,190	10.1	17	38	640
Canada	21,641	100.0	8	17	5,732

SOURCE: Financial Post Survey of Markets, 1971 (Toronto: Maclean-Hunter, 1070), pp. 44-47.

The variance among Canada's metropolises is even greater than the variance among its provinces. For example, though Canada itself had a 17 percent ten-year rate of growth, the metropolitan area of St. John showed a +1 percent rate, whereas the metropolitan area of Calgary showed a 48 percent ten-year rate of growth. In the ten-year period to 1970, the population of Canada increased by over three and a half million persons. This is enough to fill Canada's largest and third largest metropolitan areas of Montreal and Vancouver combined.

Another way of looking at this dramatic ten-year growth is to say that the increase was sufficient to fill all but five of Canada's twenty-one, 100,000-plus, urban areas. That is, the increase in ten years was sufficient to create in total the urban areas of St. John's, St. Catharines, St. John, Sudbury, Thunder Bay, Victoria, Kitchener, Saskatoon, Regina, Halifax, London, Windsor, Calgary, Edmonton, Quebec and Hamilton. It is expected that by 1975 at a 1.7 percent annual growth rate, the population of Canada will be over 23,000,000 persons, over 25,000,000 by 1980[1] and over 28,000,000 by 1984.[2] Incidentally, these are lower estimates than ones made in earlier years, because of the sharply reduced birth rates of the 1960's. The reduction may be due to delayed parent-hood decisions rather than to the Pill alone.[3] However, this population growth rate is still amongst the highest of the industrial countries of the world.[4]

Age Groups

The rates of growth also vary considerably among age groups, as they do among provinces and metropolitan areas. Table 2-2 esti-mates the distribution of population by age group for 1971 and 1976. The biggest population share is found in the age groupings under 20 years old[5] and the median age has been steadily falling from its high of 28 in 1951, to 25 today.

TABLE 2-2 Population Distribution by Age Group, 1971 and 1976

Age Group	Population (millions)		% of Total Population	
	1971	1976	1971	1976
0 – 14	6.6	6.5	30.2	27.6
15 – 19	2.1	2.4	9.7	10.0
20 – 24	1.9	2.2	8.8	9.2
25 – 34	2.9	3.6	13.1	15.2
35 – 44	2.7	2.7	12.1	11.6
45 – 54	2.3	2.6	10.6	10.9
55 – 64	1.7	1.9	7.7	8.1
65 and over	1.7	1.7	7.8	7.4
Total (Canada)	21.9	23.6	100.0	100.0

SOURCE: Financial Post Survey of Markets, 1969 *(Toronto: Maclean-Hunter, 1969)* p. 42.

However, despite the fact that there will be almost 1,700,000 more Canadians in 1976 than in 1971, there will actually be 100,000

[1] Economic Council of Canada, *Fourth Annual Review* (Ottawa: Queen's Printer, 1967) , pp. 56-64.
[2] Gene Fleet, "What Businessmen Should Know On The Way to 1984," *Financial Post,* 10 July 1971, pp. 11-12. This article was based on cal-culations made by the Dominion Bureau of Statistics. The 28,000,000 figure is their high estimate versus their low of 25,000,000.
[3] "Empty Cradles to Stall Marketing Bonanza," *Financial Post,* 25 November 1967, p. 17.
[4] A. D. Bruce, *Changes in the Canadian Population* (Montreal: Du Pont of Canada Limited, August 1968) , p. 9; see also E. B. Chown, "Tomorrow's Customers," *Business Quarterly* 33 (Spring 1968) , pp. 55-63; and W. H. Ellis, "Who is Your Buyer of Tomorrow?" *Canadian Business* 39 (Sep-tember 1966) , pp. 32-41.
[5] For a rather detailed analysis of the 13 – 19-year-old age group, see Serge Gouin, Bernard Portis, and Brian Campbell, *The Teenage Market In Canada* (London, Ontario: School of Business Administration, University of Western Ontario, 1967) , 103 pages.

less persons under the age of 15, whereas there will be almost 1,000,000 more between the ages of 25 and 34. The *Monetary Times'* reaction to this relative decline in the youth population is that ". . . the influence of youth on the rest of us will decline as young people become comparatively fewer. . . . In short, our society of the 1970's will be less youth dominated, but more homogenous at a relatively youthful level."[6]

Calculations made to 1984 (see Table 2-3) further confirm the relative decline in the youth population.[7] Another age group which will grow at a significantly slower rate in the 1970's and early 1980's is the 45–64-year-old mature market, though the contrast here is less severe than, for example, the teenage market which may have little or no growth after experiencing an 81 percent growth from 1954 to 1969. The greatest relative increase will come in the important 25–44-year-old family market, as well as the over-65-year-old retirement market.

TABLE 2-3 Population Growth Estimates, 1969-1984[a]

Age Group	Percentage Growth		Population (1984)	
	Low Est.	High Est.	Low Est.	High Est.
	%	%	(000)	(000)
0 – 4	22	65	2,362	3,155
5 – 14[b]	–11	9	4,061	5,010
15 – 19[c]	–4	2	1,932	2,061
20 – 24[d]	33	42	2,342	2,508
25 – 44[e]	43	61	7,566	8,482
45 – 64[f]	21	27	4,655	4,888
65 and over[g]	40	45	2,304	2,367

SOURCE: *Developed from* Financial Post, *10 July 1971, pp. 11-12.*

[a] Low and high estimates based on different assumptions about fertility rates and immigration trends.
[b] 1954-69 percent growth was 55%
[c] 1954-69 percent growth was 81%
[d] 1954-69 percent growth was 33%
[e] 1954-69 percent growth was 21%
[f] 1954-69 percent growth was 45%
[g] 1954-69 percent growth was 38%

These are just a few examples of the great variance among rates of growth. They point out the importance of making a detailed population analysis from the viewpoint of one's particular interest in the Canadian market. It is obvious that the pattern of population growth to 1976 or 1984 will have far different implications for the company selling to the under-15-year-old market, for example, than for the company selling to the 25–34-year-old market; or from the geographical viewpoint, for the company selling in the Maritime market versus the British Columbia market; or from the residence viewpoint, for the company selling to the farm population which is expected to continue its historical decrease, versus the company selling to the metropolitan market.

[6] "Too Much — Too Late," *Monetary Times* 136 (August 1968) , p. 15.
[7] Fleet, "What Businessmen Should Know," p. 11-12.

Table 2-4 provides a more detailed analysis of the population using smaller age groupings and dividing the data into male and female classes. In only one age grouping is there a relatively strong deviation from the generally even split between the female and male populations. The higher female population in the oldest age group can be accounted for by the shorter life span of the male. There has, in fact, been a gradual reduction of the male/female population ratio since 1911 when at that time it was 113 compared to less than 102 today. However, rural areas still have a relatively higher ratio of males.

TABLE 2-4 Population by Sex and Age Group, 1969

Age Group	Male (100%)	Female (100%)
0 – 4	10.0	9.6
5 – 9	11.4	11.0
10 – 14	10.8	10.5
15 – 19	9.6	9.4
20 – 24	8.0	8.0
25 – 29	6.5	6.6
30 – 34	6.1	6.0
35 – 39	6.3	6.2
40 – 44	6.2	6.2
45 – 49	5.6	5.6
50 – 54	4.9	4.9
55 – 59	4.2	4.2
60 – 64	3.3	3.4
65 and over	7.1	8.4
Total (thousands)	10,481.3	10,450.0

SOURCE: *1970 Marketing's* Media Digest *(Toronto: Maclean-Hunter, 1970), p. 6.*

Marital Status

The most significant influence on marital status is the trend to "early marriage," attributed mainly to prosperous economic conditions. This trend is of particular importance to those marketers serving the needs of young families. As an indication, it may be noted that in 1941 only 60 percent of males between the ages of 25 and 34 were married, while the 1966 census showed that this figure had moved up to 78 percent. Two-thirds of the population of Canada of the age of 15 years and over were married. For the specific age group of 35–44 years, 88 percent were married. However, there was a decline in the married proportion for the 15–24-year-old age group between 1961 and 1966 as well as a decline in the birth rate.

Ethnic Origin and Religion

It is important to understand how the market is segmented by ethnic origin and religion, since these are two more factors which could affect buying behaviour for certain products, particularly food products.

Canada is composed of two major ethnic groups: one consists of those people from the British Isles, and the other, those of French origin. These two ethnic groups comprise 74 percent of the population. All the other ethnic groups combined, German being the largest of these at 6 percent of the population, comprise the remaining 26 percent of Canada's population. It should be noted that these minor ethnic groups — i.e., those other than British or French — have increased their share of the population from 21 to 26 percent in the period 1951 to 1961. This was mainly at the expense of the British ethnic group, which declined from 48 percent in 1951 to a 44 percent share in 1961. The French ethnic share remained rather stable at 31 percent in 1951 and 30 percent in 1961.

It must be kept in mind that reference to ethnic groups is not the same as reference to language or the place of birth. In fact, 85 percent of the population is native born. (However, over 94 percent holds Canadian citizenship.) Of the 15 percent, who are foreign born, a third were born in the United Kingdom and over half in other European countries.

Most of the immigrants to Canada are concentrated in the largest cities, particularly Toronto with its very large Italian population. Indeed, half of Canada's immigrants can be found in her three largest cities (Montreal, Toronto and Vancouver).

Canada's Roman Catholic population is 46 percent of the total, of which about two-thirds are of French origin. Because of the very high growth rate in the youth market, it is of interest for marketers to realize that the incidence of Roman Catholicism is much higher in this market than in the older age group market. This is probably correlated with the fact that there is a lower incidence of British origin in the younger age group markets. Of the remaining 54 percent of the population, Protestants account for 48 percent. The largest Protestant denominations are the United and Anglican churches of Canada.

Mobility

Canadians are mobile. Hence, the marketer must direct his strategy at a moving target and so must keep track of his changing market. Mobility is reflected in the movement from rural to urban areas, in the movement to the suburbs, and in the immigration and emigration flows of the country as a whole.

A study undertaken in conjunction with the 1961 census shows that 45 percent of the population had moved at least once in the previous five years.[8] Of this group, 55 percent had moved within the same municipality, and 30 percent had moved within the province, from a different municipality. The other 15 percent had moved to their new residence from outside the province or country: roughly half of this last group were immigrants from abroad, one quarter had moved to a

[8] Leroy Stone, *Migration in Canada* (Ottawa: Queen's Printer, 1969), 407 pages.

province bordering their original province of residence, and the other quarter came from other than a bordering province.

Family and Households

Household growth, which has been faster over the 1960's than simple population growth, is often more relevant to the marketer, particularly if he sells furniture, consumer durables and furnishings. Canadian households numbered 5.2 million in 1966 (including 4.5 million families), and this is expected to reach 7.5 million by 1980.[9]

The Canadian household has on the average 3.7 individuals, but this varies from province to province, so that Newfoundland has 5.0 persons while British Columbia has an average of 3.3. Roughly, a third of the households have one or two persons in them, a third have three or four persons, and a third are composed of five or more persons. It should be noted that the definition of households embraces more individuals than a census definition of families. Indeed, the fastest growing portion of the household growth is the "non-family" household; for example, one person living alone, or a group of unrelated persons occupying one dwelling. Non-family households often call for different promotional appeals and products than do family households — "swingers" are not likely to be receptive to family-type appeals!

Approximately 30 percent of Canadian families have no children living at home; 20 percent have one child, 24 years old or younger, living at home; 20 percent have two; another 20 percent have three or four; and 10 percent have five or more children of the age of 24 years or younger living at home.

Over one-quarter of the heads of families are under 35 years of age, approximately one-quarter are between 35 and 44 years of age, another fifth are between the ages of 45 and 54, and a final quarter of families consist of a family head who is 55 years of age or more.

Education

The educational profile of a market is important to the marketer. It is a prime determinant of the needs and wants of the consumer and of his level of income, and is a major factor in economic growth and prosperity. The Economic Council of Canada, in its *Second Annual Review* came to the following six basic conclusions:

1. There has been a substantial long-term rise in the educational attainments of the Canadian labour force. But the average level of such attainments has been considerably below that of the United States and has increased more slowly than in the United States. There has been a widening "educational gap" between the two countries.
2. This gap appears to have widened particularly at the secondary school

---

[9] Economic Council of Canada, *Fourth Annual Review*, p. 61.

level in the inter-war years, and particularly at the university level in the post-war period.

3. The income of individuals is generally closely related to the extent of formal schooling. In fact, available data show that differences in lifetime earnings of individuals classified by occupational groups appear to be directly associated with differences in levels of schooling. Moreover, the additional income benefits derived from obtaining a high school or university education, in relation to the cost of such education, appear to be somewhat higher in Canada than in the United States, and the rates of return from increased investment in education would appear to compare very favourably with the returns available from other types of investment.

4. The benefits of increased education, according to certain calculations and assumptions, are estimated to have accounted for a share in the general order of one-quarter of the *increase,* both in the average standard of living and in the productivity of Canadians from 1911 to 1961. Although this is a large contribution, it is apparently substantially lower than that indicated in comparable estimates for the United States.

5. Differences in the average educational attainments appear to be an important element in the difference in living standards between Canada and the United States.

6. The potential future economic benefits to Canadians and to the Canadian economy generally from increased educational attainments are very large, but they can only be fully realized over extended periods of time.[10]

Despite Canada's relatively poor performance in comparison to the U.S.A., the education industry in this country has recently undergone a tremendous boom. Though rapid growth is continuing, the rate may slow down because of government pressures. Full-time university enrolment in 1967/68 was over the 260,000 mark, and it is estimated that this will double between 1967 and 1975.[11] At present, 9 percent of Canada's GNP (and by 1977, 11 percent) is being spent on education, and it has been estimated that university budgets alone will have reached the staggering figure of $2.7 billion by 1975.[12] In addition, almost one-third of all Canadians are attending school. Professor D. Leighton has summarized some of the effects that the increase of education will have on the consumer's value system.

The emergence of education as a significant status symbol is but one reflection of some fundamental changes in social values. For example, studies have shown pretty clearly that better-educated people devote a greater proportion of their incomes to such things as insurance,

[10] Economic Council of Canada, "Towards a Sustained and Balanced Economic Growth," *Second Annual Review* (Ottawa: Queen's Printer, December 1965), pp. 74-75.

[11] Economic Council of Canada, *Sixth Annual Review* (Ottawa: Queen's Printer, September 1969), p. 36.

[12] *Ibid.,* p. 125.

medical equipment, physicians' services; these things appear to assume a higher rank in the value systems of better-educated consumers. Savings, in the form of insurance, investments and bank accounts also appear to rank higher in the value scale of the educated consumer.

A second field to which the educated consumer devotes more attention is the home. Proportionately more is spent on the home and on home furnishings the higher the education level. Considerably more is spent on such things as baby food, baby equipment and items for the children. The educated consumer appears to be more home-centred than the consumer with less education.

Proportionately, the better-educated male does not spend more on his own clothing, but he does spend significantly more on his wife's clothing. He also spends proportionately more on his automobile.

Education also appears to be correlated with recreation and expenditures on travel, sports, art, music, and the like. The book publishing business is another that should be riding this favourable trend.

Finally, but by no means least, the educated man spends a much larger proportion of his income on liquor and beer than does the less educated. Not only does he consume more, but his tastes usually run to the more expensive premium brands, the imported wines and liqueurs.

In summary, education should provide strong impetus for the development of different and, in some respects, better tastes in many things — tastes that are coincidentally more expensive, demanding of more variety, and extremely conscious of the snob appeal inherent in the term "imported." It should also lead to better medical care, more financial security, bigger and more attractive homes — and perhaps more spoiled children.

On the negative side, education also appears from the sketchy evidence available, to be correlated with divorce, psychiatric problems, alcoholism, and juvenile deliquency.

In general, many of the old accepted customs — the housewife who tended children, washed dishes, and in general did most of the daily chores — have already gone. Wives are working, not to increase family income so much as to avoid early death due to boredom. Education has created dissatisfaction with the housewives' traditional role; woman has realized that she has a mind, she wants a chance to exercise it.

At the same time, we are finding the old moral and modest standards going by the board, and this trend will undoubtedly continue. Life is rapidly becoming more "liberal," relying less on faith, religion, dogma and the established order.[13]

Employment and Occupations

The marketer will be interested in several trends in the employment and occupational characteristics of the Canadian market. The Canadian labour force is about 8.8 million strong of which 2.9 million are women.

[13] David S. R. Leighton, "Education and the Canadian Consumer," in Isaiah A. Litvak and Bruce E. Mallen, eds., *Marketing: Canada* (Toronto: McGraw-Hill Book Company of Canada Limited, 1964), pp. 22-23.

There have been some important changes in the labour force participation rate over the years. This rate measures the percentage of people 14 years of age and over and who are working or seeking work. The most striking trend, and of important consequence to marketers, is the rapidly rising participation rate of women since 1950. This incease has held for all age groups, except women over 65. It has been particularly accentuated in the 45–64-year-old age group, where the participation rate doubled between 1954 and 1971. In 1954 the participation rate for 45–64-year-old women was 18.3 percent; this increased to 36.9 percent in 1971. In other words, while in 1954 only one out of five women in this age bracket was employed (or seeking employment), in 1971 the situation had changed to the extent that better than one out of three women of this age bracket was employed, or seeking employment. Nor is this trend confined to single women. Interestingly, the participation rate for married women is approximately 30 percent.

This trend has several implications for marketers. It is a result as well as a cause of changing values, and hence changing buying behaviour. More will be said about these implications in the section on expenditures, later in this chapter.

Ironically, the participation rate of men has been falling, primarily as a result of longer periods of schooling and earlier retirement. For example, in 1960 the participation rate for 20–24-year-old males was 92 percent, while in 1971 it was only 82 percent; in 1960 the participation rate for 65-year-old males or older was 30 percent; this had fallen in 1971 to 19.5 percent. However, Table 2-5 shows that the 25–44-year-old male group with a participation rate of over 96.5 percent still lives outside the Garden of Eden.

TABLE 2-5 Labour Force Participation Rates, December 1971, (Seasonally Adjusted)

Age Group	Male Rate %	Female Rate %
14 – 19	39.0	31.7
20 – 24	85.2	61.1
25 – 44	96.6	42.3
45 – 64	89.5	36.9
65 and over	19.5	5.1
Total	76.1	37.2

SOURCE: *Dominion Bureau of Statistics, "Seasonally Adjusted Labour Force Statistics, January 1953-December 1971," No. 71-201 (Ottawa: Queen's Printer, 1972).*

Tables 2-6 and 2-7 show some interesting and important changes in occupational patterns. It is now quite evident that the Canadian economy is becoming more and more a service rather than a goods economy — three out of every five persons in the labour force were employed in a service-producing industry. These industries have been growing rapidly over the past two decades. Notice, for example, that the service industries have more than doubled their labour force between

TABLE 2-6 Percentage Distribution of the Employed Labour Force by Industry, March 1972

Industry	1972 % Distribution	% Change 1951-1972
Goods-producing industries	36	15
Agriculture	5	−36
Other primary industries	2½	−22
Manufacturing	23	43
Construction	5½	60
Service-producing industries	64	110
Transportation and utilities	8½	43
Trade	17	83
Finance, insurance, real estate	4½	162
Services	27	179
Public administration	7	87
Total all Industries	100	58

SOURCE: *Developed from DBS*, 1961 Census of Canada *data, No. 94-511 and* Labour Force *data, No. 71-001 (Ottawa: Queen's Printer, March 1972).*

NOTE: 1951 labour force figures do not contain 14 year olds as do the 1972 figures.

1951 and 1972 while the goods-producing industries have increased by only 15 percent. The primary goods-producing industries, including agriculture, have decreased rather sharply during this period. Even the labour force of the manufacturing industries has not kept pace with the general sixty percent increase in the labour force. Some service-producing industries have had startling labour force gains — for example, the investment industries. It is obvious that such occupational changes are bound to affect the buying behaviour and buying habits of consumers.

It is possible to analyze these changing patterns by occupation, rather than by industry. This type of analysis as shown in Table 2-7 is probably more relevant, as the individual who moves from a selling job in manufacturing to a selling job in retailing (the type of trend which would be shown in Table 2-6), is probably less influenced as a consumer than the individual who moves from a blue-collar job in manufacturing to a white-collar job in that same industry (the type of trend which would be shown in Table 2-7). The occupational decline in the primary industries and the sharp increase in service and recreational occupations is again reflected in Table 2-7. Also of importance to note is the increase, over three times greater, of white-collar workers vis-à-vis blue-collar workers. This swift increase is particularly noticeable in the professional and technical category, which has expanded three times faster than all occupations in general. Since these 1951–61 figures were compiled, these trends have been further accentuated by an increase to 14.5 percent (from 9.7) in the proportion of professional and technical occupations, and a decline in the proportion of farmers from 10 to 5 percent. Clearly, the shift from blue-collar to white-collar jobs could result in major shifts in buying habits and needs, and hence create many problems and opportunities for the marketer in Canada.

TABLE 2-7 Percentage Distribution of the Employed Labour Force by Occupation, March 1972

Occupation	1961 % Distribution	% Change 1951-1961	1972 % Distribution
White-collar workers	37.3	44.3	47
Managerial occupations	8.3	28.1	10
Professional and technical occupations	9.7	63.1	14½
Clerical occupations	12.9	44.1	15½
Sales occupations	6.4	43.0	7
Blue-collar workers	29.0	13.1	29
Craftsmen, producing and related workers	23.6	17.2	25
Labourers	5.3	−1.9	4
Transport and communications occupations	6.1	18.3	5½
Service and recreational occupations	12.3	54.4	12
Primary occupations	12.8	−20.8	6½
Farmers and farm workers	10.0	−21.4	5
Loggers and related workers	1.2	−21.8	½
Fishermen, trappers and hunters	.5	−32.8	½
Miners, quarrymen and related	1.0	−1.0	½
Occupation not stated	2.6		—
Total all Occupations	100.0	22.4	100.0

SOURCE: DBS, "Labour Force: Occupation and Industry Trends," 1961 Census of Canada, No. 94-551, Bulletin Series SL-1 (Ottawa: Queen's Printer, 1966), p. 7-1; Labour Force data, No. 71-001.

Language

An analysis of the market by language spoken is of major importance when looking at the Canadian market.

The French element is very significant in this country. Four-fifths of the households in the province of Quebec are French-Canadian. Indeed, if certain portions of the metropolitan area of Montreal were eliminated from the calculations, virtually this whole province, the second largest in Canada, would be French-Canadian.

The other province with a major French-Canadian element is New Brunswick. One-quarter of the households in New Brunswick are French-Canadian. These French Canadians are usually referred to as Acadians, to distinguish them from the French Canadians of Quebec. Certain areas of New Brunswick, of course, have a much higher portion of French Canadians than the 25 percent indicated above. Although no other province in the country has more than a 5 percent French-Canadian household population, the very high French-Canadian population in Quebec is sufficient to bring the ratio of French-Canadian households in Canada to about one-quarter of total Canadian households. More will be said about this important French-Canadian market in the following chapter.

Only 12 percent of the population can speak both of Canada's official languages, English and French. Two-thirds can speak English only and one-fifth can speak French only. However, 30 percent of those of French origin are bilingual, compared to only 4 percent of those of English origin. (The latter figure, of course, is higher for Anglo-Saxons living in the province of Quebec. These people are concentrated in the western half of the metropolitan area of Montreal.) Thus, though the French comprise less than a third of the population, they account for three-quarters of bilingual persons. Ten percent of bilingual persons are of neither French nor British origin. Sixty percent (1971 census) of the population consider English their mother tongue (up from 58.5 percent in 1961), although one-quarter of the latter are not of British origin. Twenty-seven percent (1971) consider French their mother tongue, (down from 28 percent in 1961), and finally, 13 percent have a mother tongue other than English or French.

THE FINANCIAL AND ECONOMIC DIMENSION

Income

Income is a very important concept to the marketer, because it is probably the single most important determinant of buying behaviour. Indeed, for a very long time, under the misconception of the economist's rational man, income was considered the only determinant of any significance. Of course, it is now realized that there are numerous other psychological and sociological influences on consumer behaviour. These influences tend to become increasingly important as consumers' discretionary income (disposable income less necessary expenditures) grows, because as it grows, consumers have fewer and fewer constraints on the range of their buying potential. Thus, while income may at one point have been the only really significant determinant of buying behaviour, this is certainly no longer true. However, for most products and certainly for buying in general, income, though not as important a determinant as it once was, is probably still the single most important influence on buying behaviour. It is for this reason that the student of the Canadian marketing scene must have a grasp of present and future trends in income patterns.

In 1971, the Canadian national income was over $70 billion (GNP was approximately $92 billion).[14] Almost three-quarters of this, or over $51 billion, was derived from wages and salaries. The remaining portion of national income was divided between corporate profits, investment income, and net income of unincorporated businesses and farms, which were approximately $8.5, $4.0 and $6.6 billion respectively. GNP

[14] Dominion Bureau of Statistics, "National Accounts, Income and Expenditure," *Preliminary Annual, 1971*, No. 13-001 (Ottawa: Queen's Printer, 1972).

is expected to reach $135 billion in 1976.[15] By mid-1972 it was running at over $100 billion.

A most important trend in income patterns is the increase in discretionary spending power at all levels. This trend will profoundly influence buying behaviour and patterns. It will lead to an increasing variety of product mixes purchased by the Canadian consumer. ". . . . It is estimated that the portion of discretionary spending in Canada rose from 30% of total outlays in 1959 to 36% in 1969. . . . discretionary spending in Canada grew at an annual average growth rate of 9% (compared with 7% for total consumer spending) in the ten years to 1969 to stand at $15 billion in that year."[16]

More important to the marketer than national income is personal income; the basic difference between the two is that personal income does not include retained corporate profits, while it does include transfer payments. Canadian personal income reached a figure of about $73 billion in 1971. Over two-thirds of this is derived from wages and salaries, and approximately ten percent each is derived from net income from unincorporated farms and businesses, investment income, and transfer payments. Personal income is expected to reach $102 billion in 1976.[17]

An even more important concept than personal income is personal disposable income (personal income less income taxes). The 1971 figure is estimated at almost $59 billion. This means that Canadian consumers had some $59 billion to spend or save in 1971. The forecast for 1975 is $73.5 billion.[18] There was a 100 percent increase in personal disposable income between 1961 and 1971, almost all of which was spent — e.g., in 1971 it is estimated that 91.5 percent was spent on goods and services and 8.5 percent found its way into savings.

Marketers are vitally interested in per capita figures as well, because this is an indication of the comparative standard of living of consumers. Per capita personal disposable income (total personal disposable income divided by the total population figure), is estimated at $2,780 in 1972 and $3,180 in 1975.[19] On a per household basis the 1971 estimate is $10,000. The average income reported per taxpayer in 1970 was $6,447.[20] It will be seen in the next chapter, in which Canada is compared to the United States and other countries, that these figures give the Canadian consumer one of the highest (often second) standards of living in the world.

The above-mentioned totals and averages, however, hide some

[15] *Financial Post Survey of Markets, 1969* (Toronto: Maclean-Hunter, 1969), p. 42.

[16] Bank of Montreal, "The Changing Role of the Consumer," *Business Review,* 29 March 1972, p. 2.

[17] *Financial Post Survey of Markets, 1969,* p. 42.

[18] *Financial Post Survey of Markets, 1971* (Toronto: Maclean-Hunter, 1971), p. 36.

[19] *Ibid.*

[20] Department of National Revenue, "Taxation Statistics, 1970," (Ottawa: Queen's Printer, 1972).

of the important facts about the distribution of income in Canada. Income distribution is important to marketers because it highlights the various market segments, each with its unique needs, potentialities and patterns of buying behaviour. Roughly speaking, it may be said that about one-third of total income is earned by 60 percent of taxpayers, who earn under $6,500; a second third, by 26 percent who earn between $6,500 and $10,000 and the final third by the 14 percent who earn over $10,000 per annum. If total family income is examined, rather than individual taxpayers' income, it can be seen that in 1969 one-third of families earned under $6,000, one-third earned over $10,000, and the middle third earned between $6,000 and $10,000.[21]

In general, it may be said that income is tending to become more evenly distributed than in the past — i.e., more and more people from the lower income classes are moving into the middle income classes. Some of this is, of course, due to inflation rather than "real" growth.

Not only are there different income distribution patterns in an absolute sense, as noted above, but also differing patterns between provinces and municipalities, occupations, sex, life cycle groups and age. The discussion will now turn to an analysis of these differing patterns, commencing with the provincial income pattern. The diversity will serve as a warning to marketers that the Canadian market is by no means uniform, but is the sum of numerous markets, each differing from the others, and each requiring special treatment in one aspect or another.

The bulk of Canada's income is generated in Quebec and Ontario (see Table 2-8) where most of her population is centred. The only other province with ten percent or more of the total personal disposable income of Canada is British Columbia.

As was noted earlier, per capita income figures are of great analytical importance to marketers. Table 2-8 points out an interesting dichotomy: the per capita personal disposable income (standard of living) is almost evenly split at the Ontario-Quebec border. The western half of Canada — Ontario and the four western provinces — has an above-average standard of living (though lower in Saskatchewan), while the eastern half — Quebec and the four Atlantic provinces — has a standard well below the Canadian average. This split would be accentuated if Montreal, only forty miles from Ontario, was eliminated from the calculations. Therefore, the search for high income markets must lie in Montreal, Ontario and the west. Furthermore, Table 2-8 shows that the range of per capita incomes is rather wide. Newfoundland's disposable income per capita, at $1,520 is only 61 percent of the Canadian average, while Ontario's per capita income, $2,820, is 113 percent of Canada's

---

[21] DBS, "Income Distribution by Size in Canada — 1969," No. 13-542 (Ottawa: Queen's Printer, 1971). For a detailed analysis of family income using over fifty classifications of families based on residence, various life cycle classes, education, origin of birth, household size, marital status etc., see Statistics Canada, *Household Facilities by Income and Other Characteristics, 1968* (Ottawa: Queen's Printer, April 1972), 180 pages.

TABLE 2-8 Personal Disposable Income by Province, 1970

Province	Total (Million $)	% of Canada	% Change 66/70	Per Capita Dollars	% of Canada Per Capita	Per House-hold[1]
Newfoundland	787	1.5	41	1,520	61	6,868
P.E.I.	188	.4	40	1,710	68	6,713
Nova Scotia	1,590	3.0	40	2,070	83	7,710
New Brunswick	1,201	2.2	41	1,920	77	7,612
Quebec	14,041	26.2	35	2,330	93	8,892
Ontario	21,572	40.3	38	2,820	113	9,680
Manitoba	2,444	4.6	34	2,490	100	7,311
Saskatchewan	1,903	3.6	4	2,020	81	7,067
Alberta	4,048	7.6	37	2,520	101	8,769
British Columbia	5,641	10.5	38	2,630	105	8,623
Canada	53,595	100.0	36	2,500	100	8,858

SOURCE: Financial Post Survey of Markets, 1971, (Toronto: Maclean-Hunter, 1971).
[1] Developed from Sales Management's Survey of Buying Power, June 1970.

average. The variation is less on a per household income basis, because there tends to be more persons per household in the lower income areas.

The Economic Council of Canada, in its Second Annual Review, (1965) has attributed the diversity of income patterns between provinces to differences in labour force participation rates, age patterns, education, capital input, industrial productivity, natural resources and public services.

Not only are there differences in income patterns among provinces, but also within provinces. For example, though the 1970 personal disposable income per capita for Ontario was an average of $2,820, the Ontario cities of Sarnia, Sudbury and Sault Ste. Marie all reported average per capita personal disposable incomes of over $3,550. In terms of average income per taxpayer (1970), Oakville, Sarnia, and Sudbury, Ontario and Sept-Iles, Quebec all reported incomes of over $7,500 with Sept-Iles' $8,100 being the highest in Canada. Canada's three largest cities, Montreal, Toronto and Vancouver, also reported above-average incomes. In fact, most of Canada's high income families are to be found in the metropolitan areas.

Income differences are, of course, to be found between occupations (see footnote 19). For example, doctors reported an average 1970 income of $34,757, lawyers over $26,700, dentists almost $22,800, consulting engineers and architects almost $22,400, accountants $19,300, employees almost $6,500, farmers over $5,250, etc. etc. There are differences in incomes between industries as well. The reported average weekly wages and salaries for employees in 1969, were the following:[22] forestry, $134; mining and milling, $149; manufacturing, $123; construction, $151;

[22] Canada Year Book, 1970-71, (Ottawa: Queen's Printer, 1971), p. 864.

transportation, communication and utilities, $131; trade, $94; finance, insurance and real estate, $114; service, $84.

Table 2-9 provides some interesting insights into income from an age and sex viewpoint. The key group here in terms of total income is the 35–44-year-old males. They, along with the 45–54 age group also constitute the highest average income market. When analyzing income patterns from a life cycle viewpoint, Table 2-10 shows that the single most important life cycle group is that of the middle-aged married-with-children-at-home. This group accounts for almost one-third of total money income. The two groups constituting the young married with school-age and pre-school-age children are also of vital importance to marketers in general.

TABLE 2-9 Income by Age and Sex, 1970

Age Group	Male Total (Million $)	Average Male Income	Female Total (Million $)	Average Female Income
Under 25	3,932	4,315	2,385	3,471
25 – 29	4,430	6,874	1,454	4,566
30 – 34	4,459	8,201	967	4,578
35 – 39	4,711	9,038	925	4,574
40 – 44	4,862	9,372	1,001	4,591
45 – 49	4,541	9,394	1,078	4,680
50 – 54	3,596	9,066	906	4,808
55 – 59	3,112	8,637	813	4,961
60 – 64	2,184	7,982	574	4,819
65 – 69	1,192	6,172	421	3,819
70 and over	1,070	5,407	643	4,431
Total	38,096	7,550	11,171	4,304

SOURCE: Department of National Revenue, "Taxation Statistics, 1970," (Ottawa: Queen's Printer, 1972), p. 14. Data include income for those supplying tax returns only.

NOTE: Columns may not add to totals because of rounding.

Younger people are becoming richer all the time, which suggests a growing market for such things as houses, consumer durables, and educational and credit services. However, as the Economic Council of Canada has warned, to sustain this trend the Canadian economy must continue to provide jobs for the ever-increasing young entrants into the labour force. Otherwise, marriages will be postponed[23] and marketers will not have the markets that early marriages generate. Marketers must not forget the older age markets as well. There are an increasing number of persons moving into the retirement age group, increasing government transfer payments to older persons, and increasing average incomes to older groups.

[23] J. K. Edmonds, "No Baby Boom Ahead?" *Financial Post*, 1 September 1962. p. 21. Ironically, the slow-down in the number of births that has actually developed since this article was written is due much more to a slow-down in the birth rate rather than the marriage rate.

TABLE 2-10 Distribution of Households and their Total Income, by Life Cycle Group, Seven Canadian Cities, 1962

Life Cycle Group	% of Total Households	% of Total Money Income
Young single people	2.8	2.0
Young marrieds with no children	6.9	6.4
Young marrieds with pre—school-age children	16.1	14.7
Young marrieds with school-age children	12.7	14.1
Young marrieds with teenage children	3.3	3.3
Middle age single people	5.3	3.6
Middle age marrieds with no children or grown-up children	16.0	16.5
Middle age marrieds with children at home	27.4	31.5
Older single people	2.2	1.2
Older marrieds with or without children	7.3	6.7
All Households	100.0	100.0

SOURCE: J. V. Poapst, 1964 Consumer Survey: Royal Commission on Banking and Finance (Ottawa: Queen's Printer, 1965), p. 105.

In spite of the excellent income performance in the 1960's, the marketer must bear in mind that a good portion of the increases mentioned were in the form of inflation or higher income taxes. For example, it is true that personal income per household in 1970 was over $11,000 or almost double the amount of 1960, and that the average weekly wage and salary rose 55 percent (23 percent after inflation) in this period; however, to cover inflation and higher income tax, a man earning $5,000 in 1960 would have had to make almost $7,000 in 1970 to stay even. The $12,000-a-year man would have needed $17,500 in 1970.[24]

Ownership and Asset Position

The Canadian consumer not only earns one of the highest average incomes in the world, but is also in possession of a considerable stock of goods. Almost two-thirds of Canadian households own their own homes, and anywhere from 86 percent to 96 percent of Canadian households have flush or chemical toilets, hot and cold running water, bath or shower, and as can be seen in Table 2-11, electric refrigerators, radios, television and telephone. The marketer will be directly interested in the stock of goods held by Canadians, if he sells consumer durables, and indirectly interested if he sells related goods or services. For example, a broadcast advertiser will be interested in the stock of radios and televisions; a telephone-order retailer will be interested in the stock of telephones; the launderer will be interested in the stock of electric washers; the record company, in the stock of phonographs; the packager in the stock of home freezers and electric refrigerators; the soap company in the

[24] "Plain Man's Guide to What's Really Going On," Financial Post, 25 April 1970, p. 15.

TABLE 2-11 Household Ownership of Consumer Durables, May 1971

Consumer Durables	% of Total Households
Electric refrigerators	98½
Radio (one or more)	97½
(Two or more radios)	(60½)
Television (one or more)	96
(Two or more televisions)	(23)
Telephone (one or more)	94½
(Two or more telephones)	(21)
Vacuum cleaner	82½
Electric washer	80
Automobile (one or more)	78
(Two or more automobiles)	(18)
Record player	70
Sewing machine	64½
Clothes dryer	60
FM receivers	57½
Floor polishers (May 1970)	53½
Lawn mowers (May 1970)	47
Home freezer	34
Colour television	18½
Outboard motor boat	8
Automatic dishwashers	8½
Tape recorders	7½
Snowmobiles	7½
Window air conditioners	5½

SOURCE: Developed from DBS, "Household Facilities and Equipment," No. 64-202 (Ottawa: Queen's Printer, May 1971).

stock of automatic dishwashers and electric washers; the carpet industry in the stock of vacuum cleaners; and numerous firms and industries in the stock of automobiles.

Marketers of consumer durables which have a high degree of ownership, such as refrigerators, radios, televisions, telephones, vacuum cleaners and electric washers, must pursue a "second-unit" or "replacement" strategy, different to that used by marketers of durables which have low ownership rates, such as air conditioners, dish washers, lawn mowers, outboard motorboats, home freezers, colour televisions, tape recorders and snowmobiles. Marketers of these commodities must induce a "first time" purchase. Some marketers, particularly sellers of radios, must even pursue a "third unit" strategy. Certainly, the type of sales appeal for the latter product will be far different than those used for products of low market saturation.

Two things must be kept in mind when using the type of data presented in Table 2-11. (1) It is important to consider the age distribution of the stock of goods. For example, if the stock of goods is on the average "old," then the "replacement" theme will be very important; if the stock of goods is "young," then the "second or more units" strategy will have greater effect. (2) A thorough examination of ownership rates will reveal pockets of particularly high or low ownership relative to the national average. It is important for the marketer to examine the regional, provincial, and municipal, and numerous other market segment data to discover the existing vacuums and opportunities.

In this regard Statistics Canada combined the results of its surveys of (a) income and (b) household facilities and equipment, both completed in 1968, and published the outcome in April 1972 (see footnote 20). One part of the analysis reported on ownership of the various consumer durables for different family types based on numerous market segment characteristics. Characteristics used included residence, owners versus renters, various life cycle classes, education, Canadians versus immigrants, size of household and marital status. In all, some 52 categories were reported on, and each of these was further divided into 13 income classes, for a total of 676 market segments for each durable! And this was only one part of the total report.

It would be impossible, of course, to summarize the findings here. Numerous relevant market potentials can be revealed from a detailed study of that document. For example, the data reveal a very high correlation between income and the ownership of colour television, two or more automobiles and automatic washing machines. In the case of automobiles, 46.5 percent of families with incomes of $15,000 and over owned two or more automobiles in 1968 versus 14 percent for all families. One of the fifty-two categories of families or market segments — families with male head aged 45 to 64 years — had a 22 percent ownership rate of two or more cars versus a 7 percent rate when the male head was 65 years or over.

Financial Assets

During the period 1962–1964 a study was undertaken for the Royal Commission on Banking and Finance,[25] with the fundamental objective of attaining greater knowledge of the pattern of household invest ment and its financing, and a greater understanding of the influences and conditions underlying that pattern. The asset, debt and net worth patterns are important financial determinants (as is income) of consumer behaviour and expenditures. The survey covered the seven metropolitan areas of Halifax, Quebec City, Montreal, Toronto, London, Winnipeg and Calgary.

As displayed in Table 2-12, households in the seven cities held average assets totalling $20,421, liabilities of $3,591 and hence, net worth of $16,830. The figures appear somewhat high, and the reader is to be cautioned against accepting them at face value. Liquid assets (11 percent), illiquid cash-producing assets (35 percent), and pensions, trusts and estates (6 percent) together comprised about one-half of reported assets, and family dwellings comprised the other half (49 percent). The

[25] J. V. Poapst, *1964 Consumer Survey: Royal Commission on Banking and Finance* (Ottawa: Queen's Printer, 1965).

TABLE 2-12 Average Balance Sheet of Households in Seven Canadian Cities, 1962

Account	$	%
ASSETS		
Cash-Producing: Liquid		
Deposits	1,425	7.0
Canada Savings Bonds	731	3.6
Total	2,156	10.6
Cash-Producing: Illiquid		
Other bonds	531	2.6
Mortgages and other loans	608	3.0
Publicly traded shares	974	4.8
Shares in mutual funds,		
investment trusts, clubs	146	0.7
Equity in own business	3,397	16.6
Real estate	1,527	7.5
Total	7,183	35.2
Pension Funds, Trusts and Estates		
Withdrawable pension funds	767	3.8
Trusts or estates	351	1.7
Total	1,118	5.5
Family Dwellings		
Owned homes	9,392	46.0
Recreational dwellings	572	2.8
Total	9,964	48.8
TOTAL ASSETS	20,421	100.0
DEBTS		
Mortgage Debt		
Family dwellings	2,752	13.5
Other real estate	331	1.6
Total	3,083	15.1
Instalment Debt	274	1.3
Other Debt	234	1.2
TOTAL DEBTS	3,591	17.6
NET WORTH	16,830	82.4

SOURCE: *Poapst,* 1964 Consumer Survey: Royal Commission on Banking and Finance, p. 8.

largest type of asset was the owned home, which averaged $9,392, or 46 percent of total assets; next was equity in own business, at $3,397, or 17 percent of household assets. Debt amounted to approximately 18 percent of assets; mortgage debt on own house alone was 14 percent of assets.[26]

[26] It should be noted that there are certain assets and debts omitted from Table 2-12. These assets include currency, life insurance, and consumer durables. It is estimated that the omitted assets exceed omitted debt by perhaps $2,500.

About 27 percent of the households had a net worth under $1,000, including zero and negative net worth; about 26 percent had a net worth between $1,000 and $7,499; 18 percent between $7,500 and $14,999; and 29 percent, $15,000 and over net worth.

As one would expect, and as confirmed by Table 2-13, there is a strong positive correlation for both assets and net worth with income and age. It is interesting to note in looking at each age category in the life cycle groupings that those with children, whether they are young, middle-aged, or older married couples, have managed to accumulate a greater asset and net worth position than those without children in the same age category. The middle-aged with children at home appear to be a particularly lucrative market because they comprise over 27 percent of households, and have a net worth position of almost $25,000. Also to be expected and as displayed in Table 2-13, occupation is an important determinant of asset and net worth position. Business executives rank first in net worth position, followed by professionals, sales, clerical and skilled labour. The strong net worth position of retired persons may indicate the growing importance of the senior citizens market.

However, one must note that these statistics are based on a sample of households in Canada's largest urban areas and therefore will tend to have an upward bias to them. Indeed a more broad-based (172 areas) survey conducted in the spring of 1964[27] shows an average asset holding of $9,000 and an average debt of $2,500 for an average net worth of $6,500. One additional reason for the lower average asset position on this survey is that the value of investments in unincorporated businesses was not included.

Consumer Expenditures

Consumer expenditures are a marketer's key guide to the understanding of a consumer market, as they lie at the crux of the meaning of the consumer market: "people with money who will spend it on consumer goods and services." It has already been seen from previous sections of this chapter that many characteristics of the consumer market will determine how, and in what quantities and proportions consumers will spend their dollars in return for the marketer's goods and services. Some of the influences that have been discussed include population, household size, education, occupation, geographic location, age group, marriage pattern, income level, assets, and so on. This section will show the net result of these influences in terms of the level and pattern of consumer expenditures in Canada.

In 1971, personal expenditures were over $53 billion, representing over $2,400 for every man, woman and child in the population, and

---

[27] DBS, "Income, Assets and Indebtedness of Nonfarm Families in Canada, 1964," No. 13-525 (Ottawa: Queen's Printer, 1967).

TABLE 2-13 Average Household Net Worth and Assets, by Selected Characteristics, Seven Canadian Cities, 1962

Characteristic	Percent of Total Households	Assets ($)	Net Worth ($)
Total Income			
Under $1,000	2.2	2,929	2,649
$1M – 1.9M	4.9	3,625	3,245
$2M – 2.9M	8.1	4,474	3,702
$3M – 3.9M	13.0	9,602	7,803
$4M – 4.9M	19.1	8,537	6,783
$5M – 5.9M	15.9	12,185	9,642
$6M – 6.9M	9.0	21,140	14,767
$7M – 7.9M	7.3	29,752	23,559
$8M – 9.9M	9.3	29,559	23,423
$10M – 14.9M	7.0	47,031	38,978
$15M – 24.9M	2.3	120,021	110,127
$25M and over	0.8	212,569	202,817
Unclassified	1.0	39,664	33,749
Age – Years			
29 and under	13.9	5,977	4,027
30 – 39	28.5	14,728	10,066
40 – 49	24.0	23,726	18,867
50 – 64	24.5	29,317	26,271
65 and over	9.1	27,598	26,742
Life Cycle Group			
Young, single	2.9	7,219	6,766
Young, married			
No children	7.0	7,457	4,570
Pre-school children	16.5	10,291	6,516
School children	13.2	18,049	12,873
Teenage children	3.3	11,130	7,308
Middle age, single	4.9	13,966	13,031
Middle age, married			
No or grown children	15.5	26,366	23,094
Children at home	27.5	28,811	24,045
Older, single	1.9	23,843	23,177
Older, married			
No or grown children	7.1	26,322	25,597
Children at home	0.2	112,006	103,962
Occupation			
Professional	9.1	31,678	26,170
Business executive	10.5	64,049	55,982
Clerical	13.0	12,450	9,899
Sales	7.2	18,393	13,147
Skilled labour	35.8	12,301	9,286
Unskilled labour	10.3	7,376	4,990
Retired	5.5	23,878	23,113
Other	8.5	16,505	14,672
All Households	100.0	20,421	16,830

SOURCE: Developed from Poapst, 1964 Consumer Survey: Royal Commission on Banking and Finance, pp. 10-12.

57.5 percent of Canada's gross national expenditures. The Maclean-Hunter Research Bureau estimated that consumer goods and services expenditures will approach $80 billion by 1976.[28] The Economic Council of Canada, in its *Sixth Annual Review* (September, 1969), analyzed the trends in consumer spending on a 1967 basis (see Table 2-14). The Council predicted that per capita consumer expenditures will grow at an annual rate of 3.6 percent between 1967 and 1975, or a total of 32.6 percent from 1967 to 1975. This means a $2,500 per capita figure (1967 dollars) for 1975. "The average standard of living would therefore increase as much in the eight year period, 1967–1975, as it did in the previous thirteen years." [29]

More dramatically, because of the increases in per capita expenditures and population, total consumer spending will grow by a total of 51 percent between 1967 and 1975 (in terms of 1967 dollars). This total growth in personal expenditures represents an average annual rate of 5.3 percent. Thus, by 1975, personal expenditures should be $59 billion (in terms of 1967 dollars), as opposed to $39 billion in 1967.

The growth rate will not be evenly distributed over all categories of personal expenditures. The broadest way of categorizing personal expenditures is into the following four classes: durables, semi-durables, non-durables and services. At present, the share that each holds is roughly 12 percent for durables, 10 percent for semi-durables, 40 percent for non-durables, and 38 percent for services.

These shares have changed over time and will continue to do so. For example, because of the highly liquid position of consumers after the war, and the low and aging stock of durables at that time, the durable share of total consumer expenditures experienced a dramatic increase from 5.5 percent of the total to almost its present position, only five years later, in 1950.

In 1971, durable goods expenditures accounted for $6.5 billion; semi-durables, $5.5 billion; non-durables, $20.9 billion; and services, $20.3 billion. The Economic Council of Canada's predictions to 1975 indicate an average annual rate of growth of 7.2 percent for durable goods, 5.2 percent for semi-durable goods (slowed down by clothing and footwear sales), 5.2 percent for services, and 4.8 percent for non-durables (slowed down by food sales). Thus, durable goods are expected to increase at one and a half times the rate of non-durable goods. Household appliances, automobile sales and recreational durables account for the strong showing of this group. The dollar predictions for 1975 (in terms of 1967 dollars) are $8.8 billion for durable goods, $6.4 billion for semi-durables, $22.2 billion for non-durables and $21.5 billion for services. "The high rate of growth in consumer purchasing power to 1975 will offer great opportunities both for expanding markets for existing goods and services and for opening up markets for new types of consumer goods

[28] *Financial Post Survey of Markets, 1969,* p. 42.
[29] Economic Council of Canada, *Sixth Annual Review,* p. 53.

TABLE 2-14 Consumer Expenditure

	Total						
	1959	1967	At Potential in 1975	1967 / 1959	1975 / 1967	1967 / 1959	1975 / 1967
	(Millions of 1967 dollars)			(Percentage change)		(Average annual percentage change)	
Durables	3,007	5,058	8,795	68.2	73.9	6.7	7.2
Furniture, carpets, etc.	566	780	1,279	37.8	64.0	4.1	6.4
Household appliances	325	495	881	52.1	78.0	5.4	7.5
Personal transportation equipment, auto repairs, and auto parts and accessories	1,691	2,841	4,971	68.0	75.0	6.7	7.2
Recreational durables	404	655	1,159	61.9	77.1	6.2	7.4
Sales tax	64	288	504	352.8	75.5	20.8	7.3
Adjusting entry	−43						
Semidurables	3,163	4,298	6,433	35.9	49.7	3.9	5.2
Clothing, footwear, etc.	2,693	3,399	4,772	26.2	40.4	3.0	4.3
All other semidurables	428	674	1,320	57.5	95.9	5.8	8.8
Sales tax	54	225	341	319.0	51.4	19.6	5.3
Adjusting entry	−12						
Nondurables	10,288	15,269	22,225	48.4	45.6	5.1	4.8
Food and nonalcoholic beverages	5,414	6,730	8,641	24.3	28.4	2.8	3.2
Alcoholic beverages	966	1,436	2,197	48.7	53.0	5.1	5.5
Tobacco	792	995	1,330	25.7	33.6	2.9	3.7
All other nondurables	3,092	5,792	9,566	87.3	65.2	8.2	6.5
Sales tax	73	316	492	332.6	55.4	20.1	5.7
Adjusting entry	−49						
Services	10,936	14,372	21,547	31.4	49.9	3.5	5.2
(Services incl. all health care services)	(10,936)	(15,780)	(25,127)	(44.3)	(59.2)	(4.7)	(6.0)
Housing	3,399	5,493	8,974	61.6	63.4	6.2	6.3
Health	1,523	1,113	588	−26.9	−47.2	−3.8	−7.7
(Health incl. all health care services)	(1,523)	(2,521)	(4,168)	(65.6)	(65.3)	(6.5)	(6.5)
Education	246	687	2,465	178.7	258.7	13.7	17.3
All other services	5,936	7,079	9,520	19.2	34.5	2.2	3.8
Adjusting entry	−168						
Adjusting entry	−106						
Total Consumer Expenditure	27,288	38,998	59,000	42.9	51.3	4.6	5.3
(Total consumer expenditure incl. all health services)	(27,288)	(40,406)	(62,580)	(48.1)	(54.9)	(5.0)	(5.6)
	(Thousands of persons)						
Population	17,483	20,405	23,285	16.7	14.1	2.0	1.7

SOURCE: *Based on data from Dominion Bureau of Statistics and estimates by Economic Council of Canada. See pp. 54-5 of the Council's* Sixth Annual Review *(Ottawa: Queen's Printer, 1969).*

NOTE: Percentage change calculated from unrounded figures.

			Per Capita				
		At Potential	1967	1975	1967	1975	
1959	1967	in 1975	1959	1967	1959	1967	
	(1967 dollars)		(Percentage change)		(Average annual percentage change)		
172	248	378	44.1	52.4	4.7	5.4	Durables
32	38	55	18.0	43.7	2.1	4.6	Furniture, carpets, etc.
19	24	38	30.4	55.9	3.4	5.7	Household appliances
							Personal transportation equipment, auto repairs, and auto
97	139	214	44.0	53.3	4.7	5.5	parts and accessories
23	32	50	38.7	55.2	4.2	5.6	Recreational durables
4	14	22	288.2	53.8	18.5	5.5	Sales tax
−2							Adjusting entry
181	211	276	16.4	31.2	1.9	3.4	Semidurables
154	167	205	8.2	23.0	1.0	2.6	Clothing, footwear, etc.
24	33	57	34.9	71.6	3.8	7.0	All other semidurables
3	11	15	259.3	32.6	17.3	3.6	Sales tax
−1							Adjusting entry
588	748	955	27.2	27.6	3.0	3.1	Nondurables
							Food and nonalcoholic bev-
310	330	371	6.5	12.5	0.8	1.5	erages
55	70	94	27.4	34.1	3.1	3.7	Alcoholic beverages
45	49	57	7.7	17.1	0.9	2.0	Tobacco
177	284	411	60.5	44.7	6.1	4.7	All other nondurables
4	16	21	270.8	36.2	17.8	3.9	Sales tax
−3							Adjusting entry
626	704	925	12.6	31.4	1.5	3.5	Services
							(Services incl. all health care
(626)	(773)	(1,079)	(23.6)	(39.5)	(2.7)	(4.2)	services)
194	269	385	38.5	43.2	4.2	4.6	Housing
87	55	25	−37.4	−53.7	−5.7	−9.2	Health
							(Health incl. all health care
(87)	(124)	(179)	(41.9)	(44.9)	(4.5)	(4.7)	services)
14	34	106	138.8	214.4	11.5	15.4	Education
340	347	409	2.2	17.8	0.3	2.1	All other services
−10							Adjusting entry
−6							Adjusting entry
1,561	1,911	2,534	22.4	32.6	2.6	3.6	Total consumer expenditure
							(Total consumer expenditure
(1,561)	(1,980)	(2,688)	(26.9)	(35.7)	(3.0)	(3.9)	incl. all health services)

and services, especially for consumer durables and household semi-durables."[30] One area of services which will have a phenomenal growth rate is education. It is expected that expenditures in education will grow at an average annual rate of 17.3 percent per year for a total of 259 percent between 1967 and 1975.

Another set of predictions projecting annual (compound) rates for 1969 to 1975 is contained in Table 2-15.[31] This table also includes estimates of percentage expenditure changes to a one percent increase in income, and a one percent increase in price (relative to other products). Certain assumptions were made in developing these projections, including the following: personal per capita expenditures will rise from 1969's $1,862 (in '61 dollars) to $2,355 in 1975; price changes for the various expenditure groups reflected a linear relationship; completion of non-apartment housing will be 4.05 per 1,000 population in 1975, vs. 4.60 per 1,000 in 1969; the marriage rate will rise from 8.65 per 1,000 in 1969 to 9.65 per 1,000 in 1975; and car registrations will go up from 308 per 1,000 population in 1969 to 356 per 1,000 in 1975.

The highest expenditure growth rates of the selected products include carpets, appliances and transportation services. The lowest include medical and pharmaceutical products, household textiles and supplies. The most sensitive products to an income increase are, in the short run, appliances and personal transportation equipment, and in the longer run, carpets. The least sensitive to an income increase are household supplies. The most sensitive products to a price increase are household supplies and services, and the least sensitive are furniture, glassware and tableware.

The geographic distribution of consumer expenditures is indicated by Table 2-16, which shows 1970 percent and per capita retail sales by province. Retail sales account for about 60 percent of consumer expenditures. The concern here is to examine the pattern of personal expenditures, rather than retail sales per se; the latter topic will be covered in some detail in Chapter 8.

It is obvious that the bulk of personal expenditures are made in the two provinces of Quebec and Ontario. The only other province of the ten that has a 10 percent or higher share of the market is British Columbia. However, Alberta also experiences above-average per capita retail sales. As is to be expected, and as noticed in the study of income patterns, there is a division at the Quebec-Ontario border. West of that border the per capita expenditure figures are (with one major and one very minor exception) higher than any province in the east. Several of the metropolitan cities in three of these five western provinces had particularly high per capita figures. London, St. Catharines and Toronto, Ontario; Calgary and Edmonton, Alberta; and Vancouver, British

---

[30] *Ibid.*, p. 71.
[31] "How Some Key Markets May Look by 1975," *Financial Post*, 13 March 1971, p. 13.

TABLE 2-15 Estimates of Growth Rates and Income and Price Influences for Selected Product Categories

Product Categories	Annual Aggregate Compound Growth Rate to 1975 (%)	Annual Per Capita Compound Growth Rate to 1975 (%)	Expenditure Rise (%) for Each (one time) % Rise in Personal Disposable Income Short Term (1 Year) %	Longer Term %	Expenditure Drop (%) for Each 1% Price Rise Relative to Other Products Longer Term
Household supplies (cleaning) and hardware	6.0	4.2	.3 – .4	.7 – .8	2.0
Carpets and floor coverings	11.3	9.5	1.23	4.3	–
Household services[1]	7.7	5.9	.72	1.27	2.0
Personal transportation equipment	6.7	4.9	4.32	1.4	.15
Furniture	8.6	6.8	2.67	–	Insignificant
Glassware, tableware utensils	7.5	5.7	1.2 – 1.3	1.1 – 1.2	Insignificant
Transportation services	9.6	7.8	.98	2.88	.7
Household textiles	5.6	3.8	2.34	.8	.2
Medical and pharmaceutical products	5.2	3.5	.7	2.5	1.33
Household appliances	9.8	8.0	5.0	1.4	Insignificant

SOURCE: Developed from "How Some Key Markets May Look By 1975," Financial Post, 13 March 1971, p. 13. (Financial Post in turn developed these data from a study completed by T. T. Schweitzer for the Economic Council of Canada.)

1 Includes domestics, baby sitting, property insurance, laundry and dry cleaning, rental of furniture and appliances, and janitor services.

TABLE 2-16 Retail Sales, 1970

Province	% of Total Retail Sales	Per Capita
Newfoundland	1.8	$ 940
Prince Edward Island	0.5	1,220
Nova Scotia	3.4	1,220
New Brunswick	2.7	1,180
Quebec	25.5	1,180
Ontario	39.0	1,420
Manitoba	4.3	1,200
Saskatchewan	3.7	1,080
Alberta	8.0	1,390
British Columbia	11.1	1,440
Canada	100.0	1,300

SOURCE: Financial Post Survey of Markets, 1971, p.55.

Columbia, all had per capita retail sales over 19 percent higher than the national average.

Table 2-17 presents a detailed picture in terms of millions of dollars, of the personal expenditure on consumer goods and services for the period 1961 through to 1967. In 1967, food, tobacco, and alcoholic beverages accounted for 28 percent of the total; shelter and household operation, 27 percent; transportation, 12 percent; clothing and personal furnishings, 9 percent; personal and medical care, 9 percent; and miscellaneous, 15 percent. The major single expense, food, which in 1967 held 21 percent of expenditures, seems to be subject to Engel's law — in spite of the fact that the population is spending more dollars on food for increased variety and more expensive food items, with increasingly higher income at all levels, the food expenditure share dropped from 27 percent

TABLE 2-17 Personal Expenditure on Consumer Goods and Services, 1961-67

	1961	1962	1963	1964	1965	1966	1967
	millions of dollars						
Food	5,829	6,123	6,414	6,724	7,114	7,620	8,073
Tobacco and alcoholic beverages	1,683	1,782	1,840	1,911	2,079	2,225	2,431
Tobacco products and smokers' accessories	744	785	800	814	881	935	995
Alcoholic beverages	939	997	1,040	1,097	1,198	1,290	1,436
Clothing and personal furnishings	2,432	2,526	2,643	2,803	2,972	3,141	3,365
Men's and boys' clothing	533	567	603	648	696	733	781
Women's and children's clothing	1,028	1,069	1,118	1,191	1,261	1,334	1,426
Footwear	311	326	330	340	358	383	414
Laundry and dry cleaning	193	197	206	221	236	249	258
Other	367	367	386	403	421	442	486
Shelter[1]	3,812	3,996	4,323	4,595	4,907	5,323	5,790
Gross rents paid by tenants	1,030	1,079	1,177	1,260	1,362	1,498	1,672
Expenses (taxes, insurance, etc.) paid by owner-occupants	1,501	1,641	1,772	1,922	2,063	2,292	2,476

TABLE 2-17 Personal Expenditure on Consumer Goods and Services, 1961-67
(concluded)

	1961	1962	1963	1964	1965	1966	1967
	millions of dollars						
Shelter[1] (cont.)							
Net imputed residential rent and imputed residential capital consumption allowances	1,029	1,007	1,089	1,115	1,165	1,193	1,276
Other	252	269	285	298	317	340	366
Household operation	3,032	3,202	3,352	3,576	3,836	4,170	4,522
Fuel	423	470	473	460	473	480	510
Electricity	347	366	384	401	419	469	540
Gas	123	140	153	171	188	201	213
Telephone	332	359	386	420	453	490	539
Furniture	314	328	338	358	381	407	424
Home furnishings	285	298	319	356	388	424	457
Appliances, radios and television sets	490	507	529	571	619	686	734
Other	718	734	770	839	915	1,013	1,105
Transportation	2,872	3,160	3,430	3,730	4,120	4,262	4,549
Street-car, railway and other fares	418	446	459	483	537	590	704
New automobiles, used automobiles (net) and house trailers	1,262	1,441	1,648	1,846	2,107	2,108	2,171
Automotive operating expenses	1,192	1,273	1,323	1,401	1,476	1,564	1,674
Personal and medical care and death expenses	2,045	2,204	2,396	2,613	2,841	3,078	3,381
Medical and dental care	415	458	497	547	600	629	691
Hospital care, private duty nursing, accident and sickness insurance, prepaid medical care	906	995	1,118	1,250	1,376	1,512	1,676
Other	724	751	781	816	865	937	1,014
Miscellaneous	2,761	2,933	3,089	3,714	4,192	5,029	5,603
Motion picture theatres[2]	62	61	64	69	75	83	94
Newspapers and magazines	242	253	261	285	308	329	363
Net expenditure abroad	209	90	29	84	80	93	−367
Other	2,248	2,529	2,735	3,276	3,729	4,524	5,513
Grand Totals	24,466	25,926	27,487	29,666	32,061	34,848	37,714
Durable goods	2,716	2,960	3,246	3,592	4,001	4,169	4,365
Major durable goods[3]	2,351	2,574	2,834	3,131	3,494	3,625	3,785
Miscellaneous durable goods[4]	365	386	412	461	507	544	580
Non-durable goods[5]	12,178	12,965	13,518	14,389	15,438	16,930	18,488
Services[5,6]	9,572	10,001	10,723	11,685	12,622	13,749	14,861

SOURCE: *DBS, "National Accounts, Income and Expenditure," No. 13-001 (Ottawa: Queen's Printer).*

1 Excludes transients' shelter.

2 Excludes amusement taxes.

3 Includes house trailers, new automobiles, net expenditure on used automobiles, home furnishings, furniture and appliances, radios and television sets.

4 Includes jewellery, watches, clocks, silverware, toys, sporting and wheeled goods, and tools and garden equipment.

5 The items electricity and gas are now classified to non-durable goods and not to services. This treatment differs from that used in "National Accounts, Income and Expenditure, 1926-1956."

6 Includes net expenditure abroad.

of the total in 1951 to 21 percent in 1967. Perhaps the groups which will increase most rapidly in the years to come are household operation, and personal and medical care.

TABLE 2-18 Average Urban Family Expenditure Patterns, Eleven Cities, 1967

Selected Characteristics	Food	Shelter	Hsld. Operation	Furns. & Equip.	Clothing	Transportation
	%	%	%	%	%	%
By Income						
(Families of two or more)						
$2,500 – $2,999	27.4	22.8	4.4	3.4	5.4	9.7
$5,000 – $5,499	24.5	19.1	4.2	3.6	6.9	10.6
$10,000+	16.8	12.9	3.9	4.3	8.9	11.4
By Family						
1 adult	18.2	20.8	4.4	3.0	7.0	12.7
2 adults	17.0	17.0	4.0	4.6	7.6	11.3
2 adults/1 child	18.6	17.4	4.3	5.0	7.4	12.8
2 adults/2 children	19.1	17.0	4.8	5.3	7.5	11.2
2 adults/5+ children	26.8	18.0	3.7	4.2	7.8	11.8
By Age of Head						
(Families of two or more)						
25 – 34	18.8	16.9	4.7	5.0	7.7	11.2
45 – 54	19.4	13.4	3.2	4.2	9.4	12.0
65 – 69	18.7	16.6	4.4	5.6	6.9	10.3
By Occupation						
(Families of two or more)						
Managerial	17.4	14.9	4.1	4.9	8.9	11.0
Clerical	19.4	17.2	4.0	4.3	8.4	10.8
Labourer	26.4	16.8	3.7	3.7	8.7	8.9
By Education						
Primary partial	24.7	17.6	3.8	4.3	9.0	10.1
Secondary complete	18.8	16.7	4.0	4.4	8.5	12.0
University complete	14.4	14.1	4.2	4.7	7.6	10.8
All Classes	19.4	15.9	4.0	4.2	8.4	11.7

SOURCE: *Selected statistics compiled from DBS, "Urban Family Expenditures, 1967," No. 62-530 (Ottawa: Queen's Printer, 1971).*

NOTE: Percentages, which are additive horizontally, do not total 100 percent as only certain selected expenditure categories were included in this table.

Table 2-18 reveals some interesting expenditure patterns. This table analyzes expenditures by income, family type, family head age, occupation and education. The income analysis confirms the conclusion about food expenditures drawn from Table 2-17. That is, very low income families spend over one-quarter of their total expenditures on food, while those with incomes of $10,000 or more spend only one-sixth of their total expenditures on this important item. The latter also spend relatively less on shelter, but more on clothing and transportation.

When expenditures are analyzed by family type, it is noted that the largest relative spenders on food are the largest families. Thus, a one- or two-adult family spends less than 20 percent on food, but the family with five or more children spends almost 27 percent of its total expenditures on food. Note that the one-adult household, with a very different life style, understandably has a unique expenditure pattern.

The age analysis reveals one important fact: the relatively high percentage of total expenditures that those in the young family group spend on furnishings, shifts to clothing in the 45–54 age group. Occupational and educational analysis points to relatively high food expenditures for labourers and lower education groups. Obviously, this is related to the income patterns. Though the absolute dollar expenditures are not shown in the table, more actual dollars are spent in every category by the higher income groups. This statement even includes expenditures for food.

The importance of women as purchasing agents for their husbands is indicated by certain statistics provided by the annual Canadian Consumer Survey.[32] The 1967 figures show that 61 percent of the women buy their men's shirts, 65 percent their socks, 67 percent their underwear, 45 percent their ties, 44 percent their sports shirts, 43 percent their sweaters, 40 percent their sleeping wear and dressing gowns, and so on.

When discussing consumer expenditures, few marketers can afford to disregard the growing youth market. From the previous discussion about population trends it was noted that half of the population is under 25 years of age. Indeed, certain products are almost completely dependent on teenage acceptance. Among these can be included records, a good portion of motion pictures, soft drinks, clothing for youth, a good portion of beauty products, and so on. Since the older portion of this youth market — those in their early 20's — comprises a very important segment of the young marrieds market, many consumer durable manufacturers are vitally concerned with this market.

It has been estimated, for example, that brides, either through direct purchases or as a result of receiving wedding gifts, account for the following percent of sales of durable products:[33]

Mixers	46%	Irons	29%
Bedspreads	44%	Blankets	23%
Toasters	42%	Soft surface rugs	19%
Towels	35%	T.V. sets	17%
Clock radios	34%	Refrigerators	15%
Coffee makers	30%	Vacuum cleaners	13%

The size of the total consumer market is not only expanding in terms of quantity and dollars and cents, it is also expanding in terms of the range of products being bought. There is an increasing variety in product offerings, and in the pattern of the consumer's product mix — the consumer market is becoming more diverse. As the previous analyses

[32] *The Canadian Consumer Survey of 1967* (Toronto: Canadian Daily Newspaper Publishers Association, 1967) , p. 247.
[33] "The Youth Market," *Marketing* 71 (24 June 1966) , p. 22.

have shown, this increasing diversity is due to such causes as: changes in the age structure, immigration influx, greater world communication to the average consumer, a move to the urban areas, reduction of the prices of many durables, the growth of consumer credit, and particularly important, the rapid growth in discretionary income. These factors along with others, have had fundamental influences on the consumer market: for example, earlier marriages along with higher household formation rates, working wives along with higher family incomes, increasingly sophisticated technological innovations and education along with changing values.

Hence, there is greater emphasis on and variety of products incorporating convenience features such as frozen foods; increasing use of restaurants; and greater emphasis on personal care products, fashion items, synthetic fibres and plastic, and on luxury items such as aeroplane travel, swimming pools, sports cars, and a whole range of recreational products attuned to the increasing leisure time of consumers.[34] These latter products include sports equipment, travel products, casual living products (e.g., home barbecues), and cultural items. Indeed, one author predicts that "two-thirds of household spending in the mid-70's will be for luxuries, compared with less than half in 1964." [35]

The quality of food purchases, as the single largest expenditure, is changing rapidly. Food purchases in general, along with other products, are becoming more variety- and convenience-oriented. There is also a greater emphasis on low-calorie protein food, rather than carbohydrates. Frozen food sales, for example, are over two and a half times their level ten years ago. Fruit juice, poultry, coffee, cheese, margarine, and beef are all up in sales, from 10 to 65 percent in the past decade, while tea, butter, rice and flour sales have declined from 10 to 5 percent in the same period.

Canadians are spending more, for numerous products that were not on the market even ten years ago. There is an increasing opportunity for the marketer following a policy of specialization and market segmentation.

URBAN MARKETS AND THE MEGALOPOLIS

Urban Markets

Canada's population is now 75 percent urban and by 1980 it is estimated that this figure will increase to 81 percent.[36] Montreal and Toronto lead in this urban concentration with a present combined

---

[34] For an excellent elaboration of this latter point see, Canadian Imperial Bank of Commerce, "Leisure Time in Perspective," *Commercial Letter*, no. 2, 1970, 8 pages.

[35] John Kettle, "Life's Essentials Keep Pace With the Population Rise: Luxuries are Moving Twice as Fast," *Monetary Times* 135 (October 1967), p. 49.

[36] Economic Council of Canada, *Fourth Annual Review*, p. 186.

TABLE 2-19 Profile of the Largest Urban Areas, 1970-71

	10-yr. Rate of Growth %	Population, Apr. 1, 1971			Personal Disposable Income, 1970					Retail Sales, 1970		
		Total No. (000)	% Can. Total	House-holds No. (000)	Income Rating Index %	Total ($ millions)	% Can. Total	Per Capita $	Market Rating Index %	Total ($ millions)	% Can. Total	Per Capita $
Canada	17	21,641.0	100.00	5,732.1	100	53,595.0	100.00	2,500	100	27,792.9	100.00	1,300
Metro areas & population 100,000+:												
Montreal	12	2,720.4	12.57	765.7	112	7,554.9	14.10	2,810	105	3,659.1	13.16	1,360
Toronto	36	2,609.6	12.06	724.3	120	7,598.3	14.18	2,990	121	4,011.1	14.43	1,580
Vancouver	33	1,071.0	4.95	330.0	112	2,921.3	5.45	2,800	119	1,617.1	5.85	1,550
Ottawa	28	596.2	2.75	160.1	135	1,973.4	3.68	3,390	108	815.9	2.93	1,400
Winnipeg	11	534.7	2.47	154.4	122	1,615.0	3.01	3,050	108	741.3	2.67	1,400
Hamilton	22	495.9	2.29	139.1	120	1,458.0	2.72	2,990	111	701.0	2.52	1,440
Edmonton	36	490.8	2.27	137.6	122	1,450.7	2.71	3,040	121	754.0	2.71	1,580
Quebec	20	476.2	2.20	114.9	99	1,163.7	2.17	2,490	106	646.0	2.32	1,380
Calgary	48	400.1	1.85	117.1	128	1,236.2	2.31	3,190	124	623.7	2.24	1,610
London	27	284.5	1.31	83.7	115	793.2	1.47	2,870	122	442.5	1.59	1,590
Windsor	15	255.2	1.18	71.7	115	721.1	1.34	2,860	109	357.6	1.29	1,420
Kitchener	38	224.4	1.04	63.2	109	596.4	1.11	2,740	114	322.6	1.16	1,480
Halifax	11	220.3	1.02	53.7	113	618.6	1.15	2,830	120	340.4	1.22	1,560
Victoria	19	193.5	0.89	62.2	110	523.3	0.98	2,750	114	281.6	1.01	1,480
Sudbury	28	153.9	0.71	38.2	144	511.8	1.01	3,600	110	215.2	0.77	1,430
Regina	10	138.9	0.64	40.3	120	414.2	0.77	3,010	108	194.0	0.70	1,410
St. John's	22	129.3	0.60	26.3	78	246.3	0.46	1,940	118	195.4	0.70	1,540
Saskatoon	17	125.1	0.58	36.3	116	356.3	0.66	2,890	108	172.6	0.62	1,400
Thunder Bay	11	111.5	0.51	30.6	117	320.3	0.60	2,910	114	162.5	0.58	1,480
St. Catharines	23	109.6	0.51	31.4	127	340.5	0.63	3,160	135	188.3	0.68	1,750
Saint John	1	105.2	0.49	27.8	95	249.6	0.47	2,380	112	153.6	0.55	1,460
Total		11,446.3	52.89	3,208.6		32,698.1	60.98			16,595.5	59.70	

SOURCE: Financial Post Survey of Markets, 1971, p. 48.

population of almost five and a half million (and an expected combined population of seven million by 1980) ; almost a quarter of Canada's total population. Half of Canada's population, or two-thirds of its urban population, lives in the twenty-one urban centres with populations of 100,000 or more. Half of this large city market is found in the two cities of Montreal and Toronto combined. The annual population growth rates indicate a continuing trend from rural and smaller urban areas to large urban centres.

The Dominion Bureau of Statistics defines a metropolitan area as a geographically small region centred economically upon a large city and containing a number of additional cities, towns and unincorporated urban settlements whose economies are closely linked with that of the large central city. These usually consist of one major city and surrounding suburbs. There were, in 1966, nineteen such DBS Census metropolitan areas. The nineteen metropolitan areas plus two other cities with over a 100,000 population are profiled in Table 2-19. Though Montreal and Toronto lead in this urban concentration, with a combined population of 5.3 million, Calgary and Kitchener are growing faster than Toronto, and in addition, all but five are growing faster than Montreal.

It should be noted, however, that almost half of the urban dwellers in these large cities live in the suburbs. This is a significant fact, since in 1941 only 25 percent of the metropolitan dwellers lived in the suburbs, while in 1951 this had increased to 33 percent.[37] Indeed, three-quarters of the metropolitan area growth between 1951 and 1961 took place within the suburban areas. In certain cities, such as Toronto, Halifax, Quebec and Saint John, all of the growth between 1956 and 1966 took place within the suburban sector, and the city proper actually had negative growth. Only Calgary, Regina and Saskatoon, because of the vast spaces available in the city proper, experienced a relatively large percentage of their total growth in the latter area. Table 2-20 presents a break-down between the city proper and suburban populations as of 1961. In 1961, 50 percent of the metropolitan area residents lived in suburban areas. This figure was as high as 69 percent for Toronto and reached 50 percent or more for the cities of Halifax, Quebec and Montreal. Growth (1961–66) in the metropolitan areas could be attributed slightly more to natural increases than to net migration. Net migration, of course, was a more important factor in the population growth of the suburban areas, as would be expected, while natural increase was the major factor in the growth of the city proper (net migration actually showed a negative figure for the city proper).

The fastest growing of these cities, Calgary, is growing at almost triple the rate of Canada in general, and Vancouver, Toronto, Saskatoon, Edmonton, and Kitchener are not too far behind. These metropolitan areas also account for an even greater percentage of Canada's income than

<hr />

[37] DBS, "General Review, Rural and Urban Population," No. 99-512, *1961 Census of Canada,* and "General Population Trends," No. 99-601, *1966 Census of Canada* (Ottawa: Queen's Printer) .

TABLE 2-20 Population Distribution in Canadian Metropolitan Areas, 1961

| Metropolitan Area | Percent of Total in | |
	City Proper	Suburban Area
Calgary	89.5	10.5
Edmonton	83.3	16.7
Halifax	50.3	49.7
Hamilton	69.3	30.7
Kitchener	48.1	51.9
London	93.5	6.5
Montreal	56.5	43.5
Ottawa	62.4	37.6
Quebec	48.1	51.9
Saint John	57.7	42.3
St. John's	70.1	29.9
Sudbury	72.4	27.6
Toronto	36.9	63.1
Vancouver	48.7	51.3
Victoria	35.6	64.4
Windsor	59.1	40.9
Winnipeg	55.8	44.2
All Metropolitan Areas	54.7	45.3

SOURCE: DBS, *"General Review, Rural and Urban Population,"* No. 99-512, Vol. 7, Part 1, Census of Canada *(Ottawa: Queen's Printer, 1963), pp. 2-14.*

do their populations. In other words, their per capita income is higher than the general per capita income prevailing in Canada. Metropolitan areas' income includes about 61 percent of Canada's personal disposable income. Toronto, Ottawa, Hamilton, Calgary, Winnipeg, Regina, St. Catharines and Sudbury have particularly high per capita disposable income. Expenditures, as measured in terms of retail sales, also account for a higher percentage of Canada's total than does the population figure — i.e., per capita retail sales are higher than the average. Montreal and Toronto alone account for over one-quarter of Canada's retail sales. Edmonton, Calgary, London, and St. Catharines all have very high per capita retail sales.

It is obvious from these tables that the Canadian marketing strategist must be particularly concerned with his big city markets. They appear to play an even more important role in Canadian marketing than they do in many other countries.

Canada's Megalopolis

A large number of these large city markets, i.e., metropolitan areas, form the "megalopolis." Montreal and Toronto form the axis for this megalopolis which stretches some 750 miles. The megalopolis starts in Quebec City, runs down through Three Rivers, the Eastern Townships, Montreal, Ottawa, Kingston, Toronto, the Niagara Peninsula, London, and ends in Windsor, some 240 miles southwest of Toronto. Table

FIGURE 2-1 Canada's Megalopolis

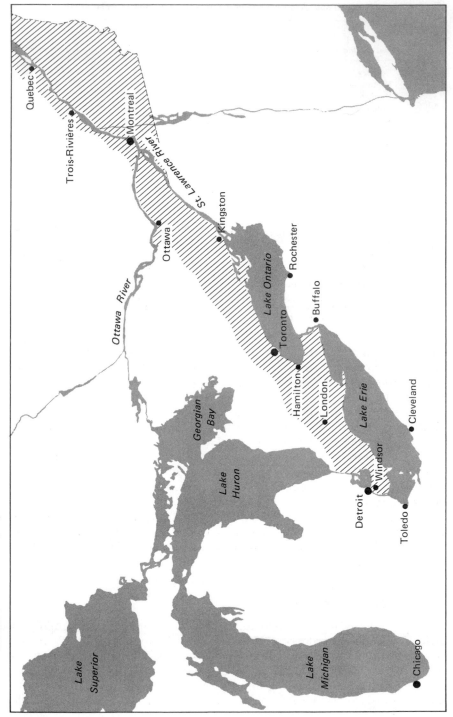

2-21 shows that though the megalopolis occupies a minute portion of Canada's total land area it contains a huge share of her population (54 percent), income (57 percent) and consumer expenditures (56 percent). In addition, it is growing faster than the rest of Canada. This area represents over 55 percent of the total Canadian market, a most important factor to consider when planning marketing programmes.

TABLE 2-21 Characteristics of Canada's Megalopolis

| Economic Areas | % of Canada's | | |
	Population (1971)	Disposable Income (1970)	Retail Sales (1970)
Quebec, Quebec	3.35	2.79	2.96
Three Rivers, Quebec	1.37	1.12	1.08
Eastern Townships, Quebec	2.25	1.62	1.91
Montreal, Quebec	4.18	3.50	3.54
Metro Montreal, Quebec	11.48	13.03	12.17
Hull, Quebec	.95	.82	.66
Eastern Ontarlo, Ontario	4.33	4.97	4.57
Lako Ontario, Ontario	1.74	1.71	1.75
Metro Toronto, Ontario	13.21	16.09	15.39
Niagara, Ontario	4.28	4.75	4.64
Lake Erie, Ontario	2.27	2.14	2.43
Lake St. Clair, Ontario	2.52	2.64	2.63
Mid-Western, Ontario	2.26	2.20	2.30
	54.19	57.38	56.03

SOURCE: *Developed from* Financial Post Survey of Markets, 1971, *pp. 116, 193.*

Canada's megalopolis, which has been referred to as the St. Lawrence Seaway corridor, the Great Lakes–St. Lawrence corridor, and the Grand Trunk, actually spills over into the U.S. and can be projected through Detroit, Chicago and St. Louis. Though the urban areas within the megalopolis do not account for the entire population, it can be safely assumed that most of the non-urban areas within this region are urban-minded.

Traditional campaign planning held to the idea of market areas growing in ever-widening circles around cities sprung from pioneer settlements. But that situation has changed. Today's planner must cope with a mushrooming metropolitan spread that melds groups of towns and cities into single, sprawling communities.

The new theory is that markets grow in broad ribbons or corridors. Super-cities spring up at corridor intersections and reach out towards each other with an inexorable gravitation pull.

For the marketing man, this trend to large, municipal units which can include some farm land, as well as built-up cities, sweeps away the old distinction between farm and city. More than ever, he is finding that the same promotional appeal will work with today's business-oriented farmer, as with the sophisticated city-dweller.

The individual has difficulty in identifying himself with his newly expanded community. He lives in a certain township, he works in the city, he bowls in another township, he attends church in the village, his children go to an area school in a town, and he and his wife do their shopping in one of the new super-complexes in a metropolitan area's suburb.[38]

Another writer states that "The potent role played by the heartland in the Canadian economy stems, in large part, from its impressive industrial base, which many observers foresee as one of the world's prime productive centres, much like England's Midlands and West Germany's Ruhr."[39]

---

[38] Edward G. Pleva, "The Marketing Corridors of Southern Ontario," *Marketing* 67 (5 October 1962) , pp. 60-64.
[39] Thayer C. Taylor, "Seven Million Customers All in a Row," in Isaiah A. Litvak and Bruce E. Mallen, eds., *Marketing: Canada*, p. 42.

3

The Cultural and Comparative Dimensions of the Canadian Consumer Market

Another environmental factor within which the marketer must operate as mentioned at the beginning of this book is the ethical-sociological-philosophical one. This ethical-sociological-philosophical environment will be termed, for purposes of brevity, the cultural environment — a term denoting the "way-of-life" of a market. Certainly, this is a key environmental factor to which the marketer must adjust, and through which he must appeal to his market.

It is the purpose of this chapter to describe the cultural environment of the Canadian consumer market, and to compare it to other similar markets. The discussion focusses first of all on Canada's two major cultures, those of English- and French-speaking Canada, and concludes by examining some of the marketing implications of Canada's bicultural aspect. In the second part of the chapter, the Canadian market is compared to other markets, notably those of the United States and Europe.

THE CULTURAL DIMENSION

Demographic and economic statistics and profiles certainly contribute to an understanding of the needs and structure of a market. However, in order to get at the "flavour" of a market, one must understand its cultural environment. This added dimension will aid the marketer in obtaining a greater depth of understanding than he would if he were simply to rely on the bare statistics of the situation.

Unfortunately, the definitive work on Canadian society has yet to be written. The literature still does not provide a scholarly research which describes the Canadian "way-of-life" in all, or at least in most of its ramifications. There have been a number of works, however, which examine small sections of the society, and one can obtain a "feel" for the Canadian cultural environment by generalizing about these many sociological studies. It must be noted, though, that the most the reader can expect from such an approach is an impressionistic view. It is the purpose of this section to provide the reader with a "feel" for the environment, rather than a clear-cut description. The approach, then, is to isolate those key concepts which the literature seems to provide.

Canada, of course, lies in the mainstream of Western civilization and culture. It has been, and is, a blend of British, American and French values. The values of these three cultures themselves are relatively similar. For example, all three are basically Christian and democratic cultures, and spring from the Judeo-Christian-Greco-Roman tradition. All three place a high value on the individual, are "this-worldly," and are to a greater or lesser degree materialistic — i.e., place relatively high emphasis on increasing the standard of living. Describing the Canadian culture as an entity distinct from these has proved perennially difficult. It has been particularly difficult to distinguish the Canadian character from the American one. Indeed, it may be added that this constant attempt to distinguish our culture from the U.S. culture, or for that matter, from any other culture, is itself a national trait which may be referred to as "negative nationalism."

During the past decade, events of paramount importance have taken place in Canada. These events have been altering Canada's social structure and have placed this country in a state of social flux. The prolonged parliamentary debates on obtaining a distinctly Canadian flag, the antagonisms between French Canadians and English Canadians, the Canadian fears of American economic domination and cultural absorption are expressions of the economic and cultural flux in Canada. There is a rising feeling of nationalism among English Canadians vis-à-vis the United States, and among French Canadians vis-à-vis English Canada. It appears that English-speaking Canadians are starting to feel more like Canadians and French Canadians more like French Canadians. There is social unrest within these groups. French Canadians are demanding a larger role in the economic and business affairs of Canada.

The English-Canadian Cultural Environment

This section will deal with the Canadian culture in general, emphasizing the English-speaking aspect of it. However, the following section will deal with French-Canadian culture. It is important to look at these two sub-cultures separately because the marketer, in evolving a marketing strategy in Canada, must realize that for a given product offer, French and English Canadians often have different buying motives and habits. The reason for these differences may frequently be found in the differing cultural environments. And further, it is important to remember that French Canadians account for almost 30 percent of the total Canadian market.

This description of the Canadian cultural environment will concentrate on its differences, particularly the difference from the American environment. It must be remembered throughout that the similarities are much more prevalent. But to mention these similarities is beyond the scope of this chapter and would really serve no useful purpose, since most of them are recognized, consciously or unconsciously, by the marketer. There are, however, as will be seen, some important differences beyond simply superficial ones such as spelling and the meaning of certain words.

CULTURAL TRAITS

Four key concepts, or traits, appear to distinguish the Canadian cultural environment:

negative nationalism
conservatism
mosaic diversity
biculturalism

Canadians, living so close to the most powerful nation on earth and constantly being bombarded with American ideas through their own media, or just as likely American media, are concerned with the possibility of cultural absorption. In order to meet this threat there is a strong tendency to point out, consciously or unconsciously, how the Canadian culture differs from the U.S. It is as if the Canadian culture had created a defense mechanism against cultural oblivion. "Canadians enjoy what may be called a 'negative nationalism.' Whereas other nationals talk about what they are, Canadians pride themselves on what they are not."[1]

Most studies on Canadian cultural society have noted the pervasive, socially conservative attitude held by many Canadians. This conservatism has both positive and negative dimensions and portrays itself in many ways.

Canadians are said to be more stable and orderly, and to have more respect for authority. For example, the "West" was never quite as unruly in Canada as it was in the United States. This was probably due to the strength of the Northwest Mounted Police. One sees less violence and strife on the labour scene, on the political scene, and on the social scene (excluding the recent unrest in Montreal). These traits have led one authority to label Canada a "sophisticated democracy."[2] Another authority sees these characteristics as being derived from the tradition of the English model which stands for stable political forms, for public dignity, and for social orderliness.[3]

It is also said as part of this conservatism that Canadians tend to be more realistic, practical and prudent. However, this often means

[1] Richard Laskin, "Canada as a Society: Some Observations," in Richard Laskin, ed., *Social Problems: A Canadian Profile* (Toronto: McGraw-Hill Company of Canada Limited, 1964), p. 20.
[2] Scott Symons, "The Meaning of English Canada," *Executive* 6 (July 1964), p. 31.
[3] Kaspar D. Naegele, "Canadian Society: Further Reflections," in Bernard R. Blishen, Frank E. Jones and Kaspar D. Naegele, eds., *Canadian Society* (Toronto: Macmillan Company of Canada Limited, 1964), p. 502. See also

they are less optimistic of the future and so less willing to take the required risks for development. They tend to be quieter, to be less emotional and impulsive and to possess a greater degree of humility. The latter traits often label them as a duller and a drabber people, less sociable, overly reserved and less expressive.

A third culturally-differentiating trait is that of mosaic diversity.[4] This aspect of Canadian society is very closely associated with biculturalism, a discussion of which will be reserved for the following section.

By mosaic diversity or, to use another term, cultural pluralism, is meant the slower rate of cultural assimilation of Canada's different ethnic groups. Whereas in the United States the ideal for the ethnic minorities is to assimilate as quickly as possible, there is not this kind of pressure on the New Canadian. Indeed, the very term "New Canadian" suggests the existence of this trait. One seldom hears of a New American. Compared to the U.S., Canada is by and large a mosaic, not a melting pot.

Certainly, one very important contributing factor to this situation is the importance and numerical strength of the French-Canadian minority. Their culture was assured a separate existence through the British North America Act which ostensibly provided for the respect of their separate language, religion, political rights and institutions. This has probably led to a similar type of respect for the minor ethnic groups. Perhaps another determinant of this mosaic diversity is the absence of strong overt patriotism. Canadians, unlike the Americans, are not flag-wavers (and only finally designed one after 98 years of existence). One does not hear of a Royal Commission into un-Canadian activities. Nor, for that matter, does one hear talk of the "Canadian way of life."

Another approach to the study of national cultural traits is an

J. Bartlet Brebner, *Canada: A Modern History* (Ann Arbor: University of Michigan Press, 1960), p. 522; Bruce Hutchison, "The Canadian Personality," in Malcolm Ross, ed., *Our Sense of Identity* (Toronto: Ryerson Press, 1954), pp. 42-43; Claude T. Bissell, "The Image of America in Canada," address delivered at the Canadian Studies Seminar, University of Rochester, 16 March 1962; F. G. Vallee and D. R. Whyte, "Canadian Society: Trends and Perspectives," in B. R. Blishen, F. E. Jones, K. D. Naegele and J. Porter, *Canadian Society* (Toronto: Macmillan Company of Canada, 1968), pp. 833-52; John Porter, "Canadian Character in the Twentieth Century," *The Annals of the American Academy of Political and Social Science* (March, 1967), pp. 48-56; Seymour Lipset, "Canada and the United States — A Comparative View," *Canadian Review of Sociology and Anthropology* 1 (November 1964), pp. 173ff, also in W. E. Mann, editor, *Canada: A Sociological Profile* (Toronto: Copp Clark Publishing Company, 1968), pp. 488-98.

[4] Many authors have made comments on this trait. A sample of these comments can be found in the following: Dennis Wrong, "Background for Understanding," in Laskin, *Social Problems: A Canadian Profile,* p. 28; Brebner, *Canada: A Modern History,* p. 526; Malcolm Ross, *Our Sense of Identity* (Toronto: Ryerson Press, 1954), p. ix; Vincent Massey, *Speaking of Canada* (Toronto: Macmillan Company of Canada Limited, 1959), pp. 33-35.

analysis of six "pattern variables." Kernan, Dommeruth and Sommers have analysed national differences using six scales or sets of pattern variables adapted from the individual works of Talcott Parsons and Seymour Lipset. The pairs of variables as defined by Kernan et al. are:

1. *Equality-elite:* whether to accord to all persons and objects (which includes products) a general level of respect or consideration (equality) or to accord respect or consideration on the basis of status or class. (elite).

2. *Performance-quality:* whether to treat a person or product on the basis of the results that flow from his or its actions (performance) or on the basis of inherited or inherent attributes (quality).

3. *Material-nonmaterial:* whether to rely upon products (material) for personal expression and evaluation of others, or to rely upon other (nonmaterial) factors.

4. *Objective-subjective:* whether to treat and evaluate a person or product in terms of a general norm applied to people or products in a category (objective) or to treat or evaluate people or products in terms of some particular personal or group relationship (subjective).

5. *Intensive-extensive:* whether to consider and evaluate involvements with a person or product in terms of a limited range of activities and attributes (intensive) or to be concerned with all aspects of a person or product (extensive).

6. *Individual-collective:* whether to evaluate people or products in terms of their potential for personal benefit or gratification (individual) or to evaluate them in terms of their appropriateness for the evaluator as a representative of a group or category such as a social class (collective).

The relative positions of the United States, Australia, Canada and Great Britain for each pair of pattern variables are illustrated in Table 3-1.

In Canada, class structure (elite as opposed to equality) is stronger than in the United States, but probably much less an accepted

TABLE 3-1 Estimates of Rankings of Countries According to Strength of Six Pattern Variables (Ranked According to the First Term in Each Pair)

Pattern Variable	U.S.	Australia	Canada	Britain
Equality-elite	2	1	3	4
Performance-quality	1	2.5	2.5	4
Material-nonmaterial	1	3	2	4
Objective-subjective	1	3	2	4
Intensive-extensive	1	2.5	2.5	4
Individual-collective	1	3	2	4

SOURCE: *Jerome B. Kernan et al., Promotion: An Introductory Analysis (New York: McGraw Hill Book Company, 1970), pp. 58-59.*

NOTE: Five of the pattern variable rankings are adapted from Seymour Lipset, "The Value Patterns of Democracy: A Case Study in Comparative Values," *American Sociological Review,* 28 August 1968, p. 521; the sixth (material-nonmaterial) is from Talcott Parsons, *The Social System* (New York: The Free Press of Glencoe, 1964), pp. 101-112.

fact of life than in Great Britain. Materialism, objectivity and individualism are all traits that the Canadian character shares with that of the American. The more or less equal concern both of Canadians and Australians with quality versus performance, and extensiveness versus intensiveness, is perhaps to be expected in these two countries that have been greatly influenced by both the United States and Britain.

REGIONAL DIFFERENCES

English-speaking Canada can be divided regionally into (1) the eastern Atlantic provinces of Newfoundland and the Maritimes (Nova Scotia, Prince Edward Island, New Brunswick) ; (2) the central province of Ontario; (3) the western provinces of British Columbia and the Prairies (Manitoba, Saskatchewan and Alberta). Each of these regions and provinces has its own specific deviations from the average. Many of these differences were seen in the tables of the preceding chapter. An examination of that data will show differences in both demographic and financial profiles. Differences are also reflected in the cultural aspects of these regions. The comments which follow are impressionistic rather than being based on exhaustive empirical research; nevertheless, in keeping with the rest of this chapter they are designed to give the reader a "feel" for the Canadian culture and its various components.

The Atlantic provinces tend to be more conservative and provincial-minded (it is strange to an Ontarian to hear his province referred to as Upper Canada by a Maritimer, or the Mainland by a Newfoundlander), and more U.K.-oriented (and so less U.S.-oriented). Atlantic inhabitants appear to take life easier.

Ontario as the richest region also contains the most sophisticated consumers, and in itself represents a cross-section of the total of Canada. These consumers are more partial to new innovations and products than their more cautious counterparts in the Atlantic region.

The western provinces have a different ethnic mix than do the three regions lying to their east (Ontario, Quebec, Atlantic). The minor ethnic groups (all those other than the French and British) play a much larger role here, and affect market strategies through their varying cultural backgrounds (this is not to dismiss the very important role of these groups in the cosmopolitan cities of Toronto and Montreal). Western hospitality and informality are two dominant traits of this region. It has four large cities which contain most of the urban population of their respective provinces: Winnipeg, Manitoba; Vancouver, British Columbia; and Edmonton and Calgary, Alberta. This of course implies on a smaller scale the kind of problems that were mentioned about the country as a whole (a megalopolis of dense population and then a scattering of centres over the country). Many marketers will concentrate on the large cities and use outside agencies to service the rest of the region. British Columbia is very much oriented to the U.S. West Coast as it is somewhat at a physical handicap (the Rocky Mountains) when dealing with the Canadian market.

SOCIAL CLASS

Table 3-2 presents an estimate by N. K. Dhalla of the percentage distribution of the Canadian population over the various social classes by province. The estimate is derived by combining years of schooling with income.[5] These two variables are multiplied together and then grouped into the five classes.

According to this estimate, approximately 72 percent of the population falls into the lower class, 23.5 percent into the middle class, and 4 percent into the upper class. Ontario, at 5 percent, has the largest relative (and absolute) upper class, Saskatchewan at 28.5 percent has the largest relative middle class, and Newfoundland with 82.3 percent has the largest proportion in the lower class. (However, if this lower class was subdivided into its parts, Nova Scotia with 58 percent in the upper-lower and Prince Edward Island with 37.4 percent in the lower-lower would hold the latter distinction.)

These figures should not come as a surprise to the reader, as they are simply a reflection of two of the features examined in the last chapter: income and education. For the marketer of luxury items, they reinforce the basis for his strategy to concentrate the bulk of his effort on the western half of the country.

TABLE 3-2 Social Class Estimates by Province, 1961 (Percentage Distribution)

Province	Upper-Upper & Lower-Upper	Upper-Middle	Lower-Middle	Upper-Lower	Lower-Lower	Total
Canada	4.2	8.5	15.0	54.1	18.2	100
Newfoundland	1.7	5.9	10.1	53.8	28.5	100
P.E.I.	2.0	5.8	11.9	42.9	37.4	100
Nova Scotia	2.7	7.3	11.1	57.9	21.0	100
New Brunswick	2.7	7.0	11.3	52.9	26.1	100
Quebec	4.2	7.6	13.9	56.0	18.3	100
Ontario	5.0	9.4	15.8	55.5	14.3	100
Manitoba	3.3	8.6	16.1	51.0	21.0	100
Saskatchewan	2.6	7.3	21.2	42.7	26.2	100
Alberta	4.6	9.1	17.2	47.8	21.3	100
British Columbia	4.3	9.5	13.7	55.8	16.7	100
Yukon & N.W.T.	3.0	5.5	11.0	54.0	26.5	100

SOURCE: N. K. Dhalla, These Canadians (Toronto: McGraw-Hill, 1966), p. 197

The French-Canadian Cultural Environment

The following section will not present a statistical profile of the French-Canadian market. The reader should refer to the statistics for Quebec presented in Chapter 2, which, though including English

[5] A more sophisticated method, placing emphasis on occupational status, may be found in Bernard R. Blishen, "A Socio-Economic Index for Occupations in Canada," Canadian Review of Sociology and Anthropology 4:1 (February 1967), pp. 41-53.

Canadians on the one hand, and excluding French Canadians outside of the province of Quebec on the other, still reflect the vast majority of the French-Canadian market. The rest of this market is to be found in extreme eastern Ontario, northern New Brunswick, and a scattering of outposts in the rest of Canada. It is of interest to note that the U.S.-Canada border itself is not culture-proof — there is quite a large French-Canadian market in the New England states. An excellent, statistically-oriented study of the French-Canadian market has been prepared by Pierre Lefrançois.[6] An analysis of the statistical profile he derives will show variations from the Canadian average in the distribution of income, age, education, population, expenditure, family size and other demographic and financial factors.

HISTORICAL PERSPECTIVE

It is impossible to comprehend the cultural environment in French Canada without at least minimal knowledge of the political and social events of Quebec since 1959. These events are frequently grouped under the label *Quiet Revolution.*[7]

The Quiet Revolution can be expressed as a nationalistic renaissance into the world of 20th Century materialism. French Canada has had a long history of nationalistic movements. But the Quiet Revolution is a French-Canadian nationalistic movement with a big difference. It is an outward-looking, rather than an inward-looking movement, a movement towards the acceptance of the materialistic way of life of the American and English-Canadian cultures, rather than a movement away from these ideals. This is reflected in a shift of slogans from *Je Me Souviens* (I remember) to *Maîtres Chez Nous* (masters in our own house) .

French Canadians have always been fearful of assimilation in a sea of English-Canadian and American culture. Like the negative nationalism discussed in the previous section, French-Canadian history is a struggle to prevent cultural oblivion. However, the French Canadian has taken a much more positive attitude to this problem than has the English Canadian. He has been able to define himself in terms of what he is, rather than in terms of what he is not.

The French-Canadian culture has shaped itself into a homogeneous society with far less variations on the basic themes than one finds in the English-Canadian culture. This, too, can be interpreted as a defense mechanism against cultural oblivion. The mores and folkways of French-Canadian society have been more rigid — less amenable to assimilating forces. For example, while the English Canadian is quite ready to accept one of his culture who is Catholic, it has been quite

---

[6] Pierre C. Lefrançois and Gilles Chatel, "The French Canadian Consumer: Fact and Fancy," *Annual Conference Proceedings* (Chicago: American Marketing Association, published in June 1966) .

[7] See, for example, Hugh B. Myers, *The Quebec Revolution* (Montreal: Harvest House Limited, 1964) .

difficult for a French Canadian to recognize another French Canadian, but of the Protestant faith, as truly a part of his society.

The reader will see, however, that much of this is changing. It is mentioned now and will be worth repeating again, that the sociology of French Canada is a sociology of change. This change is affecting the culture's philosophical and psychological outlook, its power structure, its educational forms, its internal relationships and its social stratifications.

Mr. Claude Castonguay, Minister of Social Affairs for Quebec, in a speech analyzing the fundamental sociological cause of the "October 1970 Crisis" in Quebec (in which the British Trade Commissioner, Mr. James Cross, was kidnapped, and the Minister of Labour of Quebec, Mr. Pierre Laporte, was kidnapped and murdered, by F.L.Q. separatists-terrorists) reflects the atmosphere of change and tension in the culture.

> . . . we have emerged from one type of society, not to enter an established society, but to enter a new society which is on the way to developing itself . . . We have, therefore, in the past few years, noted a very speedy rejection of many traditional values . . . We have emerged very rapidly from an extremely closed world to enter in a world where communications know practically no limits, technically, which means that in a very short while, our society opened itself on the world.[8]

The urbanizing and industrializing forces which have affected all of the North American continent since the war had, and are having, a profound effect on the French-Canadian culture. These two forces are prime determinants in the growing shift and movement towards the English-Canadian ideology. Paradoxically, however, it must be remembered that the growing acceptance of the English ideology is being accomplished through a nationalistic bent. That is, the French Canadian is as determined, if not more determined than ever, to maintain his cultural identity.

These forces of urbanization and industrialization built up for a generation enormous pressures which were held in check by the reactionary Duplessis regime. The Duplessis regime made use of several futile nationalistic moves in order to provide a safety valve for these increasing pressures. However, these "safety valves" were rather superficial. The dam burst with the death of Maurice Duplessis in September, 1959, and the final vestiges of the retaining wall were washed away with the provincial liberal election of 1960 and the ascendency of Premier Jean Lesage. *Le Chef* was gone, the Roi Negre was no longer on the scene.[9]

---

[8] As reported in the *Montreal Gazette*, 20 November 1970, p. 7.
[9] The Roi Negre was a theory that English Canada, though abhoring the internal political manoeuvres of Duplessis, nevertheless collaborated with him and allowed him to do pretty much what he wanted within Quebec, so long as he didn't directly restrict the freedoms of the English-speaking Canadians. This idea is based on the pattern of British Colonialism in Africa by which the British controlled the external policies of a Negro leader, but allowed him to behave as he wanted with his own people.

The renaissance men, the intellectuals, now seized the power and initiative. The age of patronage seemed to be at an end. In June 1966, the Lesage government lost its majority in the Legislature to the Union Nationale: however the latter party either would not or could not return completely to its reactionary policies of the Duplessis era. In any case, in April 1970 the Liberal party was returned to power.

Quebec's Quiet Revolution has initiated changes on many fronts. Probably the two most important and far-reaching fronts are the educational and industrial. The provincial Liberal government nationalized the Shawinigan Power Corporation in order to provide a basis for wide industrial development. Several large industries were thus attracted to Quebec and the government endeavoured to spread the benefits of industrialization to areas other than Montreal (though hopefully, not at the expense of Montreal). Educational reform has been no less progressive. The recommendations of the Parent Commission — the implications of the Bill 60 legislation and establishment of the Department of Education — have had profound effects on the French Canadian culture. It will be better able to participate in the highly industrial and urban society of this era.

CULTURAL TRAITS

The following discussion explores some of the cultural characteristics of French Canada. Again, the reader should bear in mind that it is most difficult to describe in the static terms available, a society which is undergoing such rapid change. Many French Canadians are caught in a tension between the older traditional ways and what may be termed the newer, urban and industrial emancipated way of life. This has shown itself, for example, in some loosening of the traditionally strong family bonds and a move towards the North American equalitarian and democratic family type, rather than the maintenance of the authoritarian form. French-Canadian culture, as any culture in a period of rapid change, is experiencing a fuzzy collective self-image. French Canadians can no longer identify with the traditional stable image generated by their former religious, educational, kinship, stratification, and philosophical characteristics, and yet they certainly cannot identify with the culture of English Canada. They have moved from the one but have not (and may not and probably do not want to) reached the other.

One must also bear in mind, in discussing the cultural characteristics of French Canada, that though there are many differences, this culture is still very much a part of the North American culture, (though less so than English Canada).

> . . . the French-Canadian shares with his neighbour to the South part of his world outlook, as for example, his admiration for science and technology, his hopes with regard to living standards, his definition of comfort and of the beautiful and of the good.
> . . . the Americanization of French Canada is an absolute fact.

> . . . the French-Canadian masses are deeply Americanized in their tastes, their attitudes, their interests and their life styles.[10]

Again, the discussion will concentrate on the differences, but as with English Canada, the similarities are much more prevalent. In addition, the following point must be considered:

> Income and education being two important determinants of the social class, we may conclude that on the average French Canadians belong to a lower social class than English Canadians. . . . It is our opinion that much of the difference in attitudes between French and English Canadians can be explained by differences in social status.[11]

Thus it may very well be that as the income and educational gaps are closed, French-Canadian consumer behaviour may become identical with English-Canadian behaviour. However, this hypothesis has yet to be thoroughly tested. Indeed Kristian S. Palda, after subjecting expenditure data to statistical tests came to the conclusion that ". . . consumption patterns do indeed differ importantly between Quebec and Ontario households of similar size and income." [12]

The French-Canadian culture has certain distinguishing characteristics. Obviously, one of them is the language itself. It will not do simply to translate promotional material from English into French. Certain English expressions are nonsensical when translated into French, and vice versa. For example:

> "To murder the King's English" should be translated as: "To speak French like a Spanish cow." [13]

Of course, it is not the language differences that are of fundamental importance. It is the more basic cultural differences which will now be discussed. Biculturalism is the real issue, not bilingualism.

The French-Canadian philosophical and psychological outlook tends to be more humanistic, more historically-oriented, more emotionally-based, and less pragmatic (though as mentioned, this is changing rapidly).[14] "The English Canadian tends to lead a relatively ascetic existence and leans heavily towards Puritanism. But French Canadians are

[10] John Richmond, trans., "Stars, Stripes and FleurdeLys," *Montreal Star*, 15 January 1972, pp. D-1, D-2 (translated from an article by Guy Rocher in *Revue de L'association Canadienne D'education de Langue Française*).
[11] Lefrançois and Chatel, "The French-Canadian Consumer," p. 715.
[12] Kristian S. Palda, "A Comparison of Consumer Expenditures in Quebec and Ontario," *Canadian Journal of Economics and Political Science* 33 (February 1967), p. 26.
[13] Maurice Brisebois, "Industrial Advertising and Marketing in Quebec," *The Marketer* 2 (Spring/Summer 1966), p. 10.
[14] For a short discussion on these points, see Jean Falardeau, *Roots and Values of Canadian Life* (Toronto: University of Toronto Press, 1960); and Mason Wade, *Canadian Dualism* (Toronto: University of Toronto Press, 1960), p. 415.

rather hedonistic in their approach to living and enjoyment for its ownself is common-place." [15]

A distinguishing characteristic of the French-Canadian culture is the strong sense of religious authority.[16] Again, this sense appears to be diminishing. "Religion is the greatest source of disagreement between young people and their parents." [17] However, it is probably nevertheless still true that the religious institution is still a powerful (though certainly not all-powerful) factor in French Canada.

> Religious and rural values are changing. The Church in Quebec is now in the avant-garde of reform. It has abandoned its leading role in education and in many cases today's priests foster a new approach in social and family problems. This, combined with more education and the mass media has led, for instance, to changes in the birth rate, family size, and the presence of married women in the workforce and in higher education; developments of much significance to marketers.[18]

Thus, the parish is still one of the fundamental social units in French-Canadian culture. The other fundamental social unit, the family, though also undergoing change, is still of importance. "The role of the family as the pillar of society and the main sociological formative influence is questioned by few respondents." [19] The French-Canadian culture assigns a major role to the family.[20] Family ties are close and wide. Indeed, one can say in general that French Canadians are used to a social relationship which is of a highly personal and emotional character. This is sometimes in conflict with the English relationship and the economic world where "efficiency" is what matters. Nepotism is not considered the evil that it is in the English-Canadian culture.

One related aspect, however, deserves special attention. The

[15] Richard Gelfand, "It's Much More Than Language," *Marketing* 74 (9 June 1969) , p. 20.

[16] C. A. Jeanneret, in Douglas Grant, ed., *Quebec Today* (Toronto: University of Toronto Press, 1960) , p. 308; Raoul Blanchard, *Le Canada Français* (Montreal: Librarie Artheme Fayard, 1960) , p. 296, quoted in Thomas Sloan, *Quebec, the Not-so-Quiet Revolution* (Toronto: Ryerson Press, 1965) , p. 30.

[17] BCP Advertising, *The 20-year-old French-Canadian Consumers* (Montreal: BCP Advertising, 1971) p. 55.

[18] Robert McGoldrick, "The French-Canadian Consumer, The Past is Prologue," speech delivered at the 54th Annual Conference of the Association of Canadian Advertisers, Toronto, May 1969. R. McGoldrick is Professor of Marketing at Laval University in Quebec City. For comments on this cultural trait and others see Yves Menard, Vice-President Marketing, Air Canada, "Quebec — The Decisive Decade," speech delivered to the Toronto chapter of the American Marketing Association, 27 April 1970.

[19] BCP Advertising, *The French-Canadian Family as a Consumer Unit* (Montreal: BCP Advertising, 1971) , p. 53.

[20] For an analysis of internal roles and responsibilities within the French-Canadian family see P. Garigue, *La Vie Familiale des Canadien Français* (Montreal: University of Montreal Press, 1962) , pp. 33-56.

extended kinship system in Quebec in the past was a phenomenon of major significance. Under the stresses of mobility and changing values, it has lost much of its usefulness.

> I sometimes think that the notion of kinship, of common values, and common interests, still remains, but at the collective national level. While modern life has disrupted the smaller group, the advent of mass communications and mobility has made the whole French Canadian society akin to a "family" in the context of the larger North-American or world community. This explains the present feeling of solidarity with traditional family pride being transformed into national pride.
>
> Evidence of the value of this analogy can be seen in the interest and affection with which television personalities are considered in Quebec, the proliferation of gossip-heavy weekly newspapers, or the adulation given to writers, actors or singers, irrespective of whether they are or are not equally successful in Paris or Toronto. For the Quebec family the outside world is not really expected to fully appreciate its members.
>
> One of the implications of this in the commercial world is the frustration which French Canada often feels when the "products" of its culture must be diffused through organizations and establishments whose management doesn't appreciate their importance. Films and books are cases in point. Because of this, government intervention may be demanded.[21]

The greatest sociological change that appears to be taking place in the French-Canadian culture lies in the area of social class and stratification. The Quiet Revolution, together with the basic trends to urbanism and industrialization and "vocational" education (engineering, economics, business), is leading to a shift in prestige amongst the various occupations. No longer can the traditional professions of clergy, law and medicine continue to preempt the elite positions in the social hierarchy. The growing new middle class, which is less tradition-oriented, wealthier, and more attuned to youth and big business, is moving into the limelight those occupations and professions associated with economic power.[22]

> Today almost everything is changing, and there is general agreement that it should change. Quebec is in the midst of a social revolution, all the more explosive for having been long repressed. But one thing

[21] McGoldrick, "The French-Canadian Consumer."

[22] For a discussion of the new middle class, see Jacques Brazeau, "Quebec's Emerging Middle Class," in Isaiah A. Litvak and Bruce E. Mallen, eds., *Marketing: Canada* (Toronto: McGraw-Hill Book Company of Canada Limited, 1964). See also Hubert Guindon, "Social Unrest, Social Class, and Quebec's Bureaucratic Revolution," *Queen's Quarterly* 71 (Summer 1964), pp. 150-62. Guindon feels that the Quiet Revolution is in fact a revolution of the new middle class public and semi-public employees pursuing economic goals.

has not changed: French Canada's preoccupation with survival, with preserving its own identity, with remaining stronger than ever, despite the vastly increased pressure of outside forces upon Quebec in the post-war period.[23]

Conclusions for the Marketer

There are a number of marketing implications which can be derived from the differentiating traits we have examined in both the English and French markets. Knowledge and understanding of these traits are particularly important in the promotional segment of the marketing mix, since there are some obvious taboos associated with such traits. For example, many U.S. appeals which emphasize characteristics opposite to the ones discussed above could boomerang. Thus the appeal to patronism, the loud, gaudy appeal, the selling of completely new concepts, the disregard of ethnic minorities and their cultural requirements, are only samples of the tactics that will alienate, if the marketer does not incorporate into his strategy appeals which match the needs of a cultural environment which is at once similar and yet dissimilar to that of the United States, the United Kingdom, or France.

Marketers must particularly understand that French Canada is different and must adapt their marketing strategy to meet the needs arising from this difference. Language obviously is an important factor to consider. For example, the U.S. media overflow into Canada has relatively minor effect on French Canada, and thus cannot be depended upon, as it often is in English Canada, to support U.S. subsidiaries' advertising campaigns. And, of course, as mentioned above, promotional material and appeals cannot without considerable danger be translated directly from the English. Marketers must consider the element of humanistic and Latin outlook on the part of the French Canadian. The cold, rational appeal may be the wrong answer. Also, the strongly religious and family overtones of the French culture must be integrated into the marketer's plans. There are obviously religious and kinship taboos which the marketer must not inadvertently break. A "family" appeal may still have greater strength in this market than in the English Canadian market, particularly when one defines "family" in the wider sense in which it is regarded by the French Canadians. Above all, the marketer must be completely aware of the flux this society is in, and must keep himself informed of the changes and trends that are coming and will come about.

Two studies on French Canadian consumers' (28–35 years old) attitudes were conducted in 1970 by B.C.P. Advertising Limited.[24]

[23] From *The French Canadian Outlook* (Preface to the Carlton Library Edition) by Hugh Mason Wade, copyright 1946 by Hugh Mason Wade. Reprinted by permission of The Viking Press, Inc.

[24] BCP Advertising, *The 30-year-old French-Canadian Woman as a Consumer*, and *The 30-year-old French-Canadian Man as a Consumer* (Montreal: BCP Advertising, 1970), 78 pages each.

The emergence of new values is testified by her attitudes towards sex and the role of women in society. However, in other areas, she shows conflicting attitudes which temporarily affect her sense of equilibrium. . . . It is imperative that neither old-fashioned, stereotype or too avant-garde approaches be used to appeal to this consumer.

We can now state definitely that 30-year-old French-Canadian women are not prototypes of their mothers. Neither are they identical to 20-year-olds.[25]

We established the fact that they [men] like large cars. In the areas of sports and leisure, their aspirations lean to costly merchandise and activities. It was also established that women are not alone in wanting to live in a suburb, in their own home. Men would like to, as well.[26]

French Canadians do show some interesting differences in their buying behaviour. They tend to have low home, bonds, stock, car, camera, and electrical ownership, while having high gasoline, car accessories, liquor, food and clothing consumption. Perhaps because of their strong traditionalism they tend to shop less in chain stores, but are, however, more loyal once they do shift.

—There is better acceptance in Quebec of premium-priced products.
—In Quebec, 60 percent of food sales are made by independent grocers; in Ontario, only 38 percent.
—Home-made soup is served in 80 percent of all French-Canadian homes.
—Margarine has not caught on in Quebec.
—The French consumer has a greater affinity for perfume.
—French Canada's consumption of beer is divided 90 percent ale, 5 percent lager; Ontario's is 55 percent ale, 45 percent lager. 95 percent of Geneva Gin sold in Canada is consumed in Quebec, where it is properly known as Gros Gin.
—Premiums and coupons are much more popular in Quebec.
—Quebec housewives have a particular fetish for bonuses in this form.
—Quebec leads all other provinces in per capita sales of soft drinks, corn syrup, maple syrup, molasses and several other sweets and delicacies. In other words, Quebec has a sweet tooth.
—In Quebec homes, a full meal is served both at noon and in the evening.
—Quebec people are inclined to spend much more time with their radio sets in use and in watching television than are people in other parts of Canada.
—Decaffeinated coffees are more popular in Quebec than elsewhere.
—In a sample of thirty-one food store commodities, fourteen are above Canadian average consumption level, and fifteen are below.[27]

[25] Idem, *The French-Canadian Woman*, p. 72.
[26] Idem, *The French-Canadian Man*, p. 71.
[27] Brisebois, "Industrial Advertising," p. 10.

Additional studies have shown the following:[28]

1. The French Canadian's emphasis on "joie-de-vivre" is indicated by the fact that Quebec leads all other provinces in per capita sales of clothing, cosmetics, premium grades of gasoline, and high-priced liquor.

2. The Quebecer's preference for convertible and high performance cars loaded with accessories is in startling contrast to the choice of standard models by his supposedly richer neighbour in Ontario.

3. The farther west you move in Canada, the more milk people drink. When the Quebec housewife buys milk, she is less likely than her English-speaking counterpart to buy skim milk or two-percent milk.

4. The Quebec housewife buys about twice as many olives as her Ontario counterpart, but only one-quarter the amount of pickles. The French Canadian's olive must be unstuffed and unpitted.

5. Anything lemon does not sell in Quebec; anything chocolate does.

6. Quebec drinks three times more fresh orange juice than the rest of Canada, and eats less frozen food than the rest of Canada.

7. French Quebecers drink five times more straight liquor than English Quebecers.

8. Quebec has more automatic dishwashers and more automatic laundry machines than its relative average; it has more T.V. sets and sewing machines as well.

9. Quebec buys more than its share of headache remedies.

Yet another study came to the following conclusions:

—The French-Canadian woman sees herself strongly in the role of homemaker, much more so than her English-speaking counterpart. She is much more involved with children, cooking, and cleaning. She is also less concerned with convenience in preparing foods. Gourmet foods, therefore, have a greater potential in Quebec. She is also super clean, and sees a greater need for disinfectants, bleach, etc.

—The French-Canadian woman is more fashion conscious and more concerned with external impressions. Thus, she is more aware of the latest fashions and hairstyles and is more prone to purchasing such things as the options on automobiles, refrigerators and ranges.

—However, she is more conservative than her English-Canadian sister and less readily associates with the "swinging life," and such youth symbols as long hair and the drug culture.

---

[28] See for example, J. Walter Thompson Co. Ltd., *A Comparative Study of Buying Habits in Quebec and The Rest of Canada* (Toronto: Unpublished, 1969) ; Lucien Roy, "How Do We Motivate the French Canadian Buyer," (address presented to the 54th Annual Conference of the Association of Canadian Advertisers, Toronto, May 1969) ; Pat Annesley, "The Ups and Downs of Pleasing Canadian Palates," *Marketing* 73 (13 December 1968) , p. 3.

—The French woman searches for more "value." Special promotions
that stress value — whether by the addition of worthwhile premiums
or by the reduction of price — are more enthusiastically accepted.[29]

At the same time, one must recognize that many of the differences
between French and English preferences, taste, and purchasing behaviour,
can be attributed to external facts. They do not necessarily represent the
symptoms of a deep-lying ethnic-based assimilarity. For example, while
French Canadians have sometimes been cited for slowness in taking to
new products, this could be due to inadequate media exposure.[30]

COMPARATIVE CONSUMER MARKETS

Tables 3-3 and 3-4 compare the Canadian consumer market
with the U.S. consumer market. Table 3-4 also includes the western
European market.

Demographic Comparisons

Obviously, the most striking difference is the size of the various
domestic markets. Canada has by far the smallest market, about 10
percent of the U.S. and under 7 percent of western Europe. Canada's
small domestic market creates many manufacturing and marketing
productivity problems. However, the Canadian consumer market is growing at a faster rate than the other two markets, with a population of over
twenty-three million predicted for 1975. The ten-year rate of population growth, 1960–1970, was over 25 percent faster than the U.S. rate,
though both had slowed down considerably in the latter part of the
decade.

In spite of the declining farm population, Canada's relative
population in this area is significantly larger than that of the U.S. This
is an indication of the higher stage of economic development that the
U.S. has reached. This development is also reflected in the higher percentage of the labour force working in service industries in the U.S.,
though Canada's percentage is higher than western Europe's. Though
a greater percentage of Americans live in the larger urban areas (50,000

---

[29] Study by Vickers & Benson, (Toronto Advertising Agency), as reported
in "Cherchez la Femme," *Marketing* 77 (31 January 1972), p. 2. (This
study is in turn based on a research design by Dr. D. J. Tigert).

[30] Verne Atrill, "Don't Dig Too Deep for French Disparity," *Marketing*
69 (20 November 1964), pp. 36-37; see also Verne Atrill, "Attitudes of the
French-Speaking Housewife Towards New Products," in W. H. Mahatoo,
Marketing Research in Canada (Toronto: Thomas Nelson, 1968), pp. 96-
103.

persons and over), only one out of the thirty-five (3 percent) Standard Metropolitan Statistical Areas in Canada was under 96,000
in population, while forty out of the three hundred (13 percent) SMSA
in the U.S. were under that population number. In 1970, half the Canadian population lived in cities of over 100,000. Thus, the two extremes of
the urban-rural market classification tend to play a relatively more
important role in Canada.

The Canadian consumer market is younger than the American
market, and much younger than the western Europe market. Many Canadian marketers must gear themselves to a population in which half are
under 25 years of age. The relative youth of the population may explain
Canada's lower marriage rate and higher relative number of single
persons. In any case, the higher number of single persons in turn will
explain the greater number of persons per household in Canada. This
affects consumer durable purchasing. In addition, the household purchasing head, i.e., the housewife, may be a relatively more important person to whom to appeal than the U.S. housewife, because she tends to influence the purchases for more individuals than her U.S. counterpart.
However, the Canadian housewife's larger family may be one reason
why she tends to participate less in the labour force than do U.S. and
western European housewives. Thus, the Canadian housewife may be
more dependent on her breadwinner's purchasing decisions for a variety
of items. For example, she may not have the same freedom in personal
purchases, because of her lack of an independent income.

The Canadian market is far less educated than the American.
For example, the percentage of the U.S. male labour force which
has completed university is twice that of Canada. This fact, of course,
will affect the sales of many products which are correlated with education; for example, books. This lower educational attainment may also
create a greater reluctance in Canadians to change and so to accept new
products and marketing institutions.

Income Comparisons

Though Canadians have one of the highest standards of living
in the world (sometimes second), their income is still well behind that of

TABLE 3-3 Comparative Profiles of Canadian and U.S. Consumer Markets

	Canada	U.S.A.
Demographic Characteristics		
Population — Canada as % of U.S. (1970)	10.4%	100.0%
Ten-year rate of population growth (1960 — 1970)	18.0%	14.3%
Percent farm population (1966)	9.6%	5.9%
Percent standard metropolitan area (50,000 population and over, 1970)	61.5%	73.5%
Percent under 15 years (Canada 1969), under 16 years (U.S. 1969)	31.0%	31.0%
Percent single marital status (Canada over 14 years, U.S. over 13 years)	28.0%	24.0%

TABLE 3-3 Comparative Profiles of Canadian and U.S. Consumer Markets
(concluded)

	Canada	U.S.A.
Demographic Characteristics (cont.)		
Persons per household (1970)	3.7	3.2
Percent Roman Catholic religion		
(1960 U.S. — 1961 Canada)	45.7%	26.0%
Percent labour force (male) — completed		
4 years high school only	8.7%	24.6%
Percent labour force (male) — completed university	5.6%	11.1%
	(Percent or Can. $)	*(Percent or U.S. $)*
Economic Characteristics		
Effective buying power (1970)		
per capita (personal disposable income)	$2,481	$3,308
per household (personal disposable income)	$9,895	$10,565
Median income of individuals completed		
1 – 3 years high school (1960)	$4,233	$4,936
Median income of university graduate (1960)	$7,956	$7,693
1971 GNP (estimate by *Business Week*)	$87.7 (Bil.)	$1,045 (Bil.)
Average annual percentage increase in		
real GNP (1960 – 1967)	5.5%	4.7%
1971 over 1970 Gross National Product (estimate)	6.7%	7.0%
1969 over 1965 Disposable Income	44%	33%
1971 over 1970 Consumer Price Index (estimate)	3.3%	3.5%
Personal savings as % Personal		
Disposable Income (1969)	6.7%	6.0%
Households with 2 or more cars (1969)	16.0%	29.0%
Consumption Characteristics		
1969 Per capita personal expenditures	$2,216	$2,834
Durable goods	$ 520	$ 441
Nondurable goods	$ 854	$1,200
Services	$ 842	$1,194
1967 Percentage distribution of personal expenditures		
Food, beverage and tobacco	27.8%	23.8%
Clothing, accessories	8.9%	10.4%
Shelter	15.4%	14.9%
Household operation	12.0%	14.3%
Transportation	12.0%	12.8%
Personal and medical care	9.0%	8.7%
Recreation and other	14.9%	15.1%
Soft drink consumption: 8 oz. bottles		
per capita (1964)	190	243
Tea consumption: pounds per household (1964)	24	17
Beer consumption: Imperial gallons per		
capita (1963) % ale of total beer	58.6%	2.8%
Canadian and Scotch whisky — Consumption per capita	.66 Imp. gals.	.24 Imp. gals.
Cigarette consumption — per capita (1962)	2,083	2,743

SOURCES: *David Sutherland, "The U.S. Marketer in Canada,"* Sales Management, *10 June 1963, pp. E-2 and E-5; DBS, 1961 and 1966* Census of Canada *(Ottawa: Queen's Printer); 1963, 1969 and 1970* Statistical Abstract of the U.S.A. *(Washington: Department of Commerce); Economic Council of Canada, Second (1964) and Sixth (1969)* Annual Review *(Ottawa: Queen's Printer); Sales Management, Survey of Buying Power, 10 July 1971; Business Week, 2 January 1971, p. 21 (GNP estimates); DBS, "Personal Expenditures,"* National Accounts *(Ottawa: Queen's Printer).*

TABLE 3-4 A Comparative Profile of the North Atlantic Area Consumer Markets

	Canada	U.S.A.	Western Europe	
Percent of population 0 – 14 (1960)	33.7	31.0	24.9	
Estimated 1970 population (thousands)	21,877	211,430	332,050	
Estimated 1975 population (thousands)	24,223	230,415	342,715	
Marriage rates (per 1,000, 1963)	6.9	8.8	7.5	(U.K.)
Percent female population in the labour force (1962)	19.5	25.9	27.2	
Percent of labour force in service industries (1960)	49.5	55.8	38.2	
Indexes of "real" earnings in manufacturing (1963) ('53=100)	125.1	123.1	135.4	(U.K.)
Per capita GNP (1962)	$2,007	$2,981	$1,205	
Per capita consumption expenditures	$1,281	$1,870	$753	
Consumption expenditures as percent of GNP (1963)	63.8	62.4	62.9	
Index of Gross National Product at constant price (1963) ('53=100)	168	155	181	
Private consumption expenditures % distribution by components (1962):				
Food, beverage, tobacco	29.9%	26.2%	40.8%	(U.K.)
Clothing	8.6%	9.1%	9.4%	(U.K.)
Rent	16.0%	31.3%	9.6%	(U.K.)
Fuel and light	3.6%	3.6%	4.9%	(U.K.)
Furniture and household equipment	4.4%	6.7%	6.8%	(U.K.)
Transportation and communication	13.9%	14.3%	10.3%	
Other	23.6%	26.8%	18.2%	
Number of radio sets in use (per 1,000 population — 1962)	504	1,006	246	
Number of T.V. sets in use (per 1,000 population — 1962)	235	322	105	
Number of telephones in use (per 1,000 population — 1962)	341	434	127	

SOURCE: *Bernard Mueller*, A Statistical Handbook of the North Atlantic Area, © 1965 by *The Twentieth Century Fund, New York. The data above were derived from the following Tables: I-4, I-5, I-12, II-2, II-5, II-10, III-3, III-5, III-6, IV-3, IV-11, IV-12, IV-13.*

Americans. The only Canadian group which has an income similar to its U.S. counterpart is that of university graduates. Indeed, because of their short supply, their 1960 income was actually higher (though this was probably a temporary condition). This lower standard of living relative to the U.S.A. but far higher relative to western Europe, is seen when the figures for per capita disposable income, per capita gross national product, median income of individuals (exluding university graduates) and ownership of radios, televisions, telephones and cars are analyzed. However, the roles are reversed when one looks at the trends in income rather than absolute figures. In Europe and Canada, in that order, there has been a higher rate of "real" income growth in the past fifteen years, than in the U.S.A.

The lower standard of living relative to the U.S.A. is of paramount importance for those marketers who must appeal to the high income groups. Those firms marketing luxury items and products related to leisure or "expensive" participation sports will be at a greater disadvantage north of the border, although this is certainly not to say that there is not a growing and significant market in Canada for these items.

Expenditure Comparisons

It is to be expected, because of the differences in income and demographic characteristics, that Canadian expenditure patterns will differ from U.S. and western European patterns. Certainly this will be true for particular products, but one can also generalize on broad product groupings. Engel's Law is probably at work here. Note that western Europe spends the greatest percentage of its income on food, while the U.S., with the highest income, spends the least on food relative to other markets. Canadians spend relatively less on clothing (surprisingly, considering the weather!), furniture and household equipment than the two other markets, while they spend more on rent and almost as much as the U.S. on communication (because of the vast distances involved). The most striking difference, of course, is that Americans spend 30 percent more per capita than Canadians, while the latter spend 70 percent more than western Europeans.

If particular products are examined there will of course be a very wide range of differences. For example, Table 3-3 indicates some of the per capita consumption rates for each of the two countries. There are many products, such as ale, for which Canadians consume a great deal more than Americans. Thus, a careful examination of the Canadian market must be made before a marketer can assume that the U.S. experience is in any way similar.

Cultural Comparisons

There are studies which have attempted to analyze the difference in certain qualitative, sociological characteristics between Canada and the U.S.A. For example, it has been stated that the Canadian is more cautious and uncertain about how he spends his money because of his more recent affluence. Thus, there is a greater reliance on known-brand names, quality and durability, and a more critical attitude towards advertising.[31]

As has already been noted, Canada's ethnic groups tend to have a slower rate of cultural assimilation than those in the U.S.A. Each country has a different ethnic structure and therefore has different needs in the marketplace. Thus, different ways of appealing to these needs are required. Perhaps the major indicator of this differing ethnic structure is

[31] David Sutherland, "The U.S. Marketer in Canada," *Sales Management,* 10 June 1963, p. E3.

a much larger percentage of Roman Catholics in the Canadian consumer market than in the U.S. market. Of course, French Canada is the main contributor to this particular difference. The French-Canadian segment accounts for about 30 percent of the Canadian market. The last section discussed the distinguishing characteristics which directly affect the purchasing behaviour of this segment. These include its language, philosophical and psychological outlook, politics, religious views, family structure and social structure.

Dr. Irving Gilman's motivation research has revealed the following differences between American and Canadian consumers:

—The Canadian consumer of goods of all kinds has to learn to live with his affluence whereas the U.S. consumer is more relaxed, even blasé, about his.

—The Canadian consumer is more cautious in the marketplace, weighing each dollar before making a purchase decision. The U.S. consumer, smug and secure after two decades of affluence, spends liberally without much concern about what his dollar is buying.

—The Canadian consumer, uncertain about the stability of his affluence, needs to rely on symbols of reassurance such as brand names. He is less sophisticated about brand importance than is his U.S. counterpart. The latter is outgrowing brand dependency and is turning in increasing numbers to private brands.

—The caution of the Canadian purchaser is reflected in a more critical attitude toward advertising and promotion than is the case with the U.S. consumer of goods, services and ideas. As a consequence, the Canadian manufacturer-advertiser is more dependent on believable ads than is the businessman south of the border.

—While seeking variety and new adventure in purchasing, the Canadian consumer insists on good quality and durability. The U.S. consumer, by contrast, is not as *worried about shoddy quality; if the material wears out, he can afford to buy something better.* Besides, it enhances his affluent image if he can throw away a shirt or garment after wearing it a few times.

—While the long-affluent U.S. consumer is receptive to products from all over the world as well as those of domestic manufacture, the Canadian consumer is more likely to buy Canadian. This insularity in the market-place is particularly apparent with respect to U.S. products. Here is revealed an ambivalence that is expressed in the Canadian consumer's desire to purchase U.S. goods as verification of his own improved economic status and in the parallel need to cut the psychological and economic bonds that tie him to the U.S.

—Canadian consumers, because of sectional and ethnic differences which are underscored by the influx of New Canadians, present a stratified market. Consumers in the U.S. whose ethnic differences were integrated as far back as World War I, exhibit little or no significant differentiations among the various market groupings. Differences due to ethnic or national background tend to be fused into a general "American" mosaic.

—In Canada, the geographical differences in terms of consumer attitudes and expectations regarding products, services and ideas are marked between each section of the country. Sharp market differentiations appear in the provinces of Quebec and Ontario, the Maritimes, the Prairies, and the West. This market condition is largely absent in the United States, where consumer attitudes and anticipation are substantially the same in all sections of the country, despite some regional variables.[32]

[32] Adapted from Irving Gilman, "Motivation Research in the Canadian Market," in W. H. Mahatoo, ed., *Marketing Research in Canada* (Toronto: Thomas Nelson & Sons Ltd., 1968) , pp. 118-19.

4

The Economic Dimension of the Canadian Industrial Market

Industrial marketing is concerned with the marketing of goods and services to businesses and other organizations for use in the goods and services which they in turn produce. The basic distinction between industrial goods that go to the industrial market and goods that go to the consumer market is that industrial goods are used for producing other goods, and consumer goods are used by household members to satisfy their wants.[1] For example, oil used for fueling a motor or a plant is classified as an industrial good, while the same oil bought for heating your home would be considered a consumer good.

This chapter contains two sections. The first provides a general definitional framework of the industrial market. Also, inter-industry transaction flows in Canada are illustrated, and their relationship traced to final demands and Gross National Product. This is done via an input-output model. The second section describes the magnitude and trends in the Gross Domestic industrial market by major segment. These major segments have been selected because of their importance to marketers. The major segments dealt with are the goods-producing industries, the capital goods market, the government sector and the reseller trade sector. The latter part of this section pertains to the special case of the manufacturing sector; its growth, problems and future.

DEFINITIONAL FRAMEWORK OF THE INDUSTRIAL MARKET

The marketing literature is not exact as to what segments should be included in the industrial market. An omnibus definition is to distinguish intermediate customers from ultimate consumers. This definition would include those customers in agriculture, forestry, fisheries, all other industries, and trade and government, excluding only the consumer market. In addition, sales for export are often classified as industrial market sales. A narrow definition would limit the industrial market to the agriculture, forestry, fisheries and all other industries groups. Figure

[1] See *Marketing Definitions* (Chicago: American Marketing Association, 1960), pp. 11 and 14. The term goods, here and in the rest of the chapter, stands for both goods and services.

FIGURE 4-1 Definitional Framework of the Industrial Market

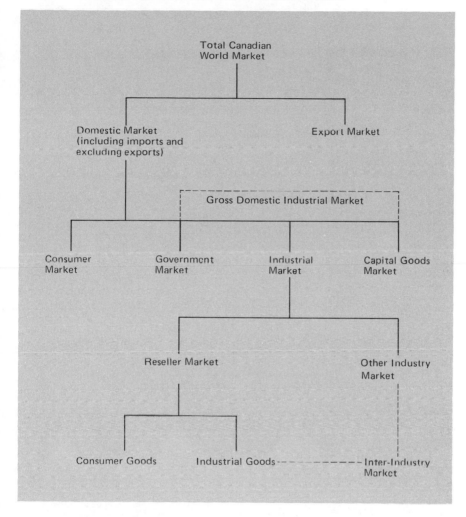

4-1 breaks down the total Canadian world market into its components and then illustrates what is being considered the industrial market by this study.

The term industrial market in the rest of this chapter refers to the domestic industrial market as differentiated from the Gross Domestic industrial market. The industrial market comprises sales to intermediate customers in agriculture, forestry, fisheries, all other industries and reseller trade in Canada. For convenience, imports will not be explicitly added and exports specifically subtracted, but a net external trade figure will be included in our term Gross Domestic industrial market. It should be noted that this net external trade figure usually amounts to less than five percent of the industrial market as defined above. Furthermore, our broader definition of the Gross Domestic industrial market will include the industrial market plus the final demand sector expenditures for investment goods and government purchases.

Industrial Market and Gross Domestic Product

The demand for industrial goods is derived, in general, from the final demands of consumers in the sense that industrial goods are purchased to produce or to assist in producing goods for personal use.

FIGURE 4-2 Gross National Expenditure, 1970

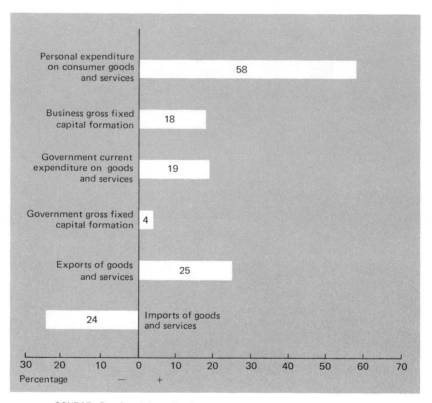

SOURCE: *Developed from Dominion Bureau of Statistics, "National Accounts, Income and Expenditure," No. 13-001 (Ottawa: Queen's Printer, First Quarter 1971).*

Derived demands generate a large number of transactions among firms in primary materials, and intermediate manufacturers. As an accounting convention, final demands as measured in the Gross National Expenditure accounts include personal consumption demand, investment demand, government demand and export demand. Gross National Product at market prices of Canada in 1970 was a little under $84.5 billion. In terms of Gross National Expenditures, this breaks down as shown in Figure 4-2.

Conceptually, to arrive at a description of the size and structure of the industrial market, one proceeds in the following manner. At first it is necessary to convert GNP to Gross Domestic Product. GDP is the actual product produced in Canada. GNP is arrived at by adding to GDP income received from non-residents and subtracting income paid out to non-residents. Since foreign investment is high in Canada, the payout of dividends and other income flows to foreigners is substantial and thus GNP is lower than GDP. In 1970, income received from non-residents was $1,074 million, while that paid out was $2,320 million, a net overflow of $1,246 million above GNP.[2] Thus, GDP or GDE* at $85.7 billion was $1,246 million above GNP.

Gross Domestic Expenditure is a "gross" measure because the cost of fixed capital consumed during the year has not been deducted. It is however a "net" output measure, and therefore avoids duplication to the extent that intermediate goods and services used by industries in the production of other goods and services are excluded. For example, the value of flour used by the baking industry to produce the bread which is purchased by persons is counted only once — as part of the value of the bread. Similarly, the measure of GDP avoids duplication by excluding the intermediate inputs of industries in the form of goods used in production. This is appropriate because, for each industry, these inputs represent the accumulated values of GDP originating in domestic industries at earlier stages of production, plus the value of imports used at earlier stages of production.

Thus, one has to disaggregate the GDP total to find out the net output originating by industry. Also, one has to relate this net output to the intermediate and final goods and services produced by respective industries to obtain a picture of the size and structure of the industrial market. To clarify this picture further, one must study the flow of transactions and this requires an input-output model, which is a model showing the input of all industries and their outputs. This is the model that will be used to describe seller and buyer industries.

GDP at factor cost is the most frequently used measure of output originating by industry. The measure is GDP at market prices excluding indirect taxes less subsidies.[3] Table 4-1 shows GDP at factor cost by industry for 1961 and 1967. As can be seen, there is little difference in Canada's industrial structure between those two years except for the marked increase of the service sector.

[2] Dominion Bureau of Statistics, "National Accounts, Income and Expenditure," No. 13-001 (Ottawa: Queen's Printer, First Quarter 1971).

* **GDP** is the income measure and **GDE** is the expenditure measure.

[3] The deduction is compelled because it is very difficult from a data point of view to distribute indirect taxes by industry. Much depends on the routing and valuation of commodities. See DBS, "The Input-Output Structure of the Canadian Economy 1961," No. 15-501 (Ottawa: Queen's Printer, October 1969).

TABLE 4-1 Gross Domestic Product at Factor Cost

	$ Billion	% Distribution	
	1967	1961	1967
Agriculture	2.479	4.7	4.7
Forestry	0.563	1.1	1.0
Fishing and trapping	0.146	0.3	0.3
Mining, quarrying, and oil wells	2.212	4.3	4.1
Manufacturing	13.606	25.5	25.1
Construction	3.304	5.5	6.1
Transportation	3.190	6.5	5.9
Storage	0.129	0.3	0.2
Communication	1.364	2.4	2.5
Electric power, gas and water utilities	1.757	3.4	3.3
Wholesale trade	2.585	4.6	4.8
Retail trade	4.776	9.3	8.8
Finance, insurance, and real estate	5.516	10.6	10.2
Public administration and defence	3.961	7.5	7.3
Service	8.578	14.0	15.8
	54.166	100.0	100.0

SOURCE: *DBS, "National Accounts, Income and Expenditure," No. 13-001, 1962 and 1968 issues.*

Industrial Market Size

To obtain industrial market size and structure, it is necessary to relate the goods produced by industries to the net output figures given by disaggregating GDP. The entire system with its links to GNP can be visualized via an input-output model. Table 4-2 is a description of this model.

In the final demand sector, columns going through Quadrants I and IV, sales to persons ($47 billion) plus sales to governments ($22 billion) plus sales of investment goods ($13 billion) plus net foreign trade (exports minus imports equals —$2 billion) equals GNE ($47 + 22 + 13 − 2 = $80 billion). This, it may be noted, is equal to GNP. The net foreign trade figure adds exports and deducts imports since the model is related to GNE/GNP statistics. To obtain the Domestic Industrial Market, one would subtract exports and add imports, i.e., reverse the net foreign trade figure. The GNP figures are given by the totals of the rows going across Quadrants III and IV. They comprise indirect taxes ($19 billion) plus wages ($47 billion) plus surplus* ($14 billion).

The larger total output figures are the sales to intermediate industries plus the sales by these industries to final demand. These figures are the totals of the rows going across Quadrants II and I. The total for industries A + B + C equals $108 billion ($46 + 35 + 27).

---

* **Surplus** is defined as the sum of the "costs" of, or incomes accruing to, capital employed in production in the form of profits and other investment income, plus depreciation.

Consequently, to avoid double-counting, only the final demands are totalled on the product side of the accounts to arrive at GNE; and similarly, only the value added by wages, surplus and indirect taxes goes into GNP.

TABLE 4-2 Schematic Description of Input-Output Model ($ Billions)

| | | Intermediate Demand | | | Final Demand | | | |
| | | QUADRANT II | | | | QUADRANT I | | |
	A	B	C	Persons	Govt.	Invst. (Govt. + Bus.)	Net Trade	Total
A	13	9	4	16	3	4	−3	46
B	7	10	4	11	—	3	—	35
C	3	3	1	11	4	4	1	27
		QUADRANT III				QUADRANT IV		
Indirect Taxes	3	2	1	9	2	2	—	19
Wages	14	8	12	—	13	—	—	47
Surplus	6	3	5	—	—	—	—	14
Total	46	35	27	47	22	13	−2	XXX

SOURCE: *Developed from hypothetical data given in DBS, "The Input-Output Structure of the Canadian Economy 1961," No. 15-501 (Ottawa: Queen's Printer, October 1969).*

The total size of Gross Domestic industrial goods production (note: "production," not "market") is given by the sales of all industries to other industries, (that is, the row totals of industries A + B + C in Quadrant II), and is equal to $54 billion, plus sales by these industries of investment goods equal to $11 billion, plus, by convention, sales to government of $7 billion, plus net trade equal to −$2 billion (the figures for investment, government and net trade are given by the respective column totals of these sectors in Quadrant I). The total size of Gross Domestic industrial goods production is thus $70 billion ($54 + 11 + 7 − 2 = $70 billion). This $70 billion excludes indirect taxes.[4] When such taxes are included for all sectors except the sale of final goods to persons, the figure rises to $80 billion ($10 billion indirect taxes equals the raw total for taxes of $19 billion minus $9 billion for such taxes on final goods sold to persons). To obtain the Gross Domestic industrial market, one reverses the magnitude of net foreign trade, i.e., one adds $2 billion instead of subtracting $2 billion since one adds imports and subtracts exports. Thus, the Gross Domestic industrial market is larger than Gross Domestic industrial production since imports are larger than exports.

[4] Because the hypothetical example is structured to correspond to real statistical difficulties, it is difficult to apportion indirect taxes by industry. See DBS, "Structure of the Canadian Economy," No. 15-501.

The actual 1961 input-output tables yield a Gross Domestic industrial market as defined above of approximately $45.2 billion. The industrial market inclusive of indirect taxes totals approximately $35.1 billion, the investment sector — business plus government — accounts for $8.2 billion, government current expenditures on goods from industry $2.1 billion, the net trade account +$0.2 billion and the net change in inventories —$0.04 billion. In comparison, GDP at market prices was $39.6 billion and total output of all industries inclusive of indirect taxes was $69.6 billion.[5]

Canada has only had two input-output series. One was for 1949 and the other for 1961. These tables require very detailed statistics and are time consuming to compile and reconcile with trade and national income accounting statistics. Therefore, the 1961 tables, for instance, were not issued until mid-1970. To obtain industrial market sizes for other years, one builds on the 1961 statistics. This is quite valid as long as the structure of the economy has not undergone fundamental changes. From the percentage distribution of GDP at factor cost for the years 1961 and 1967 it can be seen that such fundamental changes have not occurred.[6] Applying the 1961 ratio of the size of the industrial market to 1961 GDP at market prices, one can obtain a 1970 industrial market of $74.1 billion. The 1970 Gross Domestic industrial market is obtained by adding to this figure final demand from the investment sector of $18.0 billion, plus government current expenditures on goods from industry of $5.7 billion, plus the net trade account of —$1.1 billion and the net change in inventories of $0.1 billion.[7] The resultant Gross Domestic industrial market is $97.9 billion. In comparison, GDP at market prices was $85.7 billion and total output of all industries was $148.0 billion.

MAGNITUDE AND TRENDS IN THE GROSS DOMESTIC MARKET

Importance of the Industrial Market

For marketers, it is essential to understand the importance of the industrial market to the overall economy, in order to better forecast and plan marketing activities. Their estimates are more accurate of the extent of the movements of our modern complex economy and of the size, degree and timing of new marketing opportunities.

Growth in GDP at factor cost by industry of origin provides

[5] Industrial market of $45.2 billion plus personal expenditures on consumer goods and services of $24.4 billion. The latter figure is from DBS, "Structure of the Canadian Economy," No. 15-501.

[6] See Table 4-1.

[7] Figures for the investment, government, trade and inventory sectors are from "National Accounts, Income and Expenditure," No. 13-001. The figure for government current expenditures on goods from industry is an estimate based on past years.

a good measure of overall growth. It also reflects changes in structure. Table 4-3 gives real domestic product index figures by industry of origin. The word "real" is related to the concept of constant dollars.

TABLE 4-3 Real Domestic Product Indexes

		1961 % Weight	1970 Index Value	Average Annual Growth Rate (%)	
				'46 – '68	'61 – '70
A.	Real Domestic Product	100.00	160.7	4.7	5.4
	Goods-producing industries[1]	43.767	161.8	5.0	5.5
	Goods-producing industries less agriculture	39.210	166.1	5.8	5.8
	Service-producing industries[2]	56.233	159.8	4.4	5.3
B.	1. Agriculture	4.557	124.1	1.7	2.4
	2. Forestry	1.257	144.2	2.3	4.2
	3. Fishing and trapping	0.262	112.9	1.2	1.4
	4. Mining, quarrying and oil wells	4.298	172.9	8.5	6.3
	5. Manufacturing	24.741	167.3	5.1	5.9
	6. Construction	5.840	149.8	6.1	4.6
	7. Electric power, gas and water utilities	2.812	191.7	9.3	7.5
	8. Transportation, storage and communication	9.985	171.8	4.8	6.2
	9. Trade	12.721	160.4	4.6	5.4
	10. Finance, insurance and real estate	12.013	150.5	N.A.	4.6
	11. Community, business and personal service industries	13.789	174.5	4.3	6.4
	12. Public administration and defence	7.725	129.3	N.A.	2.9

SOURCE: DBS, "The Index of Industrial Production," No. 61-005 (Ottawa: Queen's Printer, various issues).

[1] The goods-producing industries are defined as B1 to B7.

[2] The service-producing industries are defined as B8 to B12.

These statistics are a relatively recent addition to the store of statistics being developed in Canada and throughout the modern world. For example, the scope of this total index covers the entire economy. In contrast, the index of industrial production only covers approximately one-third of the domestic product.[8]

As can be seen from Table 4-3 the real domestic product has been growing at the rapid rate of 4.7 percent a year from 1946, and the

[8] DBS, "Indexes of Real Domestic Product by Industry of Origin," No. 61-505 (Ottawa: Queen's Printer, May 1963). It should be noted that for statistical reasons the real domestic product contribution as shown in index weights is reasonably close to, but does not quite correspond to the percentage contributions to GDP given in Table 4-1, nor to the value-added relationships in Table 4-4. The input-output model has a dummy industry category for the production of miscellaneous commodities which cannot be classified elsewhere. See DBS, "Structure of the Canadian Economy," No. 15-501.

pace quickened in the decade of the 1960's. As a matter of fact, the
pace from 1960 to 1966 was even faster, since the period 1966 to 1970
witnessed a recessionary slowdown largely caused by a similar slowdown
in economic activity in Canada's main trading partner, the U.S. Nevertheless, Canada's high performance in the decade 1955–1965 was excelled
by a number of industrial countries. In the post–World War II period the
changes which have taken place in the industrial countries can only be
described as sweeping. Accelerating technological change has revolution-
ized methods of production and the types of goods and services produced.

**FIGURE 4-3 Growth of Productivity, Employment and Real GNP of Selected
Industrial Countries, Average Annual Growth Rate, 1955 – 65**

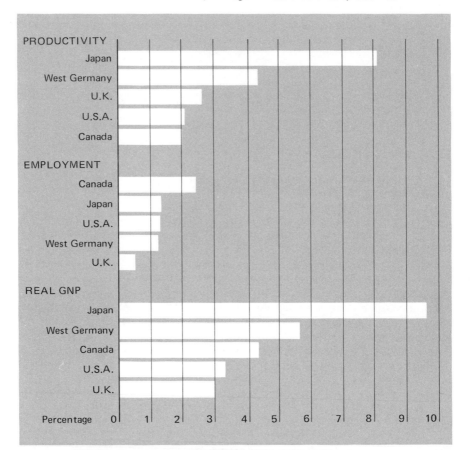

SOURCE: *Economic Council of Canada*, Third Annual Review *(Ottawa: Queen's Printer,
September 1966), p. 16.*

Increased capital investment and energy consumption have gone together
with increasing scale and specialization of output in the form of mass
production systems in industry. Further, there has been a substantial

upgrading in the quality of manpower; also, greatly extended and strengthened educational systems have provided the basis for a "knowledge boom," which has contributed to rising living standards and productivity. Canada has shared in all this but its productivity growth has lagged, as indicated in Figure 4-3.

Certainly the industrial structure of the country's economy must influence growth in productivity. Non-agricultural goods production has represented an advancing sector of economic activity, though more in terms of an increasing share of total output than of total employment.[9] On the other hand, the service sector tends generally to encompass relatively highly labour-intensive activities. Thus, the growth in employment in services has been even more marked than the growth of output among the rapidly industrially-advancing countries.[10] In this context, it is worth noting that the Canadian service-producing industries sector is larger than the goods-producing industries sector.[11]

Structure of the Industrial Market

Inter-industry quantitative relationships are best seen through the Canadian input-output model. It provides the only comprehensive and detailed presentation of the origin and disposition of industrial commodity groups and of the cost structures of individual industries. The accounting relationships describe the structure of demand and of productive activity in a particular year. It has been found that many of these relationships have considerable stability even when the conditions under which they were first observed change.[12] Therefore, the structure will be sketched for 1961 since this is the latest year for which a comprehensive input-output model exists. Then available statistics will be used to describe the position in recent years.

Fifteen industries are ranked in order of dollar gross input in Table 4-4. The table also shows the value of goods purchased by these industries, except for capital equipment purchases. Thus the industries are shown both as sellers and buyers. The table also shows the value-added or the net output added by these industries to the goods they processed. The value-added is the component contribution to GDP at factor cost by the industry. This is a measure of the effect of the industry on the economy, for it is the value-added component which pays for labour and capital utilized by the industry.

The next task is to show what these industries sell domestically and abroad. Selected major commodities sold are detailed in Table 4-5. Imports are also shown in order to facilitate reconciliation between gross sales by industry with demand from industries, final goods markets and exports.

[9] Economic Council of Canada, *Third Annual Review* (Ottawa: Queen's Printer, September 1966) , p. 16.
[10] DBS, "Structure of the Canadian Economy," No. 15-501.
[11] See Table 4-3.
[12] DBS, "Structure of the Canadian Economy," No. 15-501.

TABLE 4-4 Industry Input and Goods Purchases, 1961 ($ Millions)

	Gross Input	Goods Purchases	Value-Added
Communications and other service industries	11,742	3,152	8,590
Transportation, storage and trade	10,628	3,604	7,024
Construction	7,017	4,059	2,958
Food, feed, beverage and tobacco	5,474	3,984	1,490
Primary metal and metal fabricating	4,931	3,203	1,728
Agriculture, forestry, fishing and trapping	4,070	1,674	2,396
Transportation and electric equipment manufacture	3,372	2,055	1,317
Chemical, rubber and petroleum products	3,080	2,033	1,047
Paper and allied industries	2,229	1,262	967
Other manufacturing industries	2,220	1,123	1,097
Textile	2,217	1,352	865
Wood and furniture	1,426	1,075	551
Mines and quarries excluding coal mines	1,379	343	1,036
Electric power, gas and water utilities	1,262	404	858
Mineral fuel mines and wells	877	350	527

SOURCE: DBS, "The Input-Output Structure of the Canadian Economy 1961," No. 15-501.

TABLE 4-5 Products Sold, 1961 ($ Millions)

Industries and their major products	Gross Sales	To Industries	To Final Demand	To Exports	To Imports
1. Communication and Other Service Industries					
A. Financial services	6,857	1,823	5,097	20	−83
B. Business services	2,684	1,290	1,470	9	−85
C. Personal services	1,785	538	1,348	6	−107
D. Communications	1,055	605	443	25	−18
2. Transportation, Storage and Trade					
A. Transportation, storage and trade	10,507	3,902	6,016	670	−81
3. Construction					
A. Construction	6,964	1,052	5,912	—	—
4. Food, Feed, Beverage and Tobacco					
A. Fruit, vegetable, feed and miscellaneous food products	2,204	926	1,335	247	−304
B. Meat, fish and dairy products	2,490	640	1,844	94	−88
5. Primary Metal and Metal Fabricating					
A. Iron and steel basic product	2,184	2,394	70	150	−430
B. Non-ferrous metal basic products	1,641	871	—	887	−117
C. Machinery and equipment	1,090	939	864	114	−827

TABLE 4-5 Products Sold, 1961 (concluded)

Industries and their major products	Gross Sales	To Industries	To Final Demand	To Exports	To Imports
6. Agriculture, Forestry, Fishing and Trapping.					
A. Other agricultural products	1,232	909	413	113	−203
B. Live animals	1,073	943	73	66	−9
C. Forestry products	850	783	38	44	−15
D. Grain	908	324	—	625	−41
7. Transportation and Electric Equipment Manufacturers					
A. Vehicles and parts	1,230	607	1,173	49	−599
B. Electrical and communication equipment	1,126	665	797	75	−411
C. Other transportation equipment	701	194	718	238	−469
8. Chemical, Rubber and Petroleum Products					
A. Other chemicals	1,439	1,201	414	219	−395
B. Petroleum products	1,227	814	540	11	−138
C. Rubber products	306	250	108	8	−60
9. Paper and Allied Industries					
A. Paper and allied products	2,199	1,085	103	1,119	−108
10. Other Manufacturing Industries					
A. Printing and publishing products	849	676	299	19	−145
B. Non-metallic mineral products	664	714	63	41	−154
C. Miscellaneous manufactured commodities	585	362	533	51	−361
11. Textile					
A. Leather and textile	1,165	1,059	496	62	−452
B. Clothing	1,053	124	1,019	11	−101
12. Wood and Furniture					
A. Lumber	690	368	7	354	−39
B. Other wood products	347	329	11	40	−33
C. Furniture	362	36	358	3	−35
13. Mines and Quarries excluding Coal Mines					
A. Metal ores and concentrates	1,173	781	—	519	−127
B. Non-metallic minerals	275	162	12	157	−56
14. Electric Power, Gas and Water Utilities					
A. Utilities	1,272	794	476	18	−16
15. Mineral Fuel Mines and Wells					
A. Oil and natural gas	797	801	155	209	−368
B. Coal	66	130	47	8	−119

SOURCE: DBS, "The Input-Output Structure of the Canadian Economy 1961," No. 15-501.

NOTE: Gross Sales are different from Gross Input in Table 4-4 mainly because of inventories and the treatment of imports by DBS in these statistics as a negative column of demand for the commodity rather than partially as a supply row for the industry.

The buyers' side of the market is more difficult to summarize, since most industries are multi-product industries and purchase a large number of commodities. However, the inter-industry purchase pattern is available in massive detail in "The Input – Output Structure of the Canadian Economy, 1961."[13] The Canadian input-output model in full worksheet detail has 187 industries and 644 commodities. However, published data is available only for 110 industries and 197 commodities. This is still a very detailed system. Such an accounting of the industrial market through an input-output model and the link with final demand shown earlier above has many uses for marketers. It aids in market planning and forecasting. Direct and indirect effects of changes in final demand can be foreseen for each industry. For example, if final demand for automobiles is projected to increase, the direct effect is that output of the automobile manufacturing industry will rise – but this will have the indirect effect of increasing the demand for steel required to make automobiles. This in turn means an increase in the demand for iron ore required to make steel. Thus, the model pinpoints market potentials. Firms can compare sales distributions of their own output of commodities with those of the relevant total commodity classes, and can thereby discover potential markets.

Also, the pattern of vertical and horizontal markets is made clear.[14] As mentioned earlier, the input-output model is very useful since the basic interdependence between industries tends not to alter drastically. Thus the same market share ratios of commodities and industries can be utilized by marketing planners to analyse demand statistics of future years.

Location of Industry

Marketers should know where industry is located in order to optimize the efficiency of their marketing effort initially and with a view to future expansion of their market share and/or product line. Figure 4-4 illustrates data on the value of goods purchased by province for the important goods-producing industries – agriculture, forestry, fishing and trapping; mines, quarries and oil wells; manufacturing and construction; and electric power, gas, and water utilities. Figure 4-5 breaks down the same data by industry. The total value of such goods purchased amounted to almost $32 billion in 1968.

It can be seen that Ontario provided 46.4 percent of the total value of goods purchased, Quebec 25.4 percent, British Columbia 10.4 percent and Alberta 6.0 percent; and all other provinces combined only amounted to 11.8 percent.

---

[13] *Ibid.*

[14] One way of defining vertical and horizontal markets is the degree to which the demands for products of an industry are concentrated. The more concentrated in a single industry these demands are, the more nearly vertical is the structure of the market. A horizontal market for a product exists when the product is used by many industries.

FIGURE 4-4 Value of Goods Purchased by Goods-Producing Industries, by Province, 1968

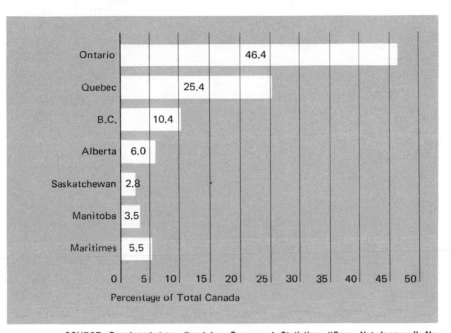

SOURCE: *Developed from Dominion Bureau of Statistics: "Farm Net Income," No. 21-202; "Fur Production," No. 23-207; "Fisheries Statistics — Canada," No. 24-201; "Canadian Forestry Statistics," No. 25-202; "Mineral Industries, Principal Statistics," No. 26-204; "Manufacturing Industries of Canada — Summary for Canada," No. 31-203; "Electric Power Statistics," No. 57-202; "Survey of Production," No. 61-202; "Construction in Canada," No. 64-201. (Ottawa: Queen's Printer, various issues).*

In agriculture, Ontario leads, followed by Quebec, Saskatchewan and Alberta. In forestry, the ranking order is British Columbia, Quebec and Ontario. In fisheries, Nova Scotia and British Columbia are by far the leaders. Ontario and Quebec lead in trapping, and the largest mining goods purchaser is Ontario, followed by Quebec. Some 52 percent of the cost of goods purchased in manufacturing arises in Ontario; Quebec is next with approximately 25 percent, and then comes British Columbia with some 8 percent. In construction and in electric power the pattern corresponds to that of manufacturing, with Ontario first, then Quebec, and British Columbia third.[15]

There are no such published breakdowns for the value of goods purchased by the service-producing sector, but in general, such values by province and industry would tend to follow the ranking pattern set by the goods-producing sector. The discussion now turns to the other market segments in the Gross Domestic industrial market.

[15] See source note, Figure 4-4.

FIGURE 4-5 Value of Goods Purchased by Goods-Producing Industries, by Industry, 1968

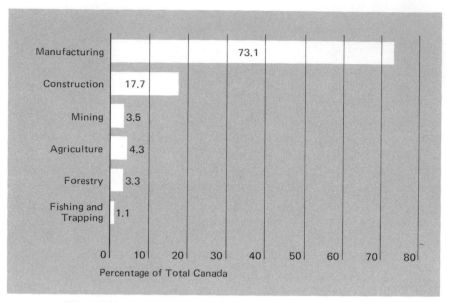

SOURCE: *See source note, Figure 4-4.*

The Capital Goods Market

Capital expenditures have constituted over 20 percent of GNE in the two decades 1950–1970. In 1970, new capital expenditures totalled $18 billion, some 21 percent of GNE and 18 percent of the industrial market.[16] More recent statistics give new capital expenditures at $19.3 billion in 1971, of which $12.7 billion was new construction and $6.6 billion was new machinery and equipment. This has been the pattern in the years since 1950. Construction expenditures generally are over 60 percent of capital expenditures.[17]

Capital repair expenditures amounted to another $5.5 billion in 1970 and $5.7 billion in 1971. These repair expenditures are considered by the input-output model and by the GDP accounts as part of the industrial market rather than a final demand sector — e.g., purchase of paint or a gear is different from a new capital goods purchase of a machine or the construction of a new plant. However, from a marketing viewpoint the machine tool manufacturer or construction firm may well be interested in the repair and new capital goods market. Figures

[16] DBS, "National Accounts," No. 13-001.
[17] Jointly prepared by the Dominion Bureau of Statistics and the Department of Trade and Commerce, "Private and Public Investment in Canada," No. 61-205 (Ottawa: Queen's Printer, various years).

FIGURE 4-6 Total Capital Expenditures (New and Repair) by Province, 1970

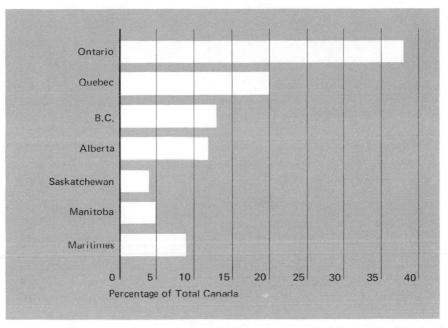

SOURCE: Jointly prepared by the Dominion Bureau of Statistics and the Department
of Trade and Commerce, "Private and Public Investment in Canada,"
No. 61-205 (Ottawa: Queen's Printer, 1971).

NOTE: Percentage figures have been calculated by the author.

4-6 and 4-7 take this into account. It should be noted that these charts
would not be significantly different if they represented only new capital
expenditures.

Another viewpoint can be obtained by noting that business
gross fixed new capital formation was $14.7 billion and direct govern-
ment new capital outlays were $3.3 billion. New capital outlays in the
goods-producing sector, including housing, equalled $12.3 billion, some
70 percent of the total. This augurs well for the productivity of the
economy and the growth of the industrial market. To complete the
picture, Figure 4-6 shows new plus repair capital expenditures in 1970
by province and Figure 4-7 shows such expenditures by sector. It is
highly probable that capital expenditures will continue to increase significantly because of the growing requirement of our advancing technological society.

It should be noted that although Ontario's total capital expenditures were 39 percent of that of Canada, the province's capital
expenditures on new machinery and equipment were 46 percent of such
expenditures for the country as a whole. This 46 percent is more in
line with Ontario's prominence in the goods-producing industries sector.

FIGURE 4-7 Total Capital Expenditures (New and Repair) by Sector, 1970

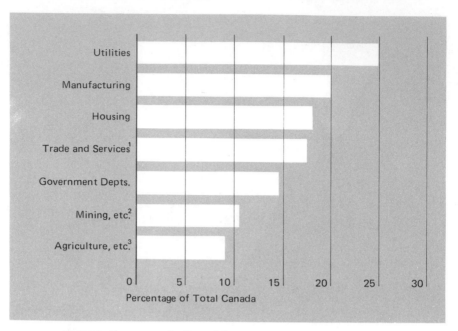

SOURCE: *See source note, Figure 4-6.*

NOTE: Percentage figures have been calculated by the author.

[1] Trade, finance, insurance, real estate, commercial services and institutional services.

[2] Mining, quarrying, oil wells and construction industry.

[3] Agriculture, fishing and forestry.

The Government Sector

Marketers should be interested in the government sector. This is a relatively large sector and the purchasing is concentrated in a few hands. As mentioned earlier, government new capital expenditures in 1970 totalled $3.3 billion. Provincial and municipal governments spent roughly 40 percent each of such expenditures, with the federal government accounting for the rest. Another view is given by noting that some two-thirds of such expenditures are direct spending by government departments, with the remaining one-third being done primarily by provincial and municipal hospitals and schools, and provincial universities. The inclusion of capital repair expenditures would have swollen government sector capital expenditures to $3.9 billion, but with the proportionate split among the various participants remaining approximately the same as that mentioned above.[18]

Aside from capital expenditures, government current expen-

[18] DBS, "Wholesale Trade," No. 63-008 (Ottawa: Queen's Printer, December 1970).

ditures on goods from business totalled roughly $5.7 billion in 1970.[19]

Municipal governments seem to do the most spending, followed by the federal government. However, if defense expenditures are excluded then the federal government would be the lowest spender of the three levels of government. In general, government current expenditures on goods from business appear to have roughly doubled through the 1960's and all environmental signs point to a continuation of this trend.[20] In most of the developed countries Big Government is getting bigger.

The Reseller Trade Sector

The reseller trade sector constitutes part of the industrial market. Nevertheless, many marketers would treat this trade sector as a special case since both industrial and consumer goods flow into it.

If we hold to our definition of an industrial good as one that is used for producing other goods rather than one used by household members to satisfy their wants, then the main sections of reseller trade that are of interest here are the wholesale industrial goods trade, and that part of wholesale consumer goods trade and retail trade where the retailer sells to industrial users as opposed to householders. It would be exceedingly difficult to break out such statistics at the wholesale consumer goods trade level or at the retail trade level. However, at the wholesale level, industrial goods trade sales (a classification by product type not by final user, and therefore including sales other than to the industrial market) amounted to roughly $9.7 million in 1970. The large industrial goods categories, in order of rank, were construction materials and supplies, including electrical wiring and lumber; industrial and transportation equipment and supplies; grain, iron and steel; junk and scrap; newsprint, paper and paper products; commercial, institutional and service equipment and supplies; farm machinery; and scientific and professional equipment and supplies.[21]

Another viewpoint may be obtained by noting that our definition of the industrial market includes reseller trade, which comprises sales to industry and sales from wholesalers to retailers as opposed to sales to final demand sectors. The input-output model for 1961 tells us that in that year less than 40 percent of total wholesale and retail sales, net of commodity and indirect taxes, occurred within the industrial market. Since total wholesale and retail sales inclusive of commodity and indirect taxes approximated some $50 billion in 1970,[22] one can make a rough

[19] This amount has been arrived at by extrapolation from ratios of total government current expenditures to government current expenditures on goods from business.

[20] DBS, "National Accounts, Income and Expenditure," No. 13-201 and "Provincial Government Finance," No. 68-205 (Ottawa: Queen's Printer, various years).

[21] DBS, "Wholesale Trade," No. 63-008.

[22] *Ibid.*, and DBS, "Retail Trade," No. 63-005 (Ottawa: Queen's Printer, December 1970), and "Structure of the Canadian Economy," No. 15-501.

estimate that less than $20 billion of these sales in 1970 formed part of the industrial market. This seems feasible in comparison with our previously estimated industrial market size of $74.1 billion in 1970. Further, one can assume reasonably that the location of reseller trade establishments that serve the industrial market conforms to the relative cost of goods purchased by province in the industrial market as depicted in Figure 4-4.

More specific detail on retailing and wholesaling in Canada is contained in Chapters 8 and 9, in the second part of this book.

Special Case of the Manufacturing Sector

The manufacturing sector is part of our industrial market, but it is being considered as a special sector because the cost of goods purchased by this sector constitutes a little over 30 percent of our estimated industrial market of $74.1 billion. Moreover, the sector is important as it provides much of the dynamism for future growth of the industrial market.

The marketer should take a keen interest in Canada's manufacturing sector despite the fact that the Canadian economy is oriented relatively more to the production of primary and processed industrial materials. In recent years Canadian manufacturing has undergone major technological developments in its methods of production. Through larger scales of production and greater specialization in many lines of production, there has been a substantial increase in the efficiency of use of productive resources. Furthermore, there has been a great proliferation in the types of products produced, with increasing exports particularly in the 1960's. The bulk of the growth of trade in nearly all developed countries since the Second World War has occurred in highly manufactured products.[23] Thus, a highly competitive posture on the part of Canadian manufacturers is required if Canada's share of such rapidly expanding markets is to grow.

However, the dominating shift in structure has been the decline in the share of the primary industries in terms of employment, and an almost corresponding expansion in the share of services. Most of the relative decline in the primary industries has occurred in agriculture. Figure 4-8 illustrates this point and gives an international comparison.

Moreover, Canada has a smaller manufacturing sector relative to its economy than most industrially developed countries, as illustrated in Figure 4-9. For Canadian manufacturing as a whole, the volume of output increased between 1947 and 1967 at a rate of about 5 percent a year, only slightly above the growth rate for the economy.[24] It is

[23] See source note, Figure 4-4.
[24] Economic Council of Canada, *Seventh Annual Review* (Ottawa: Queen's Printer, September 1970) , p. 24.

FIGURE 4-8 Employment in Agriculture, Manufacturing and Other Occupations

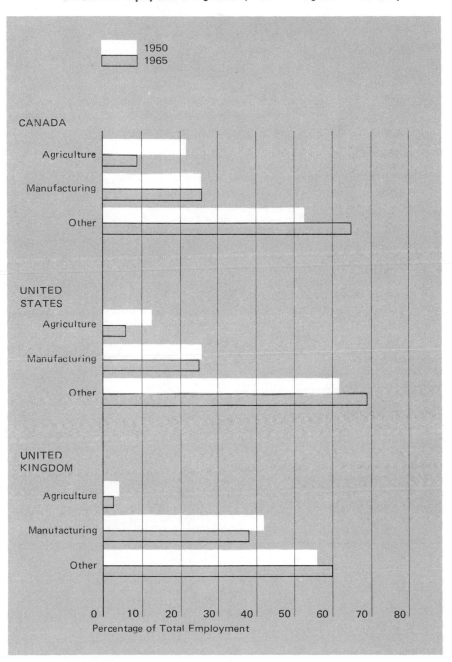

SOURCE: *Figures from Economic Council of Canada*, Third Annual Review, *p. 16.*

FIGURE 4-9 Industrial Origin of Gross Domestic Product at Factor Cost, 1968

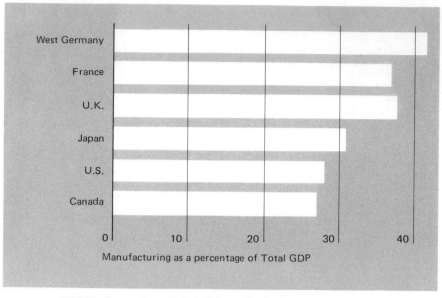

Manufacturing as a percentage of Total GDP

SOURCE: *Figures from United Nations*, Yearbook of National Accounts Statistics, 1969, *vol. II (New York: United Nations, 1969) pp. 83-97.*

highly important for the strength of the Canadian economy that its manufacturing base be expanded and the growth of this sector maintained and if possible increased.

CANADIAN MANUFACTURING SECTOR PROFILE

The total value of shipments from the secondary manufacturing sector in 1968 totalled $42 billion. Of this, the cost of materials and supplies used totalled $23 billion, and fuel and electricity used amounted to $0.8 billion, making the value-added figure $18.2 billion. Table 4-6 gives the percentage distribution of cost of goods used by province, in the manufacturing sector.

TABLE 4-6 Percentage Distribution of Manufacturing Sector, by Province, 1968

	Cost of Goods Used (%)	Employment (%)	Salaries and Wages (%)
Ontario	51.5	50.0	52.2
Quebec	27.4	31.8	29.5
British Columbia	8.3	7.4	8.3
Prairie region (Alberta Saskatchewan, Manitoba)	9.0	4.5	6.4
Atlantic provinces	3.8	4.5	3.6

SOURCE: *DBS, "Manufacturing Industries of Canada," Nos. 31-202 — 31-207 (Ottawa: Queen's Printer, various issues).*

Cost of goods used by manufacturing averaged roughly $1,113 per capita of population in 1968. The comparable regional figures are Ontario $1,635, Quebec $1,070, British Columbia $952, the Prairies $581 and the Atlantic provinces $441.[25] This illustrates the importance of the manufacturing sector in the regional economies, and is a significant indicator of economic growth in each region.

TABLE 4-7 Leading Manufacturing Industry Groups

	Average Annual Growth Rate[1] Real Value-Added (1961 – 1970) %	1968		
		Cost of Goods Used ($ millions)	Value[2] of Shipments ($ millions)	No. of Establish-ments
Food and beverage	4.5	4,971	7,674	6,361
Transportation and equipment	10.5	3,553	5,531	872
Paper and allied	2.9	1,754	3,422	635
Primary metals	6.1	1,733	3,384	405
Metal fabricating	7.1	1,392	2,900	3,983
Petroleum and coal products	4.3	1,347	1,676	95
Electrical products	7.9	1,220	2,407	689
Chemical and chemical products	7.6	1,061	2,429	1,124
Wood	3.5	1,052	1,966	3,477
Textiles	5.4	848	1,527	967
Machinery (except electrical)	8.6	735	1,480	795
Clothing	2.7	662	1,258	2,282
Miscellaneous manufacturing	7.8	563	1,258	2,810
Non-metallic mineral products	3.8	457	1,204	1,260
Printing, publishing and allied	3.1	448	1,370	3,600
Tobacco products	2.9	321	509	30
Furniture	5.9	312	660	2,300
Rubber	8.2	256	565	104
Knitting mills	4.7	209	377	342
Leather	−1.6	193	396	513

SOURCE: DBS, "Manufacturing Industries of Canada," and "Index of Industrial Products," Nos. 31-203 and 62-005 respectively (Ottawa: Queen's Printer, various issues).

[1] Based on the index of real domestic product by industry group.
[2] Value of shipments of goods of own manufacture.

For industrial marketers, it is of interest to know the major manufacturing industries of Canada and their location by region, so that they can optimize the efficiency of their marketing efforts. The major manufacturing industries in order of cost of goods used are given in Table 4-7, and the distribution of cost of goods used by region is contained in Table 4-8.

As can be seen, Ontario leads or is joint leader in every industry group except for wood, textiles, clothing and knitting. Quebec leads

[25] DBS, "Manufacturing Industries of Canada," No. 31-203 (Ottawa: Queen's Printer, 1969), and "Estimated Population by Sex and Age Group for Canada and Provinces," No. 91-202 (Ottawa: Queen's Printer, December 1968).

TABLE 4-8 Distribution of Cost of Goods Used by Industry and Region, 1967[1]
($ Millions)

	Ontario	Quebec	British Columbia	Prairies	Atlantic Provinces
Food and beverage	1,927	1,354	389	968	334
Transportation equipment	2,885	489	63	49	66
Primary metals	968	481	104	112	—
Paper and allied	612	601	313	55	133
Metal fabricating	854	327	81	102	28
Chemicals and chemical products	640	278	54	71	18
Electrical products	809	323	30	24	26
Machinery (except electrical)	554	94	30	54	3
Printing, publishing and allied	238	139	26	37	8
Wood	161	180	601	69	41
Non-metallic mineral products	237	113	31	62	13
Textiles	348	466	8	15	10
Miscellaneous manufacturing	393	139	11	7	4
Clothing	146	446	11	93	1
Furniture and fixtures	152	115	17	26	2
Petroleum and coal products	467	392	—	188	—
Rubber	186	89	—	—	—
Leather	95	60	2	6	—
Tobacco products	209	117	—	—	—
Knitting mills	59	138	—	—	8

SOURCE: Developed from data in DBS, "Manufacturing Industries in Canada," Nos.
31-202 — 31-207 (Ottawa: Queen's Printer, various Issues).

[1] $357 million is confidential in order to meet the secrecy requirements of the Statistics Act.

in the last three groups, but is otherwise behind Ontario. British Columbia leads all provinces in the wood industries, and is strong in paper and primary metals. The Prairies have a fairly diversified manufacturing range. This is due primarily to contributions from Alberta and Manitoba. The Atlantic provinces trail in almost every industry.

Ontario is especially strong in the manufacture of motor vehicles and their parts and accessories, and in the steel industry. These are two of Canada's four leading industries, the other two being food and beverages, and pulp and paper. The strength in steel gives Ontario a natural foundation for a large number of machine-based steel-user industries.

Furthermore, transportation equipment and machinery are the fastest growing industries, both of which are based primarily in Ontario.

Figure 4-10 outlines Canada's inter-regional trade flows in manufactured goods (1967). This information adds a dynamic element to the industrial market information of manufacturing locations as noted above. Some of the highlights are the following:

1. Quebec and Ontario absorb 55 percent and supply 80 percent of all manufacturing goods traded between regions.
2. Ontario and Quebec are each other's largest market, with almost half of all inter-regional trade moving between them.

FIGURE 4-10 Regional Structure of Canada's Trade in Manufactured Goods (1967)

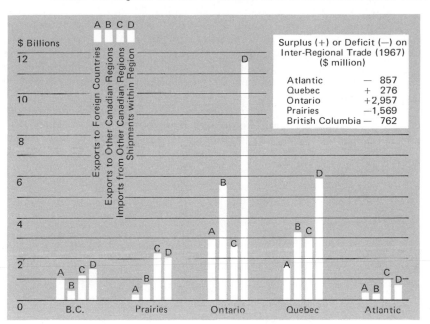

Surplus (+) or Deficit (−) on Inter-Regional Trade (1967) ($ million)

Atlantic	− 857
Quebec	+ 276
Ontario	+2,957
Prairies	−1,569
British Columbia	− 762

Legend (bars A B C D):
- A — Exports to Foreign Countries
- B — Exports to Other Canadian Regions
- C — Imports from Other Canadian Regions
- D — Shipments within Region

PER CENT DISTRIBUTION OF CANADA'S INTER-REGIONAL TRADE

	Atlantic		Quebec		Ontario		Prairies		British Columbia	
By Geographic Area:	Exports To	Imports From	Exports To	Imports From	Exports To	Imports From	Exports To	Imports From	Exports To	Imports From
Atlantic	—	—	12	4	12	5	5	1	4	1
Quebec	43	36	—	—	48	81	28	22	13	23
Ontario	44	59	64	88	—	—	37	65	26	60
Prairies	9	3	15	6	26	10	—	—	56	16
British Columbia	3	2	9	2	13	5	29	12	—	—
Total†	100	100	100	100	100	100	100	100	100	100
By Industry:	Exports	Imports	Exports	Imports	Exports	Imports	Exports	Imports	Exports	Imports
Food and beverage	33	19	11	17	12	16	60	11	24	17
Textiles	4	3	9	5	4	8	1	4	1	4
Clothing	*	7	12	2	2	9	7	6	2	6
Wood	3	2	1	2	1	4	3	4	36	1
Pulp and paper	18	4	8	5	3	9	2	4	10	2
Primary metal	X	X	6	7	6	7	X	X	2	5
Metal fabricating	2	9	7	6	8	6	2	8	5	7
Machinery	*	5	3	5	7	2	3	7	3	5
Transportation equipment	13	14	3	14	18	4	2	15	3	13
Electrical products	4	10	9	10	12	7	3	11	4	12
Non-metallic minerals	*	2	2	2	1	2	2	1	1	2
Petroleum and coal products	X	X	X	X	X	X	X	X	X	X
Chemicals	*	X	9	9	9	7	5	8	6	7
Other**	23	25	20	16	17	19	10	21	3	19
Total	100	100	100	100	100	100	100	100	100	100

SOURCE: *Bank of Montreal,* Business Review, *22 December 1971, p. 2.*

* Less than 0.5%.   † Columns may not add to total because of rounding.

** Includes: tobacco, rubber, leather, knitting, furniture, printing and publishing, and miscellaneous, as well as those industries (indicated by X) for which figures are omitted in accordance with the Statistics Act.

3. Ontario and Quebec represented the first and second most important trading partner of each of the three remaining regions.

4. Quebec and Ontario were the only two regions realizing a surplus on inter-regional trade in manufactured goods.

5. For the average Canadian manufacturer, 56 percent of total sales were made in the local market, with shipments made to other regions in Canada and internationally, accounting for the remaining 18 and 16 percent respectively.

6. The food products industry accounts for the largest proportion of both the Atlantic and Prairie provinces' total regional exports. Almost half of British Columbia's exports were composed of wood products, including pulp and paper, while Ontario and Quebec regional exports were broadly based.

5

The International Dimension of Canadian Marketing

International marketing is becoming increasingly important for Canada. Exports of goods and services from Canada totalled $22.2 billion in 1971. This was approximately 24.1 percent of the nation's GNP.[1] Exports of goods alone amounted to $18.3 billion, making Canada the sixth largest exporter of goods in the world.[2] In terms of exports as a percentage of GNP Canada stands first or second in the world among the major countries, depending on the year. The economies of some of the world's major exporters like the U.S. and Japan are far less dependent on trade. Exports are only 5 percent of U.S. GNP, and 10 percent of Japan's.

This chapter is divided into two sections. The first deals with the importance of international marketing for Canada, describing the nation's external trade, and the links between trade, capital flows and the balance of payments. Moreover the international marketing position of Canada is analyzed in the context of changing trends in world markets, and the particular position of Canada's major trading partners, the U.S., the U.K. and Japan. The second section studies the impact of foreign investment and influence in Canada and its effects on foreign trade. In particular, tariffs, the Kennedy Round and the impact of other trade restrictions are discussed. Also the specific effect of the "auto pact" and the advantages and disadvantages of having freer trade with the U.S. and other countries are outlined. And finally, Canadian aid to the Less Developed Countries (the LDCs) is examined.

THE IMPORTANCE OF INTERNATIONAL MARKETING

Canadian Foreign Trade

The resource base of a country indicates the productive activity the area can support; differences in resource endowments tend to be reflected both in such productive activity and also in the export and

---

[1] Dominion Bureau of Statistics, *"National Accounts, Income and Expenditure,"* No. 13-001 (Ottawa: Queen's Printer, Fourth Quarter 1971), p. 22.
[2] International Monetary Fund, *International Financial Statistics* XXIV (Washington, D.C.: International Monetary Fund, July 1972), p. 36.

TABLE 5-1 Canadian Exports and Imports of Goods, 1965 ($ Millions)

	Exports		Imports	
Live animals, food, feed,				
beverages and tobacco		1709.0		769.6
Wheat	840.2			
Crude materials, inedible		1763.4		1006.3
Iron ore	360.8			
Crude petroleum	280.0		Crude petroleum	312.3
Nickel in ore,				
concentrates, syrup	189.3			
Asbestos unmanufactured	158.7			
Fabricated materials, inedible		3728.8		2114.4
Newsprint	869.6		Steel, bars and rods,	
Wood pulp	493.5		plate sheet and strip	220.7
Lumber	489.9			
Aluminum	361.0			
Nickel and alloys	207.9			
Copper and alloys	194.9			
End products, inedible		1298.2		4476.6
			Transportation and com-	
			munication equipment	1613.2
			Machinery	1372.1
			Other equipment and tools	712.8
			Miscellaneous end	
			products	460.4
			Personal and house-	
			hold goods	217.8
Special transaction — trade		23.5		266.5
Total		8523.0		8633.4

SOURCE: *Dominion Bureau of Statistics, "Exports by Commodities," No. 65-004, December 1965 (Ottawa: Queen's Printer March 1966), p. 12, and "Imports by Commodities," No. 65-007, December 1965 (Ottawa: Queen's Printer, May 1966), p. 9.*

NOTE: Excludes re-exports of $241.5 million, and also exports of gold, $137.9 million.

import trade. The broad pattern of Canadian trade in 1965 shown in Table 5-1 illustrates clearly the international trade theory of comparative advantage.[3] By the end of the 1960's this broad pattern was altered by the "auto pact" with the U.S., of which more is said below.

The export figures show Canada's two main economic strengths: large natural resources and advanced resource-production technology. The import figures expose Canada's historical economic weaknesses, namely its comparatively small market and relatively high unit labour costs.[4] These are significant factors in the manufactured products trade.

[3] Developed in the 19th century by David Ricardo et al. Explained in many economic textbooks, for example, Paul A. Samuelson *Economics*, 6th ed. (New York: McGraw Hill Book Company of Canada Limited, 1964), pp. 673-83.

[4] Incidentally, it should be noted that trade in crude petroleum is the result of special factors — see Government of Canada, "National Oil Policy," *Hansard* 1960, pp. 1432-3, 1468, 1641-3, 1652, 1709.

Comparative advantages change over time. The chief change in the post–World War II years has been the relative shift of such advantages in selected manufactured goods against North America in favour of western Europe and Japan. The growth of mass markets in western Europe with the formation of the European Economic Community (EEC) and the European Free Trade Association (EFTA), and the utilization of advanced mass production technology by Japan, has enabled these areas to achieve economies of large volume output in many products.

However, Canada's secondary manufacturing sector has also been growing in absolute size as the Canadian market expands with increasing affluence and urbanization. The Canadian market is by no means small. Canadian Gross National Product in 1968 was U.S. $62.3 billion, the ninth largest in the world.[5] The growth in manufacturing has led in turn to a growth in Canadian exports of highly manufactured products at a rate of 31 percent a year from 1965 to 1971.

FIGURE 5-1 Changing Composition of Canadian Exports

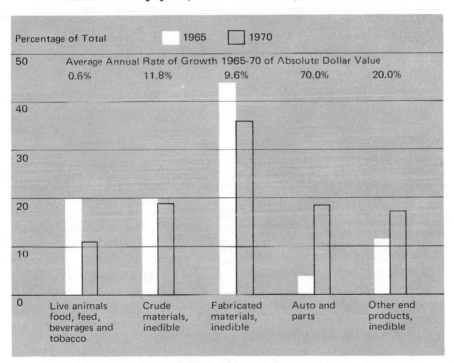

SOURCE: DBS, "Exports by Commodities," No. 65-004, December 1965 and 1970.

While much of this is due to the special circumstances of the Automotive Free Trade Agreement with the U.S., very sizable increases

[5] United Nations, *Yearbook of National Accounts Statistics, 1968*, vol. II (New York: United Nations, 1970), p. 16.

have occurred in many other fabricated materials and end products items, as can be seen from Figure 5-1.

The changing geographical pattern of Canada's international marketing position is detailed in Table 5-2. The table shows how Canadian exports to areas other than the U.K. have risen rapidly between 1965 and 1971. Figure 5-2 depicts the pattern in greater detail.

TABLE 5-2 Geographical Patterns of Canadian Exports ($ Millions)

Domestic Exports to:	1965	1971	Average Annual Rate of Growth 1965 − 71 (%)
U.S.	4,839	12,149	16.6
U.K.	1,174	1,361	2.5
EEC	626	1,101	9.9
Japan	316	791	16.5
Others	1,568	2,445	7.7
Total	8,523	17,847	13.1

SOURCE: *DBS, "Exports by Countries," No. 65-003 (Ottawa: Queen's Printer, December 1965 and 1971).*

A note on international marketing opportunities for Canadian exporters is appropriate here. The following shows what and how much Canada's main trading partners import from the world and contrasts this with the goods these important customers take from Canada. This illustrates the large potential available in these markets for resourceful Canadian international marketers.

The U.S. is the world's largest importing country. In 1968 it imported some $33 billion worth of goods, nearly 14 percent of total world imports. Manufactured goods imports were over $11 billion of this total with machinery and transport equipment comprising another $8 billion. Food, live animals, beverages and tobacco imports added up to over $5 billion, with crude materials, minerals, chemicals and miscellaneous items being the remaining $9 billion of imports. Canada supplied almost 27 percent of U.S. imports of manufactured goods and machinery and transport equipment, some 11 percent of the food, etc. category and about 33 percent of the crude materials, etc. category.

Similar figures for the EEC, U.K. and Japan are given in Table 5-3. It is obvious that Canada is barely tapping the large EEC market and that in any event complacency about export competitiveness is dangerous. Canada has to remain ever competitive, especially with the U.S. Demand from that country for Canadian goods constitutes over 14 percent of total Canadian output and now the protectionist lobby is mounting in the U.S. with the new Nixon restrictive measures coupled with a 10 percent surcharge on imports.[6]

[6] *Montreal Gazette,* 16-18 August 1971.

FIGURE 5-2 Changing Geographical Patterns of Canadian Exports

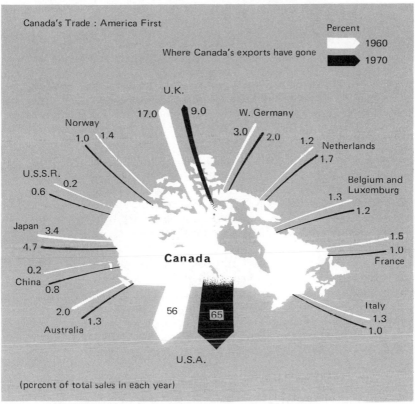

SOURCE: Financial Times of Canada, *20 September 1971, p. 9.*

TABLE 5-3 Imports from the World and Canada, 1968

	From World (Million $)			% From Canada		
	EEC	U.K.	Japan	EEC	U.K.	Japan
Manufactured goods, machinery and transportation equipment	30,176	8,819	2,828	1	4	3
Food, live animals, beverages and tobacco	9,871	3,434	1,879	1-2	8	5
Crude materials, minerals, chemicals and miscellaneous items	21,913	6,156	8,260	2	9	6
Total	61,960	18,409	12,967	1-2	7	5

SOURCE: *United Nations,* Yearbook of International Trade Statistics, 1968 *(New York: United Nations, 1970); DBS, "Exports by Countries, 1968," and "Exports by Commodities, 1968," Nos. 65-003 and 65-004 respectively.*

External Trade and Balance of Payments

The theory of comparative advantage is a far from complete explanation of world trade patterns. World trade flows are directly and significantly influenced by the flows of foreign long-term capital that precede it. Such foreign capital flows are basically of two types. The biggest of these flows has been private foreign investment made mainly through multinational companies. International foreign aid, given by governments and international institutions, constitutes the other major type of long-term capital flow. Some important factors that influence long-term foreign capital investment are attitudes, policies and needs in donor and recipient countries. Others are tariffs and impediments to trade that serve as indirect inducements to encourage foreign investments. Increasingly important are inducements offered by substantially lower wage rates in certain countries. Furthermore, world trade flows are influenced by the international flows of technology that occur through exports of products, exchanges of persons and licensing agreements. The impact of foreign investment and foreign influences on Canada's trade flows and international marketing efforts in the world market context will be discussed in the second part of this chapter.

Thus, trade is linked with capital flows and other influences which finally reflect themselves in a country's Balance of Payments or Total External account. Canada's balance of payments is influenced to a considerable extent by the size and character of its balance of international indebtedness. This is true not only through the servicing of capital, involving interest, dividends and miscellaneous income payments, but also through the influences of foreign investment on the Canadian economy and on the shape and direction of its external demands.

Canada has been among the world's largest importers of private long-term capital. The very substantial capital formation which has been a feature of the postwar pattern contributed to a rapid rate of growth in the Canadian economy, particularly in the exploitation of natural resources, and added significantly to Canadian GNP. At the same time it added substantially to the continuing burden of Canada's external debt. Gross external liabilities amounted to $46 billion with net external liabilities being $27 billion at the end of 1969.[7] This underscores the great importance of Canada achieving large merchandise trade surpluses in order to service this external debt and meet its other external payments. Thus, the fundamental necessity for Canada to develop international marketing expertise is increasing all the time in a capital-short world where Canada cannot hope to rely on an easy inflow of foreign capital as an aid to economic growth, and a rising standard of living.

---

[7] DBS, *Quarterly Estimates of the Canadian Balance of International Payments,* No. 67-001, (Ottawa: Queen's Printer, Second Quarter 1970) , p. 39.

Trends in World and Canadian Trade

World trade has had an unprecedented growth in the post–World War II period. The value of exports in current or constant dollars has risen at an average annual rate of about 7 percent.[8] This rate is faster than that of world physical output, illustrating that countries have been moving toward a higher level of economic interdependence and specialization of production.[9]

Three noticeable trends have appeared in world trade.

1. The high rate of expansion in world exports has resulted mainly from the external export activity of the industrial countries. In 1956, exports from industrial countries amounted to 66 percent of world exports. The corresponding figure for 1967 was 70 percent.
2. The bulk of world trade is made up of trade of the industrial countries with themselves, as shown in Table 5-4.

TABLE 5-4 Distribution of World Trade, 1969 (U.S. $ Millions)

Export From/To	Industrial Countries[1]	Developing Countries[2]	Soviet Bloc[3]	Total
Industrial countries	147,900	37,460	7,140	193,190
Developing countries	36,400	10,270	2,600	49,780
Soviet Bloc	6,940	4,530	18,060	29,750
World	191,240	52,260	27,790	272,710

SOURCE: *United Nations*, Yearbook of International Trade Statistics, 1969 *(New York: United Nations, 1971) p. 20.*

[1] U.S., Canada, Western Europe, Australia, New Zealand, South Africa.

[2] Regions other than 1 and 3.

[3] U.S.S.R., Eastern Europe, China Mainland, Mongolia, North Korea, North Vietnam and Japan.

Canadian exports by destination go mainly to other industrial countries. In 1969, 93 percent of Canadian exports went to other industrial countries, 6 percent to developing countries and one percent to the Soviet bloc. The latter area received mainly Canadian wheat. This basic pattern was unchanged even in 1971.

3. Manufactured goods, especially end products, formed the biggest and most rapidly growing component of world trade.

The reductions in world tariffs in the postwar period have had a much stronger impact on trade in finished goods, which were more highly

[8] United Nations, *Yearbook of International Trade Statistics, 1969* (New York: United Nations, 1971) , pp. 12-13.

[9] United Nations, *Statistical Yearbook, 1969* (New York: United Nations, 1970) , p. 54.

protected than industrial materials. Meanwhile trade in agricultural products remained shackled by a maze of tariff and other barriers devised to protect local farmers.

Moreover, actual world demand for finished goods increased more rapidly than other sectors because of greater elasticity in relation to incomes. At the same time, final demand for natural materials was restrained because of technological savings in the use of materials, the development of synthetic materials, and the demand for higher quality in contrast to quantity. Furthermore, the trend of export prices was much more favourable for manufactured goods than for primary products. In 1970 the export manufactured goods price index stood at 117 while the export primary products index was 107. (Both cases, Base 1963 = 100.) [10]

The volume of manufactured goods exports has more than quadrupled over the whole postwar period to 1968 while prices have risen 10 percent. In contrast, the volume of primary products exports has grown only two and a half times and prices are 5 percent down. Thus in 1948, manufactured goods exports were 42 percent of world exports but by 1968 this had risen to 64 percent.[11] A more detailed breakdown is shown in Table 5-5.

TABLE 5-5 Percentage Share of Commodity Groups in World Exports

	1952	1968
Manufactured goods		
Other manufactured goods and miscellaneous	30.1	30.0
Machinery	15.1	27.4
Chemicals	4.4	7.2
Sub-total	49.6	63.6
Fuels	9.4	9.6
Primary Products		
Food	22.0	14.5
Raw materials	19.0	11.3
Sub-total	41.0	25.8
Total	100.0	100.0

SOURCE: United Nations Statistical Yearbook, 1969, *p. 48.*

The percentage share of commodity groups in Canadian exports does not parallel that of world exports. Manufactured goods constituted only 9 percent of Canadian exports in 1950, and 25 percent in 1968. Although the share of manufactured goods in Canadian exports has been rising fast, the smallness of the base has meant that the impact of these exports on the Canadian total has been limited. This is a major explana-

[10] United Nations, *Yearbook of International Trade Statistics, 1969,* p. 35.
[11] United Nations, *Statistical Yearbook, 1969,* p. 54.

tion of why total Canadian exports have grown less rapidly than world exports. Canada's share of the world market was 5.1 percent in 1950. This had fallen to 4.1 percent by 1967.[12]

Another major reason for the relatively slow growth of Canadian exports is the geographical distribution of the nation's foreign shipments. Some 55–60 percent of Canadian exports go traditionally to the U.S. about 15 percent go to the U.K., with another 5–6 percent going to other Commonwealth and preferential countries. All other countries receive the balance of roughly 20 percent. In the late 1960's the share of the U.K. has declined and the U.S. share has increased markedly due to the auto pact.[13]

However, the areas of fastest growing average annual demand for imports in the period 1953–67, in order of rank, were Japan, 11 percent annually; the EEC, 10 percent; EFTA, 6.5 percent, with U.K. imports growing more slowly than the EFTA average; Canada, 5.7 percent; the U.S., 5.5 percent; and the developing countries, 5.0 percent. Trade in eastern Europe increased at an annual average of over 8 percent, but until recently it has been concentrated within the Communist bloc and its impact on world trade is very minor.[14] Thus, it can be seen from the above that the geographic concentration of Canadian exports is mainly in the slow-growing import areas. Neither is this pattern altering. For example, Canadian exports to the EEC and Japan constituted 6.8 and 4.1 percent respectively of its total exports in 1964. In 1971 the comparative percentages were 6.2 and 4.4 percent. However, the U.S. share rose from 52.8 percent in 1964 to 68.3 percent in 1971.

Although Canadian exports still exhibit substantial variations from the unfolding commodity pattern of world imports, Canada is adjusting rapidly to changes in world demand and in the period 1964 to 1971 Canadian exports have grown at an average of 12.5 percent a year under the impetus of very rapid increases in manufactured end products.[15] The improved performance of the last few years is primarily due to the auto pact and its effect on exports to the U.S. Also, in part, it is attributable to special defence and aid programmes and to a wider realization of the possibilities in economic rationalization of secondary manufacturing industries, through relevant economies of scale.

Moreover, the Government of Canada is very aware of the importance of the nation's export performance, given the large import needs that our rising standard of living dictate, and the perennial balance of payments current account deficit in an increasingly capital-short world. The government makes available a variety of services which assist in marketing Canadian products abroad. These are described in more detail in the following chapter.

[12] *Canada Year Book, 1967*, p. 957.
[13] See pp. 120-22.
[14] United Nations, *Yearbook of International Trade Statistics, 1969*, pp. 12-18.
[15] DBS, "Exports by Commodities," No. 65-004 (Ottawa: Queen's Printer, December 1964 and December 1971), various pages.

The Economic Council of Canada is optimistic about Canadian external trade growth. The Council forecasts a rise in the total value of merchandise exports of 9 percent a year between 1968 and 1975, with imports growing at 10 percent a year. However, by 1975, exports are expected to exceed imports by approximately $1 billion. In 1968 the surplus was $1.2 billion. Table 5-6 outlines the Council's forecast. Strong growth is expected in exports of industrial materials and especially of highly manufactured products, including automotive, and a wide range of other products.

TABLE 5-6 Forecasted Exports and Imports, 1975

	$ Millions		Average Annual Growth Rate
	1968	1975	1968 – 1975 (%)
Merchandise Exports Forecast to 1975			
Grain	796	900	1.7
Industrial materials	7,326	12,000	7.5
Highly manufactured products	4,244	10,200	12.0
Other	1,208	1,300	6.0
Total	13,574	24,900	9.0
Merchandise Imports Forecast to 1975			
Industrial materials	3,560	5,400	11.4
Highly manufactured products	7,630	16,900	12.1
Other	1,177	1,600	4.4
Total	12,367	23,900	10.0

SOURCE: *Economic Council of Canada,* Sixth Annual Review *(Ottawa: Queen's Printer, 1969) p. 89.*

The Economic Council makes five specific assumptions, the first being that Canada will achieve its potential average annual growth rate of 5.5 percent a year, from 1967 to 1975. Since the 1967–70 rate was only 4.0 percent a year, this assumption can hardly hold true. Second, the total output of the OECD countries will rise at an average 4.5 percent a year over the same period. Third, Canadian export and import prices will rise at an average 1.5 percent a year between 1967 and 1975. Fourth, domestic Canadian prices of tradable goods will rise no faster than such prices abroad, particularly in the U.S. Fifth, existing trade arrangements to reduce tariffs between countries will be implemented and the viability of the international financial systems maintained. No allowance is made for any changes in policy (such as free trade arrangements) that might conceivably occur.[16]

For Canadian international marketers, one event that will radically change the environment in which they operate is the entry of the United Kingdom into the Common Market. The U.K. imported $1.4 billion from Canada in 1971, making this market the second largest

[16] Economic Council of Canada, *Sixth Annual Review* (Ottawa: Queen's Printer, 1969) , p. 75.

for Canadian producers after the U.S. The agreement leading to the U.K.'s entry into the EEC was approved by the British parliament in October 1971. The U.K. became a full member of the EEC on January 1, 1973 and over the next five years will gradually impose the Common External Tariff of the EEC on its imports from the rest of the world, while eliminating its tariffs with the EEC.

Some 23 percent of Canadian exports to the U.K. comprise food, feed, beverages and tobacco, of which the largest single product is wheat. As it happens, British consumers prefer bread made of 75–80 percent of hard wheat and most of the hard wheat is imported from Canada. Climatic conditions and the quality of the soil in the U.K. and in EEC countries prevent the production of hard wheat in these areas. Thus, because of limited substitutability between Canadian and European wheat, Canada's exports of wheat should not suffer in the short run. However, other agricultural exports are likely to be widely affected.[17]

Raw material and fuel exports have constituted roughly 31 percent of Canadian exports to the U.K. It is unlikely that these exports will diminish. The tariffs in any event are low and there is little competing production from the EEC.

Manufactured goods exports comprise the remaining 46 percent of Canadian exports to the U.K. As a group these exports stand to suffer serious losses in price competitiveness, as tariffs are relatively high and there are a number of competing producers in the EEC.

On the other hand, it is hoped that entry into the Common Market will lead, through increased efficiency, to accelerated growth in the U.K. economy. Should this be the case the resultant increase in import demand may act as a beneficial influence on Canadian exports to the U.K.

It should be noted that while the growth of most countries' exports to the EEC increased in the period since 1959, Canada has been an exception to this general trend. Moreover, Canadian exports to the EEC grew at a slower rate than Canadian exports to the rest of the world. This suggests that Canadian international marketers could make good use of their long established contact with, and "presence" in the U.K. in order to expand their sales in the rest of the EEC. Should they live up to this challenge, then the growth of Canadian exports could well accelerate to this enlarged market. In 1971, Canadian exports to the EEC were over $1,100 million. Thus, the combined U.K. and EEC market absorbed $2.5 billion worth of Canadian exports, some 14 percent of Canadian total merchandise exports.

FOREIGN INVESTMENT AND INFLUENCE

Foreign long-term capital invested in Canada amounted to $34.7 billion in 1967 at book value, over 50 percent of Gross National Product,

---

[17] Bank of Montreal, *Business Review*, 30 June 1971.

and roughly one-fifth of the total capital stock in Canada. Of such foreign investment some 81 percent was owned by U.S. residents. Direct investment constituted 59 percent of the total with the balance of 41 percent being investment in government and municipal bonds and other portfolio investments.[18] Direct investment is defined here as investments in business enterprises where the investment is sufficiently concentrated so as to constitute control of those concerns. On the other hand, portfolio investments are typically scattered minority holdings of securities which do not carry with them control of the enterprises. Foreign direct investment in Canada has been rising steadily through the years. In 1926 it was only 38 percent of total foreign investment. At that time, non-residents controlled only 17 percent of the combined capital in manufacturing, mining, railways and other utilities, and merchandising. Foreign control in the above industries had risen to 34 percent by 1964, and to 40 percent by 1968. Table 5-7 shows the extent of foreign control. Foreign domination is even higher in industries such as automo-

TABLE 5-7 Foreign Control in Selected Industries (Percentages)

	1926		1964		1968	
	Total	U.S.	Total	U.S.	Total	U.S.
Petroleum and natural gas	n.a.		74	62	83	67
Other mining and smelting	38	32	59	52	54	39
Manufacturing	35	30	60	46	58	43
Total of above industries, railways, other utilities and merchandising	17	15	34	27	40	29

SOURCE: *DBS*, Canadian Balance of International Payments, *1963, '64 and '65* and International Investment Position, *No. 67-201, pp. 79-80; idem,* Corporations and Labour Unions Returns Act, Annual Report for 1968, *various pages for 1968 figures.*

NOTE: The 1968 figures are not directly comparable with the others, since the source and coverage are different.

biles and parts (96 percent), transportation equipment (80 percent), chemicals (80 percent) and electrical apparatus (78 percent).[19]

Foreign investment brings both benefits and costs to Canada. The benefits are the receipt of capital, technology, and market contacts, all of which speed economic development. The costs involve the payment of interest, dividends and fees for business services. High and rising levels of foreign investment have led to increasing concern in the 1960's with the possible consequences. However, it is imperative to see this in perspective. One question to be answered is whether the production base of the Canadian economy and its international receipts are

[18] DBS, *Quarterly Estimates,* No. 67-001, Second Quarter 1970, p. 45. Bank of Nova Scotia, *Monthly Review,* April-May 1971, estimates non-resident long-term investment liabilities to be $44 billion at the end of 1970.
[19] DBS, *Daily Bulletin,* 13 February 1970.

growing sufficiently to help finance the nation's international indebtedness. As regards the production base it should be noted that GNP in current dollars has risen about twice as fast as the total of foreign capital since the 1920's.[20]

Regarding international receipts, it should be noted that Canada's capital requirements are exceedingly high. Although the U.S. is regarded widely as the nation having the highest amount of capital per worker in the world, in fact capital per worker is generally higher in Canada.[21] A number of factors contribute to the relatively heavy use of capital in Canada. In manufacturing, relatively short production runs in many products tend to lead to more capital overhead in relation to output. Also, in many fields production is subject to wider seasonal swings in Canada, with the result that more capital facilities may be needed to meet seasonal peaks but with lower annual production rates. Climate, the wide geographic extent of this country and the sparseness of population settlement outside the major urban concentrations clearly contribute to relatively heavier capital investment in transportation and communication facilities as well as in various form of social capital, such as hospitals. Another factor is the excess capacity which is a frequent feature of the build-up of large natural resource production capabilities in Canada, in anticipation of long-run future demand increases.

To match such capital needs, Canada has one of the highest rates of national savings in relation to GNP of any country, surpassing by a substantial margin that of the U.S. and U.K., and exceeded only by Japan and a few countries of western Europe.[22] Despite this high level of savings, Canada has had to draw upon additional resources from abroad. Exports of goods and services have been below such imports; net imports of resources have averaged 2 percent of GNP over the postwar period.[23]

A closer analysis of the need for the net import of resources shows that in recent years it averages out at being broadly equivalent to the net outflow of interest, dividends and business services required to service foreign investment in Canada. Thus the emphasis on Canada's international marketing efforts directed at achieving a high positive merchandise trade balance must continue to increase. Figure 5-3 depicts the situation in the postwar period.

Foreign Direct Investment in Canadian and External Trade

A question that continuously arises with foreign direct investment is the "performance" of the foreign subsidiary in Canada. The concern here is to limit the analysis to "performance" in certain salient

---

[20] DBS, "National Accounts," and "Canadian Balance of International Payments," Nos. 13-201 and 67-201 respectively, various issues.

[21] Economic Council of Canada, *Second Annual Review* (Ottawa: Queen's Printer, December 1965) , p. 60.

[22] United Nations, *Yearbook of National Accounts Statistics, 1969,* pp. 187-214.

[23] DBS, "National Accounts," and "Canadian Balance of International Payments," Nos. 13-201 and 67-201 respectively, various issues.

FIGURE 5-3 Balances in Merchandise Trade, Services Trade, and Current Account (Billions of Dollars)

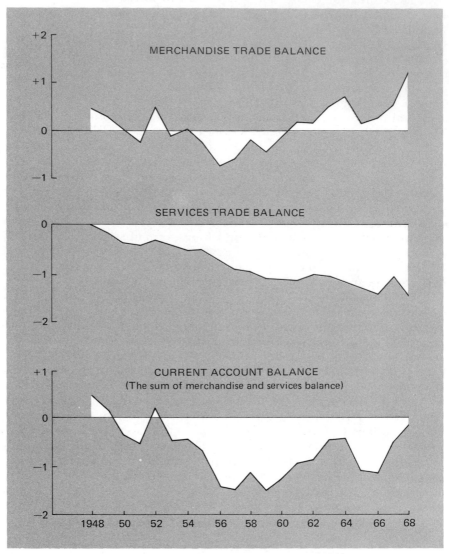

SOURCE: *Economic Council of Canada*, Sixth Annual Review, *p. 80.*

aspects of Canadian external trade and international marketing efforts. The major economic question regarding the external trade of subsidiary companies is whether the fact of foreign ownership inhibits exports and stimulates excessive imports by these companies, particularly of manufactured products.

In this regard the available evidence regarding exports shows that in 1965, American subsidiaries owned 44 percent and controlled 46 percent of Canadian manufacturing industries[24] but exported 48 percent of exports of manufactured goods from Canada. Such exports from subsidiaries amounted to $2,537 million, almost 20 percent of the total sales of such subsidiaries. Furthermore, American-controlled mining subsidiaries in Canada exported $1,005 million in 1965, some 71 percent of their total sales.[25]

On the import side we have the data from a U.S. study concerned only with American subsidiaries. The study showed that in 1969 imports by such subsidiaries in Canada from the U.S. totalled $1,840 million and were concentrated mainly in transportation equipment, machinery and chemicals. Some $1,351 million of this was from parent companies. By type of significant import this $1,351 million breaks down into $628 million for processing and assembly and $659 million for resale without further manufacture.[26]

Furthermore, this same study compared the performance of 160 non–resident-owned firms and 96 resident-owned firms with assets of $1 million or more in industries where both types of firms exist. It was found that the foreign-owned subsidiary was definitely more import-oriented.[27]

Thus, the above evidence tends to show that subsidiaries do not restrict exports, but the import content of the subsidiaries' production is likely to be substantial. Many of these subsidiaries begin and continue their existence as a partial alternative to imports. Moreover, the subsidiary tends to maintain a similar product line to that of the parent. This explains the significant volumes of products brought in for resale. It is interesting to note the external trade of these subsidiaries by industry, shown in Table 5-8.

These absolute figures do not answer directly the question of the effect of foreign ownership on exports and imports. It would seem to be difficult to get a direct answer. Some studies that have been done indicate that there is little significant difference between the export performance of subsidiaries as compared to resident Canadian companies. On the other hand, if the foreign investment had not occurred, economic growth would most probably have been slower and export growth less rapid.

Foreign investment certainly has a marked impact on external

[24] A. E. Safarian, *The Performance of Foreign-Owned Firms in Canada* (Canada: Private Planning Association of Canada, 1969), p. 23.

[25] U.S. Department of Commerce, *Survey of Current Business,* November 1966, various pages.

[26] *Ibid.*

[27] Safarian, *Performance of Foreign-Owned Firms,* pp. 37-38. However, from this it does not follow that foreign subsidiaries favour foreign suppliers to the detriment of the Canadian economy. See some arguments by Rudolph Penner, "On the Behaviour of Foreign Subsidiaries," *The Canadian Banker* 74 (Winter, 1967), p. 86.

TABLE 5-8 Exports and Imports of Larger Foreign Subsidiaries[1], by Industry, 1967
($ Millions)

	Exports[2]	Imports[2]	Balance
Transportation equipment[3]	1,748	1,966	−218
Pulp and paper	803	39	+764
Wholesale trade	548	220	+328
Gas and oil	453	469	− 16
Mining and primary metals	395	94	+301
Machinery and metal fabricating	175	379	−204
Electrical products	161	221	− 60
Food and beverages	111	201	− 90
Chemical products	99	209	−110
Other manufacturing	92	207	−115
Other non-manufacturing	14	58	− 44
Total	4,599	4,063	536

SOURCE: *Department of Trade and Commerce,* Foreign-Owned Subsidiaries in Canada, 1964-67 *(Ottawa: Queen's Printer, 1970), pp. 26-28.*

[1] Foreign subsidiaries are defined as more than 50 percent owned by one foreign parent. Larger is defined as foreign subsidiaries with assets over $5 million each. The data are from 326 such corporations.

[2] Exports represent in most cases sales to foreign buyers while imports cover only purchases made directly from foreign suppliers; i.e., they do not include goods of foreign origin purchased from a Canadian supplier. Also, imports include imports of capital equipment.

[3] The transportation equipment industry reflects the influence of the auto pact — see pp. 120-22. Exports of this industry in 1964 were $375 million and imports $715 million.

trade. The study done by the Federal Department of Trade and Commerce on 326 foreign-owned corporations in Canada shows that these companies alone accounted for more than one-third of all Canadian exports and about one-third of all imports. Table 5-9 illustrates the parental-link geography of such trade. This table shows that foreign subsidiaries sent 67 percent of their total exports to their parents and affiliates abroad, and obtained some 70 percent of their imports from such related companies. Thus intracompany trade done by multinational companies has become a major element of Canadian external trade.

Intracompany trade also has become a major force in world trade in the post–World War II period. This movement continues unabated. For instance, growth of U.S. direct investments abroad has maintained a consistent 10 percent per annum rate from the late 1950's.[28] From a modest level of direct investment of $20 billion in 1955, most of it in Canada, U.S. direct investment abroad increased to $65.7 billion by 1968 with Europe the main recipient.[29] Another viewpoint is given

[28] David S. R. Leighton, "The Internationalization of American Business — The Third Industrial Revolution," *Journal of Marketing* 34 (July 1970), p. 3.

[29] N. William Hazen, "Overseas High States of Multinational Firms," in Bernard A. Morni, ed., *Marketing in a Changing World* (Chicago: Illinois: American Marketing Association, June 1969), pp. 47-52.

TABLE 5-9 Destination of Exports and Sources of Imports of Larger Foreign Subsidiaries, 1967 ($ Millions)

	With U.S.	With Other Countries	Total
Total trade of these subsidiaries			
Exports	3,509	1,090	4,599
Imports	3,302	761	4,063
Balance	+207	+329	+536
Trade with parent and affiliate abroad			
Exports	2,775	299	3,074
Imports	2,294	560	2,854
Balance	+481	−261	+220
Percent of total trade with parents and affiliates abroad			
Exports	79%	28%	67%
Imports	69%	74%	70%

SOURCE: *Department of Trade and Commerce,* Foreign-Owned Subsidiaries in Canada, 1964-67, pp. 23-25.

by noting that world output from foreign-owned subsidiaries of international corporations was about $240 billion in 1967 while exports from major nations in that year totalled $130 billion.[30] Thus, for the whole developed world, international investment has emerged as the major channel of international economic relations. External trade is being led by foreign investment. International trade theory with its dependence on the theory of comparative advantage seems inadequate for the 1970's.

In looking at trade from a country's point of view one tends to lose sight of the fact that increasingly, countries do not trade with each other; companies do. Furthermore, a significant portion of trade is intracompany within the global sphere of multinational companies.

The above has important implications for Canada's international marketing efforts. External trade is linked increasingly to direct investment. U.S. direct investment is now no longer concentrating on Canada.[31] Moreover, in the latter half of the 1960's the flow of U.S. investment abroad has been attracted to lower wage free-world nations which are politically stable — for example, western Europe and certain nations of the Far East.[32] Thus the sectors of world trade which are outside the intracompany network of the multinational company are

[30] Dr. Sidney Rolfe is so quoted in the Toronto *Globe and Mail* "Report on Business," 2 May 1969, in a report on an international conference on trade held in Washington, D.C.
[31] Leighton, "The Internationalization of American Business," p. 3.
[32] "The Global Scramble for Cheap Labour," *Time,* 21 September 1970, pp. 67-68.

being confined. Moreover, these confined sectors are necessarily more competitive. Therefore, the task of obtaining a significant share of these sectors requires a high degree of efficiency on the part of Canadian international marketers.

Foreign Investment and Good Canadian Citizenship

In the wake of foreign investment, from time to time, problems are raised by the attempt of a foreign investor's country to obtain extraterritorial extension of its law and policy through the medium of the industry's subsidiaries abroad. Two recent and important examples concerning the U.S. and Canada are the U.S. restriction on exports by U.S.-controlled foreign affiliates to certain Communist countries, and capital restraint programmes to moderate private capital transactions in the U.S. balance of payments.

The United States Treasury's Foreign Assets Control regulations prohibit trade with Mainland China, North Korea, North Vietnam and (with some qualifications) Cuba. Canadian policy, by contrast, generally permits trade with these countries except for strategic goods. This difference in policy has led to serious conflicts of interest for some U.S. subsidiaries. Moreover, alleged cases of refusal to export which have come to public notice have aroused generally critical comments in Canada.[33] Fortunately, there have been relatively few cases, since the Communist countries concerned have not had the financial wherewithal to purchase the kinds of products U.S. subsidiaries have been manufacturing in Canada. Canada has now recognized mainland China[34], however, and the U.S. will probably follow suit.

In regard to capital restraint programmes, a number of measures have come into being in the 1960's in order to cope with the sizable and continuous U.S. balance of payments deficits that have arisen during this period.

In 1963 the U.S. Interest Equalization Tax was passed to moderate the outflow of U.S. dollar funds. Canada obtained an exemption in return for establishing as a ceiling its then existing level of foreign exchange reserves. In March 1965, U.S. companies were asked to comply with a voluntary restraint programme. Canada was exempted from restraints on U.S. direct investment but was included for purposes of the goal of repatriating short-term funds from abroad where possible. However, a few months later, Canada was included in the global arithmetic of the direct investment guidelines. Each U.S. parent company was permitted a specified annual increase in its world level of direct investment — this being defined as new outflows plus retained subsidiary earnings destined for reinvestment. The inclusion of Canada was justi-

---

[33] Walter Stewart, *Star Weekly*, 5 February 1966, pp. 2-4.
[34] *Time*, 23 October 1970, p. 14.

fied by the U.S. authorities mainly on the view that much of the increase in direct investment to Canada under the previous exemption represented funds flowing through to other countries.

The official Canadian response was multipronged. Steps were taken by the Bank of Canada and the Department of Finance to discourage new borrowing in Canada which was prompted by the guidelines encouraging U.S. firms and their subsidiaries to look outside the U.S. for funds. In March 1966, Canada issued its own guidelines to foreign subsidiaries in Canada indicating what was expected of them in terms of good corporate practice. Furthermore, information was asked from such subsidiaries on their exports, imports and selected quarterly capital transactions.[35] The long-term purpose of the Canadian guidelines was to make the subsidiaries aware of desirable patterns of performance from the Canadian good corporate citizen viewpoint.

In January 1968, the U.S. introduced a mandatory regulation on direct investment flows, including those to Canada. The timing was bad for Canada because of the domestic economic situation: there was strong pressure on the Canadian dollar. In March 1968, a Canadian-U.S. agreement was reached to exempt Canada.[36] In return Canada agreed to institute a reporting system so that no company could use Canada as a flow channel for funds destined to other countries. In effect, the cost of exemption was surveillance of capital exports from Canada to third countries.

The above history is a reflection of the interdependence of the Canadian and U.S. economies, with Canada being more dependant on the U.S. than vice versa.

Tariffs and the Kennedy Round

Forty-seven countries, including the six EEC countries bargaining as one unit, all the major trading nations and some thirty Less Developed Countries, participated in the Kennedy Round negotiations which ran from May 1964 to June 30, 1967. These countries account for around 80 percent of world trade.

The Kennedy Round was the sixth round of multilateral trade negotiations thus far held under the General Agreement on Tariffs and Trade (GATT) which was negotiated in 1967 to liberalize international trade through reduction of tariff and non-tariff barriers to the expansion of trade. The working hypothesis of the Kennedy Round was that a linear cut of 50 percent in tariffs should be made by every country. It was recognized from the start that equivalent percentage reductions in tariffs would give a greater advantage to countries with a wider spread of, and higher, tariff rates, and that 50 percent linear cuts would not be

[35] Safarian, *Performance of Foreign-owned Firms,* pp. 96-99.
[36] Sharp-Fowler letters, *Hansard* 7 (7 March 1968) , pp. 7379-80.

appropriate in all cases on account of the special features of the economies of the countries concerned. This was true of Canada, a large proportion of whose exports consist of foodstuffs and primary products with already low tariffs. It was agreed, therefore, that Canada fall in the second category of countries which should offer tariff concessions equivalent, in effect on trade, to the benefits received.

The Kennedy Round agreement included tariff concessions covering almost $40 billion or 20 percent of world trade in 1966. The agreement had four basic elements. First, it was the most far reaching tariff cut in the history of GATT. After full implementation on January 1, 1971, the average level of duties in the major western industrialized countries was expected to be in the range of $6\frac{1}{2}$ to $8\frac{1}{2}$ percent compared with the 12 to 18 percent prior to the agreement, as shown in Figure 5-3.

FIGURE 5-4 Average Tariff Levels Prior to the Kennedy Round

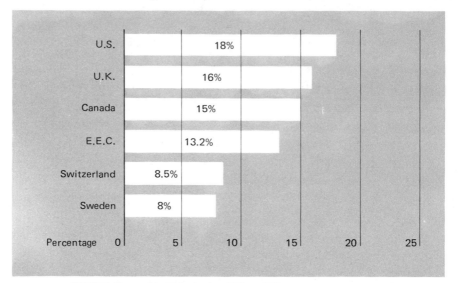

SOURCE: Economist, *10 September 1966, p. 1033.*

The tariffs shown in Figure 5-4 are nominal tariff rates not "effective" rates. An "effective" tariff is the level of protection on the value-added component. It can be markedly different from the nominal tariff rate.[37] Moreover, these arithmetic unweighted averages are misleading: they are compiled by counting every category of import as one whether it be matchboxes or automobiles. This hardly gives a true pic-

[37] D. J. Daly, B. A. Keys, and E. J. Spence, *Scale and Specialization in Canadian Manufacturing,* Staff Study No. 21, prepared for the Economic Council of Canada (Ottawa: Queen's Printer, 1969), pp. 53-59.

ture of the restrictiveness of tariffs. To correct for this, the duty on each category would have to be weighted by the goods it keeps out. But this is not possible, since the appropriate figures are just not available. Nevertheless it serves to show that the resulting tariff levels on most manufactured goods in the major western industrialized countries will probably cease to constitute any significant barrier to trade.

The second element of the agreement was negotiated higher minimum and maximum prices for wheat under the international wheat agreement. This was a concession to wheat exporters like Canada and Australia. Also a food aid programme was agreed upon whereby all developed countries, whether exporters or importers of wheat, would contribute to a pool of 4,500,000 metric tons annual aid.[38]

The third element was a new anti-dumping code to go into operation on July 1, 1968. This directly affects Canada. Previously, the only proof needed for the penalties to be applied under the Canadian dumping code was that the product was imported at a price below its fair market value, and that the product was of a class or kind made in Canada. Under the new dumping code, in addition to the above, injury to domestic industry has to be proven by the complainant. What constitutes injury is left indeterminate.[39]

The fourth element was the inclusion, for the first time, of negotiations on non-tariff barriers to trade. Discussion centred on the removal of the American Selling Price system on benzeroid chemicals.[40]

There remains a whole set of non-tariff barriers to trade such as quota requirements and special import controls which often constitute no less an obstacle to trade than the tariff structure.

It is only possible to assess the effects of the Kennedy Round for Canada in very general terms. Precise assessment by industry and commodity is difficult because the concessions that Canada received are also available to third countries under the most-favoured-nation clause of GATT. The effects of these cuts on trade would vary for different countries because of the level of the original tariff, the demand and supply elasticities, the elasticity of substitution between domestic and foreign goods, the scale of operations, technological changes, the market structure, and the changes in tastes and preferences of consumers. Thus the whole problem can better be viewed in the context of both the opportunity and the challenge to the Canadian economy and its export industries in particular.

Of the $3 billion or almost one-third of Canada's total export trade to benefit from the Kennedy Round tariff reductions, almost $2

[38] Bank of Montreal, *Business Review*, 31 July 1967, p. 4.
[39] *Ibid.*
[40] The ASP is a system under which duty is calculated on the wholesale price of the domestic product rather than on the landed cost of the imported product, resulting in considerably higher duty. The EEC took special objection to this system.

billion is with the U.S. Table 5-10 illustrates the gain. Substantial opportunities have arisen obviously in the section pertaining to the $1,358 million of exports shown in this table.

TABLE 5-10 Dollar Volume of Canadian Exports to the U.S. in 1966 Affected by the Kennedy Round ($ Millions)

	Previously Free and Now Free	Previously Duties 5% or Less, Now Free	Duties Substantially Reduced, i.e., by 50% or less
Agriculture	—	$29	65
Fisheries products group	—	92	1
Lumber and paper	—	387	72
Chemicals	—	10	85
Minerals:			
Nickel	176		
Others bound free[1]	46		
Copper and products	—		
Molybdenum, magnesium	—		
Indium	—		122
Aluminium ingot	—		174
Non-metalic minerals	—	9	11
Pig iron and sponge iron	—	22	—
Iron and steel group	—	—	95
Manufactures			700
Others		7	33
	$222	$558	$1,358

SOURCE: Canada Year Book, 1968, pp. 949-950.

NOTE: Columns may not add to totals because of rounding.

[1] A bound rate of duty is a rate the country concerned undertakes not to increase.

About 95 percent of Canada's exports to the U.K. were already duty-free. The U.K. made an average reduction of 38 percent in its most-favoured-nation rates of duty. Thus the margin of preference enjoyed by Canada and other Commonwealth country exporters to the U.K. will be reduced. In regard to the remaining 5 percent of Canadian exports, the U.K. has agreed to adjust preferential rates of duty so as to maintain the existing ratios of preference enjoyed by Commonwealth countries.

Canadian exports to the EEC in 1966 were $160 million plus $144 million of wheat exports which are covered by the new agreement on cereals. Of the non-wheat exports, 50 percent reductions will apply to $37 million and smaller reductions to the remaining $123 million. Canadian exports of manufactures to the EEC, about $54 million in 1966, are small but growing. Tariffs in this sector will be reduced in general by 50 percent to a range of 5 to 8 percent, thus providing improved opportunities for Canadian exports.

Japanese tariffs have been reduced significantly on a variety of fully manufactured goods, but they are still at a high protective level.[41] Canadian exports to Japan amounted to $177 million in 1966 of which $90 million was wheat. Japan is a party to the memorandum of agreement on cereals and will reduce duties up to varying rates on Canadian exports amounting to $35 million.[42]

Scandinavia and Switzerland are low tariff countries.[43] However, they also reduced tariffs affecting some $30 million of Canadian exports. In some cases — for example, wood pulp – Canadian producers will now be able to compete more effectively with the EFTA countries.[44]

As mentioned earlier, the tariff reduction that Canada received will also apply to all most-favoured-nations. It follows that international competition in world markets will become more keen. As for the future direction of Canadian exports, since $1,358 million of Canadian exports to the U.S. will benefit from significant tariff cuts,[45] and Canada will have reduced margins of preference in the U.K. market, it is possible that Canadian exporters will tend to try to increase their sales to the U.S. In addition, Canada will receive an increased opportunity to penetrate the western European markets.

As also noted earlier, Canada did not adopt the linear reduction approach but offered concessions to cover some $2.5 billion of imports in 1966. Rates on final manufactures will now generally be in the range of $17\frac{1}{2}$ to 20 percent. On intermediate products the rates will be 15 percent or less, while some basic materials will be free or almost free.[46] Machines and control equipment have been consolidated into one tariff item. Full remission of duty should occur for machines not produced indigenously. The overall effect will be an average rate on machines of 9 percent or less.

Thus Canada has reduced the level of protection but in addition, the cuts tend to make imported components available at cheaper costs. To the extent this lower cost is passed along, reduced prices will benefit the consumer. Moreover, the government has implemented an Adjustment Assistance Program to help industry offset short-run difficulties.[47] In the long run, intensified foreign competition should lead to progressive revisions in Canadian industry towards greater specialization, longer production runs and other economies of scale made possible by an expanding world market. This should aid improvements in productivity and Canadian economic growth.

---

[41] Duties generally range up to 40 percent. However, most raw materials are duty-free or at moderate rates. In addition, commodity taxes ranging from 5 to 40 percent are applied on many consumer and luxury type goods sold in the Japanese market. See U.S. Department of Commerce, *International Commerce* 74 (14 October 1968), p. 11.

[42] Bank of Montreal, *Business Review*, 31 July 1967.

[43] See Figure 5-4.

[44] *Canada Year Book, 1968,* pp. 951, 968.

[45] See Table 5-10.

[46] Bank of Montreal, *Business Review*, 31 July 1967, p. 3.

[47] Government of Canada, Department of Industry, *Annual Report,* 1 April 1968 — 31 March 1969, pp. 2-4.

The Auto Pact

The Automotive Trade Agreement with the U.S. has been the largest single influence on the level and balance of Canada's external trade from 1965. In 1964, exports of automotive equipment were $187 million, imports $838 million, and therefore the trade deficit on such products was $651 million. By 1968 such exports had climbed to $2,638 million, some 20 percent of total exports, while similar imports were $3,056 million, roughly 25 percent of total imports, yielding a trade deficit of $418 on automotive account.[48] By 1968 automotive trade had become the most important component of trade in highly manufactured products, constituting 60 percent of exports and 40 percent of imports of such goods. The impetus of this agreement now seems to be coming to an end. Auto and auto part exports in 1970 were only 6 percent greater than in 1969. Barring any special arrangements, such exports may henceforth be expected to expand only in line with the growth of the North American market.

The main economic criteria by which the agreement should be judged, however, are its effects on productivity and on relative prices and costs of products.

The auto pact provided for free trade between Canada and the U.S. in automobiles and parts, with two classes of exception. First, several automotive products such as replacement parts and tires were excluded from duty-free treatment.[49] Second, on the Canadian side only, manufacturers of motor vehicles who complied with the following conditions could avail themselves of the duty-free privilege.

1. To maintain the ratio of the net value of their production in Canada to the net value of their sales in Canada at not less than the ratio in the model year 1964. Thus, as their sales in Canada grow, there had to be at least proportionate growth in their production of finished vehicles.

2. To maintain, in the production of vehicles in Canada, a level of Canadian value-added in absolute dollar terms that is at least as great as that achieved in model year 1964. As Canadian production of vehicles expands the relative importance of this requirement declines.

3.(a) To increase the total Canadian value-added in vehicles and in original equipment parts by an amount equal to 60 percent of the growth in the value of their automobile sales in Canada (and by 50 percent of their commercial vehicle sales).

3.(b) To increase Canadian value-added in vehicles and original parts by a total amount of $260 million over and above that achieved in model year 1964 and that required to fulfill condition 3 (a). This increase was to be accomplished by the 1968 model year. The larger commitments included in the $260 million are: General Motors, $121 million;

---

[48] *Ibid.*
[49] However, tires when mounted on new automobiles could pass duty-free.

Ford, $74.2 million; Chrysler, $33 million; and American Motors, $11.2 million. Conditions 3 (a) and 3 (b) cover Canadian value-added in Canadian-built cars and also Canadian content in exported original equipment parts.

Conditions 1 and 2 are in the treaty, while conditions 3 (a) and 3 (b) are side commitments by the automobile companies.[50]

The agreement places a floor on assembly (condition 1) with no similar floor on parts production. Hence the pact seems to encourage assembly, since firms simultaneously satisfy two restrictions: the ones on assembly and value-added.

For Canada, the results show that the merchandise trade deficit is less than would have occurred under previous protection. Here one assumes that under previous protection the growth in North American auto markets and production would have been reflected in a roughly proportional growth in the Canadian auto deficit with the U.S. The gain to the U.S. is in the elimination of the possibility of Canada's implementation of a high tariff policy to reduce automobile imports, which would thereby greatly reduce the U.S. trade surplus.[51]

Canada also gained the full benefits of large scale production, and fair participation in the North American vehicle market. In the 1968 calendar year Canadian production of passenger vehicles was 161 percent higher, and of commercial vehicles 250 percent higher, than that of 1964. Average levels of employment in the Canadian automotive industries rose to a monthly average of 84,500 in 1968 compared to 69,000 in 1964. Moreover, during the period 1964 to 1968, average annual investment was approximately $160 million, which was five times higher than during the years 1960 to 1963.[52] It may be noted that despite this, and the rationalization of production that continues to take place, total capital per worker is still below the comparative figure in the U.S. automotive industry. Thus, although the most modern Canadian plants are achieving productivity levels and efficiencies equal to the best in the U.S., for the Canadian industry average to match that of the U.S., continuing major new investments will be needed, to take advantage of the new opportunities to produce for the much larger market.

The price index for automobiles has declined since the initiation of the auto pact. In 1964 the new car component of the consumer price index was 99.0; by 1968 it had declined to 98.6. In comparison, the consumer price index had risen from 104.8 to 120.1 in those four years.

[50] Government of Canada, Department of Industry, *News Release*, 15 January 1965, contains the text of the agreement. Letters of undertaking embodying conditions 3 (a) and 3 (b) were sent by the four major Canadian auto manufacturers to the Canadian government. These letters were published in the *News Release*, 26 April 1965.

[51] For further detailed comments see Paul Wonnacott and R. J. Wonnacott, "The Automotive Agreement of 1965," *Canadian Journal of Economics and Political Science* 33 (May 1967) , pp. 269-82.

[52] Department of Industry, *Annual Report*, p. 16-22.

Furthermore, Canadian factory wholesale prices were 8 to 10 percent above those in the U.S. for similar vehicles in the years immediately prior to the pact. By the end of 1968, this price differential had been reduced to 4 to 5 percent. However, the fact is that new car prices for Canadian consumers remain substantially above those in the U.S. This is a critical issue which has become a matter of public controversy. The argument has arisen that initially the auto companies benefited by the revision tariffs at the expense of the Canadian consumer as long as consumer prices remain unchanged. The auto companies say this gain is being passed on from the 1966 model year in the form of a reduced price in Canada relative to the U.S. The Canadian consumer, therefore, may be about as well off as without the agreement.[53] However the auto companies have since benefited by the cost reductions that are made possible through increased scale of production. This is a windfall gain going to the auto companies exclusively. If such gains do not go to the consumer in the form of a price reduction to U.S. levels, but remain as company profits, then the unions may partially expropriate them by getting wage parity with the U.S. The crux of the matter is that if price parity is achieved first, the Canadian industry should be in a position to compete effectively under unrestrained free trade, and the unions could bargain for near wage parity later. However if wage parity comes first then this may slow down industry growth. As it is, some inputs to the auto industry come from other protected Canadian industries. Such inputs are by definition at high cost. Thus, a move to further increase Canadian costs by wage parity prior to full rationalization may jeopardize the future possibility of an internationally competitive industry capable of operation under unrestricted free trade. This in turn would mean that the Canadian government would find it difficult to eliminate the tariff and the Canadian consumer would always pay higher prices.

Canadian Aid to the Less Developed Countries

Canada's aid to the Less Developed Countries (LDCs) helps Canadian international marketing efforts both directly and indirectly. The direct effect is through tied aid or other aid which leads to the purchase of Canadian goods and services by the LDCs. The indirect effect is more difficult to quantify but its qualitative effects can be considered a pool of goodwill. In turn this pool becomes utilizable over time for the furtherance of Canada's international marketing efforts.

The 1960's have been named the "Development Decade" to highlight the United Nations objective of transferring one percent of the Gross National Product of advanced countries to the LDCs, and achieving a 5 percent annual rate of growth of total output in the latter group. The

---

[53] Wonnacott and Wonnacott, "The Automotive Agreement of 1965." The authors say this took the form more of a U.S. price increase than a Canadian price decrease.

growth and aid targets are being carried forward into the 1970's, as a second development decade.

The flow of aid (official and private) from the OECD industrial countries to the developing countries in 1967 amounted to about three-quarters of one percent of their combined GNP. Since these funds were made available, the imports of the LDCs have increased, but much of the trade thus created is tied to particular donor countries as suppliers.[54]

Canadian aid disbursements have been of the order of less than one-half of one percent of GNP but are growing in line with Canadian government policy of striving to meet the U.N. aid target. In 1967 such aid amounted to $275 million, in 1968 it was $317 million[55] — approximately six-tenths of one percent of GNP — and in 1969 it rose to $338 million. It is expected to increase to $500 million by 1975.[56]

It must be realized that the single statistic "one percent of GNP" is somewhat misleading. It is heavily biased in favour of "ex-colonial" powers because they can and do include all sorts of vestigial colonial activities whether of an investment or an educational and administrative type. Moreover the current private investment abroad of a normally capital-exporting country is often, perhaps usually, included. Thus in 1965, the only countries to exceed the one percent target in order of extent of increase were the Netherlands, the U.K. and Portugal.[57]

Aid consists of three basic types. First, there are grants, which are the best form of aid as they have no financial strings. Second, there are loans made on more or less commercial terms and with the primary objective of aiding the donor country's exporters. Third, there is the "soft loan," on the terms used by the International Development Association (50 years, no interest, $3/4$ percent service charge, repayment to begin after 10 years). Canada has eliminated the service charge and also has introduced a semi-soft loan (30 years, 3 percent interest, repayment to start after 7 years).

Aid is basically given as "tied" — bilateral aid under which the recipient country has to purchase Canadian goods and services — and "untied" — multilateral aid given largely by way of Canadian contributions to support the programmes of the World Bank, the development agencies of the United Nations and regional lending institutions such as the Asian Development Bank. In 1964 about 15 percent of Canadian aid was multilateral.[58] In general it is politically easier to justify tied aid to

[54] Economic Council of Canada, *Sixth Annual Review*, p. 79.
[55] Maurice F. Strong, "Overseas Opportunities through the Canadian International Development Agency," *The Commerce Man* 24 (Kingston, Ontario: Queen's University Business Student Publication), p. 47.
[56] *Globe & Mail*, 13 January 1970, p. 29.
[57] A. F. W. Plumptre, "Perspective on Our Aid to Others," *International Journal, 1966-67*, vol. 22, p. 442.
[58] Strong, "Overseas Opportunities through the Canadian I.D.A.," p. 49.

donor's taxpayers. On the other hand, over the years, expenditures by international aid agencies in Canada have probably been broadly equal to Canadian contributions to the same international agencies.[59] This would remain true for the future only if a wide range of Canadian goods and services remained fairly competitive, when judged by world standards.

In addition to aid, in 1969 the Canadian Exports Credit Insurance Corporation extended long-term financing at low interest rates to foreign buyers to the tune of $64 million.[60]

Aid loans and export credits have brought in their wake some complex problems. For many developing countries the external indebtedness issue is very serious. Their debt-service ratios (ratio of service payments to foreign exchange earnings on current account) have risen sharply. For example, in many countries of Latin America the debt-service ratio moved from below 10 percent in the mid-fifties to over 20 percent by the 1960's.[61] Moreover, export credits superimpose two problems on the debt-service ratio, namely, that export credits are relatively costly, and that they have maturities which are often inappropriate to the nature of the project and the economic and financial conditions of the developing country concerned.[62] Export credits are by no means insignificant in quantity. By 1964, net government guaranteed medium and long-term export credits granted to developing countries by the DAC members amounted to $744 million, representing almost 25 percent of the aggregate net flow of private capital to those countries and over 8 percent of the total net flow of financial resources from DAC members to those countries.[63] In comparison, total imports by developing countries amounted to $21 billion in that year.[64]

Export credits have also brought a series of problems to the developed countries. There is a widespread concern regarding "unfair competition" in the provision of such credits and its degeneration into a disruptive race. It is generally felt that although no exporting country can now compete successfully in the world market for capital goods without being able to offer long deferred-payment terms, excessive credit competition should be avoided.

Obviously the search for an international solution to export credit competition must be undertaken within the context of the accepted need for a sustained and indeed increasing net flow of financial resources into developing countries. Thus, the aid and export credit issues are interlinked, and the trend might well accentuate towards greater multilateral efforts. The task of Canadian international marketers will be

[59] Plumptre, "Perspective on our Aid to Others," p. 496.

[60] *Ibid.*

[61] U.N., *Export Credits and Development Financing* (New York: 1967), p. 4.

[62] *Ibid.*

[63] OECD, *Development Assistance Efforts and Policies,* 1965 Review (Paris, 1965), p. 42.

[64] United Nations, *Yearbook of International Trade Statistics, 1968,* (New York: United Nations, 1970), p. 12.

increasingly to remain competitive and to stay knowledgeable as to the form of assistance and aid being given under the growing Canadian aid programme.[65]

CONCLUSION

Canada, like many other industrial countries, has come to rely more and more on external trade to sustain and improve its economic performance. Exports now equal about half the output of Canada's goods-producing industries, and nearly half the goods supplied to Canadians are imported.[66]

In the past, Canadian commercial policy focused strongly on two themes: first, the negotiation of reduced tariff and other barriers in foreign countries, particularly for resource-based products in which Canada had a natural advantage, and second, the maintenance of Canadian protection for a considerable range of manufactured products. The result of the second theme is that Canadian manufacturing industries are often characterized by small scale, rather unspecialized production, and by high unit costs.[67]

Today one of the principal features of the trading world is that most industrial nations, singly or in groups, now comprise tariff-free markets of at least 100 million consumers each. Furthermore, the U.K. and other western European countries will join the EEC in the early 1970's, forming an enlarged industrial free trade unit with common tariffs against nonmembers. This enlarged unit would account for about 50 percent of Canadian exports outside North America.

In the 1970's, advancing technology will mean that large markets will become more important than ever for productive and competitive performance of manufacturing industries. Also, large multinational firms are playing a rising role in organizing world production and trade and the number of such firms indigenous to Canada is small.

The fundamental issue is how Canada will respond to the pattern of big industrial markets, accelerated technological change and big multinational firms.

Many Canadians believe that Canada and the U.S. are heavily interdependent even now. Thus, Canadian free trade with the U.S. is one

---

[65] An interesting recent development is the move to form a Canadian International Research Centre for $30 million with an annual budget of 5 percent of the total effort. It will be the largest such centre in the world. See *Globe and Mail*, 13 January 1970, p. 29.

[66] Economic Council of Canada, *Seventh Annual Review* (Ottawa: Queen's Printer, 1970), p. 75.

[67] A detailed analysis of why this occurs is given by H. Edward English, *Industrial Structure in Canada's International Competitive Position* (Canadian Trade Committee, 1964), p. 36.

answer. Free trade, Canada-U.S., would raise Canadian productivity and average real living standards substantially. The cost of North American tariffs to Canada prior to the Kennedy Round was estimated at 10.5 percent of Canadian GNP.[68] On the other hand, many more Canadians fear the far-reaching economic, political and national consequences of such a move. A limited answer is for more special trade arrangements on the lines of the auto pact and the defense production-sharing arrangement which aims at improving productivity and minimizing trade deficits in defence-related goods. These agreements have built-in production safeguards. Other practical possibilities are a long-term overall agreement for increased Canadian oil and natural gas flows to the U.S. mid-west and western regions. The possibility of bilateral arrangements for energy could be explored in depth.

However, in the near future, Canada's posture has to be competitive and flexible. World currencies are in a state of flux as the U.S. attempts to reduce its huge balance of payments deficit by increasing its exports and reducing its imports. In August 1971, President Nixon imposed a 10 percent surcharge on a large group of U.S. imports. No exemption was given to Canada although we had unpegged our dollar in June 1970, and our export prices had already effectively risen by over 4 percent.[69] In exchange for a realignment of world currencies plus some outright trade concessions, the U.S. dropped the surcharge in December 1971, although the U.S. attitude seems to remain protectionist. A new DISC (Domestic International Sales Corporation) programme is now in operation, which gives tax advantages to U.S. corporations to encourage export from the U.S. Moreover the U.S. wants Canada to cut its trade surplus with the U.S.; however Canada needs this surplus to pay its interest and dividends on U.S. capital invested in Canada. Therefore we are also unwilling to peg our dollar well above the U.S. dollar. Trade negotiations are continuing.

Furthermore, research is needed in the development of efficient exports, efficient import substitution and their relationship to development.[70] It must be remembered that foreign subsidiaries in Canada are today part of growing multinational parents whose investment patterns are trending away from Canada.[71]

In any event, the efforts of Canadian international marketers will have to be ever more efficient in a low tariff and more competitive

[68] J. H. Dales, *The Protective Tariff in Canada's Development* (Toronto: University of Toronto Press, 1966), pp. 110-25, and Wonnacott and Wonnacott, *Free Trade Between the United States and Canada: The Potential Economic Effects* (Cambridge, Mass.: Harvard University Press, 1967), pp. 290-99.

[69] DBS, *Quarterly Estimates of the Canadian Balance of International Payments*, No. 67-001 (Ottawa: Queen's Printer, Fourth Quarter 1971), p. 7.

[70] For these relationships, see William Gruber et al., "The R & D factor in International Trade and International Investment of U.S. Industries," *Journal of Political Economy*, February 1967, pp. 20-38.

[71] See page 112.

world market, since the country's economy is so dependant on exports. Moreover, the Canadian export product line is trending towards increasing diversification. The widening of the product line makes possible steadier export growth as Canada is no longer so dependant on primary exports,[72] which are vulnerable to relatively large fluctuations in world demand and supply conditions. On the other hand, increased competition is precisely the challenge inherent in export diversification, because world-wide competition in manufactured goods is more intense than in primary products. Thus far, Canadian international marketers are reacting favourably to this challenge. World exports of manufactured goods other than automobiles grew by 112 percent from 1960 to 1968 whereas corresponding Canadian exports grew by 107 percent.[73] Furthermore, attempts are being made to expand Canadian trade in new areas. For instance, there has been a marked recent rise in Canada's trade with California and the more important countries bordering the Pacific. These countries absorbed some $2 billion worth of Canadian exports in 1970 or 12 percent of Canadian total exports. Sales to Japan have trebled between 1960 and 1971.

Since World War II international marketing has progressed from the pure export decade — the era of the straight bilateral transaction, which ended in the mid-1950's. The export sales manager did not have to travel; customers came to him. Then with the industrial recovery of Europe and Japan, competition in the world market really commenced. The large flow of foreign investment into Europe and the growth of multinational marketing with world-wide sources of products has dominated international trade in the 1960's. Competition is likely to become even keener in the 1970's and it is up to Canadian international marketers to meet this challenge with competitiveness and greater marketing skills.

[72] See Figure 5-1 on p. 99.
[73] Bank of Montreal, *Business Review*, 21 December 1970.

6

The Governmental and Legal Dimension of Marketing in Canada

This chapter covers another part of the external environment as outlined in the preface — the political-legal-governmental environment.

The government affects marketing as a buyer and seller of goods and services, as a collector and dispenser of information, and as a regulator. The Canadian federal government and the two major parties, Liberals and Progressive Conservatives, are, next to the United States government, probably the strongest proponents of the private enterprise system and market economy. However, as in the United States, there are regulations which affect all aspects of marketing and of which marketing men must be aware.

Government regulations and statutes which apply to one or more areas of the marketing activity are numerous. A complete discussion of these areas would be beyond the scope of this book. For example, both federal and provincial governments regulate many of the products that may be sold. Thus, Canada and her provinces have special laws, acts and regulations which affect foodstuffs, drugs, poisons, explosives, firearms, feeding stuffs, fertilizers, precious metals, fish products, farm machinery, bedding, and a host of other products. These governments, including municipalities, have regulations which influence the method of sale and advertising of goods and services. Thus, there are laws pertaining to lottery sales, trading stamps, packaging, door-to-door selling, special promotional sales, etc. Other areas of marketing in Canada which are affected by government regulations include trademarks, designs, copyrights, commodity taxes (excise and sales tax), transportation laws, and tariff and import regulations.

There are laws which must be considered by the advertiser who would, for example, imitate a well-known voice over a broadcast medium, broadcast interviews with the man-in-the-street, make use of a common first and family name in an advertisement, mention competitors' names for purposes of comparison with his own product, and use a medium which cannot be avoided by the listeners — e.g., mobile loudspeakers parading through the street. There are also laws which affect sales promotion methods, such as coupon premiums, the sending-in of a label or wrapper, contests and prizes.

This chapter will be limited to a description of the more general and significant regulations and laws which affect marketing. The first section will deal with several activities administered through the Department of Consumer and Corporate Affairs: consumer protection, patents, trademarks, industrial design law, copyright and standards. One important activity of this department will be described and discussed in a section of its own; this second section will describe and analyse the single most important Canadian statute which affects marketing, and in particular, competition and pricing — the Combines Investigation Act. This is an all important framework within which pricing strategy must operate. The Act deals with restraint of trade, combines, mergers, monopolies, discriminatory discounts, resale price maintenance, illegal allowances, misleading advertising and price misrepresentation. The third section will provide an overview of selected federal legislation and programmes administered by several departments and government agencies with the exception of activities carried on by the Department of Consumer and Corporate Affairs. The final section will deal with the law of sale and agent-principal law.

THE DEPARTMENT OF CONSUMER AND CORPORATE AFFAIRS

Consumerism

The issue of consumer rights has been prevalent in recent years. Though the issues that come under the encompassing title "consumerism" — e.g., misleading advertising, high prices, confusing packages, labels and weights — have been discussed and argued over for many years by such groups as the Consumers Association of Canada and the Better Business Bureau, it is only in recent years that large segments of the general public have become quite vocal and active in the "fight" for consumers' rights. This great interest on the part of the public has, in part, led to important federal and provincial government legislation, culminating in the establishment of the Department of Consumer and Corporate Affairs and parallel government organizations at the provincial level.

In theory, a market economy operates in such a manner that consumers have tremendous power in deciding which products and companies will thrive and survive, and which products and companies will wither and leave the marketplace. The assumption here, of course, is that consumers are in a position to make rational decisions, and after considering all factors will buy the products that give better value; therefore the producers of these selected products will fare far better than those who are not so patronized. Only the most radical consumerists will deny that this system is, at least in theory, far superior to a controlled economy, such as one finds in a socialist state. Indeed, the fundamental objective of the consumer movement is that of allowing the consumer to be able to make the rational decisions so necessary for a free market economy to operate properly. The consumerists would argue that, though business-men may say that consumers will naturally select the best products under a free market system, in practice it does not work that way because con-sumers do not have the necessary knowledge and expertise to make such decisions in the very complicated present-day world of services and products. Though consumerists will admit that perhaps the consumer was in a position to make rational decisions in a simpler past era, the compli-cations of modern-day production and consumption make him a "babe-in-the-woods." The basic argument continues that because of the in-creased complexity of products and services there should be a shift in responsibility from the consumer to the producer, i.e., from "let the buyer beware" to "let the seller beware." Ron Basford, former Minister of Consumer and Corporate Affairs, termed this idea "the doctrine of visibility in consumer affairs."

> The aim will be to permit consumers to look behind the cardboard and plastic, to get clear and simple warnings of the hazards in danger-ous household products, to provide for better understanding of the terms and conditions of legal documents and to prevent the dissemina-tion of misleading statements and impressions in advertising. If con-sumers can see and appreciate clearly all the aspects of the things they buy they will be able to operate much more effectively in the market-place.[1]

Though the more radical consumerists would portray the con-sumer as completely passive and susceptible to the manipulations of the marketing man, and further, suggest that there is a fundamental conflict of interest between consumers and producers, those who have given it more careful objective thought have concluded that both of these assump-tions are false.[2] One author takes a very strong stand against the myth of the manipulated consumer and even goes so far as to call today's con-sumer a "super-consumer":

> The Canadian consumer today is vastly different from his counterpart of twenty-five or even ten years ago. He is better informed, better educated, more articulate, more discriminating, more demanding. He is more mobile, has more money, lives a better life, has more leisure time. He is healthier, lives longer, he is more urbanized, more sophisti-cated, more confident. He is more concerned about his fitness, his appearance, his "style." He possesses a fuller grasp of his own identity,

[1] Ron Basford, "The Doctrine of Visibility in Consumer Affairs," *Canadian Marketer*, Winter 1969-70, p. 6.
[2] David S. R. Leighton, "The Challenge of Consumerism," *Canadian Marketer*, Winter 1969-70, pp. 4-6. Dr. Leighton was Chairman of the Cana-dian Consumer Council.

understands his own motives better, has better insights into his own personality and how he relates to others.

As a sort of "super-consumer," today's version of the consumer is less likely than ever before to be hoodwinked by manufacturer or retailer. Housewives, for example, smile indulgently when advertisers go too far in making their claims. They are aware that they themselves, along with the advertiser, are role-playing in a gigantic game. They obviously know that white knights do *not* exist, that sex does *not* reside any more in this brand of cigarettes than in that brand, that blondes do *not* invariably have more fun, that there may be a little more involved in maintaining a satisfactory marital relationship than using the right brand of mouthwash — or toothpaste — or deodorant — or, for that matter, coffee. And yet such messages are daily fare. Moreover, a great deal of research has been conducted showing that many of these patently "fictional" messages seem somehow to work. People *do* buy that brand of mouthwash — and they keep on buying it even in the face of their dissolving marriage. One way or another, the advertiser is forgiven his implied promise. Similarly, the fact that switching to a particular brand of deodorant does not always catapult one to instantaneous popularity is overlooked. How could it really? It was all a big spoof. No one meant any harm, and no one was hurt.[3]

However, whether one considers the present-day consumer to be much more sophisticated than the consumer of the past or not, few would deny that even this increased sophistication is not very useful without the proper facts, and protection in areas which require specialized training in order to interpret these facts. ". . . there exists deception in the marketplace, it exacts a heavy toll on Canadian citizens, [and although] individuals and governments do attempt to regulate the activities of the deceivers, more can still be done."[4]

Another study concluded that Canada's major industrial firms are myopically insensitive to consumerism's demands. "These firms exhibit a high degree of sensitivity to government legislation affecting their operations, but little sensitivity to societal pressures having no legal sanction."[5]

Organization

The Department of Consumer and Corporate Affairs was created in December, 1967. Recommendations for its creation came primarily from two sources:

[3] Richard W. Crosby, "The Consumer and His Attitudes," *Canadian Marketer*, Winter 1969-70, p. 7.

[4] Ronald I. Cohen, *The Regulation of Misleading Advertising in Canada: A Comparative Approach* (Ottawa: Canadian Consumer Council, November 1970), p. 8.

[5] Isaiah A. Litvak and Peter M. Banting, "Societal Pressures: How Big Business Perceives Them," *Business Quarterly* 36 (Spring 1971), p. 36.

1. The Special Joint Committee of the Senate and House of Commons on Consumer Credit (prices) (the Croll-Basford Committee)[6]
2. A study of the Economic Council of Canada[7]

Canada was the first country to consider consumer affairs important enough to be represented by a cabinet minister. Many sections of the new department are in fact a regrouping, rationalization and consolidation of divisions that existed in other departments such as Industry, Trade and Commerce, Health and Welfare, Registrar General, Justice, Agriculture, and Fisheries.

The department is divided into three basic bureaus: Bureau of Consumer Affairs, Bureau of Corporate Affairs, and Combines Investigation and Research Division. The Bureau of Corporate Affairs is further divided into four branches — Corporations Branch, Bankruptcy Branch, Trade Marks Branch, Patent and Copyright Branch. Trademarks, patents and copyrights will be discussed later in this chapter because of their interest to the marketer. The Combines Division itself is composed of five branches — Combinations Branch, Merger and Monopoly Branch, Trade Practices Branch, Research Branch, and a Legal Branch. The Combines Investigation Act will be described in some detail later in this chapter. The Bureau of Consumer Affairs includes an Information and Services Branch, an Operations Branch and a Standards Branch. In addition, it has Legal and Research branches. Associated with, but theoretically independent of the department, are the Canadian Consumer Council, the recently disbanded Prices and Incomes Commission which dealt with the problems of inflation, and the Restrictive Trade Practices Commission, which is involved with the combines apparatus and will be discussed under that topic.

The Information and Services Branch of the Consumer Bureau deals with consumer complaints and with publishing bulletins and other literature for consumer education. One innovation of this branch was to establish Box 99, Ottawa, to which consumers could write for information or to complain.

In 1969, 6,683 complaints were processed through Box 99.[8] The main product areas of complaint were foods, motor vehicles and accessories, wearing apparel, real estate/housing and appliances. The main categories of complaint were prices, quality, compensation, alleged unethical practices and advertising.

[6] See "Proceedings of the Special Joint Committee of the Senate and House of Commons on Consumer Credit (prices)," *Progress Report* (Ottawa: Queen's Printer, April 1967), p. 3454.
[7] Economic Council of Canada, *Interim Report of Consumer Affairs and the Department of the Registrar General* (Ottawa: Queen's Printer, July 1967), 53 pages.
[8] Consumer Service and Information Branch, *Second Annual Report of Complaints and Enquiries* (Ottawa: Department of Consumer and Corporate Affairs, 1970), p. 2.

The Operations Branch includes a team of hundreds of inspectors spread across the country to check products at the retail level. In addition to these inspectors (formerly from such departments as Fisheries, Agriculture, and Health and Welfare), there are provincial liaison officers who work with the provincial governments, and consumer consultants who hear consumers' complaints and provide direct information.

The Standards Branch of the Consumer Bureau is concerned with packaging, labelling, and administering such legislation as the National Trade Mark and True Labelling Act, the Precious Metals Marketing Act, the Weights and Measures Act, and the Hazardous Products Act. Recently, the responsibility of the Food and Drug Directorate of the Department of National Health and Welfare relative to economic fraud on the sale of food (not drugs) was transferred to the Department of Consumer and Corporate Affairs. Thus, the responsibility for supervising the broadcast advertising of food, on behalf of the Canadian Radio-Television Commission, now rests with this department.

In 1969 the Hazardous Products Act was enacted giving the department the authority to ban certain hazardous products and to regulate the sale, distribution, advertising and labelling of others. Beginning on June 1st, 1971, as a regulation under this act, consumer chemical products ranging from bleaches to anti-freeze must be labelled according to a system developed by the department. The system is based on a set of easily understood symbols which show what the hazard is and how injurious it is. Four hazards have been pinpointed: poison, inflammable, explosive and corrosive. In addition, three degrees of hazards have been determined: danger, warning and caution, leading to a combination of twelve basic symbols.

Bill C-180 to regulate labelling and packaging has recently been passed by Parliament. It requires the standardization of information, package sizes, net contents and shapes. Labels will have to clearly provide information on net quantity, the name and address of the manufacturer, the generic term of the product, the product's origin, its composition and performance standards. The bill will provide the Department of Consumer and Corporate Affairs with powers to prosecute false and misleading labels, e.g., "big gallon," and slack-fills.

The National Trademark and True Labelling Act requires that manufacturers who label certain specified products such as fur garments, textiles, hosiery, turpentine, and watch jewels, must do so accurately to avoid public deception. In addition, if a manufacturer has produced to a prescribed specification he may make use of Canada's national mark "Canada Standard." This is a voluntary programme. Manufacturers who label articles of precious metals must adhere to the Precious Metals Marking Act. Again these manufacturers (jewellery, watches and flatware, and gold, silver and platinum products) need not make quality claims — but if they do they come under this act.

The Weights and Measures Act describes legal standards of

weight and measure for use in Canada; it also regulates weighing and measuring devices used for commercial purposes in order to eliminate sales by short weight or short measure.

Apparently, the Bureau of Consumer Affairs will continue to be very active. Programmes for the future include looking into consumer credit, packaging, labelling and grades — particularly textile labelling — and door-to-door selling.[9]

Along with the development of the Department of Consumer and Corporate Affairs, an advisory council to the Minister of Consumer and Corporate Affairs called the Canadian Consumer Council was created in November, 1968. The Council has developed the following terms of reference:

1. The Council is designed to bring a wide variety of viewpoints to bear on issues of concern to consumers. It does not represent any single group or segment within our society.
2. The members of Council, although chosen in some cases because of their membership in certain groups, are not representatives of those groups. The views they express are their own, and are sought because of the individual's personal expertise or experience. The relative criterion to be applied is that of the overall public interest.
3. The Council is an *autonomous* body, speaking independently of the views of government or other bodies. While cognizant of the problems of different jurisdictions, it does not consider itself limited in its interests by constitutional constraints.
4. The Council, while offering its advice and counsel first to the Minister, retains the right to publish its views in a form and manner which members themselves determine.
5. The fundamental goal of the Council's activities is to improve the consumer environment, and to remove those imperfections which operate contrary to the most efficient and productive allocation of resources.[10]

During its first year of operation, the Council issued a Report on Consumer Credit calling for a comprehensive consumer credit act that would include sweeping changes to the Small Loans Act, credit card legislation and provisions for the regulation of consumer notes. Other

[9] For additional literature on the Department of Consumer and Corporate Affairs see the following: C. J. Maule, "Consumer Affairs," *Executive* 11 (June 1969), pp. 54-55; "Consumers' Watchdog," *Financial Post,* 30 November 1968, pp. 13-14; Robin Schiele, "Basford's Bureaucracy for Consumers," *Canadian Business* 42 (August 1969), pp. 16-23; Graeme Hughes, "Is There Still a Caveat on the Emptor," *Industrial Canada* 70 (December 1969), pp. 11-16; "Consumer Affairs Conference: The Corporation and the Consumer," *Industrial Canada* 70 (July 1969), pp. 59-68; Jacob S. Ziegel, "Consumerism in Canada," *The Canadian Banker,* November/December 1971, pp. 4-6.
[10] Canadian Consumer Council, *First Annual Report* (Ottawa: Canadian Consumer Council, December 1969), pp. 10-11.

problems studied by the Council included misleading advertising, product standards and testing, a charter of consumer rights, problems of the low-income consumer, and consumer education.

In the Council's *Second Annual Report* (December 1970), a broadening of consumerism aims was noted. "Increasingly, consumer groups were heard speaking out on subjects such as environmental protection, inflation, combines, taxes and tariffs, in large measure because many of the traditional concerns of consumers were seen as less crucial to consumer well-being than these broader issues."[11]

Projects undertaken and reports made to the Minister by the Council during 1970 covered such diverse consumer concerns as referral sales and other deceptive selling practices, the elimination of the federal sales tax on margarine, competition policy and revisions to the Combines Investigation Act, hearing aids, food store self-help projects, two studies on consumers' attitudes towards their rights in the marketplace and the development of two new consumer publications.

Provincial Consumer Protection Acts

Several provinces have also enacted consumer legislation in recent years. Fairly typical of these is the act passed by Quebec in 1971, which established a Consumer Protection Bureau to apply the act and to investigate consumer complaints. Also created was the Consumer Protection Council to study consumer problems and act as an advisory body. The provisions of the act include the following:

1. A consumer who signs a contract for more than $25 with a door-to-door salesman will be able to cancel the agreement within five days of signing.
2. No person may issue a credit card to a consumer who has not applied for it.
3. Any goods furnished by a merchant must comply with the description of them given in the contract and in any advertisements for the product.
4. The consumer who buys an item for a specific purpose has the right to demand that a warranty be circulated in the contract indicating the article may be normally used for the purpose indicated.
5. Consumers have the right to examine their credit files on demand and to obtain copies of these files.
6. Pyramid sales contracts are outlawed.

A number of other sections on preparing contracts, installment buying and the repayment of loans are included.

---

[11] Canadian Consumer Council, *Second Annual Report* (Ottawa: Canadian Consumer Council, December 1970), p. 7.

Patents

A patent may be applied for "any new and useful art, process, machine, manufacture or composition of matter, or any new and useful improvement in any art, process, machine, manufacture or composition of matter." The "thing" must be an invention, rather than a simple workshop improvement. This means that an obvious and easy innovation capable of being created by any skilled workman, would probably not be patentable. Nor can it be a simple, obvious rearrangement of a known and old product. However, one can usually obtain a patent for a similar product if it was invented through a very different method. Improvements on a previously patented product can themselves be patented, but the new inventor cannot use the original product without permission of the holder of the original patent.

Applications for a patent, together with specifications, are made to the Commissioner of Patents in the Department of Consumer and Corporate Affairs, and once granted, anyone may examine a patent. Of course, the applications themselves are kept secret as are patents pending. The government will issue a caveat which provides protection before application while experimentation is under way. However, an application must be filed within three months if another person has already filed, and within one year of the caveat issuance. Failing this, the caveator is no longer considered protected. Assuming the invention is patentable a patent will be granted if it was not in public use or for sale in Canada more than two years before the application. (U.S. patent laws only allow up to one year.) Those who filed in foreign countries have an additional year to file in Canada. This means, that if a patent was filed in the United States on January 1, 1970, it will be considered filed on that date in Canada, so long as the inventor files in Canada at any time during 1970. The reverse situation also holds for the Canadian inventor who wishes to patent his invention in the United States, i.e., he has an extra year of grace. If the holder of a patent does not make commercial use of his invention within three years from the granting of the patent, the Commissioner of Patents may allow another company to produce and distribute the product. Of course, a reasonable royalty must be paid by the latter firm to the holder of the patent.

Patent rights may be assigned to another company by the patentee in any case and at any time. Patent provides protection for seventeen years and any company or person infringing on this patent can be sued for damages as well as having an injunction secured against him. Infringement would usually include the selling of a similar, but not really new product. In 1970, over 28,900 patents were granted, 66 percent of these to U.S. firms or persons, and 5 percent or 1,461 to Canadians; 31,360 applications were issued, 229 caveats were granted, and over 28,200 patent assignments were registered.

In 1969 an amendment to the Patent Act gave the Commissioner of Patents the power to give a license to others to import or manufacture a patented drug, in order to increase competition.

Trademarks

Trademark regulations are described in the Trade Marks Act and are administered by the Registrar of Trade Marks. A registered trademark provides protection for fifteen years; however, this can be renewed for subsequent fifteen-year periods ad infinitum. A company need not register a trademark, as the basic right is found in "use." However, an unregistered trademark holder cannot sue for infringement on that trademark but may sue for "passing-off." The latter term means that any firm can sue another if it is felt that the defendant is attempting to confuse his product with that of the other firm. When a trademark is registered, the complainant needs only to prove that the defendant is using a similar mark and need not prove "passing-off." Of course, the holder of a trademark may arrange, with the approval of the Registrar of Trade Marks, to have another firm become "a registered user." For example, soft drink bottlers may be registered as users of a soft drink company's trademark.

The first user of a trademark is protected if he registers within six months of use. "Use" means that the product is being sold commercially and that buyers can see a close association between the trademark and the product being sold. Advertising, for example, using the trademark before the product is actually available for sale, will not be considered "use." A firm can apply for a trademark in anticipation of "use" — but no final registration will be issued until the product is actually "in use."

A trademark or name may be registered if it is not confusing with regard to a previous one that is being used, or one for which an application for registration has been filed, and provided it is not on the list of prohibitive trademarks. This list includes marks or names which are: overly descriptive, deceptively descriptive, similar to symbols of the Royal Family, Governor-General, Canadian governments, Red Cross, United Nations, Armed Forces, Royal Canadian Mounted Police, or an individual who is living or who has died within the preceding thirty years.

Trademark registrations provide somewhat less protection in Canada than in the United States. Usually, a firm producing a substantially different product may use the trade name of another, but dissimilar product. However, in another respect there appears to be more protection in Canada with regard to trade names becoming generic and therefore no longer protectable. For example, Bayer's Aspirin is still protected in Canada, while the word "aspirin" has become a generic one in the United States. Approximately 6,700 trademarks were registered in Canada in 1970.

Industrial Design Law

The regulations which govern the protection of industrial designs, contained in the Industrial Design and Union Trade Marks Act, are usually only applicable to ornamental features on the surface of a product. If the design or part of it can be considered "useful" then protection must usually be sought under the patent regulations. In addition, the act does not usually apply to the distinctive shape of the product itself, unless its shape becomes well-known as such — e.g., the Coca-Cola bottle. In the latter case, a "passing-off" action can be taken. As mentioned previously a "passing-off" action is taken when it is felt that the defendant is trading on the goodwill of another product and is confusing his product with another in the mind of the public. Unlike other regulations mentioned in this chapter, the act does not prevent a firm copying a design of another firm if the latter did not register its design (perhaps because it was not registerable) and if it cannot be considered as "passing-off." Industrial designs are registered with the Commissioner of Patents for a maximum of two successive five-year periods. 1,026 such designs were registered in 1970.

The Copyright Act

This act should be of particular interest to those involved with producing and using advertisements. Canada belongs to the Berne and Universal Copyright Conventions, both of which provide for reciprocal copyright protection. The Universal Copyright Convention includes the United States. Copyright protection lasts for the life of the author plus fifty years, although in the United States the protection lasts twenty-eight years plus one renewal, and American writers must first publish in their own country. In order to be protectable the material must be set down in a permanent form. For example, to protect broadcast material it would probably be necessary to have it taped. Copyright protection is in force even if the material has not been registered. Injunction and damage actions can be taken if copyright material is plagiarized; however, only an injunction alone may be issued if the copyright material was not registered, as it could not be considered feasible for the defendant to have been aware of the original material's existence. In 1970, there were 8,611 copyright registrations in Canada.

The Copyright Act does not protect ideas per se. Thus, an advertising scheme is not itself protectable; however, particular advertisements can be protected. It is interesting to note, though, that slogans appear to be protectable in Canada, while this is not the case in the United States. Slogans are defined as a single sentence or disjointed fragment in an advertisement. Incidentally, advertisements are owned by the advertiser, not the agency.

There are a number of other ways that copyright law affects marketing. For example, a mailing list can be copyrighted; however a firm working from original sources may compile the same list without contravening the Copyright Act, so long as no use is made of a copyrighted list itself.

THE COMBINES INVESTIGATION ACT[12]

The purpose of this section is to describe and comment on the single most important piece of legislation affecting the marketing community in Canada, the origins of which go back to 1889 — the Combines Investigation Act.

Introduction to the Act

The purpose of the act is to maintain competition and achieve economic efficiency, maximum output and employment, and so, ultimately and ideally, a maximization of the standard of living with the given level of available scarce economic resources. To accomplish this task, a range of restrictive trade practices are outlawed. The Combines Investigation Act is analogous to the various anti-trust acts of the United States such as the Sherman Act, Clayton Act, Federal Trade Commission Act, and the Robinson-Patman Act. Although the Combines Act covers many of the marketing practices regulated by these U.S. acts, it is by no means identical in content or administration.

As in most other areas, the Canadian economic environment is itself enveloped in that of the U.S. In the area of combines many Canadian subsidiaries of U.S. firms are in fact also subject to the aggressive U.S. antitrust laws. In 1954, one of Canada's largest companies was split in half by an antitrust decision in the United States. The U.S. decision was based on the fear that other U.S. exporters to Canada would have difficulty in selling to the Canadian market because of the existence of this large U.S.-owned firm in Canada. The result was the creation of two new firms from the old: Canadian Industries Limited and DuPont of Canada.

It should be clearly understood that the act does not attempt to regulate prices, and identical prices as such are not considered an offense. There are no positive demands for competition in the act, only demands for a situation which would allow for competition. In other words, the business community is not told in the act that "thou shall compete" but only "thou shall not do such and such because that will hurt any competition which might take place." Competitors are not forced to put on the gloves and get into the boxing ring, but are only outlawed from throwing the match.

The CIA, with a few exceptions, does not apply to services unless they are so closely related to goods that competition in such goods would be affected if the related services were subject to restrictive practices. Professional services are, of course, exempt unless they are closely

[12] From Bruce E. Mallen, "The Combines Investigation Act: Canada's Major Marketing Statute," *MSU Business Topics*, Spring 1970. Reprinted by permission of the publisher, Division of Research, Graduate School of Business Administration, Michigan State University.

related to goods, such as the services of a pharmacist. Thus professional accountants, lawyers, medical doctors, and the like, may take advantage of their professional associations or societies and agree on prices, rates and fees. Unions, also, are not subject to the provisions of the act. Finally, the CIA takes a back seat to other legislation. Where an industry is under provincial legislation, the provincial regulations and not the regulations of the act usually apply.

Administrative and Court Procedure

The act provides for a director of investigation whose duty it is to begin an inquiry if he has reason to believe that an offense has been committed. Administratively, the director reports to the Federal Minister of Consumer and Corporate Affairs. The director may be required to start an inquiry if he receives a formal request from the responsible minister or six citizens. In practice, the director or his department initiates almost all inquiries, although action may also be generated by information received from businessmen. Since the act is rather vague in many sections, and since there is very little or no jurisprudence on many of the points raised in the act, the situations in which the director feels he should start an inquiry are of great interest to businessmen. Director D. H. W. Henry, Q.C., has delivered addresses and written articles for various audiences over the past few years indicating the kinds of practices he feels would impel him to start an inquiry.[13]

At any point during the investigation, the director may discontinue the inquiry if he feels that an offense has not been committed or that there is insufficient evidence to support the accusation. The discontinuation is subject to the minister's approval and the approval of the Restrictive Trade Practices Commission, if the evidence has already been submitted to them. If the director is of the opinion that an offense has been committed, and time is not of the essence, he may refer the case to the Restrictive Trade Practices Commission, and perhaps eventually through it to the Attorney General, or he may refer the case directly to the Attorney General. The direct route to the Attorney General will usually be taken if swift court action is important; for example, in cases involving a formal charge under Section 33C "misleading price advertising." The basic function of the commission is to hear and appraise the evidence of the director and the accused and then issue a report which would include its recommendations. This report is available to the

---

[13] D. H. W. Henry, "The Combines Act — Background of the Unfair Trade Practices Provisions," *Industrial Canada* 61 (February 1961), pp. 39-42; "The Combines Investigation Act," *The Canadian Chartered Accountant* 88 (May 1965), pp. 352-57; "Here Are Advertising Perils, Pitfalls," *Financial Post,* 23 February 1963, p. 27; "In Pricing, Marketing Buying, Here Are the Purlieus of Legality," *Financial Post* 14 April 1962, pp. 28-29; "Address to the New York State Bar Association, Anti-Trust Law Section," (New York City, 30 January 1964); "Address to the American Marketing Association, Montreal Chapter," (Montreal, 12 May 1970).

public, although the hearing is usually held in private, and is considered one of the methods of fighting restrictive trade practices through the process of public exposure.

As a result of this report the Attorney General may take the case to court. The case may be taken through the provincial courts, or with the permission of the accused, to the Exchequer Court of Canada. Judgments of these lower courts can be appealed to the Supreme Court of Canada. If the courts find the defendant guilty they may issue a restraining order or an injunction, dissolve a merger, adjust patent and trademark rights of the accused, impose a fine (there is no maximum), or order a jail sentence with a two-year maximum (in practice, the latter has not yet happened). In addition, the government may adjust tariff rates to increase the competition in the industry in question.

Unlike the antitrust authorities in the United States, neither the director of investigations nor the Restrictive Trade Practices Commission has legal powers to impose penalties or adjustments. The director may only start (sometime he may be formally required to commence) an inquiry. The RTPC, unlike the Federal Trade Practices Commission in the United States, can only hear evidence and submit recommendations. Only the courts have legal powers in combines matters. An inquiry *cannot* be avoided because the director or the RTPC feels there are good sound economic reasons for a given practice which happens legally to appear to be an offense under the act. For example, rationalization of production in a given industry, through adding efficiency to the economy, may be of benefit to the public, but this still does not provide an excuse for not starting an inquiry if such rationalization offends a section of the act.

Professor H. E. English suggests that the RTPC should be replaced with a more flexible type of structure which would allow for administrative decisions (such as the Federal Trade Commission in the United States) and which could consider economic as well as legal viewpoints in making decisions.[14]

Under Section 42 of the act, the director may also undertake general research into business practices and industrial structures for the purpose of making recommendations for legislation. In addition, the director has in the past number of years undertaken a programme of compliance under which businessmen may ask his advice on specific contemplated action (a merger, for example) to see if such action would elicit an inquiry. Because of the relative lack of guidelines in terms of clear wording of the act or jurisprudence, such advice can prove invaluable and also act as an excellent deterrent. Indeed, there is agitation for more effective preventative legislation than now exists. Legislation for preapproval of mergers that would be legally binding (unlike the

---

[14] H. E. English, "Competition and Policy to Control Restrictive Practices," in T. N. Brewis et al., eds., *Canadian Economic Policy* (Toronto: MacMillan Company of Canada Limited, 1961), pp. 28-67.

director's compliance programme), and wider use of injunctions have been suggested.[15]

It should be understood that the director does not have the legal power to bind himself to this promise of *not* starting an inquiry. However, the programme of compliance has appeared to work fairly well. Apparently, two large mergers have taken place with the approval of the Combines Branch: Canadian Chemical Company and Canadian Celanese merged to form Chemcell Limited, and the latter firm and Canadian Industries Limited merged their marketing and sales fibre organizations (only) to form CelCil.

The director of investigations and research issues an annual report outlining discontinued, ongoing and completed inquiries, prosecutions, proceedings, and administrative changes of the branch (published by the Queens Printer, Ottawa).

Sections of the Act

The core sections of the act can logically be discussed in three groups:

1. Combinations (Section 32).
2. Mergers and monopolies (Section 33).
3. Unfair trade practices — price discrimination (Section 33A); promotional allowances (Section 33B); misleading price advertising (Section 33C); misleading advertising (Section 33D); and resale price maintenance (Section 34).

COMBINATIONS

Section 32 forbids actual or attempted collusions or combinations in production and distribution that unduly lessen competition. Thus combinations which have not been realized but only attempted, as well as those (realized or attempted) which only *may* unduly lessen competition are also considered an offense under this section.

A key word in this section is *unduly* and its presence makes the section operate under an "abuse" principle rather than the principle behind the U.S. Sherman Act, where this kind of practice is an offense per se. Of course, *unduly* is a vague term which may be defined in several ways. Critics have called for a clear definition of the term. The tendency of the courts to interpret the word as "too large a market share" has not helped to placate the critics. It appears that until competition is completely eliminated, or until the accused can act in a manner completely unaffected by competition, the courts will not rule against the defendant. The collusion or combination need not take the form of a formal agreement or arrangement to constitute a breach of this section.

---

[15] Arthur Brydon, "Archaic Combines Laws Set for Revamping," *Executive* 7 (August 1965), pp. 37-39.

A "gentleman's understanding" will be sufficient. However, true price leadership without collusion or without a gentleman's understanding does not constitute an offense, according to the director of investigations.

In spite of these problems, this section is probably one of the more effective ones in the act. The offense it has been most efficient in combating is price fixing. Other offenses under this section include market sharing, profit sharing, group boycotts in selling, buying or distribution, and horizontal agreements on discounts and submission of tenders.

The section does allow for the exchange of statistics, agreement on product standards and definition of trade terms, credit information, cooperation on research and development, and agreement to restrict advertising. Firms may even exchange price lists so long as such exchange is not used for price-fixing purposes. All this is done with the understanding, of course, that such exchanges do not lessen price competition, production, distribution, number of competitors, or ease of entry into an industry for new competitors. The section also allows for export trade agreements between firms, so long as such agreements do not lessen export volume or hurt Canadian buyers or sellers. This special agreement for export trade is similar to the Webb-Pomerene Act in the United States.

MERGERS AND MONOPOLIES

Unlike Section 7 of the Clayton Act, which has allowed the Federal Trade Commission and U.S. courts to have a very aggressive merger policy by breaking up mergers in the very early stages of concentration in an industry, Section 33 of the Combines Act has been rather ineffective. This is one particular section which many feel requires greater flexibility in administration and a greater regard for the economic consequences of a merger. This is particularly important because the relatively small Canadian domestic market often can efficiently support only a very few firms in a given industry.[16]

Section 33 forbids horizontal and/or vertical mergers that lessen or are likely to lessen competition and that have harmful economic effects on sellers and/or consumers. This section also forbids monopolies (excluding those holding patents or those which are regulated in another manner by the federal or provincial governments) that are detrimental to the public. Note that a monopoly as such is not an offense. For example, internal growth by a firm which ends up as a monopoly may be quite legal.

A monopolist must be careful in restricting the distribution of his products, or in creating tying arrangements whereby he makes it a requirement that other products be purchased if the buyer wishes to also receive the ones for which the seller has the monopoly.

[16] See the interesting argument presented in W. G. Phillips, "Canadian Combines Policy — The Matter of Mergers," *The Canadian Bar Review* 42 (March 1964) , pp. 78-99.

PRICE DISCRIMINATION

Section 33A is the first of the various substantive sections of the act which deals with unfair trade practices. The sections which are of most interest to marketing men are 33A to D and 34 because they deal basically with marketing practices. Section 33A forbids price discrimination. According to the provisions of this section the supplier must usually give all competitors the same price deal if these competitors buy the same quantities and quality. Although the supplier may discriminate in his pricing on odd occasions, such as a store opening of a customer, he may not make a practice of so doing. Of course, the words used in this section tend to beg the question — for example, what is a competitor? what is a practice?

There is no simple answer to these questions, Administratively, interpretation is left to the director of investigations, and legally to the courts. However, there is still no definite jurisprudence on this section. Section 33A has been most difficult to enforce because even minor differences in quantity of purchase can provide a solid defense. Unlike Section 3 of the Robinson-Patman Act and the Clayton Act, the Canadian supplier is not required to justify, on a cost basis, the differences in his selling price between one buyer and that buyer's competitor. He need only show that there was some difference in the quality or quantity purchased. Of course, the lack of the cost justification defense is a two-edged sword in that the offending supplier cannot use such a defense to justify any discrimination when the quality and quantity are the same.

Scales or schedules of quantity volume discounts are quite permissible under the act. However, since volume discounts are discounts of quantity accumulated over a reasonable period (for example, a year) it is important that the supplier inform all competing buyers well in advance of the availability of these volume discounts. This will avoid his being accused of discriminating against those whom he did not inform until it was too late for them to plan their purchasing accordingly.

Since the cost justification is not applicable under the act, discounts for performing special functions, such as maintaining high inventories of slow turnover brands, are illegal. In other words, functional discounts are not permissible in Canada.

Quantity and volume discounts may be based on the total purchases of a corporate chain even though deliveries are made to the individual store. It is important for voluntary and cooperative chains, if they wish to take advantage of the central discount that the corporate chain receives, to actually establish a central buying firm which takes title to the merchandise and then distributes it to the members. It is necessary that their central agency be legally structured in this manner because quantity and volume discounts can apply only to purchases of a single buyer and not to the total volume of several, even if they place orders through a single agency. Section 33A specifically excludes consumer cooperative dividends as a potential form of price discrimination.

The Combines Branch does not restrict its interpretation of competition to competition at the same level of distribution. For example, it is quite conceivable that a wholesaler and large retailer may be considered competitors if they are operating in the same market. Buyers must also realize that they can be a party to any offense under Section 33A if it can be shown that they applied pressure on sellers to make a practice of discriminating in their favour.

PREDATORY PRICING

An important part of Section 33A stipulates that a supplier may not have a policy of pricing in such a manner that he substantially limits competition or competitors. The act forbids an unreasonably severe price-cutting policy with the purpose of lessening or trying to lessen competition and competitors. Notice that it need only be a tendency to so lessen competition and competitors, and that the policy need not succeed to be considered an offense. For example, a financially strong and geographically- or product-diversified company which is making a sound supporting profit in one area cannot price unreasonably low in another area in order to eliminate local competition, or have the objective of so doing. This is a form of regional price discrimination and is an offense under the predatory pricing clause of Section 33A. Retailers should note that discount store pricing is not considered predatory, because there are sound economies to their operations which naturally allow for the price cuts associated with this form of retailing.

PROMOTIONAL ALLOWANCES

Another of the unfair trade practices portion of the act, under Section 33B, has certain similarities with Sections 2D and 2E of the Clayton Act. There has been no jurisprudence under Section 33B, and as with Section 33A, enforcement is made quite difficult because this section can be bypassed by applying the allowance *directly* to the selling price. The latter action means that the allowance in question would come under the terms of Section 33A rather than Section 33B.

A supplier must not only make available, but must actually offer all competing buyers the same allowance deal in proportion to their volume of purchases. However, under Section 33B the discrimination need not be a practice to be an offense. One incident of such discrimination will be sufficient. For example, allowance arrangements given to a buyer for the purpose of a buyer's anniversary sale must still be offered to all that buyer's competitors. Competitors are interpreted, as in Section 33A, as firms competing for the same customers regardless of whether the firms are, for example, mail order versus store retailers or wholesalers versus large retailers.

A key word in this section is "proportionate." Any allowances provided by the supplier, and services provided or expenses incurred in return by the buyer, must be proportionate to the latter's purchases from the supplier. A supplier may not demand a larger amount of services by a buyer if the latter did not receive a greater promotional allowance, nor can a supplier eliminate or drastically reduce a promotional allowance to a buyer who has not purchased a stipulated quantity. If, for example, buyer A purchases twice as much from the supplier as buyer B, then buyer A may receive an allowance twice that of buyer B. In this example, buyer B can be expected to provide only half the services (for example, half the expenditure on advertising the supplier's product) that buyer A is expected to provide. The supplier may only reduce the promotional allowance in proportion to the difference in purchases between the buyer who received the maximum allowance and the competitor in question. Note that this is unlike Section 33A, where a supplier may completely eliminate the price discount if competing buyers have purchased different quantities. If a buyer is willing to perform a certain service to receive a promotional allowance but for one reason or another cannot do so, then the supplier must provide the buyer with an alternative proportional service which the buyer can perform. Of course, the supplier is off the hook if the buyer can but will not perform a stipulated service which would qualify him for a promotional allowance. A supplier, for example, cannot use time periods which tend to discriminate between buyers, and then turn around and use the inability of specific buyers to perform a service as an excuse for not providing a proportionate allowance. In principle the allowance need not be the same kind but must have proportionate *value*. Buyers may pocket the allowance without performing any service, but the supplier cannot discriminate between buyers by allowing some to do so while others must provide services to qualify for the allowance.

MISLEADING PRICE ADVERTISING

Section 33C refers to misleading price advertising. A most frequent offense under the CIA happens when a retailer quotes a regular price which is really nonexistent and uses that inevitably higher price as a comparison to his lower offering price. According to the director of investigation, if a reasonable shopper would draw the conclusion from any expression used, that the figure named by way of comparison is a price at which goods have been, are, or will ordinarily be sold and that such a higher figure is in fact a misleading one, then an offense has been committed under this section. Normal sales must have taken place or must take place at the designated regular price. An offering of the product at that so-called regular price or a few accidental sales at that price is not good enough. In order to avoid an inquiry, it is important that a special low price used to launch a new product and stipulated as such in advertising, be marked up within a reasonable time period and the product sold at the stipulated regular price. Regular-priced sales must have been realized by the seller in question or most of his competitors. A plea of ignorance of the ordinary price is not a defense to a charge brought under this section. The medium carrying the misleading advertising is normally excluded from responsibility, assuming it was printed or broadcasted in good faith.

Manufacturer's suggested or list price, or use of such devices as pink ticketing and "cents off" deals must be valid. The list price may only be used if the products are ordinarily sold at that price, or else the retailer or manufacturer may be prosecuted.

Comparisons may only be made between packages of the same size. Thus it would be considered an offense under this section if a manufacturer or retailer were to list as the regular price of a large package, the per unit price of a small package multiplied by the number of units in the large package, if that large package is not ordinarily sold at the price derived from these calculations.

MISLEADING ADVERTISING

As of July 31, 1969 legislation concerning misleading advertising, formerly part of the Criminal Code, officially became Section 33D of the Combines Investigation Act. Contained in the Criminal Code, enforcement of this legislation was the responsibility of the provincial attorneys general, and, under their direction saw only rare application because of their preoccupation with more serious criminal matters. It is expected that now that this legislation is part of the Combines Act, which falls under the jurisdiction of the Department of Consumer and Corporate Affairs, it will enjoy much more vigorous enforcement.

Enforcement will at least be brought against the following practices. (1) False or misleading product guarantees. (2) The statement or guarantee of the performance or life of any product that is not based upon adequate or proper tests by recognized testing organizations. (3) Deceptive use of contests; for example, indicating that an individual is a winner of first prize when in fact many others receive the same information. (4) Free offers that are not in fact free; for example, when receipt of the free gift is contingent on the purchase of other articles which could be purchased through conventional channels at lower prices. (5) "Bait-and-switch" operations where the item is used as bait and is not in fact held for sale by the advertiser, or the advertiser used the advertised article to help switch customers to other goods. (6) A contest purporting to award prizes where such prizes are not in fact available. (7) Misrepresentation as to origin; for example, "Made in Canada" when in fact it is not made in Canada. (8) "Clip-and-paste" solicitations. This is a direct mail device in which typically the customer is invited to verify by return form-letter mail, a listing of his address in a directory but which, when signed and returned, amounts to an order for which he may be invoiced.

For some of these sub-sections of the act, defenders face fines at the Court's discretion, jail terms up to five years, plus a court injunction.

RESALE PRICE MAINTENANCE

Section 34, which is an outcome of the MacQuarrie Committee of 1951, forbids actual or attempted resale price maintenance at any level, whether these are attempts at resale price control by the manufacturer over the wholesaler or retailer, or attempts at resale price control by the wholesaler over the retailer. Section 34 forbids specified or minimum price setting, be it through establishing exact price or minimum price in dollars, markups or markup minimums, or discount maximum arrangements. However, the section does not forbid maximum price setting or even inducements to sell below this price, so long as such inducements do not specify a price to be established below the list. Nor does this section prohibit resale price control through the technique of consignment selling. Legally such selling is not reselling, as the buyer keeps title to the merchandise. The petroleum companies make wide use of this technique for resale price control purposes. In addition, suggested prices are considered an offense, if such prices are used to enforce resale prices.

REFUSAL TO SELL

The supplier may not refuse to sell to actual or potential resale price cutters for purposes of enforcing a resale price maintenance policy. However, this restriction does not require a supplier to sell to any interested buyer in any circumstance. He may refuse to sell to any interested buyer, especially newcomers, for any reason except for the purpose of resale price control, if he is not doing this in collusion with other suppliers (this collusion would be against the combination section of the act), or if he is not a monopolist. The latter firms have a greater obligation to distribute more widely, and so allow competition within the channel. The Eddy Match Company was convicted on this basis, and Canadian Industries Limited was "persuaded" to ease its distribution policy in the Ammunition case.

A supplier may also refuse to sell to a buyer who is making a practice of using the former's product as a loss leader, or is involved in misleading advertising, or is providing insufficient service to the consumer on the supplier's product. Under these circumstances it is felt that the manufacturer's product is being used for the purpose of advertising or traffic creation and not for the purpose of direct profit. Thus the manufacturer may be justified in refusing to sell to that buyer. However, price cutting by a reseller to meet competition or weak demand for the product may not be considered a form of loss leading (even if he must sell below cost) and so may not be used by the supplier as an excuse for refusing to sell to him.

Future Developments

There are pressures to have the Combine Investigation Act clarified and expanded in order to have it apply to services, labour unions, professions, and marketing boards as well as to the goods to which it now applies.[17] There are also pressures to have the act's administration

[17] L. A. Skeoch, "The Case for Changes in the Combines Laws," *Industrial Canada* 67 (July 1966), pp. 220-23.

modified to allow more room for economic considerations, perhaps through a tribunal (see footnotes 14 and 15) rather than to allow the strictly legal factors to influence the final decisions. Recommendations have also been made to take the Combines Act out of the criminal law arena and place it under civil law.[18] Despite these recommendations, two authors hold to the thesis that the history of Canadian legislation in this field shows that legislators do not really want to have a strong anticombines statute on the books. In their opinion the only reason for its existence at all is to avoid the poor public image that would be created for the legislators, if they openly supported restrictive trade practices.[19]

Not all authors are for a stronger Combines Act. J. W. Younger in an article thoroughly blasting the act,[20] questions the government's interpretation (as he sees it) of the basic premise of the act, that is, competition as a "good" in itself rather than as a means to a freer society. He feels that though the Combines Act comes under the criminal law, the courts are not demanding the usual stringent evidence required by criminal law. He also questions the courts' interpretation of Section 32, in particular the narrow product-oriented definition of a "market." The trade practices sections, particularly 33A, 33B, and 34, he considers to be illogical and anti-competitive, detrimental to the small retailer and to orderly distribution, and inconsistent. He is particularly disturbed by the illegal status of functional discounts and concludes:

> It may well be that in the World of 1968, the Combines Investigation Act is a rather useless anachronism which should be repealed entirely. . . . The real criterion, therefore, by which the legislation must be judged is whether or not it contributes to a free society, and weighed in this balance the Combines Investigation Act must be found wanting.[21]

On June 30, 1971 Parliament gave first reading to Bill C-256 — the Competition Act — which when passed will replace the Combines Investigation Act. The new act, which is based on the recommendations of an Economic Council of Canada report,[22] is at this writing still under public debate and will be somewhat modified upon final reading. The Council made three basic recommendations. (1) The act should apply

---

[18] Because of the provincial rights outlined in the British North American Act, which constitutionally hampers federal civil law legislation in this area, the CIA is criminal law. However, since criminal law requires evidence of guilt beyond reasonable doubt, it has severely hampered enforcement of the act.

[19] G. Rosenbluth and H. G. Thorburn, "Canadian Anti-Combines Administration, 1952-1960," *Canadian Journal of Economics and Political Science* 27 (November 1961), pp. 498-508.

[20] J. W. Younger, "A Fresh Look at the Combines Investigation Act," *Business Quarterly* 34 (Spring 1969), pp. 75-84.

[21] *Ibid.*, p. 83.

[22] Economic Council of Canada, *Interim Report on Competition Policy* (Ottawa: Queen's Printer, July 1969), 244 pages.

to the service industries and the professions, including the banks and professional sports. (2) Except for five specific business practices (mentioned in the next point), the act should come under civil rather than criminal law and a "competitive practices tribunal" should be established with power to make administrative decisions based on economic welfare as well as legal considerations. This would especially apply to the mergers and monopoly sections of the act (section 33). (3) For the five specific business practices, stronger penalties and enforcement should be available. These business practices include: collusion of various sorts (Section 32), misleading advertising (Sections 33C and 33D), and resale price maintenance (Section 34).

In addition to accepting the three broad recommendations listed above, the Competition Act incorporates various new administrative procedures, clarifies the meaning of a number of terms used in the old act, introduces additional terms, and in addition to the Competitive Practices Tribunal's merger powers (all mergers involving combined assets and/or sales of five million dollars will have to be registered), provides it with powers in disallowing certain trade practices, some of which were disallowed under the Combines Act, and some of which are introduced for the first time.

The trade practices which the tribunal may disallow include: price differentiation, promotional allowance differentiation, delivered prices (forcing a customer to pay delivery cost as part of the price even if the buyer is willing to pick-up the merchandise at the supplier's warehouse), tied sales, exclusive dealing, reciprocal buying, trading area reselling restrictions, and refusal to supply by a monopolistic or oligopolistic supplier to a credit-worthy customer. However, a number of these practices are to be allowed under certain circumstances. For example, price and/or promotional allowance differentiation will not be considered discriminatory if one or more of the following exist: there is a proportionate saving in delivery cost, the difference assists market entry of buyer or seller, the buyer (s) is of insignificant size, the difference offers an insignificant advantage, the difference will help to lower the general price level of that commodity, there is strong import competition, it is for customer's private brand (so long as other customers have a proportionate price opportunity for their private brands), or the difference reflects a volume discount rate available to all buyers.

In addition to the trade practices over which the tribunal has discretionary powers, there are a number which are outlawed per se, as broadly noted above in the third recommendation of the Economic Council: collusion, misleading advertising and price maintenance. Some important new aspects of the latter two offences include the following:

1. The defense under a price maintenance charge, that a supplier refused to sell to a buyer because of the latter's loss leader, bait, misleading advertising or lack of servicing practices, is no longer a valid one.

2. Suggested resale prices will constitute proof of a price maintenance offence if it was not made clear to the reseller that he was under no obligation to use the suggested price.

3. Prior permission is required from an individual or organization, if their testimonial is to be used.

4. Pyramid selling is illegal if the potential gain to the buyer is misrepresented.

5. Referral selling is illegal.

6. Merchandise may not be displayed at a price higher than that advertised.

7. Promotional contests must publicly disclose the odds of winning in each trading area and must distribute prizes in a random and prompt manner.

The new Competition Act provides for a commissioner (to replace the director of combines investigation). Penalties include imprisonment of up to five years and/or maximum fines of two million dollars for second convictions under the collusion and monopolization clauses; two years imprisonment and/or fines at the court's discretion for a price maintenance offence; imprisonment for one or two years or one year and a two thousand dollar fine maximum for a misleading advertising offence; and imprisonment for one year and/or a maximum fine of ten thousand dollars for offences regarding pyramid selling, testimonials, referral selling, bait and switch selling, higher-price displays and promotional contests. The Courts could also impose special remedies such as the removal of patent rights and the ordering of payment of double damages to any other persons who suffered as a result of the offence.

AN OVERVIEW OF OTHER FEDERAL LEGISLATION THAT AFFECTS MARKETING

It is useful to think of federal legislation affecting consumers as falling into four categories:[23]

1. Protection against fraud and deceptions
2. Protection against hazards to health and safety
3. Promoting the development of suitable quality standards and grades
4. Providing information of assistance to consumers

Figure 6-1 shows the existing distribution of federal government duties affecting consumers and marketing. In the first group — protection

[23] Economic Council of Canada, *Interim Report of Consumer Affairs and the Department of the Registrar General* (Ottawa: Queen's Printer, July 1967).

FIGURE 6-1 Existing Distribution of Federal Government Activities Affecting Consumers

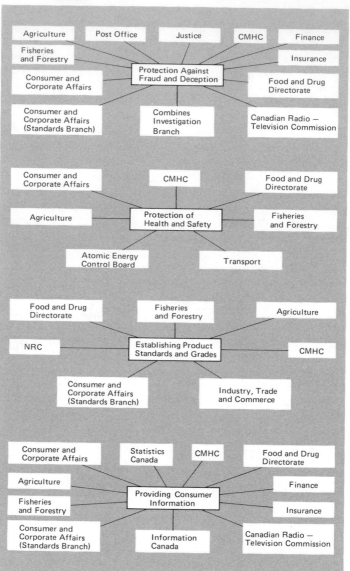

SOURCE: *Economic Council of Canada,* Interim Report: Consumer Affairs and the Department of the Registrar General *(Ottawa: Queen's Printer, 1967),* p. 13.

NOTE: This chart has been revised to take into account the Department of Consumer and Corporate Affairs and the branches transferred to it; the new Canadian Radio-Television Commission; the merger of the Department of Industry with the Department of Trade and Commerce; the name-change of the Dominion Bureau of Statistics to Statistics Canada; and the establishment of Information Canada.

against fraud and deception — the Department of National Health and Welfare (the Food and Drug Directorate) plays a role in the area of drug legislation; the Combines Investigation Act provides protection against misleading advertising; the Post Office provides protection against fraudulent direct mail selling or advertising; the Department of Consumer and Corporate Affairs is involved in the area of weights and measures, and provides protection against deceptive descriptions for food products; and the Canadian Radio-Television Commission regulates broadcast advertising.

The Food and Drug Directorate of the Department of National Health and Welfare along with the departments of Agriculture, and Fisheries and Forestry all play an important role in providing measures to protect the health and safety of consumers. These departments, and the Standards Branch of the Department of Consumer and Corporate Affairs, are also active in establishing products standards and grades. The Central Mortgage and Housing Corporation along with the National Research Council, two federal government agencies, have also helped to establish standards for home building. Governmental agencies such as the Dominion Bureau of Statistics and the departments of National Health and Welfare, Consumer and Corporate Affairs, Agriculture, and Fisheries and Forestry provide information helpful to consumers.

A brief discussion now follows of the role of each department and agency (with the exception of the Department of Consumer and Corporate Affairs which was discussed in the previous two sections) ; this is of interest to marketers, not only with regard to consumers, but throughout every sphere of marketing activity.

Department of National Health and Welfare

The main section of the department which is of particular interest to marketing men is the Food and Drug Directorate. It is concerned with the administration of three statutes: the Food and Drugs Act, the Proprietory or Patent Medicine Act, and the Narcotic Control Act. The first act provides protection to consumers in the sale of foods, drugs, cosmetics and medical devices. Regulation of standards, packaging, labelling, advertising, drug manufacturing, selling and sampling are all provided for under the act. Misrepresentation in food labels, packages, selling or advertising are specifically outlawed. The act also prohibits fraudulent or deceptive promotion of drugs. Furthermore, drugs that present a significant hazard can only be sold on prescription. The directorate also controls the licensing of proprietory or patent medicines.

The directorate contains a Bureau of Operations which is concerned with the approval of all drug advertising materials for radio and television, the examination of labels and advertising materials, handling of consumer complaints, and other matters. A small consumer division is responsible for disseminating information to Canadian consumers and their organizations. In addition, this division obtains feedback from consumers. Recently, the responsibility of the directorate relative to economic fraud in the sale of food (not drugs) was transferred to the Department of Consumer and Corporate Affairs.

On June 10, 1971, the Health Minister introduced legislation to Parliament which placed a total ban on cigarette advertising in Canadian newspapers, magazines, radio and television as of January 1, 1972. Cigarette advertising is restricted to exposure in retail outlets, basic information on vending machines and signs at the plants and on the vehicles of manufacturers. There are labels on all cigarette packages and on vending machines which say: "Warning: The Department of National Health and Welfare advises that danger to health increases with amount smoked."

Department of Agriculture

The department provides a Canada Grade designation which indicates a product quality for a wide range of agricultural food products. The Canada Agricultural Standard Products Act covers the regulation of grading, labelling and package sizes for a broad range of these commodities. The consumers' section of the department includes a consumer education and information service.

The two most important agencies responsible for the grain trade are the Board of Grain Commissioners for Canada and the Canadian Wheat Board. The former, acting under the Canada Grain Act, regulates grain transportation, grade names, Canadian Government grain elevators, licensing of elevator operators, grain commission merchants, grain buyers, grain dealers, grain weighing, etc. The Canadian Wheat Board, by entering into agreements with owners of distribution facilities, tends to bring about an orderly flow of grain through each of the steps involved in distributing the grain from the producer to the domestic or overseas buyer. The Canadian Wheat Board actually reports to Parliament through the Minister of Industry, Trade and Commerce, rather than the Minister of Agriculture.

The Canadian Dairy Commission, established in 1967, has the power to purchase any dairy product and package, and to process, store, shop, insure, import, export, or sell or otherwise dispose of any dairy product purchased by it. Another federal act, the Agricultural Products Cooperative Marketing Act, aids farmers in pooling the returns from sale of their products by guaranteeing initial payments and thus assisting in the orderly marketing of the product.

Provincial government agencies are also very active in the field of food regulation. Included in this labyrinth of controls are milk control legislation which regulates milk prices through milk control boards, producer marketing boards which may set production quotas for particular commodities such as hogs, dairy products, poultry, wool, tobacco, wheat, soy beans, sugar beets, potatoes, vegetables, fruits, seed corn, white beans, honey, maple products and pulpwood.

Department of Communications

The Department of Communications was formed in 1969 and incorporated the Post Office department as well as certain telecommunication powers formerly held by the Department of Transport. The Minister of Communications is responsible for the regulation and control of all technical matters relating to the planning and construction of broadcasting facilities, but the Canadian Radio-Television Commission (described below) is responsible for all other matters. The Minister of Communications, through the Canada Post Office, also affects the distribution facilities of print media — that is, the use of the mails to distribute media in Canada.[24]

A recent Senate Committee[25] recommended that advertising in the Canadian editions of U.S.-owned *Time Magazine* and *Reader's Digest* (together, these two periodicals have over half the consumer magazine advertising market), or on U.S. television stations near the Canadian border, should no longer be treated as a deductible business expense for tax purposes (a condition which already exists for other foreign periodicals), thereby reserving that treatment exclusively for Canadian-owned media.

CANADIAN RADIO-TELEVISION COMMISSION

This commission, established under the provisions of the Broadcasting Act of 1968, has the authority to regulate and supervise all aspects of the Canadian broadcasting system. It is the licensing body for operating a broadcasting station in Canada. It is also responsible for the character of advertising and the amount of time that may be devoted to advertising. The CRTC reports to Parliament through the Minister of Communications. Reporting to Parliament through the Secretary of State is the Canadian Broadcasting Corporation, which is the largest broadcasting network in Canada. Established in 1936, it is wholly owned by the Government of Canada.

Department of Industry, Trade and Commerce

This department is very much involved with export marketing. It includes the Trade Commissioner Service which has numerous offices around the world, promoting Canadian trade; the Canadian Government Travel Bureau which encourages tourist travel to Canada; the Export Credits Insurance Corporation which provides export credits insurance and, in certain cases, long-term export financing; and the National Design

[24] For a complete catalogue of governmental activities influencing the mass media in Canada see Bruce E. Mallen, *Report on Legislation, Acts, Regulations and Controls of the Federal and Provincial Governments which Affect The Mass Media in Canada* (Montreal: Sir George Williams University, 1969), 63 pages.

[25] Hon. Keith Davey (Chairman), *The Report of the Special Senate Committee on Mass Media* (Ottawa: Queen's Printer, 1970).

Council which was established to promote improvement of product design.

The Department of Trade and Commerce also has various operating branches. There is a Trade Fair and Mission branch whose function is to co-ordinate the department's annual programme of participation in trade fairs abroad and of outgoing and incoming trade missions. In 1966, Canadian exhibits were sponsored in forty-five trade fairs abroad, and twenty-six trade missions were organized.

The department's Transportation and Trade Services Branch handles international freight transportation matters and the provision of general guidance to firms seeking entry into the export field. Further, it administers the controls established under the Export and Import Permits Act.

The Commodity branches provide the main link between industry and the department. They search out products and services, the sale of which can be promoted abroad.

There is a Trade Policy Service which consists of the Office of Trade Relations and the Office of Commodity Trade Policy. The former is concerned with the negotiation and administration of trade agreements, endeavouring to find practical solutions for tariff and other problems, and provides expert information on foreign import and exchange controls and other regulations. It also has responsibilities in relation to the export financing facilities for the development of Canadian capital equipment exports. The Commodity Trade Policy division makes detailed export commodity studies and is responsible for international commodity policy work.

The Trade Publicity branch has the function of stimulating interest in Canadian products in foreign markets and encouraging Canadian manufacturers to look beyond domestic horizons. The branch produces *Canada Courier,* an international trade promotion newspaper published monthly on behalf of Canadian exporters to promote products and services abroad. It has a circulation of over 100,000 and is distributed in more than 100 countries. Also published are the magazines *Foreign Trade,* a bi-monthly and *Commerce Exterior,* a monthly. These journals, designed to help Canadian exporters, contain information on overseas markets, tariffs, exchange rates and other pertinent trade data.[26]

In addition, exporters can get expert help from various other sources. For example, all Canadian provinces engage in trade promotion and are ready to assist their exporters. Generally their assistance is co-ordinated with that of the federal government. Further, there is a Canadian Export Association which has been in existence since 1943. The association provides information and assistance to member firms and publishes a number of magazines. The Canadian Manufacturers Association is also a source of reference on all export matters. It maintains several specialized departments concerned with exports. Moreover, it runs

[26] See *Canada Year Book, 1967,* p. 999.

Export Study Clubs and supports a variety of export education programmes. Also, the boards of trade of Montreal, Toronto and Vancouver offer assistance and information on a wide range of export questions.

Dominion Bureau of Statistics

Recently renamed Statistics Canada, this organization is the central source of Canadian government statistics both at the national and provincial level. DBS reports cover all aspects of the national economy, and range from full censuses to a weekly supplement entitled *The Canadian Statistical Review* which contains the most recent economic statistics. DBS publishes a Canadian Government Publication catalogue which lists all such publications, including many hundreds of its own. Moreover, DBS has recently built a computerized information bank containing historical series data on a number of main economic aggregates, and this bank is available for users at a moderate charge.

DBS also publishes a *Market Research Handbook* which provides summary statistics on selected economic indicators; various types of merchandising; advertising and media; housing, motor vehicles and household facilities and equipment; and small area market data. Further, the federal government publishes the *Canada Year Book* which has DBS statistical information supplemented by social and legislative data from other departments of the federal government and from the provinces.

The Economic Council of Canada

This is a council appointed by the federal government to recommend how Canada can achieve the best possible economic performance in the medium and long run. The Council issues an *Annual Review* on the Canadian economy, plus staff studies at intermittent intervals, on various aspects (many of them directly affecting marketing) of the economy.

Department of Justice

Sections 303 and 304 of the Criminal Code prohibit persuasion based on misrepresentation of the facts. Section 306 prohibits false advertising or guarantees of performance (now, see Section 33D of the Combines Investigation Act). Section 324 specifically prohibits the use of the mails for purposes of deception or fraud. Sections 349 and 350 prohibit trademark forgery. Section 351 makes it an offence to substitute in delivery goods other than those ordered and to give a false description of a product with regard to its mode of production, performance, geographical origin, quality or composition. Section 354 specifically prohibits the passing-off of second-hand goods as brand new merchandise.

Department of Transport

Historically the railroads, being a monopoly, tended to be highly regulated in Canada. However, with the advent of other competitive modes of transportation some of this regulation had proved to be too restrictive and in 1967 it was revamped by the National Transportation Act. The Department of Transport and the transportation companies owned by the government are responsible for railways, canals, harbours, shipping, and civil aviation. Pipelines are the responsibility of the National Energy Board. Highway and road transportation falls under provincial or municipal jurisdiction, though in theory the federal government has authority over interprovincial and international highway transportation. The two key regulatory agencies affecting transportation in Canada are:

1. *The Canadian Transport Commission.* This commission has jurisdiction over railway and inland water transportation and air. (It also has jurisdiction over communications by telephone and telegraph.) Perhaps its key function for the marketing man is regulation of railway and air freight rates and inland water transport tolls. Under the new National Transportation Act, railways are, with certain exceptions (for example, "captive shippers"), allowed to set their own rates.
2. *The National Energy Board.* This board's key function for the marketing man is its regulatory powers over the tolls charged for transportation by oil and gas pipeline. It reports to Parliament through the Minister of Energy, Mines and Resources rather than the Minister of Transport.

Other Federal Government Departments and Agencies

There are several other departments and agencies which affect marketing in Canada. They include the Department of Finance in the area of consumer credit, the Department of Insurance with regards to the Small Loans Act, the Central Mortgage and Housing Corporation in the area of housing, and the Department of Fisheries and Forestry for products in these categories.

Sale and Advertising of Alcoholic Beverages

Among the many products that are directly controlled by the provincial governments (see for example, the marketing boards mentioned under the Department of Agriculture), alcoholic beverages in particular come in for some very specific and strict laws with regard to their retailing and advertising. In most provinces alcoholic beverages, when sold in unopened bottles for off-premise consumption, are marketed through retail outlets owned by the provincial government. However, in some provinces beer and wine are sold through regular grocery stores, and similar outlets.

Liquor advertising is also tightly regulated. Table 6-1 summarizes these advertising regulations for the various provinces and media.

CONTRACT OF SALE

The law of sale or sales contract is a crucial legal area for the marketer because of the all-important central role of the sales transaction in marketing. The following discussion should be recognized as a general one, excluding the variations from the main theme from province to province (particularly Quebec). There are basically four types of sales, of which this section is primarily concerned with the first two:

1. *Absolute sales* — the buyer acquires ownership and possession at the time of sale.
2. *Conditional sales* — the seller retains ownership until he is paid in full, and the buyer obtains possession.
3. *Bulk sales* — for example, where a merchant sells out most or all of his inventory in one sales transaction.
4. *Bills of sale* — the seller retains possession and the buyer obtains ownership.

Absolute Sales

Absolute sales refer only to sales of personal (movable) property and exclude real property, consignment sales, barter and work contracts. Unless otherwise specified, the buyer, not the seller, is responsible for taking delivery, and payment is expected at the time of delivery. However, the seller cannot break the contract if payment is late. Goods are accepted if the buyer has received them and acts in a manner which would infer that he is the owner, e.g., if he makes use of the goods. Ownership of the goods passes at the time that the contract is made, if the specific items have been selected by the buyer and are in a deliverable state. This is an important point, because any losses must usually be incurred by the owner even if the goods are still at the seller's location. If the goods are not in a deliverable state, (e.g., alternations are necessary, or the specific items have not been selected out of a batch, or no final approval has been given on goods accepted on approval), then title is considered not to have passed to the buyer until: the goods are put in a deliverable state, the exact items are specified, and the buyer is notified of this.

"Conditions" and "warranties" are stated or implied terms of a contract. A "condition" is a major point, such that if there is a breach of a condition the buyer may break the contract and may in addition sue the seller. Warranties are more minor points in a contract, which do not allow a buyer to break the contract even if there is a breach of warranty. However, a warranty breach allows a buyer to seek

TABLE 6-1 Liquor Advertising Regulations, by Province

MEDIUM	ALBERTA	BRITISH COLUMBIA	MANITOBA
(1) NEWSPAPERS	PERMITTED, brand and institutional advertising only. All ads for all media require Liquor Control Board approval.	NOT PERMITTED	PERMITTED, maximum of 1,250 agate lines without inserts or supplements. Frequency limited to one advertisement per issue.
(2) MAGAZINES	PERMITTED as above.	NOT PERMITTED	PERMITTED, maximum size of one page, without foldovers, inserts or supplements. Frequency limited to two advertisements per issue.
(3) TV & RADIO	NOT PERMITTED	NOT PERMITTED	PERMITTED, brand and institutional advertising in accordance with CRTC regulations for brewers and wineries, but only between 10 p.m. each evening and 7 a.m. the following morning.
(4) BILLBOARDS & POSTERS	NOT PERMITTED	NOT PERMITTED	NOT PERMITTED, except on premises where product is manufactured, on manufacturer's vehicles and on signs at the International Airport.
(5) EXTERIOR SIGNS	NOT PERMITTED, except on premises where product is manufactured and corporate name only on manufacturer's vehicles.	NOT PERMITTED, except on premises where product is manufactured and on manufacturer's vehicles.	NOT PERMITTED, except on premises where product is manufactured and on manufacturer's vehicles.
(6) CAR CARDS	NOT PERMITTED	NOT PERMITTED	PERMITTED, brand, corporate and institutional advertising on cards inside the bus, one card per company in each bus, and not to exceed 56 inches long and 11 inches high. Also signs at airports not exceeding 50 inches in length and 40 inches in width.
(7) DONATIONS	PERMITTED	B.C. does not control donations for charitable purposes by manufacturers.	PERMITTED
(8) CIRCULARS, PRICE LISTS, PROGRAMS	NOT PERMITTED	NOT PERMITTED	NOT PERMITTED
(9) NOVELTIES, CALENDARS (Handouts)	NOT PERMITTED	NOT PERMITTED	PERMITTED, novelties of minor value only as approved by the Commission, showing only the corporate name, or portion thereof and/or its emblem or insignia.
(10) P-O-S Advtg. (Where liquor consumed)	NOT PERMITTED	NOT PERMITTED	NOT PERMITTED
(11) BRAND ADVERTISING	PERMITTED	PERMITTED, with certain restrictions.	PERMITTED, as well as corporate and institutional advertising. May show bottles and glasses but no family scenes or drinking scenes.

Saskatchewan law prohibits liquor advertising or promotion with the exception of public service ads in newspapers by Saskatchewan breweries only. The brewer may include its name at the base of the ad.

Yukon Territory law requires all ads to have Liquor Control Board approval. Ads or notices displayed by electric or illuminated signs, or on any boarding, signboard, billboard or other place in public view, advertising liquor, are prohibited. But, subject to the approval of an inspector, a sign or poster relating to the sale of liquor may be displayed in or on licensed premises. Newspaper ads must not be larger than 8 x 10 in. and must not carry the baseline 'This advertisement is not published or displayed by the Government of the Yukon Territory'.

Radio and TV advertising by distillers is forbidden by CRTC regulations.

This chart was prepared on the basis of information obtained from provincial liquor commissions.

	ONTARIO	QUEBEC	NEW BRUNSWICK*	NOVA SCOTIA**
(1)	PERMITTED, brand, corporate, and institutional advertising only. All ads for all media require Liquor Control Board approval. Maximum size is 1,250 lines. Frequency is limited to one insertion per issue.	PERMITTED, with certain size and frequency limitations. Maximum size is 1,200 lines. Frequency is limited to two insertions per issue.	PERMITTED, institutional advertising only. All ads require Liquor Control Commission approval.	PERMITTED, service and brand advertising only. Manufacturers may now show full bottle or can, with or without glass or decanter, and not more than five brands per advertisement.
(2)	PERMITTED, brand, corporate, and institutional advertising only. Maximum size is one page. Frequency is limited to two insertions per month.	PERMITTED, same as above.	NOT PERMITTED, unless approved by the Commission.	PERMITTED, as above.
(3)	PERMITTED, brand and institutional advertising only, in accordance with CRTC regulations, for brewers and wineries. NOT PERMITTED, for liquor manufacturers, by Federal regulations.	PERMITTED, brand and institutional advertising only for beers, cider and wine. NOT PERMITTED for liquor manufacturers.	NOT PERMITTED	PERMITTED, after 8 p.m. on TV, brand and institutional advertising only, in accordance with CRTC regulations, for brewers and wineries. NOT PERMITTED for liquor manufacturers.
(4)	NOT PERMITTED	NOT PERMITTED, except on premises where product is manufactured and limited to brand and institutional advertising only.	NOT PERMITTED	NOT PERMITTED
(5)	NOT PERMITTED, except on premises where product is manufactured or sold and on manufacturer's vehicles.	NOT PERMITTED, except on premises where product is manufactured and on manufacturer's vehicles.	NOT PERMITTED, except on premises where product is manufactured and on manufacturer's vehicles.	NOT PERMITTED, except on premises where product is manufactured and on manufacturer's vehicles — after approval by the Board.
(6)	PERMITTED, brand, corporate, and institutional advertising only. Bottles and glasses up to 10% of space per bottle.	PERMITTED, in prior car cards only.	NOT PERMITTED	NOT PERMITTED
(7)	PERMITTED	PERMITTED — only scholastic awards and bursaries.	NOT PERMITTED	NOT PERMITTED
(8)	NOT PERMITTED (circulars and programs). Price lists are permitted.	Circulars are prohibited except for company reports, commercial association booklets, etc.	NOT PERMITTED, unless approved by the Commission.	NOT PERMITTED
(9)	NOT PERMITTED, except bottle openers to purchasers of beer.	NOT PERMITTED for advertising or promotional purposes. PERMITTED as bona fide gifts.	NOT PERMITTED	NOT PERMITTED
(10)	NOT PERMITTED, but exceptions may be made during recognized festivals.	PERMITTED, provided such advertising is not visible from outside premises, such as grocery stores and other retail outlets. NOT PERMITTED in licensed premises.	NOT PERMITTED	NOT PERMITTED
(11)	PERMITTED, but only one bottle per brand can be shown.	PERMITTED	NOT PERMITTED	PERMITTED, with certain restrictions.

SOURCE: Marketing, 1 November 1971, pp. 12D, 13.
* New Brunswick, in theory, permits liquor ads which must carry the commission's authorization. In fact, the commission has given no approvals to date and has no plans to give any.
** Nova Scotia also permits production and showing of educational films, provided that credits and announcements are not more than allowed for radio and TV, and that presentations are confined to non-profit and non-commercial showings. The province permits newspaper notices of changes of address, telephone numbers, etc., as well as distribution of factual pamphlets produced by trade associations with commission approval. Newfoundland radio and TV are bound by CRTC regulations. Newfoundland has no regulations governing advertising or promotional restrictions. Prince Edward Island prohibits any form of liquor, wine and beer advertising.

damages from the seller. Proper delivery is usually considered a condition. For example, a buyer may cancel an order if he receives more or less items than originally ordered. One important and implied condition is that a seller owns the goods he is seeking to sell. Incidentally, stolen goods are considered owned by the original victim, even if the third party has bought them in good faith. (This is not true for money.) Another implied condition is that delivered goods will correspond with goods purchased through description of a sample.

The rule of *caveat emptor*, "let the buyer be aware," has exceptions regarding quality and fitness of products sold. If the buyer relies on the seller's expert skill and judgment in selecting goods, the seller is responsible for the fitness of such goods for the intended purpose. Thus, a retailer is responsible if he gives advice on a purchase to a customer, and the customer buys the product because of that advice. Of course, if the buyer relies on his own skill and judgment in making a selection, the retailer cannot be held responsible if the product does not work, or is not useful under conditions for which the buyer wishes to use it. The manufacturer is usually held responsible if a purchase is made by brand name without the advice of the retailer. There is an implied condition that food for sale is edible. Caveat emptor applies if a buyer has had a full opportunity for an inspection and if it can be considered reasonable that defects could have been discovered prior to purchase through reasonable inspection.

An unpaid seller can take several courses of action. He may reserve control over the goods until certain conditions are filled, (e.g., C.O.D.); this is known as a right of disposal. The seller may retain ownership of the goods until they are paid for, if no credit arrangements have been made, i.e., he has the right of lien. If the goods are in transit and the seller learns that the buyer is insolvent he can order the carrier not to deliver the goods to the buyer. An unpaid seller may resell the goods if he has retained them through his right of lien, if the goods are perishable, or if he has served notice on the buyer and has allowed a reasonable time lag for the buyer to respond. If ownership and possession of the goods have passed to the buyer, and the latter refuses to pay, the seller may sue for the price; however, if they have not passed, the seller may sue only for breach of contract.

Conditional Sales

In a conditional sale the buyer gets immediate possession of the goods and the seller retains ownership until the full price is paid. Usually the latter is paid in the form of instalments. The conditional sales contract usually provides for the right of the seller to re-possess the goods in the event of payment default, and the right to retain any payments made up to that point and to resell the merchandise, with the provision that the original buyer is liable for any deficiency between the retail price plus payments already made and the original selling price. In the unlikely event that there is a surplus on resale, such surplus will go to the original purchaser. As a rule the original seller must wait a stipulated amount of time (about twenty days) before reselling the merchandise, and after that period he must give the buyer an option to meet his defaulted payments and recoup the repossessed goods.

In most provinces a conditional sales contract must be registered in order to protect the original seller from losing ownership of goods sold by the original buyer to a third party who is buying merchandise in good faith. If a contract was not registered, the third party takes legal title to the goods. In several provinces it is not necessary to register conditional sales contracts on manufactured goods in order to provide this protection to the original seller, if the original seller's name is placed on the merchandise. Note that this protection does not apply when a manufacturer is selling to a wholesaler or retailer. Buyers and consumers who purchase in good faith from the latter resellers take title to the merchandise and the manufacturer loses his right of repossession. Of course, in all the above situations it is possible that the original buyer can be charged with either or both fraud and damages.

The Legal Relationship of Principal and Agent

Many marketing relationships are of an agency nature, and as such, Canadian laws pertaining to this special relationship are of interest to marketers. This section deals with the more general regulations involved. There are several special provincial statutes dealing with specialized agents such as commission agents, common carriers, auctioneers, brokers, etc. These statutes delve into such arrangements as licensing, bonding, reporting and inspection.

Basically, an agent is a person or firm who represents his principal to third parties. Incidentally, an adult can appoint a minor as his agent, and the latter's action in this relationship would be binding on the former. However, the reverse situation need not be binding.

An agent may be appointed "expressly," "implicitly," or by "necessity." "Expressly" means that he is appointed by an oral or written contract. "Implicitly" means he is appointed because of the conduct of the principal who acts in such a manner as to imply that he has given authority to his agent. "Necessity" is brought about by special circumstances — e.g., a deserted housewife buying goods on her husband's name. A principal may appoint an agent who has acted on his behalf without actual or even apparent authority and retroactively bind a third party. Thus, for example, if a firm sold a principal's merchandise to a third party without actually being the principal's agent at the time of sale, the principal may retroactively ratify that firm as his agent and bind the buyer. Of course, if the principal so wishes, he is not bound by the selling firm's act and need not ratify them as his agent. In order to so ratify, the principal must have been in a position to have been able to have made these arrangements at the time that the merchandise was sold — for example, the principal must have at least existed at the time.

The agent is liable to damages to his principal for any losses brought about by a lack of claimed skills. An agent may not sell his own goods to his principal without the latter's knowledge. The principal may claim any secret profits or commissions made by the agent, and can break the contract with third parties providing such "payola." If an agent acts beyond his authority, he may be liable to his principal for any losses to the latter. An agent can deduct his commissions before forwarding proceeds of a sale and can be compensated for any losses that he has had if they are not his fault. A principal is responsible to third parties for the agent's acts, even if the latter operates with apparent rather than express authority. The principal and agent can be sued by third parties if the agent does not tell the third party of the existence of the principal. The principal must officially notify third parties of the cancelling of an agent's contract, or else he may continue to be liable for the agent's acts.

Part Two

THE INTERNAL ENVIRONMENT:

Marketing Problems
Practices
and Institutions

7

Distribution in Canada

This chapter and the next two deal with the first of the "marketing mix" categories mentioned in the preface and listed below:

1. The variables dealing with channel and physical distribution management
2. The variables dealing with pricing and product (goods and service) management
3. The variables dealing with information, advertising and personal selling

As is the case throughout this book, these chapters will *not* attempt to cover the basic material so well covered in many introductory marketing textbooks. Rather, the purpose here is to limit discussion to those aspects of distribution which are different or peculiar to the Canadian scene.

THE COST OF MARKETING AND DISTRIBUTION BY THE CANADIAN ECONOMY

The percentage of the Gross Domestic Product for which marketing accounts is a most elusive figure to establish. The basic problem for estimating purposes is that not only do the distribution industries (retailing, wholesaling, freight transportation, etc.) generate marketing costs or "value-added" but so do the nondistribution industries, particularly manufacturing. If distribution industries were the only creators of marketing value-added, the estimate would be reasonably simple to develop, since these are "pure" or total marketing industries and hence, by definition, their total value-added is marketing value-added. Thus, one need only use the value-added figures for these industries to discover their marketing value-added, and these are readily available. However, the nondistribution industries' value-added consists of both nondistribution and distribution activities, and the problems of dividing the value-added between these two categories is both difficult, and with the best of presently available data, arbitrary.

Perhaps the most comprehensive effort at developing such estimates was made by Reavis Cox for the U.S. economy.[1] Based on the concepts developed in that work, Table 7-1 is an estimate of the cost of marketing goods (excluding services) by the Canadian economy.

TABLE 7-1 Estimated Cost of Producing and Marketing Goods[a] by the Canadian Economy, 1967 ($ Millions)

	Total Gross Domestic Product at Factor Cost[b]	Non-Distribution Activities	Distribution Activities[c]	Percent of Total Distribution Activities
Agriculture, forestry, fisheries	$ 3,188	$ 2,774	$ 414	2½
Mining	2,212	2,013	199	1½
Manufacturing	11,996[d]	8,517	3,479	22½
Construction	3,304	2,974	330	2
Total Non-Distribution Industries	$20,700	$16,278	$ 4,422	28½
Transportation	$ 2,000[e]	—	$ 2,000	13
Storage	69[f]	—	69	½
Wholesale trade	2,585	—	2,585	16½
Retail trade	4,776	—	4,776	30½
Advertising[g] and marketing research	750	—	750	5
Packaging[h]	1,000	—	1,000	6
Total Distribution Industries	$11,180	—	$11,180	71½
Grand Total	$31,880	$16,278	$15,602[i]	100
Percentage	100[j]	51	49[k] [l]	—

NOTE: The figure is 45 cents rather than the 49 cents shown above for distribution out of each dollar if the advertising and packaging adjustments are not made — see Notes g and h. This 45 cents figure is the one directly comparable with the Cox estimate for the U.S. economy (see footnote 1 below, *Distribution in a High-Level Economy*).

See the appendix to this chapter for notes to Table 7-1.

Approximately half, or 49 cents (45 cents using the Cox formula, where certain advertising and packaging costs are not included) out of every dollar spent on goods of the Canadian economy is allocated to paying for distribution activities.[2] Almost three-quarters of this is paid to the distribution industries themselves — i.e., 35 cents (71½ percent of 49 cents) — with the retail trade accounting for the single largest

[1] Reavis Cox (in association with) Charles S. Goodman and Thomas C. Fichandler, *Distribution In A High-Level Economy* (Englewood Cliffs, N.J.: Prentice-Hall, 1965), 331 pages.

[2] Strictly speaking, Canadian industry creates 41 cents of marketing cost (value-added) for the Canadian market; in addition, it exports 8 cents of marketing costs, and the Canadian market imports 9 cents of marketing costs, so that the cost of marketing that Canadians incur as goods buyers is 50 percent per dollar of goods output; and as sellers, Canadians create 49 cents of marketing cost per dollar of goods output. (See the appendix to this chapter, Notes to Table 7-1, Note i.)

share at 15 cents (30½ percent of 49 cents). However, it should be noted that at 11 cents (22½ percent of 49 cents) manufacturing also plays a major role in creating marketing value-added.

Wholesale trade (16½ percent) and transportation (13 percent) are the other major contributors. The other industries — primary industry, construction, storage, advertising and packaging — account for ½ to 6 percent each, for the remaining total of 17½ percent.

The Cox estimate showed only a 42 percent share for distribution costs in the U.S. goods economy (after adjusting the value-added calculation for trade) versus 45 cents in this Canadian estimate (before adjusting for advertising and packaging). The extra 3 cents of distribution costs of the Canadian economy is accounted for by the distribution industries shown in Table 7-2. It must be noted that the Canadian market is much more scattered and less dense — hence, the greater role required of transportation and trade.

TABLE 7-2 The Number of Cents in Each Dollar Cost Added by Distribution Activities of Goods-Producing and Distributing Industries — Canada 1967, U.S. 1958

	Canada[a]	U.S.[b]	Difference
Agriculture, etc.	1½¢	1¢	½¢
Mining	½	½	—
Manufacturing	12½	14	(1½)
Construction	1	1	—
Total Non-Distribution Industries	15½¢	16½¢	(1)¢
Transportation and storage	6½¢	5¢	1½¢
Wholesale and retail trade	23	20½	2½
Total Distribution Industries	29½¢	25½¢	4¢
Grand Total	45¢	42¢	3¢

[a] Developed from Table 7-1. Note that the advertising and packaging adjustment has been excluded; hence, the 45c figure (compatible with the Cox estimate) is used rather than the 49c figure.

[b] Developed from Cox study (see *Distribution in a High-Level Economy*, p. 159).

Table 7-3 provides an estimate of the relative contributions of industrial* versus consumer marketing. Consumer marketing in Canada accounts for about two-thirds of total marketing and distribution costs (33½ cents of total cost) with the distribution industries accounting for 75

---

* **Industrial marketing** is defined here as all goods marketing excluding consumer goods marketing. Perhaps the most startling finding is that four-fifths of the final cost of consumer goods consists of marketing and distribution costs.

percent of consumer marketing costs, or 25 cents of each dollar of the total costs — distribution and non-distribution — of all goods, industrial and consumer. (Note this table refers to the allocation of marketing costs, not the size of the market itself.) Retail trade takes the biggest single chunk of these costs at 15 cents. Here it can be seen that of the 11 cents that manufacturing contributed to the nation's marketing costs, 8½ cents comes from consumer manufacturing goods, and 2½ cents from industrial manufacturing goods. However, the primary industries and construction add their marketing costs to the total of industrial marketing costs, so that the non-distribution industries play a relatively greater role within industrial marketing,[3] although in absolute terms they still play a smaller marketing role than the one played by consumer non-distribution goods industries (basically, consumer manufacturing).

TABLE 7-3 Estimated Cost of Industrial Goods and Consumer Goods Marketing[a] by the Canadian Economy, 1967

	Industrial Marketing		Consumer Marketing	
	($ Millions)	Cents per Dollar of Total Cost	($ Millions)	Cents per Dollar of Total Cost
Agriculture,[b] etc.	$ 414	1½	—	—
Mining[b]	199	½	—	—
Manufacturing[c]	800	2½	$ 2,679	8½
Construction[b]	330	1	—	—
Total Non-Distribution Industries	$1,743	5½	$ 2,679	8½
Transportation, storage, packaging and wholesale trade[d]	$3,109	10	$ 2,545	8
Advertising[e]	75	e*	675	2
Retail trade[f]	—	—	4,776	15
Total Distribution Industries	$3,184	10	$ 7,996	25
Grand Total	$4,927[g]	15½	$10,675[h]	33½
Percentage[i]	31½	—	68½	—

See the appendix to this chapter for notes to Table 7-3.

Examples of total marketing cost for specific products can be estimated. The total marketing and distribution cost for white bread is at least 60 percent of the final price paid by consumers. For bread alone, excluding the value-added of the industrial portion (flour and wheat), the marketing and distribution costs are probably over 70 percent of the final price. The estimated portion of marketing costs, excluding value-added of suppliers (i.e., consumer goods portion only), is

[3] See the appendix to this chapter, Notes to Table 7-3, Note h.

| Total Economic Output | Industrial Goods Non-marketing Costs (26¢) | | Industrial Goods Marketing Costs (9¢) | Consumer Goods Non-marketing Costs (5¢) | Consumer Goods Marketing Costs (20¢) | | Services Non-marketing Costs (35½¢) | | Marketing of Services Costs (4½¢) |

| Total Economic Output | Non-marketing Costs All Goods (31¢) | | | Non-marketing Costs Service Industries (35½¢) | | | Marketing Costs All Goods and Services (33½¢) | | |

| Total Goods Output | Non-marketing Costs of All Goods (51%) | | | | | Marketing Costs of All Goods (49%) | | | |

| Total Consumer Goods Output | Non-marketing Costs of Consumer Goods (20%) | | Marketing Costs of Consumer Goods (80%) | | | | | | |

| Total Marketing Value-Added (costs) | Industrial Goods Marketing Costs (27%) | | Consumer Goods Marketing Costs Portion of Total Marketing Costs (60%) | | | | | Services Marketing (13%) | |

Total Marketing Value-Added (costs)	Primary Industries and Construction								
	Manufacturing (22½%)	Transportation and Storage (13½%)	Advertising and Packaging (11%)	Wholesale Trade (16½%)	Retail Trade Marketing Costs Portion of Total Goods Marketing Costs (30½%)				
(6%)									

Percentage   10   20   30   40   50   60   70   80   90   100

at least 85 percent for choice beef, 65 percent for home delivered milk, 70 percent for Grade A eggs, and 90 percent for fresh tomatoes.[4] Figure 7-1 shows various relationships between marketing and non-marketing value-added in industrial and consumer goods and services industries.

CHANNELS OF DISTRIBUTION OF MANUFACTURING INDUSTRIES IN CANADA

In order to reach the ultimate consumer and industrial user, products are distributed in myriad ways through a complex combination of marketing institutions and middlemen called channels of distribution. Different products require different channels of distribution. The following outlines some of the patterns that have emerged in Canada.

In conjunction with the 1961 Census of Canada, the Dominion Bureau of Statistics undertook a study, the purpose of which was to show the percentage of distribution of shipments from manufacturing plants by channel level. In other words, the study shows the percent of total shipments in a given industry that a particular channel member receives directly from a manufacturing plant. This study is summarized in Table 7-4.

The two most important links in the channel in the sense that they receive the greatest percentage of shipments directly from the manufacturing plants are (a) retailers in Canada, and (b) other manufacturers in Canada. This roughly reflects the division between consumer goods and industrial goods, respectively. In other words, very generally speaking, industrial goods are usually sold directly to other manufacturers, and consumer goods are usually sold directly to retailers in Canada. There is, of course, very little direct selling to the ultimate consumer, as can be seen from the total for "Households in Canada."

[4] These estimates are made here from data provided in Prairie Provinces Cost Study Commission, *Report of the Royal Commission on Consumer Problems and Inflation* (Prairie Provinces, 1968), p. 145. For white bread: retail margin of 17.2 percent plus wholesale margin of 28.3 percent plus manufacturing costs of 6.1 percent for packaging, .9 percent for advertising and promotion, and 1.7 percent for transportation, equal 54.2 percent. In addition there are the manufacturer's labour and other expenses and profits which are not allocated between marketing and non-marketing. There are also cost of materials which incorporate marketing and distribution costs incurred by suppliers and suppliers' suppliers. Out of the remaining 45.8 percent, at least 6 percentage points (and probably much more) can be considered marketing and distribution costs and can be added to the 54 percent, to bring the total to at least 60 percent. Eliminating the value-added of suppliers (mainly wheat and flour) of 18.2 percent and readjusting the percentage base, a figure of 66 percent for the retail and wholesale margins and allocated manufacturing marketing and distribution expenses is arrived at. To this may be added some portion of the unallocated labour and other manufacturing expenses, perhaps 4 percent, bringing the total to at least 70 percent. Similar estimating procedures were used for the four other products mentioned. Note of course, that the basic data was only collected for the Prairie provinces for 1966.

TABLE 7-4 Distribution of the Shipments of Manufacturing Plants in Canada by Type of Buyer, 1961

Industry	Percentage Distribution of Shipments to Buyers Outside the Ownership of Respondent's Firm								Percentage Distribution of Shipments to Branches of Respondent's Firm			
	Wholesalers in Canada	Retailers in Canada	Households in Canada	Other Manf. in Canada	Govt. Depts.	Others in Canada	Buyers in Other Countries	Through Agt. and Brokers not Identified	Wholesale Branches in Canada	Retail Branches in Canada	Foreign Branches	Branch Plants in Canada
Food and beverage	21	34	7	6	4	5	5	2	10	1	1	4
Tobacco products	82	2	—	6	—	—	1	—	—	—	2	7
Rubber	22	16	—	27	3	5	1	1	20	4	—	—
Leather	12	58	—	19	1	1	5	—	1	2	—	—
Textile	17	11	1	53	1	3	4	1	1	—	—	8
Knitting mills	21	61	—	12	1	—	—	—	3	—	—	1
Clothing	8	81	4	2	1	1	—	—	1	1	—	—
Wood	23	8	5	7	1	10	27	6	8	1	1	3
Furniture and textile	9	64	6	7	2	8	1	1	1	—	—	—
Paper and allied	11	3	—	21	—	4	33	5	9	1	7	5
Printing, publishing and allied	13	24	12	17	6	23	1	3	—	—	—	—
Primary metal	7	—	—	33	2	11	30	—	—	—	5	11
Metal fabricating	20	5	2	28	5	32	2	1	3	—	—	1
Machinery	11	7	1	18	4	26	10	1	11	2	7	2
Transportation equipment	5	36	—	11	11	8	8	—	13	—	1	6
Electrical products	22	18	1	11	6	24	4	—	9	1	—	3
Non-metallic mineral products	18	10	3	20	3	3	2	1	6	—	3	1
Petroleum and coal products	10	4	7	5	1	6	—	—	65	—	—	—
Chemical and chemical products	16	19	1	31	2	10	10	1	5	—	2	3
Total Canada	17	20	3	18	4	10	11	1	9	1	2	4

SOURCE: DBS, Census of Canada, "Manufacturing Industries Channels of Distribution," No. 97-544 (Ottawa: Queen's Printer).
NOTE: "—" means less than ½ of 1 percent.

The basic pattern ranges widely in the different industry group-ings as shown in Table 7-4. The tobacco industry is the greatest user of wholesalers in Canada, reflecting the great need for wide distribution and convenience-buying by the consumer. In other words, the tobacco manu-facturers require the vast distribution system that only a large whole-saling sector can provide. The fashion industries, particularly clothing, knitting and shoe industries, require more direct distribution to retailers, because of the perishability of styles. This is particularly strong in the clothing industry where Table 7-4 shows that 81 percent of shipments from manufacturing plants in the clothing industry go to retailers in Canada. The publishing industry shows a rather high direct-to-consumer distribution system, reflecting in part the ability to distribute its goods through the mails.

Industrial products, almost by definition, show the greatest strengths in direct-to-other-manufacturers distribution. Products offered by such industries as rubber, leather, primary metal, fabricating, mineral and chemical, constitute important inputs for other manufacturers. Note in particular the high distribution of textile industries to other manu-facturers in Canada. This phenomenon is the result of textiles being the key input of the large garment and clothing industries.

Government departments and agencies are important buyers of transportation equipment, as is reflected in the study. The wood and paper industries are two very important Canadian exporters and this shows up in their 27 and 33 percent distribution respectively to buyers in other countries.

In general, the distribution of shipments to branches of the shipping manufacturer is relatively unimportant compared to shipments to buyers outside the ownership of the firm. However, by far the most im-portant exception to this generalization are the petroleum and coal products industries, which ship two-thirds of their volume to their own wholesale branches. This basically reflects the vertical integration of petroleum refineries. Indeed, petroleum refining as a sub-industry in this industry grouping ships 93 percent of its volume to its own wholesale branches. The rubber industries ship a significant amount of their volume to their own retail branches, reflecting some forward vertical in-tegration of rubber tire and tube manufacturers. In a slightly different manner the transportation equipment industries show a high degree of distribution to independent retailers. However, this is basically due to the franchising operations of the motor vehicle manufacturers.

Channels of Distribution — Canadian Examples[5]

STEEL PLATES

Canadian steel mills sell directly to industrial users and manu-facturers, providing the latter groups can meet minimum quantity and

---

[5] Some of the information in this section comes from student research papers completed as part of the requirement for the course "Marketing Channels" at Sir George Williams University. Modifications in distribution structure may since have been effected for some industries.

credit requirements, and are able to order in advance of production. Canadian steel mills also sell to middlemen known as steel service centres. These centres service small manufacturers and maintenance users as well as the large users who need "fill-in" orders. They also import steel plates from foreign sources. The most important user industries are the fabricating structural metal industry, the motor vehicle and parts industry, the ship building and repair industry, the machinery and equipment industry, the metal stamping and coating industry, and the boiler and plate works industry. About three-quarters of the steel plate distribution is made direct from Canadian producer to Canadian user, approximately 20 percent of the distribution goes through steel service centres, and another 5 percent is imported directly by the Canadian user. Included in the 20 percent distribution by steel service centres is approximately 7 percent of imported goods.

ALUMINUM

Of the aluminum produced in Canada, 85 percent is exported. The remaining 15 percent is distributed to Canadian users in several ways. Approximately 85–90 percent of the domestic portion goes directly to the industrial user market through two basic flows: three-quarters of this direct distribution is in the from of primary aluminum which actually flows to extruders before it is passed on to the user in a semi-fabricated state. The other one-quarter is semi-fabricated material (secondary aluminum, which has been semi-processed into sheet, flat-rolled, cable, rod, wire, bars, extrusions, forgings, castings, and other products. Approximately 15 percent of the domestically produced and consumed aluminum moves through independent warehouses. In addition, roughly 15 percent of the aluminum consumed in Canada is imported and these imported goods either move through the warehouses or direct to the industrial user. Sometimes an additional middleman involved on some of the imported aluminum is a broker who may in turn sell either to the warehouse or to the industrial user. The most important user industries for aluminum in Canada are: the building and construction industry, the electrical industry, the transportation industry, the machinery and equipment industry, and the canning and packaging industry. There are of course a range of consumer goods industries that use aluminum; however, the total usage is less than 10 percent of total Canadian consumption.

OIL

Approximately half of the Canadian-produced oil is exported and about the same figure is imported. The exports leave from the west and the imports arrive in the east. The oil industry is vertically integrated: crude oil moves to the refineries and the refineries in turn move the goods along to ultimate consumers, retail outlets, bulk plants, and jobbers. The bulk plants may in turn move the goods to retail outlets, ultimate consumers and jobbers. And, once again, the retail outlets and the jobbers sell the goods directly to the ultimate consumer.

PRIMARY TEXTILES

There are two major types of processors in primary textiles as shown in Figure 7-2. First, there are the integrated mills that perform all the stages (spinning, weaving and finishing) to most of their output. Secondly, converters will arrange to buy from weaving mills, goods which are made in patterns they have specified, or will buy greige goods* and dye or print them with patterns they have designed. The dyeing or printing can be performed either by converters or by contract finishers. Customers of Canadian processors have been, and are potential customers of foreign suppliers. Table 7-5 shows the products foreign

TABLE 7-5 Imported Textiles: Products and Buyers

Customers	Products		
	Yarn	Greige Goods	Finished Fabrics
Integrated mill	X	X	X
Weaver	X		
Knit mill	X		
Converter		X	X
Clothing manufacturer			X
Wholesale jobber			X
Retail jobber			X
Dry goods and clothing wholesaler			X
Large retailer			X

suppliers import, and the type of Canadian firms that purchase these products. Imported items can enter the Canadian market through a number of distribution channels:

1. Export merchant and import merchant
2. Foreign buying office
3. Export agency
4. Subsidiary company or branch
5. Buying and selling trips
6. Trading company (Japan)

The export agency method of distribution is the most widely used in textiles. Such agencies are usually given an exclusive distribution for a region or even for all of Canada, and will usually not sell competing lines. Exclusive regions are not normally granted by domestic processors.

Canadian integrated mills sell only about 10 percent of their volume to wholesale jobbers. However, the wholesale jobbers do perform the necessary function of selling domestic and foreign fabrics to small clothing manufacturers, small retailers, dry-goods and clothing whole-

*Greige goods are unfinished (non-dyed, non-printed) goods.

FIGURE 7-2 Canadian Primary Textiles Industry, Sellers and Buyers

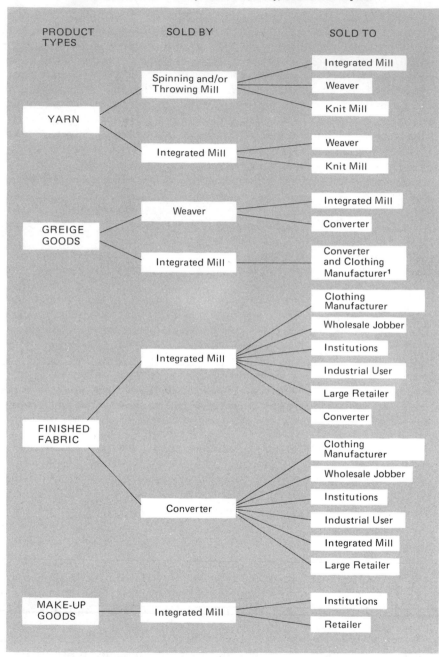

[1] The clothing manufacturer takes ownership of the goods but does not take possession. The greige goods remain at the integrated mill to be finished
at a specified date in the future; the finished fabric is then delivered
to the clothing manufacturer. The purpose of buying the greige goods
in advance is to ensure supply of finished fabric when it is required.

salers, retail jobbers, and to the large manufacturer or retailer if he is in need of a special and/or rush order. Arrangements are usually made between the wholesale jobber and his mill supplier whereby the jobber will not attempt to sell fabrics to the mill's direct customer. Furthermore, the retail jobber and the dry goods and clothing wholesaler will occasionally buy direct from the domestic mill.

ELECTRONICS

There are two basic types of manufacturing firms in the Canadian electronics industry — the manufacturer of component parts, and his principal customer, the producer of end-use products (radios, appliances, television sets, etc.). To a large degree, this producer performs an assembling function, although assemblers also manufacture certain components. Figure 7-3 shows that the component parts manufacturers sell directly to industrial users, to the Canadian assembler, and also to jobbers and through manufacturers' representatives. The jobbers do not restrict their sales to assemblers, but also sell components to other buyers. Despite a recent increase in the number of these jobbers, the method of sale between component and assembling manufacturers is still very direct due to the larger units of purchase and the technical nature of the products.

Large assembly manufacturers normally use their own sales force, and sometimes manufacturers' representatives, to sell their products. However, manufacturers' representatives are used mainly by the smaller assembly manufacturers, and are usually the same ones that are used by the component manufacturers. It is quite possible to encounter a situation whereby the manufacturers' representative is selling parts to an assembler for the component producer, and selling end products for the same assembler. Besides jobbers and retailers, the assembling manufacturer also sells to vending machine companies (who place automatic electronic tube dispensers in retail outlets), industrial users, and repair shops.

The foreign component parts manufacturer sells to the same customers as the domestic component parts manufacturer. However, the manufacturers' representatives who buy from this manufacturer take title to the goods. These representatives are frequently the same ones who perform an agency function for domestic component parts manufacturers. In addition to the above, the foreign assembly manufacturer sells to general merchandise importers and domestic assembly manufacturers themselves. The large jobbers will handle import merchandise from foreign assembly manufacturers, but imports usually move through the domestic assembly manufacturer who performs the wholesaling function for the foreign product. Imports by industrial users are infrequent. And large retail outlets which import a shipment of electrical products usually do so for a specific promotional programme.

Between the component part and assembly manufacturers and a consumer lie several types of middlemen (see Table 7-6) : general merchandise importers, manufacturers' representatives, jobbers, sub-jobbers,

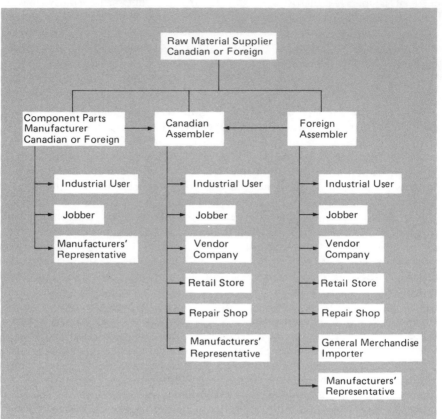

FIGURE 7-3 Sales by Electronic Producers (Canadian and Foreign) to Canadian Customers

TABLE 7-6 Canadian Customers of Canadian Electronics Middlemen

	Customers								
Middlemen	Domestic Assembler	Mfrs' Reps.	Jobber	Sub-Jobber	Industrial User	Vending Machine Company	Repair Shop	Retailer	Consumer
General merchandise importer		X	X		X			X	
Manufacturer's representative	X		X		X				
Jobber	X			X	X	X	X	X	X
Vending machine company									X
Sub-jobber								X	X
Repair shop									X
Retailer									X

vending machine companies, repair firms and retailers. Sub-jobbers are special retailers, usually located in smaller urban centres, who pay a lower price for merchandise purchased from a large jobber and in turn resell to other retailers within the area. Furthermore, the sub-jobbers will also sell to the public. Usually when a retailer's sub-jobbing business becomes large enough, he will break his ties with the jobber and become a full-fledged jobber on his own.

REFRIGERATORS

Canadian manufacturers of refrigerators may sell all of their products under their own brand name and/or sell all or some under a private brand label. In addition, there are manufacturer-distributors in the appliance industry who do not produce refrigerators themselves but sell, under their own brand name, refrigerators manufactured for them by the stencil (private) brand manufacturers. However, the large majority of manufacturers sell some or all of their products under their own brand name.

There are three different types of wholesalers:

1. *The wholesaler* who is owned by the manufacturer, but is actually operated as a separate and distinct company.
2. *The manufacturer's direct sales office* which merely sells a product for the manufacturer.
3. *The independent distributor* who is used mainly in western Canada. Manufacturers using these distributors believe it is not profitable, because of distance and population, to use either company-owned wholesalers or branch offices in that part of the country.

Finally, the retailers selling refrigerators include department stores, chain stores, independently-owned stores, and kitchen specialty shops. The latter sell mainly to building contractors, and occasionally to the contractors' clients as well as to the general public. Contractors can, in some cases, purchase their refrigerators directly from wholesalers, but when they are not in a position to do so they go to the kitchen specialty shop. Contractors may retain ownership of the dwellings in which the refrigerators are installed, or they may sell the dwellings, and hence the refrigerators, to the landlord (in the case of an apartment building), or to occupants.

The large national-brand manufacturers who account for 40 percent of the total volume of the industry deal exclusively with their manufacturer-owned wholesalers who in turn sell about 55 percent to independent retailers and about 40 percent directly to contractors. The remaining 5 percent goes to other kinds of retailers, including the kitchen specialty shop. Manufacturers who produce some or all of their refrigerators under private brand sell a much greater percentage of their output to the department stores. In addition, they also sell some of their output to distributors who in turn sell to chains and independent retailers.

ADHESIVE BANDAGES

The distribution system for adhesive bandages is fairly straight-forward. The four major producers sell to independent drug wholesalers, food wholesalers, mass merchandise wholesalers, industrial wholesalers and hospitals. And in addition, one of the producers sells directly to drug retailers. The drug wholesalers in turn sell to drug retailers, the food wholesalers to food chain retailers, the mass merchandise wholesalers to mass merchandise retailers, and the industrial wholesalers to industry. The large majority of the output moves through drug retailers and food chain retailers. The food wholesalers and mass merchandise wholesalers are usually wholly-owned buying divisions of the large food chains and mass merchandisers.

SPRING MATTRESSES

Spring mattresses are distributed through department stores and furniture stores, and through wholesalers who in turn sell to such institutions as hospitals and hotels. Approximately 25 percent of the output moves to institutions and slightly over 35 percent each moves through department and furniture stores. Marginal amounts move through other types of retailers.

ETHICAL PHARMACEUTICAL PRODUCTS

The distribution system for these products involves manufacturers, wholesalers, retailers, hospitals, physicians, and of course, consumers. The bulk of these products moves from manufacturers to wholesalers to retailers and finally to consumers. There are almost one hundred wholesalers in Canada; however, two of them — one a cooperative and the other a corporate organization — each account for about one-third of wholesale sales. Manufacturers also distribute a substantial amount direct to hospitals which in turn dispense the products to consumers. An equally-large amount moves directly from manufacturers to retailers, and a small percentage moves to physicians who pass it on to consumers. Although they sell the bulk of their volume to retailers, wholesalers also sell approximately 8 percent direct to hospitals. Figure 7-4 shows the distribution of these goods.

NYLON CARPETING

Excluding the sales to the automobile industry, about 60 percent of the output of manufacturers moves through distributors who in turn sell about one-quarter of their own volume to building contractors and three-quarters to retailers. Approximately 40 percent of the manufacturers' output goes directly to retailers. A very insignificant amount moves directly to contractors. However, substantial amounts do move directly to the automobile manufacturers. Approximately 20 percent of the retailers' carpet sales move to contractors and 80 percent to consumers.

FIGURE 7-4 Physical Distribution of Pharmaceutical Products, 1967

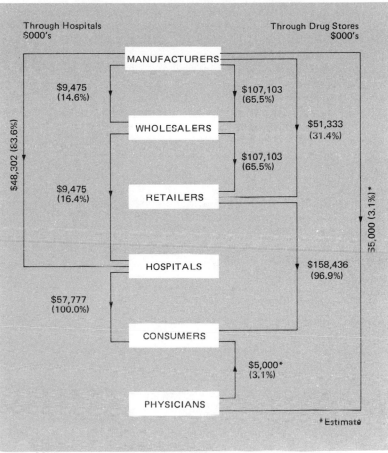

SOURCE: *D.K.K. Canada, 31 March 1968.*

NOTE: The dollar volumes as shown above are based on the price paid by either
          the drug store or hospital and do not include the mark-up or service
          charge added immediately prior to the consumer purchase.

SOFT DRINKS

There are several marketing institutions involved in the distribution of soft drinks:

1. *Company plants* — owned by the soft drink manufacturers themselves, they produce approximately 30 percent of the total output.
2. *Bottlers* — independent businessmen who are franchised to bottle and distribute by one or more soft drink manufacturers.
3. Some of the smaller manufacturers and bottlers use distributors rather than their own fleet of trucks. This is particularly true for the rural areas.

4. An additional form of distribution is through vending distributors who use machine distribution. Actually vending machines are not only owned by distributors: some are owned by the soft drink companies themselves, and others by the proprietors of the machine location.

5. Syrup is sold to wholesalers who in turn distribute this to restaurants and soda fountains. This method is mainly used by the Coca-Cola Company.

6. Retailers are divided into two main categories: *On Premise* retailers (restaurants, bars etc.), which sell their product "open" for consumtion at point of purchase, and *Take Home* retailers or those who sell the product "closed" for consumption at some place other than the point of purchase.

TURBINES

Because of the technical and expensive nature of the product, turbines are usually sold directly by the electrical manufacturer to the utility. However, in the case of smaller electrical manufacturers, use is made of sales agents. These agents do not take title to the product but only act as initial contacts with buyers, i.e., "door-openers," and receive a commission for their efforts.

SUGAR CONFECTIONERY

The marketing middlemen include:

1. *The agency* — if a firm is located in one area and would like to sell in another but does not have an extensive line an agent may be used. For example, a firm manufacturing in Toronto may have an agent in Winnipeg. The agent would have exclusive representation for the product in the Winnipeg area.

2. *The distributor* — this is a firm which acts as an intermediary between the manufacturer and the retailer or jobber. The distributor may handle imported items or local items or both. Some distributors will sell the product under the manufacturers' brand label and others will bag their own product and sell under their own brand. The distributor sells to the major chain stores.

3. *The jobber* — the jobber distributes to service stations, restaurants, corner stores and so on. Jobbers purchase their goods from manufacturers, distributors and importers.

4. *Cash and carry* — a cash and carry wholesale store represents a type of wholesale supermarket for the small store. A small retailer may go to the cash and carry store, purchase his items for a lower price than he would have to from the jobber and take them back to his store for sale.

5. Large department stores like Eaton's and Simpsons maintain *foreign buying offices*. This means, for example, that a resident buyer is located in Britain to make purchases for these particular companies.

6. As a rule, imported sugar confectionery is brought into the country by *import middlemen*. These importers then resell the goods to an agent or distributor.

In the confectionery field the largest volume of output reaches consumers through the jobbers who in turn sell to the various corner-store operations. The next largest volume passes through food chain stores. The jobbers' clientele and the food chain stores together account for about three-quarters of all confectionery sold at the retail level. Department stores, variety stores, specialty stores, tobacconist shops, and miscellaneous outlets like theatres, vending machines, etc., account for the remaining 25 percent.

PHYSICAL DISTRIBUTION

The physical and geographic factor is another environmental consideration affecting marketing in Canada. The country's population, as was noted in Chapter 2, runs in a 4,000 mile east-west direction paralleling the U.S. border. However, its topographical barriers run in a north-south direction, so that mountains, large bodies of water, and forests tend to isolate the different market segments from each other. For example, Newfoundland is isolated from the mainland by the Cabot and Belle Isle Straits, New Brunswick by forests from Quebec, Ontario by forests from the prairies, and of course British Columbia from Alberta by the Rocky Mountains. Further, it has been noted[6] that the average distance to the closest city of 50,000 population or over is 145 miles in Canada versus 56 miles in the U.S. The average distance to the second closest city is 257 miles in Canada versus 87 miles in the U.S. Thus, it is obvious that storage and transportation facilities are of vital concern to the marketing effort in Canada. An efficient marketing system cannot be such without an efficient storage and transportation system.

The various modes of freight transportation divide the ton-miles into the following shares: railway, 41 percent; water transport, 25 percent; pipeline, 24 percent; and truck, 10 percent.[7]

Rail Transport

The railway system is still the principal mode of freight transportation in Canada. It is composed of two enormous trans-continental systems: the Canadian National and the Canadian Pacific railways. The former company is a Crown Corporation, owned by the Government of Canada. In addition, there exist a number of small, regional, independent railways.

Canada has over 59,000 track-miles in operation. In 1969, with over 188,000 freight cars, the Canadian railway systems operated almost

---

[6] By J. D. Forbes, Associate Professor, University of British Columbia, in an address to the First Canadian Marketing Workshop (held at York University, 1 June 1972.)

[7] Dominion Bureau of Statistics, *Canada Year Book, 1969* (Ottawa: Queen's Printer, 1969) , p. 802.

95 billion freight ton-miles. Mine products (almost half being iron ore) accounted for approximately 42 percent of the total tonnage, manufactured and miscellaneous products for about 35 percent, agricultural products (more than half being wheat) for about 12 percent, and forest products (almost half being pulpwood) for about 11 percent.[8]

There have been several developments in railway transportation which have enhanced this mode's service to shippers. Included are the trend to larger and more specialized freight cars; intermodel operations, e.g., cement tube blown from a hopper car to a tank truck; piggyback, express terminals and centralized traffic control; unit trains, i.e., one product moved constantly between two points, like a pipeline; and containerization, which ". . . is on its way in. Canadian manufacturers whose products suit this method of shipping should be taking a careful look at it."[9]

Road Transport

Though the areas that most marketing men will be interested in are well endowed with highways and roads, there are several outlying areas in Canada which have either private roads operated by primary industry companies, or no roads at all. Canada has almost half a million miles of highways and rural roads. The Trans-Canada Highway, which was officially opened on September 3, 1962 (but is still not completely finished), is the prima donna of the Canadian highway system. It is now possible to drive its entire length of some 4,827 miles.

In 1968 there were reported to be 2,787 common motor carriers and over 1,600 contract motor carriers. Traffic congestion in urban areas and government restrictions remain major problems.

Water Transport

All Canadian waterways, including those inland, are open to foreign ships, except for transportation between two Canadian ports. In 1968, over a quarter of a billion tons of cargo were loaded and unloaded at Canadian ports from vessels in international sea-borne and coastal shipping. Wheat and iron ore were the most important commodities in this category.

The National Harbours Board is a Crown Corporation which operates facilities at Canada's nine principal harbours. This includes the operation of wharves, piers, transit sheds, grain elevators, cold storage warehouses, terminal railways, etc.

Canals in Canada, including the St. Lawrence Seaway Authority system, comprise a series of waterways providing navigation for 1,875

---

[8] DBS, "Railway Freight Traffic, Year Ended Dec. 31, 1969," No. 52-203 (Ottawa: Queen's Printer, 1971).

[9] R. G. McGrath, "Transportation In Canada: Containers," *Industrial Canada,* September 1969, p. 16.

miles inland from salt water. Almost 20,000 vessels with over 97 million tons of freight passed through these canals in 1969. The St. Lawrence Seaway, which opened in April 1959, is a system of facilities between Montreal and Lake Erie, which allows 27-foot navigation to reach the geographic heart of the North American continent. In 1969, approximately 4,550 ships carried over 25 million tons of cargo up and another 35 million tons down through the Seaway. 24 percent of this cargo was carried by ocean-going ships and lakers carried 76 percent. Mineral products accounted for 50 percent of the tonnage, and agricultural products some 23 percent. Wheat at 9 percent, coal at 18 percent and iron ore at 25 percent were the three largest single commodities.

Water carriers are beset with problems such as rising costs, foreign competition, toll increases, closing shipyards and strikes.

Civil Air Transport

There are two main airlines in Canada: Air Canada, and Canadian Pacific Airlines. These companies have divided up the world market between them as follows: CP Air serves the Pacific area, Asia, Australia, New Zealand, south-eastern Europe and Latin America, and Air Canada serves Britain, western, northern and eastern Europe, and the Caribbean. Air Canada is a Crown Corporation, owned by the federal government, and CP Air is a subsidiary of CP Rail. In addition to these two main carriers, there are five domestic air carriers licensed to operate scheduled regional commercial air services in Canada: Eastern Provincial Airways Limited, Quebecair, Nordair Ltd., Transair-Midwest and Pacific Western Airlines Ltd. In all, Canadian carriers transported approximately 315 million ton-miles of goods in 1969.

Oil and Gas Pipelines

The Canadian network of oil pipelines is the third largest in the world after the U.S. and U.S.S.R. systems. In 1968, almost 15,000 miles of oil pipelines were in operation. The key segments of the system are the lines operated by the Inter-Provincial Pipe Line Company and the Trans-Mountain Oil Pipe Line Company. The first company carries oil eastward from Edmonton and the second carries it westward from that city. In 1969, there was a total of almost 55,000 miles of gas pipelines. These, however, are not common carriers but are operated by gas pipeline companies who own the gas they transport.

Warehousing

In 1970, 135 firms were reported as engaged primarily in the public warehousing of general merchandise and refrigerated goods.[10]

[10] DBS, "Warehousing (General Merchandise and Refrigerated Goods), 1970," (Ottawa: Queen's Printer, 1972), 13 pages.

This figure does not include firms engaged mainly in household goods storage; nor does it include organizations operating warehouses for members, companies operating storage facilities in connection with their own businesses, small food lockers, cold storage and storage of food, storage of petroleum and petroleum products, customs warehouses, and licensed grain storage. In 1970, the 135 firms had over 163 million cubic feet of general merchandise storage facilities; to this could be added another 17 million cubic feet in household storage and motor carrier firms, for a total of over 180 million cubic feet of facilities for general merchandise. The 135 firms also had 47 million cubic feet of storage facilities for refrigerated goods.

DECISION-MAKING AND ATTITUDES OF CANADIAN FREIGHT TRANSPORTATION BUYERS

Canadian carriers' value-added accounts for about one-eighth of the total costs of marketing and distributing goods in the Canadian economy (see Table 7-1). This is a high proportion compared to other nations, and is a reflection of Canada's scattered and thin domestic market. More to the point, freight transportation is perhaps the most pervasive industry in Canada, in the sense that it is the one which interacts with the largest number of other (goods) industries. It is in many ways the jugular vein of the Canadian economy. A breakdown in the transportation industry would bring several industries to a standstill, and cripple, in various degrees, all other industries, eventually bringing even their production to a halt.

Since freight transportation is such a pervasive and vital industry, a study of decision-making procedures and factors and the attitude of transportation buyers, should be of interest to marketers in all industries. Perhaps the views of those who often know best — the customers — can provide a basis for improving the marketing productivity of this industry, and hence the productivity of all the buying industries, i.e., the economy.

Between July 1, 1970, and June 30, 1971, under the direction of the author,[11] some 500 depth interviews were conducted with freight transportation buyers throughout Canada. Though the predominate representation came from traffic managers, the whole range of executives involved with transportation decisions was included in the sample. The sample consisted virtually of a census of all of Canada's largest corporations (in some cases several individuals were interviewed in one company) and a sample of smaller firms. Almost all industries and regions were included.

The purpose was to detail the decision-making process of the

[11] See Bruce Mallen and Jean François Pernotte, *Decision-Making and Attitudes of Canadian Freight and Cargo Transportation Buyers* (Montreal: Sir George Williams University, 1972) , 50 pages.

buyers and to elicit their general attitude towards the carriers and their specific attitudes towards the carriers' marketing efforts. The following is a summary report of the findings, divided into four sections: (a) decision-making; (b) general attitude toward modes; (c) attitudes toward carriers' specific marketing efforts; and (d) decision-making and attitudes of different buying industries.

Decision-making

ORGANIZATION FOR DECISIONS

The importance of transportation as a managerial function depends on:

1. The share it represents of the total cost of a given product.
2. Its influence on the "marketability" of the product.
3. The "criticality" of the supply of raw materials.

The greater its "criticality," cost share and/or "marketability" influence, the greater importance, status and attention devoted to the transportation function within the organization.

Since it appears that the transportation function is increasing its cost share and "marketability" influence in the average company, more importance is being attached to the function. This is reflected in a number of basic ways:

1. The emergence of a concept of "total physical distribution systems" where all elements in transportation and storage are seen as part of an interacting system in which various trade-offs are required to obtain the lowest overall costs. This means paying more for one activity in order to obtain savings in another which more than compensates for the higher costs in the first — e.g., fast delivery and small inventory. This trend also means that far more sophisticated management tools are to be used — for example, operations research models.
2. The organization of strong centralized traffic departments. This trend ties in with the above move to total physical distribution, as it integrates a number of different functions under the responsibility of the traffic manager, or superimposes a central distribution department over existing traffic, warehousing, etc., departments. Consolidation of shipments in order to cut down costs is one outcome of this trend.
3. In a significant number of organizations, transportation decisions are based on a consensus between representatives from traffic, sales, purchasing and production. This trend is a first step towards an effective integration of traffic decisions as noted above, and a greater recognition of the importance of the transportation function. Transportation is increasingly being tied to marketing, as its cost may have a critical influence on the firm's competitiveness, and thus it is more and more regarded as vital part of the service offered by a manufacturer to its customers.

It must be stressed that, though there is a strong trend towards the integration of physical distribution decision-making, very few firms have actually achieved a high degree of such integration. In a majority of relatively small firms, there is no traffic unit nor even an individual specializing in transportation problems. In such companies, as well as in a number of larger ones, customers control most traffic decisions, and so it is very difficult for these companies to establish and to follow any consistent transportation policy. Further, a few very large firms have passed through the integration stage and have decentralized because of size. In this case, there is usually a central transportation group that deals with corporate transportation problems, and regional groups that deal with the day-to-day operating problems.

FACTORS IN DECISION-MAKING

There are a number of factors which transportation buyers take into consideration in selecting a mode and specific carrier. All of these decision-makers operate within a framework of certain inherent constraints which often severely narrow down the range of choice. These constraints include the location of the origin and destination, the volumes involved, the characteristics of the product, as well as the ability of carriers to meet these constraints (in terms of direct shipment, through rates, points served, special equipment, availability of a siding or dock, etc.).

Besides these constraints, some combination of costs (including a favourable trade-off between transit and inventory costs) and service is the basic criterion for the selection of a carrier. Service includes such factors as reliability, total transit time, pick-up and delivery, damage and claims experience, and flexibility of schedule. Note that many companies are more concerned with reliability, i.e., "getting there at the time you promised to get there," than speed. However, because of the feeling that most carriers lack reliability and therefore make effective planning difficult for shippers, speed is becoming a more important requirement for a growing number of industries.

Very few shippers have formal or written transportation policy statements, although a number do have informal principles that they follow, such as "no run out," "no captive traffic," "not too many carriers," "ship the same day as orders received." However, in large companies, standing procedures are widely used. Two developments that shippers must increasingly take into account in their decision-making are containerization and palletization, both of which have gained widespread acceptance. However, shippers are now faced with implementation problems during the transition period and they look to the carriers to help with such problems.

General Attitude Toward Modes

Respondents had both positive and negative comments to make in comparing each of the basic modes of transportation. However, it was also felt by many that different modes serve different needs and should not really be competing for the same business. In general, transportation buyers felt that marine carriers give very good service, truckers offer relatively good service and railroads offer just adequate service. Pool car service and forwarding agents have a very good image in the transportation industry.

Part of the reason that truckers rank ahead of railroads is that the respondents were ranking the specific carriers they use, and since the choice is much broader in the trucking field, these respondents usually used what they considered to be the best of the truckers. Thus, their judgment does not reflect their opinion of the whole trucking mode versus the railroad mode. Such a comparison would certainly have lowered the rating of truckers.

Certain selected truckers are said to be much more flexible than railroads, easier to deal with and with very competitive "door-to-door" service. Most traffic managers also like road transport because they feel they can keep very close control over the operations of this carrier type. However, it was felt that truckers often fail to make the best use of their flexibility and are frequently paralyzed by provincial regulations, labour problems and poor equipment.

The main complaint about the railroads is that there is a "communication blockage" with the average shipper, which is felt to be caused by their heavy organizational structure, excessive centralization, and so, diminished responsibility of men in the field. A number of respondents stressed that the real problem at the operating level is not the railroads' in-transit performance but their disorganization and slowness in terminals and railyards, or movement from these points to the final destination. This is negatively affecting their reliability.

Though marine transportation offers the lowest rates and usually provides good service, the huge volumes it presupposes involve high inventory costs. Seasonality, weather, damage rate, slow speed and poor pick-up and delivery service reduce the advantages of this mode. Thus, the rate differential is often insufficient compensation for these disadvantages.

Attitudes Toward Carriers' Specific Marketing Efforts

SALESMEN

Carriers' sales representatives can fulfill important needs, according to the respondents. However, they often lack proper training or specialization, or adequate authority and support from their companies to be really efficient and helpful, despite a recent improvement in their quality. A good sales representative can be of critical importance for many transportation buyers and their traffic decisions. The respondents felt that sales calls should be problem-oriented service calls. Salesmen should act as problem solvers for shippers and develop tentative solutions to a shipper's problems before calling on the client, rather than limiting themselves to "order-taking." It was noted that a good sales representative must have enough authority and company support to act as a "problem solver."

PRICING

A majority of shippers indicated no special problems with the carriers' prices. However, a fairly large minority strongly criticized the existing price structure. Their criticisms included the following:

1. Railroads lack a true cost and market orientation to pricing in spite of the recent legal flexibility allowed to them. Their "class rate" or "cubic content" systems are arbitrary and lack an economic rationale.[12] Their agreed-charges contracts require more flexibility.
2. Truckers have far too complex a pricing structure. Large truckers dictate rates to small ones through the "tariff bureaus," in spite of the keener competition existing in this segment of the industry.
3. Steamship carriers are the most cost-oriented, but on many occasions they tend to use a "rail-rate minus differential" approach and lack consistency in pricing.

ADVERTISING

Respondents felt that advertising has very little impact on transportation decisions, particularly "brand" advertising. Informative advertising holds more interest. However, shippers' information needs are too variable to be effectively reached through advertising without too much waste. Nevertheless, there was a consensus that advertising is useful to the transportation industry for its image with the general public. It was also seen as being somewhat useful to small buyers of transportation.

SPECIAL SERVICES

Such services as intermodal arrangements, distribution consulting and site development advice are slowly gaining acceptance in the traffic community at the conceptual level. Some form of site development advice has historically been a railroad company function. However, because (a) small firms feel their decision variables are quite simple, (b) large companies can provide these services internally, and (c) medium-size firms feel there could be a conflict of interest for the carrier, the present environment is not ready for the implementation of these services

---

[12] In considering this particular criticism, certain individuals with railroad experience have stated to the author that technically speaking, class rates are set according to the economically sound principles of inherent value and handling characteristics of the product. Unfortunately, new products are assigned to classes according to often unrealistic and unrevised precedents, while old products are never re-classified except downwards. Rail rates are very cost oriented where volumes from one shipper are large.

on a large scale. In any case, the offering of such services seems to have only minimal influence on most transportation decisions. Intermodal transportation, or the offering of a "total transportation package," seems to be the special service with the greatest potential in the near future.

Decision-Making and Attitudes of Different Buying Industries

The objective of this section is to indicate to what extent each transportation-buyer industry group differs from the general profile established in the other sections of this discussion.

MINING INDUSTRY

Mining companies tend to have strong centralized traffic units because of the weight of transportation costs in the total cost of their products. They are heavy rail users, but competition is now coming from steamship companies through intermodal movements. Reciprocal buying considerations, loading and unloading facilities and adequate car supply are particularly important decision-making factors. The respondents are interested in more flexible agreed-charges contracts, and would like to see more unit trains.

GRAIN INDUSTRY

Given the large volumes shipped every year, transportation is considered an important managerial function. Some of the most sophisticated transportation units are found in this industry. The respondents in this industry are concerned about the problems of car supply and cleanliness.

LUMBER, PULP AND PAPER INDUSTRY

To most pulp and paper companies, traffic management is very closely related to their own marketing effort. Transportation costs have a strong bearing on the ability of Canadian companies to compete in the U.S. market. Thus cost considerations and reliability are of utmost importance in their traffic decisions. Respondents in this industry consider they are subject to "captive" rail rates and feel they should benefit from "public interest rates" as do grain shipments.

OIL INDUSTRY

Again, this is an industry in which transportation plays a crucial role. Heavy use is made of pipelines to the refinery, rail to the bulk plants and trucks to industrial users and retail outlets. There is a possibility that rail will play a diminished role in the future as pipeline-truck intermodal systems are developed. The main railroad problem is the lack of special equipment and poor allocation of such equipment that is available.

CHEMICAL INDUSTRY

Because of the nature of the product, special "safety" equipment, direct shipments (which reduce the competitiveness of marine transport and increase that of road transport) and strong carrier security service are required.

STEEL INDUSTRY

For manufacturers of standard steel products (steel bars, sheets, etc.) cost is the main consideration because of their own competition; thus summer marine transport is a favoured mode. Manufacturers of structural steel elements, because of the non-standard nature of their products, consider the most important selection criteria to be the ability of the carrier to physically handle the product and to provide reliable scheduling; the last factor is important because of the cost of the erection crews who remain idle on the job site if the steel element is not there on schedule. Thus, road transport is a favoured mode for this segment of the industry.

BUILDING PRODUCTS AND GLASS INDUSTRIES

Handling problems are the prime transportation concern of these industries. Thus traffic managers in these industries select the mode or carrier offering the best handling technique and claims settlement, and lowest damage rate. Marine transport is not favoured because of these considerations, though carriers of this mode have recently and are now developing improved handling methods for such products. Truckers have the flexibility required to carry shipments to remote construction sites.

OFFICE EQUIPMENT AND CONSUMER DURABLE INDUSTRIES

These two basic industry groups have a number of common transportation needs, and so attitudes. Transportation is a far less critical function in these industries than most of those outlined above. Thus, transportation activities tend to be non-integrated and there is seldom a specialized traffic unit. The production, product or sales manager is usually the responsible executive. In fact, in most cases decisions are made by customers, who are generally more interested in the service element than in cost. Respondents in these industries basically want "trouble-free" movements and want carriers that can take the entire problem "off their backs." The only important requirements are speed and a low damage rate.

FOOD AND BEVERAGE INDUSTRIES

Since transportation is considered an important element in the operation of such companies, the industry contains sophisticated traffic departments. Many of these companies have developed large and well-equipped internal transportation facilities. They are very favourably disposed to intermodal movements, standardization and fast return of pallets. There appears to be a trend to speedier transit which, despite higher costs, is more than compensated for by lower inventory costs.

MISCELLANEOUS INDUSTRIES

Because too few interviews were conducted in certain industries, some industries have no specific differences from the profile and general attitudes expressed, or there is a conflict of opinion within certain industries, not all industries are covered above. However, there are a few which deserve some attention because of one basic difference from the general profile:

1. In the automotive industry, companies are very large; they "get what they want" and so have few criticisms regarding carriers' service.
2. In the retail industry, the trend is towards increasing use of private truck fleets for both cost and safety reasons. Such firms are more interested in punctuality than speed.
3. The textile industry has achieved little sophistication in handling transportation problems. Basically, customers make the decision, considering speed critical because of fashion perishability; and since most firms are small, they find good service hard to obtain from the carriers.

Summary

1. The greater transportation's cost share and "marketability" influence on a company's products, the greater its importance, sophistication, and status as a managerial function.
2. There is a trend towards a "total physical distribution systems" approach to transportation decision-making and to the organization of strong centralized traffic departments, with marketing and production executives providing these departments with critical information required for decision-making.
3. These are some very basic constraints within which a transportation buyer must operate in making carrier selection decisions. These include the location of origin and destination, the volumes involved, the product's characteristics and the ability of a carrier to meet these constraints.
4. Given these constraints, some combination of costs and services, especially reliability, forms the basic criterion for carrier selection. Formal policies are seldom developed.
5. Different modes serve different needs. In general, marine and "selected" trucks give better service than the railroads. Part of the railroads' problems stem from poor communication with customers caused by a heavy bureaucracy. However, the other two modes also have significant criticisms directed towards them.
6. Carriers' sales representatives in general are of poor quality and do not serve their basic role as problem solvers.
7. Most respondents voiced little dissatisfaction with pricing. However,

a significant minority were most vocal about the lack of economic rationale in the pricing methods of all three modes.

8. Respondents felt that advertising has very little impact in transportation decisions but could be of use in creating a good public image.

9. Carriers' special services such as intermodal arrangements, distribution consulting and site development advice are slowly gaining acceptance, especially the first. However, it is unlikely that the transportation market is ready for these services on a large scale.

10. There are enough differences in requirements between different types of buyers — not only in terms of industries, but in terms of size and sophistication — that a need exists for carriers to adapt their "products," more than they have in the past, to each different market segment.

APPENDIX: Technical Notes to Tables

Technical Notes to Table 7-1

[a] Excludes service, utilities, communications (but see Note g), public administration, finance, insurance and real estate industries. These industries account for approximately 39 percent of Gross Domestic Product at market prices, excluding indirect taxes less subsidies. The other 61 percent is accounted for by the "goods-producing and distributing industries" listed in the table. A small proportion of the goods-distribution industries' output would in fact be distribution or "production" of services. However, it is felt that this effect is offset by the production and distribution of goods by the non-goods industries. The basic format is that all value-added created by goods-producing and distributing industries is so reflected, even if a good reaches the final demand point as part of a purchase from one of the excluded industries. In addition, the value-added of some service industries for services provided to help market the goods of the goods industries, are also included as part of the value-added of the goods economy. This latter point specifically applies to advertising (see Note g). Unfortunately, it was not possible to extend this concept to other service industries — e.g., auditing services provided to the retail trade — because the data are not available. One possible approach would have been to use gross margin rather than value-added for the trade industries. However, that would have included payments made to other goods-producing and distributing industries, (as well as the service industries, including advertising), and since it was not possible to separate these payments, a double-counting would have ensued. Such calculations, if possible, could probably raise marketing and distribution costs on the order of 5 cents per dollar of goods output, i.e., from approximately 49 or 50 cents to 55 cents.

[b] Excluding figures on advertising and packaging industries, these figures are derived from Statistics Canada, *National Accounts, Income*

and Expenditure (Ottawa: Queen's Printer, 1968). However, adjustments are made to manufacturing, transportation and storage. (See Notes d, e and f.)

e Allocation between nondistribution and distribution activities is based on the Cox split (see *Distribution in a High-Level Economy*, p. 159). Distribution has 13 percent for agriculture, forestry, fisheries, etc.; 9 percent for mining; 29 percent for manufacturing; 10 percent for construction; and 100 percent for all distribution industries.

d $610 million for print and outdoor advertising and $1,000 million for packaging are removed from the manufacturing total value-added and placed in advertising and packaging industries respectively. (See Notes g and h.)

e $1,190 million estimated highway and bridge maintenance passenger (versus freight) value-added removed from transportation (air, rail, urban transit, inter-city bus and taxi passenger business). Note that value-added remaining ($2,000 million) does not include the internal transportation costs of the other industries — e.g., salary of delivery truck driver — as these would be reflected in the marketing costs of these industries.

f $60 million estimated household storage firms (and others) removed from storage. Note that the value-added remaining ($69 million) does not include the internal storage costs of the other industries — e.g., salary of warehouse foreman — as these would be reflected in the marketing costs of these industries.

g It is more in keeping with the definition of marketing to include advertising expenditure payments to other goods-producing industries, in particular the printing and publishing industries, in distribution activities rather than non-distribution activities. In addition, advertising and marketing research expenditure and payments paid to certain service industries, to the extent that they are made to promote goods, should be included in the cost of marketing goods. These service industries include advertising agencies, marketing research agencies and in particular the broadcast industry. The total of $750 million is arrived at as follows:

Print and indoor net advertising revenue	$664 million
Less classified advertising	54
	$610 million
Broadcast net advertising revenue	200
Advertising agency revenue	73
Market research and marketing consulting revenue	17
	$900 million
Less advertising for service industries	150
Revenue for advertising industry	$750 million

Advertising revenue and advertising agency revenue is derived from *A Report on Advertising Revenues in Canada* (Toronto: Maclean-Hunter Research Bureau, 1970). Marketing research agency revenue is estimated from Winston H. Mahatoo and A. B. Blankenship, "The Status of Market Research in Canada," *The Canadian Marketer,* Fall, 1971. The estimate of advertising for service industries (non-goods industries, see Note a) is derived from the 16 percent calculation for such advertising of the total budget of Canada's 100 largest advertisers (transportation firms' advertising is allocated 100 percent to passenger marketing, i.e., services industry). This would understate service advertising somewhat, since service firms tend to be smaller on average. A very small portion of classified advertising would be business sector spending, and if possible to isolate, it would not have been deducted. All the figures are gross revenue figures rather than value-added, and so to the extent that the advertising industry pays something to the other goods-producing and distributing industries, there would be some double-counting. Thus, a somewhat smaller figure would be more appropriate. However, the difference, to the extent that it can be estimated, would lower the total cost of marketing by a fraction of one cent (per dollar). Note that the internal cost to the other industries of marketing research and advertising — e.g., the salary of the advertising manager — is not included in the $750 million, as it would be reflected in the cost of distribution activities of these other industries.

[h] Packaging is also shifted down out of manufacturing to constitute a separate distribution industry. Canadian production (value of factory shipments) of packaging is estimated to have reached $1,274 million in 1967 (Maclean-Hunter Research Bureau, *Canada's Packaging Market* [Toronto: Maclean-Hunter, 1970], 32 pages). However, a portion of this consists of firms selling supplies to each other within the packaging industry. It is difficult to ascertain the value of these internal sales. However, either by adding up the relevant items listed as materials used in each sector of the industry, or by adding up these industry sales of items which have the highest incidence of sales to other firms in the industry — e.g., wrapping paper, film and sheeting, twine and cordage, and adhesives — one arrives at a figure close to $275 million; therefore, the non-duplicated Canadian production value is estimated at $1 billion as shown. Note that even this $1 billion is not the value-added of the industry, since the packaging industry makes purchases from other industries. However, to the extent that these other industries contribute a portion of their value-added to packaging, it is felt that that portion should be reflected as part of the packaging industry. Since this other industry value-added is not eliminated from the $1 billion, and since the entire $1 billion is subtracted from the manufacturing portion (see Note d), there is no double-counting of this other industry value-added to packaging. (Some of these industries would be in the primary sector, or import material suppliers; however, the entire amount is subtracted from the Canadian manufacturing sector as it is most difficult to make the separations; nonetheless, most would probably be from other Canadian manufacturing industries, and hence the overall results would be

little affected) . Imports of packages are not included in the $1 billion figure, as the final cost reflects the cost of "Canadian marketing" and not the cost of "marketing-to-Canadians." (See Note i.)

¹ Strictly speaking, this (and all other marketing costs mentioned in this estimate) is the total cost of "Canadian marketing" and not the costs of "marketing-to-Canadians." It would include the marketing value-added by Canadian firms of Canadian exports, but would exclude the marketing value-added of foreign firms of exports to Canada. To the extent that Canada has a positive balance on merchandise trade, "Canadian marketing" costs would tend to be larger than the costs of "marketing-to-Canadians," and vice versa. In addition, to the extent that we tend to have a more marketing-intensive import mix, (a high proportion of consumer goods imports), relative to our export mix, (a high proportion of primary goods) , costs of "marketing-to-Canadians" would be higher than "Canadian marketing" costs, and vice versa.

The conversion for 1967 from the cost of "Canadian marketing" of goods to the cost of "marketing-to-Canadians" of goods would increase the latter by one cent, i.e., from 49 cents to 50 cents per dollar of goods output, estimated as follows:

(a) Net exports of crude materials was $1,651 million;

(b) Net imports of fabricated and end products was $1,614 million. (Both (a) and (b) were derived from *Canada Year Book 1969*, pp. 1,009, 1,011) ; 10 percent was applied to (a) (using Note c: 9 percent on value-added for mining and 13 percent on value-added for agriculture gives a 10 percent average cost of marketing for crude materials since they consist of one-third agricultural products and two-thirds mining products) . 29 percent was applied to (b) (using Note c's 29 percent figure for manufacturing's marketing value-added) . The difference between (a) and (b) marketing value-added is that (b) exceeds (a) by $313 million.

Thus goods marketing-to-Canadians cost is $313 million more than Canadian marketing costs; or one cent more per dollar of goods output. (Value-added rather than sales percentages allocations are used even though import and export figures are sales data, since they represent the cumulative value-added at the point of sale by foreign economies in the case of imports and the Canadian economy in the case of exports.)

Another way of looking at it is to say that the domestic marketing value-added for goods for the domestic market (the cost of Canadian marketing *to* Canadians) , is 41 cents; the domestic marketing value-added for goods for other markets, (the cost of Canadian marketing to foreign consumers) , is 8 cents; and the foreign marketing value-added for goods for the Canadian market, (the cost of foreign marketing to Canadians), is 9 cents. Thus the cost of Canadian marketing of goods is 49 cents and the cost of marketing to Canadians is 50 cents.

ᴶ Since the data exclude indirect taxes because of difficulties in allocating them by industry, for the percentage columns, indirect taxes are assumed to be allocated in proportion to the value-added of each industry, i.e., it is assumed that indirect taxes have no affect on the percentages.

ᵏ Moyer and Snyder, in the only other published estimate of this figure for Canada, arrived at 51 cents for marketing and distribution costs. (See M. S. Moyer and G. Snyder, *Trends in Canadian Marketing* [Ottawa: Queen's Printer, 1967] pp. 2–4, 245–251). This compares to 50 cents (see Note i) for this estimate. The difference of one cent between the Moyer and Synder estimate and the one calculated here is remarkably small considering the completely different approaches used. Moyer and Snyder (1) used trade industries' gross margins rather than value-added and (2) applied their calculations to household demand, rather than total final demand. These two factors would raise marketing's cost. On the other hand, they (1) did not separate the marketing costs of primary industry, (2) did not include the marketing cost incurred by manufacturers in selling to foreign buyers (although this fact is basically neutralized by using the 50 cents estimate, as in Note i, rather than the 49 cent estimate), (3) did not include inter-plant transfers (primarily transportation costs), and (4) used a significantly lower percentage, 5 percent versus the 12 percent used in the calculations here, as the portion of manufacturing's sales going to marketing costs. These four factors would lower marketing costs. The net effect, apparently is one cent more for their estimate on each dollar of goods output. As well, Moyer and Snyder did not attempt to break out advertising, packaging, transportation and storage as separate distribution industries. However, this should not have any net effect, as these costs would be reflected in their manufacturing and trade industries' marketing costs.

There is one irreconcilable difference. The percentage figures applied to manufacturing and sales to arrive at manufacturing marketing costs are different in the two estimates. As noted, Moyer and Snyder used an average 5 percent while the calculations in Table 7-1 are based on 12 percent (actually this was translated into a 29 percent on value-added; see Note c). Thus, the marketing value-added by manufacturing relative to the distribution industries is significantly smaller in the Moyer and Snyder estimate. Even using their basic assumption, one small automatic adjustment to their figure seems appropriate. This is to add an additional 5 percentage points of sales as the marketing costs to household consumers and retail outlets, including manufacturer's own retail outlets, as this represents the cost of selling to wholesalers; and a more realistic assumption is that not only wholesaler's margin must be included as an estimate of cost of marketing direct to retailers, plus retailer's margin if direct to consumers, but that the cost of marketing to wholesalers must also be included.

Different assumptions were used, and unfortunately it would require an intensive distribution cost analysis of the total Canadian manufacturing sector to resolve this question of manufacturing's total marketing cost.

¹ If 10 percent is assumed as the percentage of the "excluded" industries' (see Note a) value-added which can be attributed to their internal marketing costs (admittedly, an arbitrary but not unreasonable figure), plus the $150 million for the advertising of these industries, (as calculated in Note g), and since the value-added of these industries is approximately 40 percent (including passenger transportation) of total Gross Domestic Product at factor cost, then the total cost of marketing by the economy (*both* goods and services) is 33½ cents per dollar of total output: (.6 × 49 cents for goods plus .4 × 10 cents for services). As in Note i, indirect taxes are assumed not to affect results.

Technical Notes to Table 7-3

ᵃ Total of both derived from Table 7-1.

ᵇ Agriculture, mining and construction marketing costs allocated 100 percent to industrial marketing.

ᶜ 55 percent of manufacturing value-added considered industrial and 45 percent consumer. This is based on calculations estimated from DBS, *Census of Canada* "Manufacturing Industries Channels of Distribution," No. 97-544. Since this allocation is originally based on sales rather than value-added, it could be argued that the percentages to be applied to divide value-added may be different than the ones derived from sales figures. Specifically, consumer manufacturing may have a smaller percentage than 45 percent as above, because standing closer to the ultimate market it contains a high degree of the value-added in its gross sales of industrial goods manufacturers. Thus the 55 percent share for industrial marketing should be higher. However, a check of the value-added by different manufacturing industries does not bear this out. For example, though no manufacturing industry is entirely consumer or industrial (hence the need for this estimation of the value-added split), predominantly consumer industries, like furniture and clothing, have in practice higher value-added percentages than their prime industrial input industries of wood and textiles respectively. The one basic exception is the tobacco, food and beverage industries category which has a low percentage value added, and hence may somewhat inflate the share of consumer manufacturing when allocated on the basis of sales shares as done here.

A 4:1 ratio (consumer:industrial) in relative marketing cost percentages was assumed, using the cost ratio of Moyer and Snyder in their calculations of sales to industrial buyers versus sales to retail outlets. This ratio was applied in such a way that total marketing costs of manufacturing would be equal to the total calculation in Table 7-1. This required a 12½ percent application to industrial manufacturing value-added and a 50 percent application to consumer manufacturing value-added. (The latter percentage is about the same as 17½ percent of sales cost of internal marketing for consumer manufacturers.)

ᵈ Fifty-five percent of transportation, storage, packaging and wholesale trade costs were assumed to be a cost of industrial marketing and 45 percent of consumer marketing. This is based on the same split as in Note c and is also the same split in which DBS 1967 wholesale statistics are divided.

ᵉ Ten percent of advertising and marketing research value-added was considered industrial, and 90 percent, consumer.

e* ¼ cent.

ᶠ Retail trade allocated 100 percent to consumer marketing.

ᵍ This represents 27 percent of the total value-added ($18,606 million) of the industrial goods economy.

ʰ This represents 80 percent of the total value-added of consumer goods distribution and non-distribution activities using the allocations described in Notes c, d and e — i.e., $10,715 million marketing cost out of a total $13,434 million, for the "consumer goods economy," (not to be confused with the GNE figures for personal expenditures on goods, as these figures do not subtract the value-added of industrial goods, much of which, excluding investment and government goods, finds its way into the GNP through personal expenditure on goods).

ⁱ Extrapolating from Note 1, Table 7-1, consumer goods marketing accounts for 60 percent of total marketing costs of all goods and services by the Canadian economy, or 20 cents for each dollar of total output of all goods and services; industrial goods marketing, 27 percent or 9 cents; and the marketing of services, 13 percent or 4½ cents.

8

Retailing in Canada

THE MAGNITUDE OF CANADIAN RETAILING

The retail sector is of prime importance to both the consumer marketer and the economy in general. There are over 150,000 stores in Canada employing close to a million people (about 12 percent of the Canadian labour force) and moving $31 billion, or 35 percent of the economy, through their doors. This is expected to reach $36.5 billion in 1974,[1] and $40 billion by 1981.[2] Sixty percent of personal expenditures are punched through the cash registers of Canadian retailers. Though the retailing industry contributes approximately 9 percent of the total value-added of the economy (this figure excludes from its sales, among other things, the cost of its purchases from its suppliers), in fact, four times this amount moves through its doors. This is the institution to which mass manufacturers of consumer goods must look in order to get distribution in the Canadian market.

Retailing's Vital Statistics

Table 8-1 summarizes the key retailing statistics of the 1966 Census of Canada. The over $22.5 billion of sales in that year is the end result of an average annual growth rate of 6 percent (4 percent in "real" terms) over 40 years; or in physical terms, retailing is "5 times larger than it was 4 decades ago."[3] As one would expect, Ontario and Quebec account for the majority of store and sales volume, with a combined total of almost two-thirds of Canada's stores and retail trade. The western provinces account for another one-quarter of retailing and the Atlantic provinces, for about one-tenth. Examination of retailing by trade group reveals the large share of the retailing dollar going to food stores and automotive outlets which together account for over half of the retailing dollar. Though not shown in the table, the food group had

[1] *Financial Post Survey of Markets, 1970* (Toronto: Maclean-Hunter, 1970), p. 42.
[2] John Fell, "Growth Rate in Retailing Expected to Slow in 1970's," *Financial Post*, 3 June 1972, p. 16.
[3] Moyer and Snyder, *Trends in Canadian Marketing* (Ottawa: Queen's Printer, 1967), p. 67.

TABLE 8-1 Key Retailing Statistics, 1966

	Number of stores	%	Sales Volume ($000,000)	%
By Province				
Newfoundland	4,779	3.1	405,607.4	1.8
P.E.I.	906	.6	107,641.5	.5
Nova Scotia	6,388	4.2	752,988.9	3.3
New Brunswick	5,123	3.3	594,806.3	2.6
Quebec	46,980	30.6	5,882,110.8	26.0
Ontario	51,119	33.3	8,625,423.0	38.2
Manitoba	6,497	4.3	1,006,479.8	4.4
Saskatchewan	7,464	4.9	1,046,646.8	4.6
Alberta	10,182	6.6	1,758,076.4	7.6
British Columbia	13,948	9.1	2,462,828.5	11.0
Total	153,620	100.0	22,686,418.2	100.0
By Organization Form				
Individual proprietors	103,341	67.27	5,703,137.3	25.14
Partnerships	11,744	7.64	1,197,881.8	5.28
Corporations	35,956	23.41	14,738,380.3	64.96
Cooperatives	813	.58	251,148.9	1.11
Other	1,686	1.10	795,869.9	3.51
Total	153,620	100.00	22,686,418.2	100.00
By Trade Group				
Food group	46,220	30.0	5,905,358.2	26.0
General merchant group	9,231	6.0	3,626,300.4	16.0
Automotive group	36,262	23.6	6,943,448.1	30.5
Apparel and accessories group	19,816	13.0	1,625,415.4	7.2
Hardware and home furnishings	15,921	10.4	1,480,774.2	6.5
Other retail groups	26,170	17.0	3,105,121.9	13.8
Total	153,620	100.0	22,686,418.2	100.0
By Size of Business (Sales)				
Less than $10,000	15,530	10.11	79,436.0	.35
$10,000 – $29,999	36,149	23.53	689,501.3	3.04
$30,000 – $49,999	23,883	15.55	937,133.1	4.13
$50,000 – $99,999	35,338	23.00	2,500,922.2	11.02
$100,000 – $199,999	23,072	15.02	3,197,145.7	14.09
$200,000 – $499,999	12,491	8.13	3,742,603.0	16.49
$500,000 – $999,999	3,869	2.52	2,681,858.1	11.82
$1,000,000 and over	3,287	2.14	8,857,817.8	39.06
Total	153,620	100.00	22,686,418.2	100.00
By Number of Persons Employed				
1	52,852	34.40	1,258,661.0	5.55
2	34,122	22.21	1,816,418.4	8.01
3	19,920	12.97	1,655,039.7	7.29
4	12,514	8.15	1,426,557.6	6.29
5	8,204	5.34	1,173,173.5	5.17
6 – 10	15,555	10.13	3,426,398.5	15.10
11 – 15	4,060	2.64	1,722,172.5	7.59
16 – 20	1,866	1.21	1,183,218.2	5.22
21+	4,526	2.95	9,024,778.7	39.78
Total	153,620	100.00	22,686,418.2	100.00

TABLE 8-1 Key Retailing Statistics, 1966 (concluded)

	Number of stores	%	Sales Volume ($000,000)	%
By Number of Store Units Owned				
Single stores	134,281	87.0	14,022,471.9	61.81
Two stores	4,781	3.1	861,324.7	3.80
Three stores	1,602	1.4	322,779.5	1.42
Department and chain stores	12,956	8.5	7,479,842.1	32.97
Total	153,620	100.0	22,686,418.2	100.00

SOURCE: *Developed from* 1966 Census of Canada, *vol. VI "Retail Trade."*
NOTE: Columns may not add to totals because of rounding.

an average 18 percent gross profit (1961) and the automotive group, 21 percent gross profit in the same year. Though the general merchandise trade group showed a relatively small number of stores it did account for almost one-sixth of the retailing dollar. This group includes the department stores* and as such would reflect a relatively high average sale per store. The average gross profit for this group was 31.3 percent (1961). Hardware and home furnishings showed about the same gross profit as the general merchandising group, and apparel and accessories had a slightly higher average gross profit at 33.5 percent (1961). The overall gross profit for retailing in the same year was 27 percent. (See the next section for a more detailed discussion on operating ratios.)

In analyzing the 1930–61 data on market share by kind of retail business, the outstanding trends are these:

A marked rise in the share of the market held by automobile dealers and filling stations; a sharp decline in the market share of most omnibus outlets such as department stores, general stores, and general merchandise stores, and a moderate but unmistakable decline in the position of stores dealing in footwear and apparel.[4]

Apparently, automobile dealers owe their performance to the fact that the strong growth in automobile demand has been served almost solely by their outlets. Department stores have suffered from pre-retailing, the suburban shift and relative shift of expenditures to "non-department store type" merchandise. Grocery and combination stores have also increased their share, because of their increased sales of non-foods and increased share of the food market — this, in spite of the relatively lower share of income spent on food.

Single, independent retail outlets still accounted for the vast majority of stores, almost 90 percent, and the majority of retail sales, 62

* **A department store** is defined as a retail establishment carrying a general line of merchandise, operating with separate departments integrated under a single management.
[4] Moyer and Snyder, *Trends in Canadian Marketing*, p. 82.

percent. (This retail sales share remained at 62 percent in 1971.) Their staying power, as an institution, is derived from the personal service they can provide and in the inherent strengths of "ownership-management." However, the department and chain stores, with only 8.5 percent of store units, accounted for one-third of all retail sales. This reflects an important trend towards retail trade concentration, because in 1951, department stores and chains accounted for only 16.7 percent of total retail sales, and had 5 percent of the stores. However, as noted, the department stores *per se* have had a steadily declining share of total retail sales since 1933.[5]

The increase of market share by chain stores was almost totally at the expense of the single, independent store, which had some 78 percent of total retail sales in 1951. A further indication of this concentration trend, which has been evident at least since 1930, is the fact that in 1951, stores with sales of over half a million accounted for 1.75 percent of total stores and 34 percent of total sales volume. In 1961, these figures moved up to 3 percent of total stores and 43 percent of total sales, and in 1966, the figures stood at 4.67 percent of stores and 51 percent of sales.

This fact is again re-emphasized and reflected in an analysis of stores by the number of persons employed: in 1951, stores with twenty or more employees accounted for slightly under 2 percent of total stores and for about 23.5 percent of sales. In 1961, stores with this many employees accounted for about 2.5 percent of total stores and a significant 37 percent of total sales, and in 1966, for 3 percent of stores and 40 percent of sales.

In 1970, the Dominion Bureau of Statistics[6] reported that there were 661 corporate chains* (excluding department stores) in the country, with 15,156 stores and sales of $7.75 billion. Forty-five percent of the sales volume came from the food chains, which had 3,063 stores. The 661 chains included 189 local, 274 provincial, and 198 regional or national chains. These latter chains contributed 57 percent of total chain sales. Thirty-one chains have 100 units or more, and they accounted for 60 percent of sales. Other retail fields with a large number of chains include: shoe stores, variety stores, family clothing, women's ready-to-wear, drug stores, men's clothing stores, and service stations.

Chain operations are playing a most important role in Canadian

---

[5] M. S. Moyer, "An Exploration in Institutional Ecology," *Canadian Marketer* 6 (Winter 1971) , pp. 15-18. For the four years to 1975, department stores are expected to increase their sales by approximately 10 percent per annum in current dollars. However, the outlook appears more pessimistic after 1975 because of the possibility of overstoring becoming a widespread factor nationally; see John Robinson, "The Department Store Industry in Canada," *Research Report* (Montreal: Morgan, Ostiguy and Hudon, Inc., September, 1971) , 12 pages.

[6] Dominion Bureau of Statistics, "Retail Chain Stores 1970," No. 63-210 (Ottawa: Queen's Printer) .

* A **chain** is an organization operating four or more retail stores in the same kind of business under the same legal ownership.

retailing. However, two authors feel only mildly optimistic about their future:

> If the corporate chain becomes an even more important institution in Canada's marketing system, its displacement of other retailing forms will be gradual and moderate. Chain stores will advance in selected trades rather than across the broad front of Canadian retailing, and much of this growth will originate in shopping centres and in new areas of urban development. This rate of growth in chain store sales will hinge to an important degree on the speed and successes with which variety chains and food chains reach into new fields of merchandise and provide services not usually vended "over the counter." Finally, the future of the chain store will be shaped and perhaps circumscribed by the confrontation between [the] corporate chain and its closest imitator, the voluntary chain.[7]

One-third of total grocery and combination sales and almost 60 percent of independent grocery and combination sales took place in voluntary group stores in 1969.[8] Most (82 percent) buy at least one-half of their purchases from the group wholesaler (of which there were 72 in 1969). Average annual store sales of these firms are also growing at a significant rate. Thus, the manufacturer must recognize that to sell to independents in the food field, he must in fact deal with sophisticated voluntary or cooperative chain operations to reach half of this market. The same may be said of the drug store independents, where 67 percent of their sales took place in voluntary chains in 1968. Sixty-eight percent of these drug stores made over half of their purchases from the group wholesaler. Independent hardware stores and variety stores also qualify for this warning. The first moved 70 percent of their sales through the voluntary group arrangement, and the second, 44 percent. Seventy-five percent of these hardware stores and 84 percent of the variety stores made over half of their purchases from the group wholesaler.

Operating Ratios in Canadian Retailing

In general, Canadian retailers' ratios fared reasonably well in comparison to the economy. In 1969,[9] retailer's percentage profit (before tax) on net worth was 12.1 percent versus 14.1 percent for all manufacturing; 10.1 percent return (before tax) on net worth plus long-term debt and debt due shareholders, versus 11.0 percent; 2.4 percent profit (before tax) on total revenue (not to be confused with net margin) versus

---

[7] Moyer and Snyder, *Trends in Canadian Marketing*, p. 148.
[8] DBS, "Voluntary Groups, 1968 and 1969," No. 63-215 (Ottawa: Queen's Printer). A **voluntary chain** can be defined as a group of independent retailers franchised by a single wholesaler.
[9] DBS, "Corporation Financial Statistics," No. 61-207 (Ottawa: Queen's Printer, 1970) and Canadian Imperial Bank of Commerce, "Selected Corporate Ratios, 1969," *Commercial Letter*, May-June 1972, pp. 4-7.

6.7 percent; an average collection period of 19 days versus 44 days; a ratio of 6.9 times sales to inventory versus 5.4 times; and a current ratio of 1.6 versus 1.7.

However, retail productivity has lagged well behind the economy as a whole over the years.[10] Between 1957 and 1967, output per employed person in retail trade increased by .9 percent per year compared to 2.6 percent for the economy as a whole. The differences have been attributed to: a shortening of hours worked; a less experienced, less educated and younger work force; a lower capital stock invested per person; and a shift to suppliers of high potential productivity functions such as packaging and labelling. As will be noted in the later comparative discussion of U.S.–Canada retailing, there appears to be less opportunity to apply labour-saving technology and to achieve economies of scale in the retail industry. However, the drive to make the industry more efficient goes on, as noted in the last section of this chapter, entitled "Future Developments."

Table 8-2 provides 1969 ratios for various retail trades. These figures are useful to the retailer who wishes to compare his performance to the average in his type of retail trade. The variations between the different retail trades will, of course, reflect the different product mixes and nature of the business. Motor vehicle dealers, food stores and tobacconists have the highest ratio of cost of sales to sales, i.e., the lowest gross margin, versus the very high gross margins of such retail trades as book stores, florists and jewellery stores. Food stores and florists, given their perishable products, have a very high inventory turnover compared to men's clothing stores and jewellery stores. The latters' turnover of 2.9 means that it takes an average of four months until a piece of jewellery is sold. The florist sells his product in about ten days. Furniture and jewellery stores, both dealing in expensive items, have long collection periods, as do fuel dealers. Variety stores show the highest profit on total revenue (not to be confused with net margin) versus motor vehicle dealers who see less than ½ cent profit (before tax) on each $1.00 of revenue. Perhaps the most important ratio is profit on equity — often called return-on-investment — as this is the ultimate test of a business's performance to its owners. Variety stores had the highest ratio, with a 21.1 percent before tax profit on equity versus 12.1 percent for total retail trade, and 5.5 percent return for the poorest performer — motor vehicle dealers.

Table 8-3 presents key operating ratios for selected retail chain stores and independent businesses. All seem to fit a similar pattern except food retailing which is a high turnover, low gross margin operation. Non-food retailing stock turns range from 1⅔ for piece good chains to 4⅓ for women's ready-to-wear and variety chains. The chains generally show a better performance than independent outlets. Gross margin of non-food retailing ranges from 28 percent on sales for independent family wear

---

[10] Economic Council of Canada, *Patterns of Growth* (Ottawa: Queen's Printer, 1970) , pp. 29-34.

TABLE 8-2 Selected Corporation Ratios By Type of Retail Trade, 1969

	Cost of Sales to Sales %	Sales to Inventory %	Collection Period — Days	Current Assets to Current Liabilities	Profit (b.t.) on Capital %	Profit (b.t.) on Equity %	Profit (b.t.) on Total Revenue
Food stores	80.4	16.6	4.5	1.5	10.8	13.9	2.1
Department stores	67.3	5.9	18.7	1.8	9.2	10.3	3.1
Variety stores	66.7	5.5	19.8	2.2	15.4	21.1	6.5
General merchandise	75.4	4.8	23.4	2.5	11.7	14.1	3.7
Auto accessories and parts	71.1	6.5	40.4	1.6	8.4	9.9	2.4
Gasoline service stations	77.7	17.7	15.4	1.2	8.8	12.2	1.9
Motor vehicle dealers	88.4	6.7	13.6	1.2	3.9	5.5	.4
Motor vehicle repair shops	72.6	11.9	32.2	1.2	13.2	16.3	3.6
Shoe stores	61.5	4.5	8.4	1.6	15.0	16.0	4.0
Men's clothing stores	67.1	3.3	30.7	2.2	9.4	10.5	4.1
Women's clothing stores	65.8	6.0	36.0	1.9	13.5	14.7	4.2
Dry goods stores	67.0	4.1	25.0	2.0	12.4	13.7	3.6
Hardware stores	71.2	4.1	29.9	2.5	8.7	9.8	3.3
Furniture stores	70.6	5.0	53.5	1.7	8.7	9.6	2.4
Electrical appliances	76.7	4.0	25.4	1.1	12.8	14.7	1.5
Drug stores	67.0	4.9	9.5	2.0	14.6	16.5	4.3
Book and stationery stores	57.3	5.0	130.6	2.7	10.6	14.9	5.3
Florists	48.8	34.9	24.7	.9	9.2	12.5	2.4
Fuel dealers	69.1	14.7	62.8	1.3	8.2	9.2	3.3
Jewellery stores	56.0	2.9	53.6	2.1	4.2	15.3	6.4
Tobacconists	80.2	10.0	3.8	1.2	10.3	10.6	1.2
Other retail trade	72.2	5.3	23.5	1.5	10.7	12.5	3.2
Total	76.5	6.9	18.9	1.6	10.1	12.1	2.4

SOURCE: Statistics Canada, "Corporation Financial Statistics, 1969," No. 61-207 (Ottawa: Queen's Printer, pp. 232-35.

TABLE 8-3 Key Operating Ratios for Selected Retail Chain Stores and Independent Businesses

	DBS Cat. No.	Year	Stock Turn	Gross Margin	Net Profit B.I.T.
Chain Stores					
Clothing	63-401	1964			
Children's wear	"	"	3.16	33.08	3.68
Family wear	"	"	3.74	33.59	3.42
Men's wear	"	"	2.71	33.11	2.38
Piece goods	"	"	1.62	37.36	2.74
Shoe	"	"	2.26	37.64	2.82
Women's ready-to-wear	"	"	4.35	36.42	4.70
Drug	63-402	1965	3.37	33.08	3.75
Food	63-403	1966	14.01	21.33	4.13
Variety	63-405	1964	4.34	36.24	7.38
Independent Business Incorporated					
Men's and boys' wear	63-406	"	3.14	31.09	2.75
Women's wear	"	"	3.71	33.05	2.75
Children's and infants' wear	"	"	2.72	30.58	2.68
Family wear	"	"	2.43	28.06	4.17
Family shoe stores	"	"	2.12	34.13	3.35
Drug stores	63-407	"	2.94	34.57	6.43

SOURCE: *Selected DBS publications on operating ratios.*

stores to 37 percent for chain shoe stores. Net profit before income tax of non-food retailers ranges from 2.38 percent on sales for men's wear chain retailers to 7.4 percent on sales for variety chains.

In 1969 and 1970, data concerning gross margin was collected for the first time in the annual chain survey.[11] Information was available for only five major chain groups for 1970:

	Gross margin
Grocery and combination stores	22.7%
Variety stores	30.5%
Drug stores	36.3%
Women's clothing stores	36.4%
Shoe stores	39.9%

Compared to the chain store data shown in Table 8-3, variety stores show a substantial drop in gross margin, drug and shoe chains are up somewhat, while food and women's clothing show a stable gross margin.

Data published by the *Financial Post*[12] show that Canadian food chains made a small fraction of a percentage point more than their U.S. counterparts when net profit is taken as a percentage of sales. They made slightly less than all retail establishments taken together, and substantially less than all manufacturing.

On the basis of profit as a percentage of total assets employed

[11] DBS, "Retail Chain Stores 1970," p. 11.
[12] *Financial Post,* 29 April 1967, p. 17.

in the business, however, they made less than chains in the U.S. and only slightly more than all retailing establishments and manufacturing. In profit as a percentage of equity, i.e., of common and preferred stock and retained earnings, Canadian food chains have been in line with U.S. chains but, because of a sharp drop in the U.S. return, have more recently tended to exceed U.S. chains by about one percentage point. They are slightly below all Canadian retailing and slightly above Canadian manufacturing. Table 8-4 gives individual 1966 figures for five Canadian chains.

TABLE 8-4 Selected Ratios for Five Canadian Food Chain Stores

Store	Profit ratios (%)		
	Profit/ Sales	Profit/ Equity	Profit/ Total Assets*
Atlantic and Pacific	1.85	9.81	7.71
Dominion Stores	2.07	15.92	10.81
Loblaw Groceterias	1.17	14.66	5.10
Safeway	2.05	12.05	9.56
Steinberg's	1.37	9.06	3.59

SOURCE: Clarkson, Gordon & Co. report to joint Parliamentary committee on consumer credit. Reported in Financial Post, 29 April 1967, p. 17.

* To compute this ratio, profit was adjusted by adding back interest paid on debts.

1971 Retail Trade

1971 retail sales in Canada were over $30 billion. Table 8-5 shows the breakdown of the retailing industry by type of business, with grocery and combination stores taking the lead at almost $7.3 billion, and department stores second (excluding automotive business), with $3.2 billion of sales.

Table 8-6 shows the breakdown by province. Any distribution of selected kinds of stores by province tends to cluster around the average of the total sales by province, with, however, some exceptions. For example, Newfoundland tends to have a relatively low "clothing store" share; Prince Edward Island and Nova Scotia, a low hardware store share; New Brunswick, a high furniture share; Quebec, a high furniture store and clothing store share (and the latter is reflected visually in the sophisticated dress of men and women walking in downtown Montreal); Ontario, a low hardware store share; the Prairies a low clothing store share, but relatively high hardware store share, particularly in Saskatchewan; and British Columbia a relatively low hardware store share and a high motor vehicle share.

On a per capita basis, retail sales are approximately 12 percent above the national average in British Columbia, 10 percent above in Alberta, 15 percent below in Saskatchewan, 4 percent below in Manitoba, 10 percent above in Ontario, 11 percent below in Quebec, 17 percent below in New Brunswick, 8 percent below in Nova Scotia, 17 percent

TABLE 8-5 Retail Trade by Kind of Business, 1971

	$000
Grocery and combination	7,260,204
All other food, beverage	654,237
General merchandise stores (less than 1/3 food including department mail order)	938,822
General stores (more than 1/3 food)	616,524
Department stores	3,184,097
Variety	570,690
Motor vehicles	4,924,650
Garage, filling station	2,694,890
Men's clothing	475,586
Family clothing	423,771
Women's clothing	621,803
Shoes	345,707
Hardware	408,936
Furniture, appliance, radio and T.V.	942,255
Fuel	523,261
Drugs	907,014
Jewellery	235,972
Other	4,917,718
	30,646,137*

SOURCE: DBS, "Retail Trade," No. 63-005 (Ottawa: Queen's Printer, January 1972).
* Excludes non-store retailing, e.g., vending, door-to-door.

TABLE 8-6 Retail Trade by Province, 1971

	$000
Newfoundland	533,251
Prince Edward Island	141,027
Nova Scotia	1,022,868
New Brunswick	834,843
Quebec	7,681,439
Ontario	11,877,171
Manitoba	1,318,127
Saskatchewan	1,138,866
Alberta	2,466,603
British Columbia (Including Yukon and N.W.T.)	3,631,942
	30,646,137

SOURCE: DBS, "Retail Trade," No. 63-005.

below in Prince Edward Island, and 23 percent below in Newfoundland.[13]

Estimates of percentage changes from 1966 to 1971 were provided by D. S. McGiverin, Managing Director of the Hudson's Bay Company, in an address to the 1972 Convention of the Retail Council of Canada:

[13] From an examination of statistics provided in the *Financial Post Survey of Markets, 1970* (Toronto: Maclean-Hunter, 1970).

—Suburban department stores' share of total department retailing in 1971 was nearly 50 percent vs. only 33 percent in 1966.

—Downtown department stores accounted for 40 percent in 1971 vs. 58 percent in 1966.

—Self-service stores increased their sales by 60 percent in 1966–71. Others gained by only 31 percent.

—Department and mail-order sales rose by 41 percent.

—Chain retailing increased its share of retail trade to 39 percent in 1971 from 33 percent in 1966. Chain store sales rose by 56 percent while independents only rose by 23 percent.[14]

Estimates[15] of total retail sales made at the convention predicted $40 billion by 1981. Average annual increase in volume terms would be 2.8 percent, or a 10-year increase (1971–81) of about 32 percent (versus 3 percent per year, in 1966–71).

A Comparative View of Canadian and American Retailing

Canadian and American retailing, though quite similar, still have their differences, just as there are differences in the consumer market itself. Table 8-7 provides an analysis of Canadian and U.S. retail sales

TABLE 8-7 Comparison of Canadian and U.S. Retail Trade By Store Groupings, 1971

	Canada		U.S.A.	
Store Groups	$ Millions	Percentage Distribution	$ Millions	Percentage Distribution
Food	7,934	25.2	86,887	22.0
Eating and drinking places	1,546	5.0	29,620	7.5
General merchandise	5,292	17.0	71,784	18.3
Apparel	1,822	5.8	19,693	5.0
Furniture — Household appliances	934	3.0	16,591	4.3
Automotive	5,365	17.0	71,928	18.3
Gas stations	2,625	8.4	27,881	7.1
Lumber, building supplies and hardware	1,334	4.3	20,869	5.3
Drug	885	2.8	13,566	3.5
Other	3,586	11.5	33,768	8.7
Total	31,323	100.0	392,587	100.0

SOURCE: Developed from Sales Management Survey of Buying Power, 10 July 1972. © 1972, Sales Management Survey of Buying Power; further reproduction is forbidden.

by store groups. It should be noted that the Canadian figures will differ slightly from the 1971 figures presented in Tables 8-5 and 8-6, because of the adjustments, made by the Sales Management Survey of Buying Power,

[14] As reported in John Fell "Growth Rate in Retailing Expected to Slow in 1970's," *Financial Post*, 3 June 1972, p. 16.

[15] *Ibid.*

which were used in Table 8-7 for comparative purposes. The basic adjustment is that Table 8-7 includes certain additional eating and drinking places, automotive establishments, lumber yards and building material dealers as well as non-store retailing, and excludes certain garage and gasoline service station sales. As is to be expected in a lower income country, food sales account for a greater percentage of total retail sales in Canada; however, the U.S. market compensates for this by distributing a relatively greater percentage of the retail sales dollar to eating and drinking places. Canadian retail sales are relatively slightly greater in apparel and gas station groups and relatively smaller in general merchandise, furniture, automotive, hardware and drug groups.

TABLE 8-8 Comparative Retail Data, U.S. and Canada

	Canada (Canadian $)	U.S.A. (U.S. $)	Canada/ U.S.A. Index U.S. = 100
Total retail sales ($000,000) 1971**	$ 31,323	$392,587	8.0
Retail sales per capita, 1971**	$ 1,434	$ 1,892	75.5
Retail sales per store average Canada 1966, U.S. 1967	$147,000	$176,000	83.5*
Number of population per store Canada 1966, U.S. 1967	130	112	116.0
Retail sales as % of personal expenditures 1971**	59	59	100.0
Retail employment as % of total employment, Canada 1968, U.S. 1969	10%	14%	71.5
Retail sales per retail employee Canada 1969, U.S. 1967	$ 28,700	$ 30,000	95.5*

SOURCES: *Data estimated, developed and calculated from several sources including:* Census of Canada 1966, Statistical Abstract of U.S. 1970, Sales Management Survey of Buying Power 1972.

* Would be slightly lower if exchange rate considered.

** Sales Management Survey of Buying Power.

Table 8-8 presents some very interesting comparative retail vital statistics for the United States and Canada, and helps to indicate retailing's relative importance in the respective economies. Canadian sales are only about 8 percent of U.S. retail sales, and since the population ratio is about one-tenth, one finds that on a per capita basis, Canadian retail sales account for only about three-quarters of U.S. per capita retail sales. The average retail sales per store also tend to be larger in the United States, with the average Canadian store being five-sixths the size of the U.S. store in terms of retail sales. The latter fact would suggest that as an economy or market becomes larger, the retail sales tend to become more concentrated, perhaps in order to take advantage of increased possibilities of economies of scale. This conclusion would coincide with the concentration trend noted in the Canadian census "Retail Trade" surveys of 1951, 1961 and 1966. Moyer and Snyder report that "in 'real' terms, the growth of the average retail outlet has been impressive; about two and a half times as much merchandise now moves through the average store as in 1930," [16] a definite move towards the "mass production of sales." The population per store is slightly higher in Canada which may reflect the lower retail sales per capita, and therefore the greater need to have fewer stores per capita for efficient operation. This observation could temper the former conclusion on concentration, in that though sales are higher per store in the larger economy, there is a slightly greater concentration in the smaller economy in terms of population per store.

U.S. retailing shows a stronger picture vis-à-vis Canadian retailing in terms of retail employment as a percentage of total employment. This could be a reflection of the larger economy's greater involvement in tertiary industry, and the smaller economy's relatively greater involvement in primary industry. Retail sales per retail employee are greater in the United States, an indication of the generally higher productivity of the U.S. economy. However, Canadian productivity in retailing is over 95 percent of the U.S.'s productivity. This is relatively very

TABLE 8-9 Comparative Merchandising and Operating Results for Canadian and U.S. Department Stores, 1969

	% of Net Sales	
	Canada	U.S.
Cumulative mark-on	41.1	43.2
Markdown	7.3	7.1
Shortages	1.3	2.3
Cash discounts	.5	1.1
Gross margin	35.0	36.9
Average gross sale	5.46 (1968)	6.98
Returns (% of gross sales)	5.9	8.4
Net sales per square foot	74.91	79.65
Stock turns	2.0	3.3
Total operating expenses	34.4	31.8
Net other income	2.4	.12
Net profit before tax	3.0	5.3

SOURCE: *Canadian statistics from "Merchandising and Operating Results, Canadian Department Stores, 1969," (Retail Council of Canada, Toronto); U.S. Statistics from "Financial and Operating Results of 1969," (Controllers' Congress, National Retail Merchants Association, New York).*

high and may indicate a lack of opportunity for great productivity gains and economies of scale in an industry such as retailing, even when it reaches the enormous scale of operation found in the U.S. This comparative lack of opportunity, probably caused by the relative inability to automate and become capital-intensive, would explain why other industries in Canada have a much lower productivity ranking (under 80 percent) compared to their American counterparts in the retail trade.

Table 8-9 shows some comparative merchandising and operating results. Canadian stores tend to require smaller cash discounts and returns

[16] Moyer and Snyder, *Trends in Canadian Marketing*, p. 92.

and have less shortages. These positive features tend to be mitigated by a slightly smaller cumulative mark-on, a smaller average gross sale and sales per square foot, and higher operating expenses. These negative factors lead to a smaller gross and operating margin. However, fortunately for Canadian retailing, other income compensates somewhat for the latter.

The Retailing Giants — Concentration Statistics and Some Comparisons

Canadian retailing is significantly more concentrated than U.S. retailing; i.e., a smaller percentage of companies account for a greater percentage of total retail sales. In Canada, the department stores and food stores have tremendous strength and very few, if any, mass manufacturers can succeed in the Canadian market without the cooperation of these retail outlets. A mass manufacturer in the Canadian market cannot sidestep the large Canadian department store chain, or, if he is in the food field, the large corporate supermarket chain. Eight companies can be listed as Canadian retail giants, four in the department store field, and four in the supermarket field.

The four department store chains are Eaton's, Simpson's and Simpsons-Sears, Hudson's Bay Co., and Woodward Stores Limited; the food corporate chains are Loblaw Groceterias Co. Limited, Dominion Stores Limited, Steinberg's Limited and Canada Safeway Limited. There is very heavy concentration in the grocery business in Canada, with the four corporate chains, plus A. & P. and a few voluntary chains controlling more than 75 percent of the business in many urban areas; and their share is increasing.[17] These four corporate supermarket chains account for 44 percent of the total sales of grocery stores in Canada, or 40 percent of the food group as defined by the Sales Management Survey of Buying Power. The four largest supermarket chains in the United States account for only about half of this market share, or 19 percent of the food group. These four U.S. supermarket chains are Great Atlantic and Pacific Tea Company, Safeway Stores Inc., Kroger Company, and Food Fair Stores.

The four large Canadian department store chains account for $21\frac{1}{2}$ percent of department store merchandise. Department store merchandise is defined as all retail sales with the exception of food (including eating and drinking places and groceries) and automotive sales (including cars, garage and service station sales), and again, in the United States, their counterparts have only about half this market share at $11\frac{1}{2}$ percent. The four largest department store chains in the United

---

[17] The top four grocery retail groups in the five major Prairie metropolitan areas (which excludes Steinberg's), did in 1966 from 69 percent of the business in Calgary to $84\frac{1}{2}$ percent in Saskatoon. See "Prairie Provinces Cost Study," *Report of the Royal Commission on Consumer Problems and Inflation* (Provinces of Manitoba, Saskatchewan and Alberta, 1968), p. 163.

States are Sears-Roebuck and Company, J. C. Penney, Marcor (Montgomery Ward) , and Federated Department Stores.

In total, the eight Canadian stores account for one-quarter of non-automotive retail sales, while the eight American stores account for only one-eighth of such sales. Indeed, the eight Canadian stores account for almost one-fifth of total Canadian retail sales, including automotive sales, while it takes the fifty largest U.S. retailers, which include not only supermarket, department and mail-order stores, but also variety stores, specialty stores, etc., to account for this proportion of total U.S. retail sales.[18] In general, the U.S. ratios for the four largest stores in the department store and supermarket fields equal about one-half of the Canadian ratios. Following is a brief description of each of the largest Canadian stores with approximate figures for 1971–72:

> *T. Eaton Company.* Canada's largest retailer, Eaton's has over 20 main stores, 28 branch stores, 3 catalogue order centres, 39 heavy goods stores, and 350 sales offices, with estimated gross sales (this is a privately-held corporation) of well over $1,000 million.
>
> *Simpson's Limited,* and *Simpsons-Sears.* Simpson's operates 9 department stores in 5 larger urban centres, and also has an equal interest with Sears, Roebuck & Company in Simpsons-Sears which operates 40 retail stores and a mail-order business across Canada. Simpson's Limited and Simpsons-Sears, with combined sales of $1,100 million, form the second largest department store group in Canada.
>
> *Hudson's Bay Company.* This company is the third largest department store group. It operates 22 large department stores and 221 smaller stores in smaller communities. Estimated sales of the Hudson's Bay Company are $559 million.
>
> *Woodward Stores Limited.* Woodward Stores, the fourth largest department store group in Canada, operates 16 large department stores in British Columbia and Alberta. Large food markets are operated within or adjacent to Woodward Stores. Woodward's estimated sales are $332 million.
>
> *Dominion Stores Limited.* The company operates a chain of supermarkets and stores across Canada. In 1971, there were 400 stores in operation, with sales of $954 million.
>
> *Steinberg's Limited.* The company operates a chain of retail food markets in the provinces of Quebec, Ontario and New Brunswick. It has its own private brand lines of dairy products; delicatessen foods; vegetables, fruits and juices; bread, cakes and other baked goods; and many non-food items. In addition to food products, the company sells specialty items, such as kitchenware, toilet articles, soft goods, magazines and tobacco products. Steinberg's operates approximately 184 supermarket and 28 departmental discount stores (Miracle Mart) , as well as certain other outlets, for total sales of over $850 million.

[18] See "The Fifty Largest Retailing Companies," *Fortune,* May 1972, pp. 216-17.

Loblaw Groceterias Company Limited. In 1971 the company operated a chain of 209 stores in Ontario and western Canada. The company stores handle all kinds of groceries and foodstuffs, including several of its own private brands, and certain other commodities. The company also operates its own coffee roasting and tea packing plant. Sales are estimated to be over $700 million. (This is a very approximate estimation, as the company's reported figures consolidate revenue from many sources.)

Canada Safeway Limited. The company operates 263 retail meat and grocery stores at the head of the Great Lakes, Toronto, and in the western provinces. Sales are estimated at $686 million (excluding overseas sales).

Four other companies, though not included in the "big eight" above, could be considered emerging giants: Zeller's Limited, Canadian A & P, and the Canadian operations of S. S. Kresge Company and F. W. Woolworths. Zeller's operates a chain of about 140 junior department stores across Canada with total sales of $201 million. Canadian A & P, subsidiary of the U.S. supermarket chain, has sales ranging around $275 million.

There are approximately half a dozen other merchandising operations in Canada with sales over $200 million each, particularly M. Loeb Limited with $531 million and Oshawa Wholesale Limited with $490 million. However, most of these are wholesale-retail groups in the food field and will be discussed under wholesaling, in the following chapter.

INSTITUTIONAL AND COMPETITIVE TRENDS IN RETAILING[19]

The Discount Store

As with most other economic phenomena, the discount store has made its appearance in Canada with the usual time-lag after its appearance in the United States, and is less of a factor in this country. These stores tend to be concentrated in the large megalopolis (Quebec City to Windsor) market. The Dominion Bureau of Statistics first isolated this form of retailing in 1962, and at that time recorded total retail sales of $100 million. By 1966 this figure had increased to $345 million — in other words, an increase of 345 percent in four years, a steep rate of growth from anyone's viewpoint. The 1966 volume represented sales equal to almost 16 percent of those of their chief competitor, the department store. Note, however, that in some lines the inroads have been much

---

[19] For a shorter but more historical overview of Canadian retailing trends, see Canadian Imperial Bank of Commerce, "Retailing In a Changing World," *Commercial Letter,* no. 2, 1971, 5 pages.

more serious. For example, sales of photographic equipment and supplies were equal, in 1965, to 60 percent of the department store sales in the same line; toiletries and cosmetics totalled 37 percent of the department store sales in that same year.

By far the most important form of discount store in Canada has been the discount department store rather than the discount house. The former is basically a softgoods supermarket which carries a wide range of often unbranded goods, compared to the branded durables carried by the latter. Indeed the biggest difference between the commodity composition of discount stores and department stores in Canada is that furniture and appliances accounted for 22 percent of total sales of the department stores and only 9 percent of those of the discount store, in 1965.[20]

Fourteen companies were recognized by the Dominion Bureau of Statistics as operating discount stores. These include companies which are subsidiaries of U.S. firms, subsidiaries of Canadian chain supermarkets and of variety chains, etc. These fourteen companies include those which have leased some or all of their departments, and those which are operated by owner-merchants and closed-door discounters. For the latter, a customer must hold a membership card which can only be obtained if he is a member of a certain industry or group — e.g., the civil service.

In recent years the well-known retailers in other retail fields have established discount chains. This trend differs from an earlier one involving less-successful operators who were real-estate investors and who leased the various departments. This trend is also supplemented with a trend towards upgrading of stores, services and goods, though the Canadian discount movement has never really followed the rough decor, nonservice policies of the early U.S. operations. Indeed, many of these companies do not identify themselves as discount stores, as such, but as junior or promotional department stores. However, while the basic appeal of the latter is still that of the usual discount store — low markup and costs, and so lower prices — it becomes harder and harder to distinguish the discount store from the department store. In the last few years even the Dominion Bureau of Statistics has not been making the attempt.

The reasons for the rise of discount stores (for example, the preselling power of advertising), are well-known in the United States, and there have been no basic differences in Canada except that the strong position of the department stores helped to hold back the discount flood in the past, and in spite of the discount store's rapid rise in the past few years, will probably be able to block any very serious inroads in the future. This last statement cannot as readily be made of the U.S. department stores. The Canadian department store has moved rather rapidly

[20] Jerry Snyder, "Discounting: What's Happened?" in Isaiah A. Litvak and Bruce E. Mallen, eds., *Marketing: Canada* (Toronto: McGraw-Hill Book Company of Canada, 1965) p. 237.

in meeting the particular types of competition of the discount store, including: moving to shopping centres and the suburbs, with their convenient location, good parking and evening shopping hours; lowering markups and cost, and therefore price, through such tactics as self-service and "refusal to be undersold" policies.

The biggest mass merchandise discounters included, as of mid-1972:

Towers Department Stores Ltd., owned by the Oshawa Group Ltd., with about thirty-three stores.

K-Mart, owned by S. S. Kresge Co., with about fifty-five stores.

Miracle Mart, owned by Steinberg's Ltd., with about thirty stores.

Woolco, owned by F. W. Woolworth, with about fifty-two stores.

Private Brands

Canada is also having her battle of the brands. Private brands (retailers' brands) are making great headway in their battle with the national brands (manufacturers' brands) for both the supermarket and the department store market. Today, private store brands hold over fifteen percent of the market and this share is growing with great vigour. In some specific product lines, particularly in very stable items, this share is much higher and accounts for over half the market for such items as coffee and peanut butter.

These shares, of course, differ by geographical region and income group. For example, French Quebec is still very loyal to national brands, and high income families purchase a higher percentage of products under private labels than do low income families. The latter phenomenon is said to be the result of the greater security that higher income and therefore higher educated groups feel about their shopping habits — these groups do not need the security of a well-known national brand, which has been pre-sold through abundant advertising, to decide their buying choice. The corollary of this is that the lower income groups have greater anxieties in their attitudes towards private brands because these are not usually as well-known as the national brands.[21] This implies that in addition to other factors, private brands will continue to grow because of the growing rate of affluence and education in Canada. In addition, one must recognize that many of the private brands, such as Eaton's "Viking" brand, are certainly as well-known as the best-known national brands. Indeed, such private brands can themselves be labelled "national" brands – after all, they are distributed nationally.

Another reason for the growth of private brands is to be found in the concentrated structure of the retail industry, a situation which was noted earlier. The power of private brands is derived to a great extent from the power of Canada's chain supermarkets and department stores.

[21] David S. R. Leighton, "Who Actually Buys Private Brands," Marketing 67 (6 April 1962) , pp. 26-29.

These stores have the buying power, selling power, and other financial and human resources to establish strong private brands. These retailers are both upgrading the quality of products carrying their labels, and advertising them more. In addition, there is a trend towards the actual manufacturing of private brands by the retailers, i.e., backward integration. However, for the most part, the actual manufacturing process is still carried on by non-integrated manufacturers, very often the same manufacturing firms that produce competing national brands. These private brands can now compete on a quality basis, as well as on a price basis. It is interesting to note that not only is the Canadian retailing industry concentrated at its own level and therefore composed of several very powerful retailers, but in addition, this power is being applied with increasing intensity back through the marketing channel. Thus, not only are the smaller retailers feeling the effects of the giant retailing power, but so are the wholesalers and manufacturers themselves. Indeed, it appears that the whole focus of power of the entire food industry, from farm to consumer, is becoming more and more concentrated among about half a dozen retailing firms. This trend is particularly significant when it is noted that food, at over 20 percent of the family budget, is the consumer's biggest single expenditure.

The Senate-House of Commons Joint Committee on Consumer Prices, established in 1966, took a close look at private brands. Its findings (see Table 8-10) show that private brands do provide the consumer with substantial price savings. Indeed, some of these savings may be over 50 percent, for such products as toilet soap, liquid detergent, and bread.

TABLE 8-10 Comparison of Private and National Brands

Private brand products sell at prices below those of national brands. The supermarkets claim their private-brand products are of a quality comparable to national-brand products.

Here are examples, using private brands of A. & P., Dominion Stores (D), Loblaw (L), Steinberg's (S) and Canada Safeway (CS).

Item	Size or Quality	National Brand Price ($)	Private Brand Store	Private Brand Price ($)	Savings on Private Brand (%)
Dairy Products					
Cheese spread	16 oz.	0.75	A & P	0.69	8
Cheese — cheddars	16 oz.	0.83	CS	0.73	12
Sliced cheese	8 oz.	0.41	S	0.35	15
Powdered milk	3 lb.	1.29	S	0.99	23
Evaporated milk	16 oz.	0.18	A & P	0.15	17
Ice cream	½ gal.	1.05	S	0.89	15
Canned Goods					
Peaches	15 oz.	0.30	A & P	0.28	7
Cut green beans	20 oz.	0.22	S	0.18	18
Cut wax beans	20 oz.	0.22	S	0.19	14
Tomato soup	10 oz.	0.15	A & P	0.12	20
Tomatoes	28 oz.	0.38	S	0.35	8
Tomato juice	105 oz.	0.77	S	0.69	10

TABLE 8-10 Comparison of Private and National Brands (continued)

Item	Size or Quality	National Brand Price ($)	Private Brand		Savings on Private Brand (%)
			Store	Price ($)	
Canned Goods (cont.)					
Baked beans	15 oz.	0.24	A & P	0.18	25
Beans with pork	20 oz.	0.29	S	0.23	21
Creamed corn	15 oz.	0.20	A & P	0.17	15
Whole kernel corn	14 oz.	0.22	S	0.19	14
Apple juice	48 oz.	0.39	S	0.37	5
Pumpkin	28 oz.	0.27	A & P	0.22	19
Fruit cocktail	28 oz.	0.51	S	0.47	8
Sockeye salmon	8 oz.	0.69	A & P	0.63	9
Pink salmon	7¾ oz.	0.39	CS	0.38	3
Tuna	7 oz.	0.49	CS	0.43	12
Frozen Goods					
Peas	12 oz.	0.22	CS	0.21	4
Strawberries	15 oz.	0.49	CS	0.43	12
Orange juice	12 oz.	0.59	S	0.44	25
Bread and Cereals, Baked Goods					
Flour, all purpose	25 lb.	2.63	A & P	1.99	24
Flour	10 lb.	1.15	S	0.95	17
Macaroni	2 lb.	0.47	S	0.35	26
Quick oats	3 lb.	0.57	L	0.49	14
Rice	2 lb.	0.49	CS	0.47	4
Cake mix	19 oz.	0.51	CS	0.43	16
Bread	Loaf	0.20-0.36	L	0.16-0.24	20-56
Bread	Loaf	0.24	CS	0.14	42
Meat Products					
Sausages	1 lb.	0.82	L	0.75	9
Lard	1 lb.	0.29	A & P	0.27	7
Paper Products and Wraps					
Toilet tissue	650	0.16	S	0.12	25
Facial tissue	400	0.36	S	0.31	14
			D	0.32	11
Napkins	60	0.21	S	0.18	14
Wax paper	100 ft.	0.37	S	0.35	5
Foil	25 ft.	0.37	S	0.33	11
Beverages					
Roasted coffee	16 oz.	0.99-1.09	A & P	0.95	4-13
			L	0.87	12-20
			D	0.87	12-20
Instant coffee	10 oz.	1.69-1.89	S	1.39	18-26
			D	1.43	15-24
			L	1.53	9-19
Tea bags	120	1.63-1.67	S	1.09	33-35
			L	1.39	15-17
Tea bags	60	0.87	D	0.69	21
			L	0.73	16
			A & P	0.65	25
Instant chocolate	2 lb.	0.99	S	0.79	20
Bulk tea	16 oz.	1.37	D	0.87	36
Ginger ale	30 oz.	0.25	D	0.15	40
			L	0.15	40
Soft drinks (canned)	10 oz.	0.12	CS	0.10	17

TABLE 8-10 Comparison of Private and National Brands (concluded)

Item	Size or Quality	National Brand Price ($)	Private Brand		Savings on Private Brand (%)
			Store	Price ($)	
Spreads, Sauces, Oils					
Margarine	1 lb.	0.30-0.38	S	0.30	21
			CS	0.25	17-34
Peanut butter	48 oz.	1.29	S	1.15	11
Peanut butter	16 oz.	0.53	D	0.37	30
			L	0.43	19
Ketchup	15 oz.	0.37	S	0.31	16
Mustard	24 oz.	0.35	S	0.19	46
Salad dressing	32 oz.	0.67-0.69	CS	0.61	9-12
			S	0.59	12-14
Salad dressing	16 oz.	0.45	D	0.35	22
			A & P	0.35	22
			L	0.39	13
White vinegar	128 oz.	0.83	L	0.73	12
Apple sauce	20 oz.	0.22	S	0.20	9
Vegetable oil	32 oz.	0.93	S	0.79	15
Mayonnaise	16 oz.	0.53	A & P	0.39	26
Cleaning Products					
Powdered detergents	42 oz.	1.03	D (32 oz.)	0.59	25
Powdered detergents	King Size	1.89	S	0.99	48
Powdered detergents	King Size	1.99	S	0.99	50
Powdered detergents	Jumbo Size	3.59	S	2.49	31
Liquid detergents	24 oz.	0.89	A & P	0.45	49
Liquid detergents	32 oz.	1.09	S	0.59	46
		1.27	D	0.59	54
			CS	0.87	31
Window cleaner	20 oz.	0.45	S	0.29	36
Liquid bleach	128 oz.	0.88	S	0.69	22
Laundry rinse	64 oz.	0.88	S	0.59	33
Steel wool pads	10's	0.28	S	0.23	18
Powdered soap	King Size	1.89	A & P	1.29	32
Toilet soap	Bar	0.16	CS	0.08	50
Other					
Chocolate bars	10's	0.97	D	0.78	20
Anti-freeze	1 gal.	3.17	S	2.57	19

SOURCES: Senate–House of Commons Joint Committee on Consumer Prices (Ottawa: Queen's Printer, October, 1966); and Financial Post, 29 October 1966, p. 18.

In a "blind" taste test[22] it was found that, in general, store (private) brands rated higher than name (manufacturer national) brands, and in fact many national best-seller brands ranked poorly. Table 8-11 provides the specific ratings.

[22] Julian Armstrong, "Panelists Test Tastes," Montreal Star, 23 June 1971, pp. 33-34. The panel and method used cannot be considered as one which meets scientific methodological and sampling requirements. However, it still appears indicative of the private-vs.-national brand situation.

TABLE 8-11 Store vs. Name Brands

Product	A & P	Dominion	IGA	Steinberg	Name Brand #1	Name Brand #2
Cut wax beans, choice grade, 19-ounce can	P	E	G	P	P (Ideal)	P (Raymond)
Cream style corn, choice grade, 19-ounce can	P	E	F	G	G (Ideal)	P (Raymond)
Kernel corn, fancy grade, 12-ounce can	F	G	no entry	F	G (Green Giant)	P (Stokely-Van Camp)
Green peas, assorted sizes, choice grade, 19-ounce can	G	G	G	F	P (Aylmer)	P (Clark)
Tomatoes, choice grade, 19-ounce can	F	E	P	E	F (Aylmer)	no entry
Tomato juice, fancy grade, 19-ounce can	E	G	G	P	F (Bright's)	E (Libby's)
Peanut butter, creamy, 16-ounce jar	E	F	E	G	E (Kraft)	G (York)
Ketchup	F	E	F	F	P (Aylmer)	E (Heinz)
Salad dressing, 16-ounce jar	F	G	G	G	G (Kraft)	G (Monarch)
Canadian cheese slices, 8-ounce package	P	G	E	G	G (Black Diamond)	G (Kraft)
Tomato soup, condensed, 10-ounce can	G	no entry	P	F	E (Campbell)	P (Clark)
Instant coffee, 2-ounce jar	P	G	P	E	P (Maxwell House)	F (Nescafé)
Apple sauce, fancy grade, 19-ounce can	F	no entry	no entry	G	P (Mont-Rouge)	E (Scotian Gold)
Peaches, halves, choice grade, 19-ounce can	F	no entry	F	G	E (Aylmer)	no entry
Pears, dessert, choice grade, 19-ounce can	G	no entry	F	G	no entry	no entry
Strawberry jam, with pectin	P	no entry	F	no entry	F (Aylmer)	E (Habitant)
Apple jelly with pectin	P	no entry	P	no entry	P (Oka)	E (Scotian Gold)
Ice cream, chocolate flavor, 1-pint box	E	F	P	F	G (Sealtest)	no entry

SOURCE: Montreal Star, 23 June 1971, p. 34.

NOTE: Each product was rated Excellent, Good, Fair or Poor in three categories — flavour, appearance and consistency. The final rating summarizes the results.

Scrambled Merchandising

The phenomenon of retailers in one line moving into the lines of other kinds of retailers is also occurring in Canada. For example, the Canadian Consumer Survey (1967) published by the Canadian Daily Newspaper Publishers' Association reports that though 33 percent of respondents said they "buy most" of their drug sales at independent drugstores and 27 percent said chain drugstores, such non-drug retailers as supermarkets accounted for 14 percent of the response, department stores 7 percent, discount stores 7 percent, with additional sales through variety stores and house-to-house retailing. In cosmetics, the department store accounted for 14 percent of the total response, independent drug stores 18 percent, chain drug stores 20 percent, house-to-house retailing 15 percent, supermarkets 13 percent, discount stores 6 percent, and variety stores 2 percent, with an additional outlet through beauty parlours. Other examples can be found in the automotive segment of the industry. For example, though service stations accounted for 57 percent of responses to "where do you normally buy anti-freeze," such retail institutions as accessory stores, car dealers, department stores, discount stores, and repair garages each accounted for 5 to 10 percent of the responses. Service stations were the outlet from which 39 percent of respondents last bought a new battery, repair garages 14 percent, discount stores 3 percent, car dealers 10 percent, car accessory stores 18 percent, and department stores 9 percent. For tires, the breakdown is service stations 28 percent, tire stores 35 percent, and repair garages, discount stores, department stores, accessory stores, and car dealers — each from 3 to 9 percent. In response to the question, Where do you buy most of your cigarettes?, 41 percent of the women answered supermarkets, 21 percent answered grocer, and discount stores, drug stores, restaurants and tobacco stores each received 7 to 11 percent of the response. In answer to a similar question, 33 percent of the men answered supermarkets, 23 percent grocery, and the other outlets each received 6 to 12 percent each of the response.

The 1966 Retail Census of Canada further confirms the extent of scrambled merchandising.[23] For example, 14 percent of foodstore sales were non-food; 10 percent of men's and boys' clothing store sales were not men's and boys' clothing and accessories; 18 percent of hardware store sales were not hardware; 30 percent of household appliance store sales were not household appliances; 28 percent of drugstore sales were not drugs, drug sundries and toilet preparations; 37 percent of tobacco store sales were not tobacco products, etc. etc.

This trend is not only evident in goods but also in the service fields. For example, department stores are moving into such areas as: automobile service, secretarial service, insurance, home improvement services, home financing, recreational centres, health centres, travel

---

[23] See DBS, "Analysis of Sales by Commodity," No. 97-608 (Ottawa: Queen's Printer).

agencies, and rental of goods.[24] Thus a manufacturer must understand the diverse types of retailers through which his goods may pass to the consumer, before he commits himself to one or more types.

Trading Stamps

The trading stamp controversy has been as heated in Canada as elsewhere. Legislation outlawing, or greatly prohibiting trading stamp operations has been passed in British Columbia, Alberta and Saskatchewan. The usual arguments both pro and con, are advanced by the opposing sides. Those favouring trading stamps point out that the marketplace, not legislators, should judge the stamps; that most of the money spent by stamp companies goes for the purchase of goods manufactured in Canada; and that trading stamps increase sales of individual stores and thus reduce, rather than increase total costs. Those opposing the use of trading stamps point out that total demand cannot be increased significantly — in the long run, because all stores become competitive with each other by handling competitive trading stamps, they cannot raise total sales of the industry — so that the cost of the stamps, which runs about 2 percent of gross sales, must ultimately be borne by the consumer in the form of higher prices. However, the sellers of trading stamps will usually retort that even if this were so, the consumer wants trading stamps, enjoys the business of redeeming them and apparently because of their success is willing to continue to purchase them whether this increases prices or not.

The fact of the matter is that despite the decline in appeal of trading stamps in the U.S., they were more than holding their own in Canada.[25] It was estimated that over $25 million in premiums, at retail prices, were distributed annually. The largest trading stamp firms were: Lucky Green Stamp Company, a subsidiary of Loblaw Groceterias Limited; Gold Bond and Company, a subsidiary of the I.G.A. organization; Pinky Stamps, a subsidiary of Steinberg's; and Gold Star Sales. However, in the past several years, trading stamps have had a sudden decline in popularity amongst the users (not necessarily amongst consumers) so that their continued existence seems unlikely.

Shopping Centres*

Shopping centres have mushroomed in the past decade as a direct result of the population movement to the suburbs. The Dominion Bureau of Statistics reports that there were 499 shopping centres in 1969,

---

[24] Beatrice Riddell, "You Can Almost Live in Department Stores," *Financial Post,* 21 September 1963, p. 1.

[25] Paul Gibson, "Trading Stamps Dug in for Long Canadian Stay," *Financial Post,* 25 September 1965, pp. 1-2.

* A **shopping centre** is a group of at least five retail establishments which are designed as a unit with at least 20,000 square feet of free adjacent parking. The centre must include a food store, department store and variety store.

of which 343 contained five to fifteen stores; 107, sixteen to thirty stores; and 49, over thirty stores.[26] The smallest centres accounted for one-third of total shopping centre sales, the medium-size for one-quarter, and the largest for two-fifths, though the smallest shopping centres accounted for two-fifths of the stores, while the largest accounted for only slightly more than a fourth of the stores. Shopping centres accounted for approximately 12 percent of total retail sales in Canada, ranging from 5.5 percent in the Atlantic provinces, to almost 14 percent in Ontario. Over 32 percent of shopping centre sales consisted of sales of grocery and combination stores, while another 32 percent (approximately) consisted of sales by department stores, though these two retail institutions together comprised under 11 percent of total store units in shopping centres. Chain stores have participated to a much greater extent, particularly in the larger centres, than have independent merchants.

Some of the larger regional shopping centres are particularly impressive and rank among the most modern and complete in the world. These would include the enclosed malls (a definite architectural trend) of the Yorkdale shopping centre in Toronto and the Fairview-Pointe Claire shopping centre in Montreal. Both these shopping centres include units of Canada's two largest department store chains, Eaton's and Simpson's.

Retail Vending

Though far behind the United States on a per capita basis, automatic vending* sales have grown dramatically in Canada by increasing at an annual rate of 15.3 percent over the ten years to 1970. By the latter date, sales had reached almost $157 million.[27] Since 1961, vending sales have risen about 3½ times faster than total retail sales in Canada (although the rate of sales increase is diminishing). This increase in sales has been accomplished with some consolidation and shaking out of some marginal firms. Indeed, between 1963 and 1964, though sales increased by $11 million, the number of machines in operation and the number of firms declined, and again in 1970 the number of firms declined from the previous year. In 1970 there were over 768 firms in the field with slightly over 100,000 machines.

Among the reasons for vending growth are:

. . . Advances in refrigeration, packaging, and electric cooking led to new kinds of vending machines and made available to the consumer a wider range of uses and services. As well, the rapid growth of

[26] DBS, "Shopping Centres in Canada," No. 63-214 (Ottawa: Queen's Printer, 1969).

* **Automatic vending** is the completion of a sales transaction, without the presence of a sales clerk or cashier, by the insertion of money into a vending machine.

[27] DBS, "Vending Machine Operators," No. 63-213 (Ottawa: Queen's Printer, 1970).

secondary industry and of shift-work led to more in-plant feeding.
Finally, as the coffee break became universal, workers in both plants
and offices found it more convenient to have coffee, cigarettes, and
snacks close to their work stations.[28]

The basic business units in the industry are the machine manufacturers; the supplier of the goods, who may be a manufacturer or
wholesaler; the vendor, who is the key man in the industry and may own
or rent the machines himself; and the owner or tenant of the location. A
firm can of course be involved in two or more of the above occupations.
Industrial plants are the main location for the machines; however, hotels,
motels, restaurants, taverns and mess-halls are also important. Other significant locations for vending machines include recreation centres, service
stations, institutions and business offices.

In spite of its rapid growth, the Canadian industry is plagued
with problems to be found anywhere in vending. These include problems
of servicing of the machines, capital cost, technology (though there appear to be constant improvements in this area, with machines developed
to accept paper money and credit cards), and packaging.

Tobacco and confectionery products are by far the biggest volume items moving through these machines, with 58 percent of total sales
and two-thirds of all machines carrying these products. The next most
important product group moving through this form of retailing is hot
and cold drinks, which accounts for 32 percent of total vending sales.
Thus, 90 percent of vending sales were accounted for by tobacco and
confectionery products and hot and cold drinks — a fairly limited product
range. However, this percentage could fall slightly as other products are
adapted to retail vending.

Direct Selling

In 1968, the Dominion Bureau of Statistics undertook the first
annual survey of direct selling. The study was restricted to manufacturers
and selected agencies specializing in direct sales methods. This excludes
vending sales, department store and foreign mail-order operations, and
direct sales by wholesalers and storage outlets. In 1970, direct sales
amounted to over $718 million, or 3.8 percent of comparable retail store
and department mail-order sales.[29] The largest sales were in the dairy
products industry ($164 million), the newspapers and periodicals in-
dustry ($134 million), the electrical appliances industry ($50 million),
the cosmetics industry ($73 million), and the book industry ($55 million). Other industries which reported direct sales of over $10 million in
1969 included: frozen food plans, kitchenware and utensils, bakery products, brushes, soaps and housecleaners, phonographic records and
clothing.

[28] Moyer and Snyder, Canadian Trends, pp. 263-4.
[29] DBS, Direct Selling in Canada, 1970, No. 63-218 (Ottawa: Queen's Printer,
1972).

Almost three-quarters (71 percent) of this direct selling took place on a door-to-door basis, about 20 percent was accomplished through the telephone and/or mail-order route, and 7 percent was undertaken on the manufacturing premises. Virtually 100 percent of the sales of two of the four largest users of direct selling — dairy and cosmetic products — is undertaken through door-to-door canvassing. The book industry tends to put more weight (69 percent) on the telephone and mail direct selling method, while periodicals and electrical appliances use the latter method for 14 and 25 percent respectively of their direct selling volume. The other larger industries mentioned, with the exception of phonograph records, clothing and frozen food plans, put virtually all their direct selling emphasis on the door-to-door method. Phonograph record direct sales are made through the mail order route, while frozen food plans use two methods equally — sales on the manufacturing premises and telephone or mail — and clothing emphasizes telephone selling. Industries which show a high degree of direct selling on the manufacturing premises include meat, fish and poultry products; canvas, awnings and tents; furs and fur coats; and furniture.

The role of direct selling will probably increase in Canadian marketing as direct marketers improve their selling techniques and as consumers place more value on leisure time, and the avoidance of shopping trips (as well as the avoidance of complicated buying decisions in the face of the wide choice offered by mass merchandise stores) .[30]

Retail Trade Flow Changes[31]

Retail trade in the metropolitan areas in the past three decades has definitely not kept pace with the population shift to these areas. Canadian metropolitan retailing has become less effective over the years in generating trade from nonmetropolitan areas. In 1931, metropolitan per capita retail sales were 188 percent above those of nonmetropolitan areas, but by 1962 the difference had fallen to only 44 percent. In 1965 the closing spread reversed itself slightly by moving back to 49 percent.

The metropolitan areas' share of trade had not increased. It was 55 percent in 1930 and remained at about this same percentage in 1965. This in spite of the fact, for example, that Canada's half dozen largest cities moved in the 1950's alone from a 30 percent share of the Canadian population to a 38 percent share.

It appears that where a metropolitan area is directly surrounded by a basically rural area there results a flow of retail trade from this surrounding area to the metropolitan area. However, where a metropolitan area is directly surrounded by a nonmetropolitan urban area the

---

[30] For a summary of the current individual companies in the field and their plans, see Margaret Hilton "Door-to-Door Selling Wins New Friends," *Financial Post,* 13 January 1971, pp. 1-2.

[31] Bruce Mallen, "Retail Trade Flow Changes in Canada," in Litvak and Mallen, *Marketing: Canada,* pp. 241-52.

inflow of retail trade to the former is greatly restricted. This is because of the retailing facilities which nonmetropolitan urban populations can sustain.

As Canada becomes more urbanized, as the more rural areas are converted into nonmetropolitan urban areas, the metropolitan areas themselves will be forced to depend less and less on trade inflow.

Combining the type of store and its location, it can be said that the metropolitan retailers who would be most adversely affected by the strengthening nonmetropolitan urban retailing picture, would be those shopping stores located in suburban shopping centres which depend to an important degree on sales to consumers from surrounding towns and smaller cities. This trend of course does not apply to centres which depend on surrounding suburbs.

It would seem, then, that different types of retailers will be affected in different ways. Suburban shopping centre stores and non-metropolitan independent retailers will probably suffer. Convenience stores and specialty stores will be little affected by this movement. Suppliers themselves will tend to have a more decentralized operation, chain stores will move in ever increasing strength into nonmetropolitan areas, and wholesalers in the nonmetropolitan cities will decline in relative importance.

Shopping Hours

The laws regarding shopping hours are much more restrictive in Canada than in the United States. There are fewer evening openings and little Sunday shopping. Shopping hour legislation is a very controversial issue, with the suburban mass merchandisers lobbying for freeing hours, and downtown merchants and employee groups opposed.

As a result of an exploratory study[32] Mallen and Rotenberg put forward the following four hypotheses:

1. Consumers in Canada, particularly in large metropolitan areas, are not satisfied with controls restricting their shopping time and prefer to shop at times other than the traditional nine to six, which have been set by the retailing community and/or government legislation.

2. Total retail dollars in Canada would increase if stores were open at times which were more convenient to the consumer. The consumer would be willing to pay a premium if necessary for the convenience of shopping after 6 p.m.

3. The consumer would look upon shopping as more of a recreational outlet if he could shop at more convenient hours, and this would increase the total amount spent on each purchase.

[32] B. Mallen and R. Rotenberg, *The Costs and Benefits of Evening Shopping to the Canadian Economy* (Toronto: National Retailers Institute, 1969), 400 pages.

4. Sales clerks and employees of retail establishments would not object to more liberal hours, provided that they did not work more than forty hours per week and/or had the option of working overtime for higher rates.

Future Developments

A most comprehensive article by Mr. J. G. Kendrick, President of Zeller's Ltd., has been written about the future development of retailing in Canada.[33] Following is a summary of his twenty-nine points.

1. Greatly expanded assortments of merchandise growing out of, first, the needs and wants of a more sophisticated and educated population with a constantly improving standard of living, and, second, the introduction to the market of a growing number of new materials and products arising out of the miracles of research and technological know-how.
2. Greater concentration of retailing to the mass population in the hands of fewer and larger retail organizations.
3. Increased emphasis on the large one-stop shopping centres, often involving two or three major department store units. Incidentally, with the development of the Super Regional Shopping Centres, retailers will be faced with a new parking problem, namely, the lengthening distance from the parked car to the store.
4. By the early 1970's the suburban department stores, whether they be units of a national chain or branches of a local department store, will be transacting the largest proportion of the total general merchandise retail volume.
5. A continued revitalization of our downtowns but at a slower pace and with many suspected as well as unforeseen and difficult side problems.
6. Increasing emphasis on the display and merchandising of goods by classification rather than by department.
7. Increased emphasis on fashion and quality for both apparel and the home and with less emphasis on price as the prime sales appeal.
8. Quality will become more important too, as the standard of living of Canadians continues to advance and the demands of the better educated and sophisticated shopper are felt.
9. Greatly stepped-up efforts by all large retail organizations to improve productivity — per square foot and per employee — to help offset the continued upward pressure on the costs of doing business.
10. More intensive application of the behavioural sciences with the objective of developing ways and means of motivating employees in a constructive and meaningful manner.
11. More efficiently arranged and operated stock areas so as to move

[33] J. G. Kendrick, "Retailing in Canada: Past, Present, Future," *Canadian Marketer*, Winter 1970.

the merchandise to the sales floor more quickly and more economically, primarily through the stepped-up use of mechanical and electronic equipment. Also a concentrated effort to reduce the square footage devoted to non-selling functions such as receiving and storing.

Further, the use of several strategically located distribution centres will be intensified in order to better service stores with their rapidly expanding merchandise assortments and to effect their delivery more efficiently and at less cost.

12. Air freight will be used more extensively, especially for fashion merchandise and items with a short sales life.

13. Continuing growth in the importing of merchandise from countries around the world.

14. A greater effort by retailers to reduce the number of suppliers and work closely with a few major sources in order to improve quality, pricing, packaging, labeling and delivery.

15. The nationwide retail organizations will put greater emphasis on the quality of their field managers, supervisors and buyers, delegating to them more and more authority and responsibility.

16. An improved response to consumer satisfaction through the utilization of more quality control and inspection procedures.

17. Shopping will become more exciting and interesting not only because of broader and more interesting merchandise assortments, but also through the development of more attractive, warm and colourful stores and enclosed mall shopping centres. Further, there will be additional appeals to the customer with promotional events.

18. There will be a constant endeavour to improve and perfect self-selection through more imaginative layouts, fixturing, display, packaging and labeling.

19. Detailed study of all expense centres in an all-out effort to reduce the costs of doing business and as an offset to other developments that tend to raise costs. Retailers will, through study and research, learn more about how to anticipate cost increases and to overcome them through the early testing of new methods and procedures.

20. Increased attention will be given to the needs and wishes of three growing segments of the population: the teens, the young adults, and the over-65 group. However, retailers in the future will direct more of their merchandising and promotional skills to the 34–55 age group which accounts for well over 50 percent of the consumer market.

21. Services of many types will become even more important to the larger department stores, even to some of the so-called junior department stores such as beauty shops, shoe repair, auto centres, watch and jewellery repair, optical shops and others.

22. Better solutions will be sought to the vexing problem of servicing what the store sells, particularly in respect to major appliances and T.V.

23. The vast and growing market for leisure-time merchandise such as sporting goods, camping, boating, gardening, and other aspects of outdoor living will be given increased attention.

24. Retailers will, through diligent study and experimenting, develop new personnel programmes that will attract and hold better talent.

25. The larger retail organizations will come to realize more and more that a regular programme of re-education for their middle manage-

ment and top executives will be a requirement for developing better quality total management.

26. The giant retailers will direct more of their advertising dollars into the mass media, especially TV and magazines, with special emphasis on their own brand merchandise.

27. As Canada becomes a more industrialized nation, with more women working and the consumer market gaining in importance to the economy, store opening hours will be lengthened to allow for night shopping.

28. The executives of retail organizations will find it desirable economically and morally to give increased attention to the changing environment in the community and society of which they are a part.

29. Finally, progressive retail organizations will find it desirable to become involved and committed to electronic data processing as a means of improving sales and profits.

An Important Conclusion

An extensive survey of a wide variety of Canadian retailers in both chain stores and independents leaves no room for doubt about the powerful influence exercised by the retailer on vital aspects of volume merchandising through retail outlets.

It is quite evident that a manufacturer must establish a quality image for himself and his product in the mind of the retailer, must inform the retailer about the features of his products, must try to reach all levels of staff categories from floor clerk to owner, and must advise the retailer to a greater degree about his promotional plans. These are some of the chief requirements pointed up by the survey as a means of getting the retailer to add his weight to the consumer demand created outside the store.[34]

[34] *A Study of the Canadian Retailer: His Role in the Movement of Merchandise* (Toronto: The Business Newspapers Association of Canada, 1964), p. 11.

9

Wholesaling in Canada

Wholesaling plays a vital role in the economy of Canada. In a country of sparse population and great distances, the wholesaler's functions and the economies he creates, prove most valuable to the distribution system. In numerous cases, the ability of a wholesaler to distribute the goods of a range of producers, to users and retailers, at a cost significantly below that which any one of these producers can do on its own, provides an indispensable institutional arrangement for marketing in Canada.

Wholesaling, including sales of manufacturers' sales branches, represents as a percentage half of GNP. Though well over half of Canada's wholesale trade takes place in Ontario and Quebec, these are the only provinces in which their respective shares of manufacturing output exceed their shares of wholesale trade, because of the concentration of factors making for the most viable manufacturing base.[1] In addition, the 1966 per capita (population) wholesale sales in Quebec and Ontario combined were $1,400, compared to $1,830 for the rest of the country. Thus, wholesaling plays a relatively more important role in the other provinces. This is further supported by Tables 9-4 and 9-5 which show that manufacturers' sales branches play a relatively greater role in the east at 10 to 11 percent of the eastern total wholesale market compared to only 5 percent of the western total wholesale market. While Ontario accounts for 32 percent of total wholesale sales, it accounts for 41 percent of total sales of manufacturers' sales branches.

The above, then, tends to support the conclusion that in sparsely populated regions, whether one looks at Canada as a whole, or the less populated regions within Canada, independent wholesaling plays a relatively more important role.

Wholesaling's Vital Statistics*

Table 9-1 and the tables derived from it (Tables 9-2 to 9-6) display the magnitude of wholesaling in Canada. 1966 wholesale sales

---

[1] Isaiah A. Litvak and Peter M. Banting, "The Wholesaling Sector in Canada," *Industrial Canada* 67 (October 1966) , Table 1. This table is based on the '61 census rather than the '66 census. But the relationship should still hold.

* **Wholesale establishments** refer to accounting entities and are not synonymous with "locations" or "firms." Unfortunately, this is the only way such data was collected for the 1966 census.

TABLE 9-1 Wholesale Establishments, 1966

	Total trade		Primary product dealers		Wholesale merchants		Agents and brokers		Manufacturers' sales branches		Petroleum bulk tank plants and truck distributors	
	No. of estab.	Total sales $000	No.	Total sales $000	No.	Total sales $000	No.	Total sales $000	No.	Total sales $000	No.	Total sales $000
Canada	30,900	31,171,515.0	1,274	2,686,880.5	24,124	18,922,389.7	2,216	3,731,165.3	499	2,637,583.5	2,787	3,193,496.0
Atlantic Provinces	1,995	1,592,077.6	186	77,245.0	1,455	901,638.4	162	119,808.1	56	172,912.8	136	320,473.3
Quebec	8,336	7,791,873.1	223	156,843.4	7,152	5,336,736.1	570	769,166.5	122	768,877.9	269	760,249.2
Ontario	10,394	10,066,222.5	403	658,810.3	8,420	6,290,829.7	703	954,866.6	167	1,095,243.1	701	1,066,472.8
Prairie Provinces	6,724	8,137,142.6	325	1,703,234.8	4,517	4,096,632.2	421	1,218,569.0	79	417,325.0	1,382	701,381.6
B.C., Yukon and N.W.T.	3,451	3,584,199.2	137	90,747.0	2,580	2,296,553.3	360	668,755.1	75	183,224.7	299	344,919.1

SOURCE: Dominion Bureau of Statistics, Wholesale Census 1966 (Ottawa: Queen's Printer).

TABLE 9-2 Wholesale Trade by Type of Operation, 1966

Type of Operation	Average Sales per Establishment ($000)	Number of Establishments	Sales ($000)	% of Total No. of Establishments	% Sales
Primary product dealers	2,109	1,274	2,686,880	4	9
Wholesale merchants	784	24,124	18,922,390	78	61
Agents and brokers	1,684	2,216	3,731,165	7	12
Manufacturers' sales branches	5,286	499	2,637,584	2	8
Petroleum distribution	1,146	2,787	3,193,496	9	10
Total	1,009	30,900	31,171,515	100	100

TABLE 9-3 Wholesale Trade by Region, 1966

Region	Average Sales per Establishment ($000)	No. of Establishments	Sales ($000)	% of Total No. of Establishments	% Sales
Atlantic	800	1,995	1,592,078	6	5
Quebec	936	8,336	7,791,873	27	25
Ontario	968	10,394	10,066,223	33	32
Prairie	1,210	6,724	8,137,143	23	26
B.C., Yukon, N.W.T.	1,038	3,451	3,584,199	11	12
Canada	1,009	30,900	31,171,515	100	100

were over $31 billion carried on through almost 31,000 establishments. Wholesale merchants, with almost $19 billion in sales and over 24,000 establishments, accounted for the majority of both sales (61 percent) and establishments (78 percent). Manufacturers' sales branches were the smallest contributors at 8 percent of sales and 2 percent of establishments. The reverse ratio of sales to establishments between the two categories of wholesaling reflects the higher unit volume that sales branches have and the smaller customers that merchant wholesalers service. This fact is also reflected in the low per establishment sales of merchant wholesalers and the high per establishment sales of manufacturers' sales branches. This is in keeping with the basic role of the independent wholesaler.

Quebec and Ontario, with a combined total of almost $18 billion in sales accounted for 57 percent of sales. This is to be expected, because of the vast relative population. Note, however, that in spite of this, wholesaling plays the more important role in the other provinces, as was mentioned above. Within wholesale categories, Tables 9-4 and 9-5 show that:

TABLE 9-4 Sales as a Percent of Regional Wholesale Trade, 1966

	Primary Product Dealers	Wholesale Merchants	Agents and Brokers	Manufacturers' Sales Branches	Petroleum Distributors	Total
Atlantic	5	57	8	11	19	100
Quebec	2	68	10	10	10	100
Ontario	6	63	9	11	11	100
Prairie	21	50	15	5	9	100
B.C., Yukon N.W.T.	3	63	19	5	10	100
Canada	9	61	12	8	10	100

TABLE 9-5 Regional Sales as a Percent of Wholesale Categories' Sales for Canada, 1966

Region	Total Wholesaling	Primary Product Dealers	Wholesale Merchants	Agents and Brokers	Manufacturers' Sales Branches	Petroleum Distributors
Atlantic	5	3	5	3	7	10
Quebec	25	6	28	21	29	24
Ontario	32	25	33	25	41	33
Prairie	26	63	22	33	16	22
B.C., Yukon, N.W.T.	12	3	12	18	7	11
Total	100	100	100	100	100	100

TABLE 9-6 Fifteen-year Shift in Sales

Type of Wholesaler	1951 $000,000	1966 $000,000	Average Annual Percent Increase
Merchants	5,493	18,922	16.3
Agents and brokers	2,494	3,731	3.3
Petroleum distributors	1,020	3,193	14.6
Primary product dealers	1,518	2,687	5.2
Total	10,525	28,533	12.3

1. Primary product dealers (including cooperatives) play both a relatively and absolutely greater role in the Prairies.
2. Manufacturers' sales branches, as noted above, play a greater role in the east.
3. Agents and brokers play a relatively greater role in the west.
4. Wholesale merchants play the dominant role in all regions, with a slightly smaller relative share on the Prairies (50 versus 61 percent for all Canada) because of the strong primary product dealers' share. This is the reason for the high per establishment sales of Prairie wholesaling, as Table 9-2 shows a very low per establishment figure for merchant wholesalers.

The Wholesaler's Future

Professor S. G. Peitchinis concludes that the merchant wholesaler has passed successfully through a critical stage of readjustment during the 1940's and early 50's and has now reassumed a dominant position in the distribution system:

> He appears to have adjusted to the requirements of external pressures and in consequence has prospered. Admittedly in the process of change, some wholesalers disappeared. But what appears to have taken place is the replacement of multi-product general wholesalers by a number of wholesale merchants, each specializing in one or a small number of related products. What we have then is the emergence of a number of specializing wholesalers in the place of one general wholesaler.
>
> Independent wholesalers responded in various ways to the challenge to their position in the distribution system. Some of them attempted to resist the forces of change and lost. The majority, however, adopted counter-measures: they embarked upon direct sales to users, in addition to supplying retailers; expanded their users' service department; developed ways to improve their relations with both producers and retailers. In addition, the expansion of the market enabled many multi-product wholesalers to specialize in the distribution and service of individual lines of related products only, and some to become associated with individual manufacturers and limit themselves to the exclusive distribution of their products. Thus, it may be said that the independent wholesaler gave up a dominant position in the structure of a rigid distribution system, which could well have led him to extinction, for a position which carries less authority but assures him of prosperity.[2]

This conclusion rests on the significant fact that wholesale merchants' sales increased at over double the rate of other wholesale trades and of Gross National Product, and four times the rate of retail trade during the 1930's, fell behind the rate of increase of all other sectors of wholesale trade, of Gross National Product, and of retail trade during the 1940's, then re-emerged again in the 1950's, surpassing by several times the growth rate of agents, brokers and wholesale cooperatives; by almost double that of retail trade; and by about a fifth that of Gross National Product.

This conclusion is further supported by the 1966 census. Wholesale merchant sales increased their market share of total wholesale trade from 58 percent in 1961 to 61 percent in 1966 and of total establishments from 73 percent to 78 percent. Further, as shown in Table 9-6, the 15-year average annual increase of wholesale merchants at 16.3 percent

---

[2] S. G. Peitchinis, "The Role of the Wholesaler," *Business Quarterly* 31 (Spring 1966), pp. 33-34. This section relies heavily on these footnoted pages.

(or 245 percent for the entire period) was the highest of all other wholesale categories and well above the 12.3 percent (or 184 percent for the period) for total wholesale sales.

Operating Ratios in Canadian Wholesaling

In 1969,[3] wholesalers were showing a 13.1 percent profit return (before income taxes) on net worth, compared to 12.1 percent for retailing and 14.1 percent for all manufacturing. They showed a 2.8 percent profit (before income taxes) on total revenue (not to be confused with net margin) compared to 2.4 percent for retailing and 6.7 percent for all manufacturing. The average collection period was 50.3 days for wholesaling, 19 days for retailing, and 44 days for all manufacturing. Finally, the ratios of sales to inventory showed 6.9 times for wholesaling, 6.9 times for retailing, and 5.4 times for all manufacturing. In general, a reasonably good showing.

Table 9-7 provides various financial and operating ratios for the wholesale trades. The average gross margin (100% — cost of sales %) for all wholesaling in 1969 was 17.3 percent ranging from a high of 25 percent for drug and toilet preparations wholesale firms to a low of 3.4 percent for grain wholesalers. Inventory turned over an average of 6.9 times. Tobacco wholesalers turned over their very perishable product some 22.8 times or almost once every two weeks, while it took an average of over a year and a half to sell a unit of grain. It also took almost that long for grain wholesalers to collect payment, compared to tobacco and food wholesalers who collected in an average of three weeks (versus seven weeks for all wholesaling). However, grain wholesalers showed the highest profit on total revenue (note, this is not net margin, since investment income — and in this particular case, apparently, substantial investment income — is included). The ultimate measure, profit (before tax) on equity, showed general merchandise wholesalers with the highest return at 21.3 percent, and coal and coke wholesalers at the bottom with a 1.1 percent return (versus an average overall return on investment of over 13.1 percent before tax).

The Manufacturers' Agent

The manufacturers' agent wholesaler, like the merchant wholesaler, is going through trials and tribulations. Unlike the merchant wholesaler, the manufacturers' agent classically does not take title to the merchandise, and seldom undertakes a storage function. The traditional view

---

[3] Dominion Bureau of Statistics, "Corporation Financial Statistics," No. 61-207 (Ottawa: Queen's Printer, September 1972) and Canadian Imperial Bank of Commerce, "Selected Corporate Ratios, 1969," *Commercial Letter,* May-June 1972, pp. 4-7.

TABLE 9-7 Selected Corporation Ratios By Type of Wholesale Trade, 1969

	Cost of Sales to Sales %	Sales to Inventory %	Collection Period – Days	Current Assets to Current Liabilities	Profit (b.t.) on Capital	Profit (b.t.) on Equity	Profit on Total Revenue
Livestock	96.1	17.4	32.2	1.3	8.0	9.0	1.8
Grain	96.6	.6	414.6	1.1	9.2	12.6	8.3
Coal and coke	87.0	4.9	53.4	1.3	.7	1.1	.2
Petroleum products	78.6	9.2	62.9	1.0	5.3	6.2	3.6
Paper	85.8	19.9	60.7	1.3	15.6	16.7	1.9
General merchandise	81.1	5.1	55.5	1.5	17.3	21.3	4.0
Food	90.1	14.8	19.2	1.4	12.5	14.3	1.4
Tobacco	91.8	22.8	21.4	1.6	7.6	8.9	.8
Drug and toilet preparations	75.0	8.1	46.5	1.6	14.9	16.0	3.4
Apparel and dry goods	83.4	6.0	55.0	1.6	11.5	12.8	2.7
Furniture and furnishings	81.2	6.4	71.3	1.3	16.3	18.2	2.8
Motor vehicle and parts	78.6	4.6	39.4	1.5	12.8	14.4	3.7
Electrical machinery	79.6	5.6	62.2	1.6	13.2	13.8	3.5
Farm machinery	83.3	3.3	76.2	1.5	3.9	4.7	1.0
Industrial machinery	77.1	4.6	62.3	1.5	13.7	15.7	3.9
Hardware, plumbing and heating	79.9	5.0	53.5	1.8	12.4	13.8	3.2
Metal products	83.0	6.1	87.0	1.3	15.9	18.7	3.3
Lumber and building products	82.3	7.2	52.5	1.7	11.6	13.5	3.1
Scrap and waste dealers	80.6	14.2	28.5	1.7	15.0	18.3	3.4
Other wholesale	80.0	7.3	59.4	1.5	13.3	14.5	3.4
Total	82.7	6.9	50.3	1.5	11.5	13.1	2.8

SOURCE: DBS, "Corporation Financial Statistics, 1969," No. 61-207 (Ottawa: Queen's Printer, September 1972), pp. 232-33.

TABLE 9-8 Wholesale Sales, 1971

Kind of Business		$000,000
Total, All Trades		24,896
Consumer goods trades		12,729
Automotive parts and accessories	1,519	
Motor vehicles	627	
Drugs and drug sundries	654	
Clothing and furnishings	308	
Footwear	78	
Other textiles and clothing accessories	588	
Household electrical appliances	600	
Tobacco, confectionery and soft drinks	1,000	
Fresh fruit and vegetables	559	
Meat and dairy products	757	
Floor coverings	276	
Groceries and food specialties	3,830	
Hardware	638	
Consumer goods residual	1,295	
Industrial goods trades		12,167
Coal and coke	65	
Grain	1,002	
Electrical wiring supplies, construction materials	447	
Other construction materials and suppliers, lumber	3,115	
Farm machinery	793	
Industrial and transportation equipment and supplies	2,223	
Commercial, institutional and service equipment	593	
Newsprint, paper and paper products	421	
Scientific and professional equipment and supplies	337	
Iron and steel	1,306	
Junk and scrap	424	
Industrial goods residual	1,441	

of this wholesaling institution is that of an independent business establishment selling, on a continuous contractual basis in a limited or exclusive territory, a part of the output of two or more client manufacturers whose products are related but non-competing. The agent is paid a commission and has little or no control over prices, credit or other terms of sale.

However, things are changing. Such factors as the increased size of the market, faster communication and travel, political integration, and giantism in retailing have created pressures for manufacturers and retailers to bypass the agent middlemen and deal directly. In order to adapt to this new environment and partially overcome the "direct trend," manufacturers' agents are looking further and further away from their classical definition as non-storing, non–title-taking middlemen. More modern adaptive firms are becoming more and more like merchant wholesalers. They are providing a storage function and credit, taking title to merchandise, going into the leasing business, becoming involved in cooperative advertising, and providing reliable information feed-back to manufacturers. Some have even moved into limited manufacturing.

In general, the pure manufacturers' agent who sells on straight commission is a dying breed. The marketing-oriented agent is playing a far more extended role today, and in the future his position will be even more mixed, encompassing taking the title to goods, warehousing, financing, leasing, selling product systems, and acting as an agent for both warehouse and manufacturing principles.[4]

1971 Merchant Wholesale Sales by Kind of Business[5]

In 1971, merchant wholesale trade reached almost $25 billion (see Table 9-8). The biggest single merchant wholesale business was in the grocery and food specialties field which had 15.5 percent of the total. Five other wholesale fields had sales of over $1 billion — industrial and transportation equipment and supplies, non-electrical construction material and supplies including lumber, automotive parts and accessories, iron and steel, and grain wholesalers. Together, these above six groups accounted for over 50 percent of the total.

The Wholesaling Giants

Except for one company, all the wholesale giants in Canada (defined as those having sales over $200,000,000) are involved with the distribution of groceries. Below are listed the 1971–72 figures:

> *M. Loeb, Ltd.* The company, both directly and through subsidiaries, acts as wholesale distributor of groceries, tobacco, confectionery, produce, meats, frozen foods and other items in Ontario and Quebec. It holds an I.G.A. franchise. Approximate sales are $531 million. This includes the sales of its drug wholesaler subsidiary, National Drug and Chemical Company of Canada.
>
> *The Oshawa Group Ltd.* This company and its subsidiaries supply franchised I.G.A. supermarkets, Food City stores and other independent retailers mainly in Ontario, with a wide range of groceries and related items. The company operates discount food stores, discount department stores (Towers), drug stores and health and beauty aid centres. In addition, food and related products are supplied to institutional customers. Other operations include growing of mushrooms, and frozen food storage and distribution. The company's sales are approximately $490 million.
>
> *Westfair Foods Ltd.* The company is engaged in the wholesale and retail grocery, fruit and vegetable business in western Ontario and western Canada. The retail division operates on 40 stores under the

---

[4] Isaiah A. Litvak and Peter M. Banting, "Manufacturers' Agent — Adaptation or Atrophy," in Bruce E. Mallen and Isaiah A. Litvak, eds., *Marketing: Canada* (Toronto: McGraw-Hill Book Company of Canada Limited, 1968), p. 275.

[5] DBS, "Wholesale Trade," No. 63-008, (Ottawa: Queen's Printer, December 1970).

Shop Easy name and has over 700 affiliates including Tom-Boy, Lucky Dollar, Red & White, and United Purity food market groups. Sales are approximately $250 million.

Kelly, Douglas and Company, Ltd. The company carries on a wholesale and grocery business in British Columbia and the Yukon and retail grocery business in British Columbia. Under the name "Nabob Foods" the company makes packages and distributes food products. Through Super-Valu stores the company has 87 retail outlets in British Columbia, most of which are owner-operated. The company also covers 150 independently owned Red & White stores in British Columbia. It has plants at Burnaby, B.C. and Ajax, Ontario, for processing coffee, tea, and peanut butter. Approximate sales are $249 million.

National Grocers Co. Ltd. This company is a subsidiary of Loblaw Groceterias Co. Ltd. It is engaged in wholesale distribution of groceries in Ontario and Quebec, serving over 9,000 retail grocers. The company supplies Red & White, Super Save, Lucky Dollar and Maple Leaf group stores. It has 38 cash and carry depots and 28 service branches. Its sales are approximately $220 million.

Canadian Tire Corporation Ltd. This company, the only wholesale giant outside the food field, carries on retailing, wholesaling and mail order distribution of accessories and replacement parts for automobiles, as well as tools, sporting goods, bicycles, paints, etc. Some of the larger retail outlets also sell gasoline and provide automotive servicing facilities. The company has 260 associate stores in operation located throughout Manitoba, Ontario, Quebec, Newfoundland and the Maritimes. Sales are approximately $244 million.

10

Pricing and Product Management in Canada

This chapter brings the reader to the second of the three parts of the marketing mix. The past three chapters have dealt with the distribution function. This chapter covers the variables dealing with pricing and product (goods and service) management. The final two chapters will discuss the third part of the marketing mix: the variables dealing with information, advertising and sales management functions.

As already mentioned, this chapter limits its discussion to those aspects of pricing and product management which are different or peculiar to the Canadian scene. One very important set of differences which will *not* be discussed in this chapter are the legal differences, particularly the Combines Investigation Act. These legal aspects were covered in detail in Chapter 6.

PRODUCT MANAGEMENT

Special Canadian Problems in Product Research, Development and Design

Canada's high wage structure, small domestic market, widespread American ownership of Canadian corporations, and proximity to the United States, have all helped to create special problems in the design and development of products in this country.

Technical research is an essential prerequisite to the creation of products, and there is a critical need for more of such research in Canada. Canadian technological development is too greatly dependent upon American and European industry, and this situation is further aggravated by the continuing emigration of Canadian scientists and engineers to the United States and other countries. Canadian subsidiaries of U.S. companies have been criticized as depending far too heavily on parent company product research, development and design.

> Another obvious example of technological domination is found in the Canadian automobile industry which builds in Canada to basic Detroit or South Bend designs. A glance at Thomas' directory of products

clearly demonstrates the domination of other Canadian industrial production by U.S. ideas. This is no criticism of the United States. It does, however, indicate that Canada is a long way from that position of technological independence which a country with our degree of apparent prosperity should be. The lack of technological independence is almost entirely due to the negligible amount of industrial and technological research being carried out in Canada.[1]

Management may claim that the good profits which are made on Canadian-made goods — whose design, development and research is done in the United States — obviate the need for separate Canadian research. This short-sighted outlook has led to the almost complete commercial and technological domination of most of Canadian industry by foreign parent companies. The excuse that our population is too small to allow for the luxury of research is not valid either. One has only to think of Sweden with Saab and Volvo, Switzerland with Brown-Boveri and its watch industry and Holland with Philips, to realize that small countries can have industries which maintain excellent "in-house" research and development activities.[2]

Perhaps because the larger Canadian companies tend to be foreign-owned, there is a resistance in Canada to the use of industrial designers. However, recent years have certainly seen an improvement in this area.[3]

One author finds deplorable the lack of creative design in new products by Canadian firms. He confesses that he can not think of any industrial product which is so distinctively Canadian that the outside world will automatically expect it to come from Canada.[4]

Perhaps an additional reason for the relative lack of initiative in product development is that the Canadian manufacturers find themselves squeezed in a competitive vise between products of low labour-cost countries such as Japan and high U.S. production-run products. In other words, the Canadian manufacturers are not only beset by imports from low wage countries, but must also contend with the high productivity that American manufacturers can generate because of their huge domestic market. Very often, the relatively lower wage structure of Canadian industry vis à vis U.S. industry is not enough to offset the productivity advantage held by American exporters — even with tariffs. After providing an example of how Canadian manufacturers' development costs and risks are much higher relative to those encountered by U.S. manufacturers, B. E. Ohlson, points out:

> The only factor that favours the Canadian manufacturer is the fact that average wages in Canada are about 20% lower. Taking all these factors into account, it is not unusual to find that the pure

[1] Ralph W. Nicholls, "Research and Canadian Industry," *Business Quarterly* 28 (Autumn 1963) , p. 14.
[2] *Ibid.*, p. 20.
[3] "Watch Out — It May Pop," *Monetary Times* 134 (June 1966) , pp. 22-26.
[4] Warnett Kennedy, "Design for Bigger Markets," *Industrial Canada* 62 (July 1961) , pp. 124-28.

manufacturing costs in Canada for a complex product comes out as much as 45% higher.

For less complex and lower price goods which require little or no expenditure for development or tooling and which have proportionately low material cost, it is sometimes possible to equal or even under-cut the corresponding U.S. manufacturing costs. This type of product, in total, represents a very small portion of the entire Canadian dollar volume of sales, and for this reason, is of less significance to Canadian industry overall.[5]

However, Ohlson feels that the Canadian industrial designer who has a firm grasp of the Canadian situation can spur the manufacturer to produce new and original products which will so excel imported goods that the Canadian consumer will turn from imports, even though the price of domestic items may be higher. Other authors agree with this:

> Canadian industry can develop unique Canadian designs. . . . Such firms as Claire Haddad with high fashions, and Highland Queen, with the distinctive Maple Leaf Tartan . . . and the world-famous Bombardier Ski-Doo are a few examples.[6]

Of course, products for the Canadian market must take into consideration the relatively cold weather. They must also consider the need for bilingual appeals and labels. Very often, the French- and English-speaking portions of the country buy different brands to satisfy the same need. The manufacturer producing for the Canadian market must thoroughly understand the differences, if any, within the market for his specific product.

There are a few additional considerations in new product development which are particularly important in Canada:

—The Canadian consumer responds to the simple and graceful form. It would be wonderful if Canadian designers could develop an appealing style which would be recognized as distinctly Canadian. Avoid gaudy and over-trimmed stylings.
—Design for durability, long life, and a lasting appeal. Avoid design for obsolescence and annual model changes. A prolonged product life is a great help in reducing cost as all development and tool cost can be borne by a greater quantity produced for a longer period of time.
—Design the product so it can be easily maintained or repaired. People are tiring of products that are difficult or impossible to repair, so that it is cheaper to buy a new one.
—Design the product for the best possible quality. Quality is one of the best sales arguments and most consumers are willing to pay a higher price for superior quality products.

[5] B. E. Ohlson, "The Challenge of New Product Development," in Bruce E. Mallen and Isaiah A. Litvak, eds., Marketing: Canada, 2nd ed. (Toronto: McGraw-Hill Book Company of Canada Limited, 1968), p. 167.
[6] Peter M. Banting and Isaiah A. Litvak, "The Design Engineer and Marketing Innovation," Business Quarterly 35 (Autumn 1970), pp. 62-69.

—Design for ease of manufacture with simple and inexpensive but nevertheless efficient tools. Utilize the knowledge and experience of the practical men in Canadian factories who have learned how to make things without special equipment or complicated tools. Drawing on their knowledge, it is often possible to improve the design or construction resulting in both lower tool cost and cheaper parts.

—Design for real novelty in the product. It should possibly perform a function in a new and better way, or do it with greater efficiency. Avoid such worthless novelty which adds no useful feature, but merely supplies a "talking point."

—Utilize the possibilities of new materials for better construction or lower cost. For instance, easily produced plastic components may replace more costly metal components. Proper selection of materials can result in improved performance as well as better appearance and utility. Beware of mis-application of new materials which have not yet been thoroughly proven.

—Make a determined effort to solicit ideas for new products from all conceivable sources. Encourage employees in all occupations to speak up with their ideas and solicit comments from your customers. Do not discard ideas which at first appear impractical. They may contain the seed for a very useful and novel product. Never embarrass anyone who might suggest a "crazy idea." This is a sure way of inhibiting the free expression of new ideas.[7]

Canadian Developments in Packaging

The packaging industry in Canada must be one of the most competitive, innovative and fast-changing of any industry. There is a constant flow of new kinds of packages, new ideas and innovation. The dynamism of the industry might even be called bewildering! However, the excitement in this field has not been traditional:

> The upgraded role of packaging in the structure of Canadian business has not been achieved overnight. Bluntly, management of the packaging function has limped behind other key management functions. But that is rapidly changing. In fact, the growth of the packaging function in some companies is faster than the company's own growth. Package designers have a greater stature in these changes too, as well as determining the personality of a package.[8]

It would be most difficult to walk into a supermarket today and find a package which existed as little as five years ago. Packages have been designed to save time, reduce waste and provide convenience. The total sales value of packages in Canada (excluding the product in them) is probably somewhere around the $1.7 billion range. This averages just under 10 percent of the total cost of the product. However, some products

[7] Ohlson, "New Product Development," pp. 169-70.
[8] Eric Haworth, "Packaging: Canada's Billion Dollar Revolution," in Isaiah A. Litvak and Bruce E. Mallen, *Marketing: Canada* (Toronto: McGraw-Hill Book Company of Canada Limited, 1964), p. 155.

such as cosmetics may have a package cost as high as two-thirds of the total cost of the product and package.

In 1969, the manufacturing industries consumed almost $1.2 billion of containers and other packaging supplies (excluding self-manufacturing).[9] The food and beverage industries, e.g., canners, are the most important users, accounting for about 55 percent of the total consumption. Corrugated boxes are the most important single package product, followed by metal cans, folding and set-up boxes, and glass bottles and jars. Together these four categories account for about 57.5 percent of this consumption.

Aerosol containers, bleached board (mainly for milk cartons and frozen foods) and metal cans for the soft drink industry are among some of the popular kinds of packaging today. Indeed, the market for non-returnable containers, both cans and glass, was estimated to be about 30 percent of the total soft drink container market in 1969 compared with 3 percent in 1964.

Other recent developments include the following:

1. Glass combined with plastic to give a lighter, stronger bottle.
2. A new way of "bonding" plastic films together for a stronger, cheaper packaging film.
3. New uses for the paper milk carton and come-back for cellophane.
4. New types of aerosols to give a wider range of use in this fast growing area of packaging.
5. The take-off of the milk pouch — where last year there were only about three dairies using it — now there are about 120 throughout Canada.[10]

What does the future hold in packaging? Certainly, conventional materials will have to fight harder to hold on to traditional markets. More money will be spent on research to find new ways to compete with the exciting new materials that keep popping up. This will mean that the package and buyer will probably get more value for his packaging dollar.

Packaging's progress in Canada is a reflection of package buyer and user demands. Reduced weight, simplicity, greater convenience as well as less costs are emphasized in today's packages.[11]

Another writer[12] pinpoints two major influences which are likely to shape the course of packing in the 1970's: the battle against rising costs and the battle against environmental pollution. ". . . The

[9] Dominion Bureau of Statistics, "Consumption of Containers and Other Packaging Supplies By the Manufacturing Industries, 1969," (Ottawa: Queen's Printer, January 1972).

[10] Sheila Pattison, "Packaging Report," *Marketing* 74 (8 September 1969), p. 26.

[11] Haworth, "Packaging: Canada's Billion Dollar Revolution," p. 159.

[12] Brian C. Greggains, "Packagings In The Seventies," *Industrial Canada* 71 (September 1970), pp. 28-30.

most efficient package for the '70's will therefore be the most economical and the most disposable." Of particular importance are the strengths of corrugated cartons, shrink packaging and packaging films, e.g., bagged liquids like milk pouches. Injection blow molding for plastics, portion packaging and child-proof closures are yet more recent strong developments in packaging.[13]

PRICING

Two Canadian Pricing Surveys

1.   The following is a report of a pricing survey[14] of Canadian manufacturers selling a range of industrial (rather than consumer) goods. It provides the reader with a useful description of the Canadian situation.

The results of the survey indicate that thirty-three of the firms saw themselves as operating in a perfectly competitive market, twenty-four believed that they were in oligopolistic markets, and the remaining ten firms saw themselves as operating in other markets. The firms that placed themselves in the perfect competition category were primarily smaller firms (less than $5 million sales), whereas the larger, more sophisticated companies saw themselves operating in other competitive situations.

Although the tendency for smaller firms to evaluate themselves as perfect competitors is consistent with market structure theory, the large number of firms in this category is open to question. First, few markets in today's economy are perfectly competitive. Second, fifty-four of the sixty-seven respondents identified themselves as leading producers of their products in the Canadian market. It is therefore likely that many of the thirty-three firms who saw themselves operating in a perfectly competitive market were actually participating in a monopolistic competitive market. It may be concluded that these firms could actually enjoy far greater freedom in price setting than they believe is possible.

Ninety-four percent of the manufacturers stated they used a systematic pricing method. The most popular method reported by 55 percent of them was cost-plus. Second was supply-and-demand with 31 percent, followed by break-even point pricing with 12 percent. And least popular with one percent was trial-and-error. The tendency to use supply-demand pricing increased with the size of the firm. This reflects the

[13] Neil MacVicar, "Packaging's Precarious Peak," *Industrial Canada* 72 (April 1972), pp. 19-21. See also John Fellows, "Planning in a Pressure Cooker," *Executive* 14 (May 1972), pp. 17-19.

[14] From Isaiah A. Litvak, J. A. Johnson and Peter M. Banting, "Pricing — Art or Science," *Business Quarterly* 32 (Autumn 1967), pp. 36-45. This section is in essence an abbreviated version of the article.

fact that large firms have cost accounting and marketing research departments which enable them to employ this more sophisticated and difficult method of pricing. It should also be noted that some firms use different methods of pricing for different products.

The factors these firms considered important in setting prices are ranked in Table 10-1. Production costs and domestic competitors' prices share prime and secondary importance almost equally, whereas marketing costs are third in importance. Large firms tended to place primary emphasis on production costs, whereas small firms were chiefly concerned with competitors' prices. This difference in emphasis is attributable to the lack of detailed cost information employed by small firms, and their propensity to match or underbid prices set by the larger firms.

TABLE 10-1 Number of Times Price-Setting Factors Mentioned

Factor	Of Prime Importance	Of Secondary Importance	Of Tertiary Importance
Production costs	32	25	6
Domestic competitors' prices	30	27	2
Marketing costs	3	3	15
Foreign prices	3	7	11

NOTE: Column adds to more than 67 when two or more factors are given equal importance by a firm.

Personal interviews conducted with thirty of the firms indicated that in industrial channel relationships total marketing costs play a much less significant role in deciding whether a product is to be manufactured, than in the consumer goods market. This is primarily because buyers are more knowledgeable and place more emphasis on quality and price.

Ten of the companies surveyed stated they were price followers, twenty-seven saw themselves as price leaders, five felt they did both and twenty-four neither. However, four out of five firms stated that competition has the final say, and price must be adjusted to meet competitors' prices. This finding was the same regardless of the pricing method used, and the frequency of price audit.

Twenty-four of the firms sampled were subsidiaries of foreign companies. Twenty-one had U.S. parent organizations, two British and one German. Nineteen stated they were free of parental influence in their price decisions. In general, the attitudes and pricing methods of foreign subsidiaries were parallel to domestic firms. This confirms results of similar studies conducted on other marketing activities of U.S. subsidiaries in Canada.

Respondents named the sales department as being responsible for making price decisions in 52 percent of the cases. The financial department was identified in 26 percent of the replies, and the production department in 19 percent. The greatest influence wielded over price policy was attributed to the sales department in 71 percent of the replies, with the nearest contender being the finance department with only 11 percent. The second greatest influence exercised over price formulation was that of the finance department with a 48 percent vote, followed by the sales department with 25 percent, and the production department with 21 percent.

All sixty-seven firms affirmed that pricing decisions were made by senior management, and in 84 percent of the replies, this was a committee decision. Only 30 percent stated that once established, prices could be changed by anyone other than the people who set them.

Many businessmen assert that the finance department and financial executives of firms play the key role in pricing decisions. The contradictory results of this study prompted further investigation which disclosed that size has some influence on where the power in pricing lies. It was found that in smaller firms, sales and marketing have overwhelming importance, whereas in larger firms (more than $5 million annual sales) finance assumes a dominant role in pricing. Further, pricing is often the responsibility of the president in small firms, who is usually assisted by the chief sales executive.

In Canada the majority of the firms are small, and owner-managers have often reached the top through the sales route. Thus the president and his immediate subordinates see themselves as marketing or sales people. However, in larger firms, the wide product line, high degree of specialization, and much greater need for control brings the financial executive into price formulation.

When asked whether they regarded pricing as an art or a science, eight of the firms studied said art, twenty-one said science, and thirty-four said a combination of both. Forty-five companies felt that there are universal principles in pricing, and that, in general, they are learned by practice. The most frequently mentioned "principle" was costing.

Forty-six percent of the companies stated that they conduct no research whatever to support their pricing decision. The most frequently mentioned research by the others involved studying their cost records and competitors' prices. Studies of pricing, per se, were mentioned by only a few of the respondents.

Most firms agreed that a knowledge of economic theory would be valuable to a person making pricing decisions, and felt that the "pricing by the seat of the pants" method made no sense at all.

When asked if "practice makes perfect" in pricing, the general consensus was that it did. "Experience should eliminate errors," "less chance of overlooking basic factors involved in any price" and "only for differentiated products, where the manufacturer must guess at the market acceptance of a proposed difference" were typical replies. However, there were a good number of firms who cautioned that this is an easy way to "get in a rut," and that "fresh viewpoints are extremely important." One firm with sales between $5 and $25 million said, "The essence of pricing is flexibility and imagination, hence an art." Thus, although there was a good deal of professed adherence to the science of pricing, indications of scientific pricing were very sparse in this study.

For example, a manufacturer of lumber and building supplies with sales between $1 and $5 million stated, "Pricing in our business is often somewhat of a compromise between a proper price from a profit standpoint, and a price dictated by competition."

A metal fabricator with sales in the $5 to $25 million bracket said, "Application of any price policy depends upon the quality of competitors' management. The 'seat of the pants' method used by competition frustrates orderly pricing. Thus, a scientific approach is impossible."

Throughout the sample, one word dominated all discussion of price. That word: competition.

2.   The second survey was undertaken by the Economic Council of Canada.[15]

The interview survey was conducted among twenty-one companies engaged in manufacturing and resource production in Canada. The great majority of these firms had total assets of over $100 million, and most were in a range from $100 million to $500 million.

While bigness is clearly necessary for some kinds of pricing policy, it does not of itself appear to produce a standard pattern of such policies. One fairly broad generalization may, however, be drawn from the Canadian results, and interestingly enough it constitutes the one significant divergence from U.S.A. findings. This concerns the influence of the external sector, relatively little mentioned in the U.S. study. In Canada, by contrast, considerations of foreign competition appeared to be the broadest and most important limitation on discretionary pricing by large firms. The limitation is evident, first in the position of many exporters, particularly of primary products, who have to meet a world or North American price and have little discretion to set a price on their own; and second, in the practice among many Canadian firms producing for the domestic market of pricing to the landed (tariff-paid) price of competing imports. These two types of situations are widespread though by no means universal. There are, for example, certain exporters who are not wholly without some discretion as to price, and certain industries which price below the landed price of competing imports.

It is also noticeable that certain other types of pricing practice, such as domestic price leadership and the "building up" of a price on a cost-plus-desired-return basis, seem most to prevail where there is an appreciable degree of insulation from external competition, whether as a result of tariffs or transport costs, or both.

The following were some less general but recurrent themes:

[15] Economic Council of Canada, *Third Annual Review* (Ottawa: Queen's Printer, September 1966), pp. 132-36. This section is in essence an abbreviated version of this survey. Reprinted by permission of Information Canada.

1. Apart from foreign competition, the power of large buyers and the competition of substitute materials and products were the factors most often mentioned as tending to limit the scope for discretionary pricing. They did not usually appear to be absolute limitations, but were more in the nature of potential threats discouraging excessive upward price movements. Buyer power was generally conceived as the buyer's ability to turn to foreign suppliers to "integrate backward" and set up as a self-supplier or, in the case of a large retailer, to substitute the retailer's own branded line of goods for that of other suppliers. Competition between different materials seemed to be particularly important in textiles and in the complex of industrial markets for steel, aluminum, copper and plastics.

2. Pricing decisions often appeared to be closely mingled with other corporate decisions, notably in respect of investment. A key price decision might be taken at the same time as the decision to market a new and distinctive product and to set up the necessary productive facilities.

3. The most common company goals relevant for pricing decisions were the achievement of a certain return on investment and the gaining or maintaining of a certain share of the market. The goal of achieving a certain return on sales was also encountered. Companies varied, however, in the immediacy which they assigned to these goals. For some companies, they were serious, practical targets; for others, they were ideal goals which might actually be realized only in an occasional good year. Companies varied, too, in the degree to which they articulated their goals and assigned definite numbers to them.

4. Other things being equal, firms often appeared to have a preference for situations of relatively stable prices, with competition occurring mainly in respect of quality, style, service and advertising.

5. A desire on the part of producers of basic materials to "integrate forward" into more highly processed and fabricated forms of product was also evident. Such integration appeared to offer an ultimate prospect of more stable and certain markets for materials and somewhat greater pricing freedom.

6. The nature of the product was an important factor affecting the possible scope for discretionary pricing. The scope for such pricing appeared to be less for perishable products, and for products whose demand tends to be highly responsive to price changes. For products with a high content of technology, some signs could be discerned of a typical price history. At the outset the price might be relatively high, then decline as increased competition and a reaching out for higher sales volume developed. Differences between pricing policies and profit experience relative to "old" and "new" products could be noted within multi-product firms. The same firm was often engaged in producing newer products, in which it had some technological, patent or other "edge" over its competition, and older and more standardized products, the technology of which had become widely known and disseminated. A more discretionary pricing policy generally applied to the first type of product.

7. In a number of industries, prices of all firms tend to be much influenced by price decisions of the leading firm in the industry.

8. An interesting variant on the practice of pricing to the landed price of imports was that of pricing by suppliers to processors so that the latter would be able to meet the landed price of their import competition. Thus, product "A" might be a major ingredient of product "B." Product "A" would be priced so that product "B" could comfortably meet its import competition.

The Level of Prices — Inflation

The general level of prices is an important factor that the businessman must consider in setting his own prices. The following is a report from the *Sixth Annual Review* of the Economic Council of Canada (September 1969):

> Widespread and generally high rates of price and cost increases have continued, and remain seriously out of line with the Council's views about maintaining reasonable price stability.
>
> For a number of years prior to 1968, rates of increases in prices and costs in the United States had been below those taking place in Canada. But the accelerated general advance in the U.S. price and cost increases in 1968 brought the U.S. advances up sharply to about the rates of increase occurring in Canada, and even faster increases appear to be occurring in the United States than in Canada in 1969.
>
> Consumer price increases have become a matter of increasing concern in both countries, reaching a rate of advance of about four percent in 1968. But as the magnitude of the advance has risen over the past three years, the sources of price increases have changed considerably. Food price increases were the largest contributor to overall consumer price increases over the 1961–66 period (food items have a weight of 27 percent in the total index). But in 1966–69, the focal point has shifted to shelter costs, especially the costs of owner-occupied homes. Although the various shelter cost items have a combined weight of only 18 percent in the total index, this group has contributed some 30 percent of the total price increase in the Consumer Price Index in the last three years. In fact, its contribution rose to over 40 percent in the fall of 1968 and spring of 1969.[16]

One year later, the Council reported:

> Such increases continue to be relatively high and widespread in 1970, although some moderation in the advances of certain general price measures appears to be emerging.[17]

In 1972, the inflation rate was running at about 4.5 percent per year, and many economists were predicting a resurgence of the high rates of 1969–70.

---

[16] Economic Council of Canada, *Sixth Annual Review*, pp. 146-7.
[17] Economic Council of Canada, "Performance and Potential Mid-1950's to Mid-1970's," (Ottawa: Queen's Printer, September 1970), p. 22.

11

Promotion in Canada

This chapter and the next bring the reader to a discussion of the third part of the marketing mix outlined in Chapter One: the variables dealing with information, advertising and personal selling.

Promotion (advertising and personal selling) in Canada has a long and extensive history. In many ways, it was fairly well advanced before the country was born. The first recorded newspaper advertisement appeared in the *Halifax Gazette* on Monday, March 23, 1752.[1] The first daily paper to survive beyond its infancy was issued in 1833 in Montreal, and was in fact called the *Daily Advertiser*.[2] By 1864, three years before Confederation, with a population of less than 3,500,000 Canada had 286 periodicals.[3]

PROMOTION AND CULTURAL FACTORS

Like most cultural phenomena in Canada, promotion has evolved under the pressure of three primary external influences and several internal influences. The three external influences are those of Great Britain, France and the United States. The influences of the first two countries may have been fairly strong in colonial days when European settlers brought with them the signs of their trade such as the barber's pole, the furrier's stuffed bear, the saddler's wooden horse and the money-lender's three spheres.[4] American influence, however, has been far longer-lived and much more pervasive. Canadians, since before Confederation, have had access to American salesmen and periodicals. Many Canadians' first experience with radio and television was via programmes broadcast from those American stations situated close to the Canada-U.S. border. On a professional level, many promotion associations and organizations in Canada such as the Audit Bureau of Circulation and the American Marketing Association are either integral parts of, or closely affiliated with, their larger counterpart in the United States.

[1] H. E. Stephenson and Carlton McNaught, *The Story of Advertising in Canada* (Toronto: Ryerson Press, 1940), p. 1.
[2] *Ibid.*, p. 6.
[3] *Ibid.*
[4] *Ibid.*, pp. 5-6.

One should not however assume that the very powerful influence of the United States has eliminated the differences between the promotional environments of these two friendly, culturally close countries. Differing philosophies and historical accidents have resulted in distinguishable cultural differences which must be taken into account in both the preparation and implementation of any promotional programme in Canada. (See Chapter 3 for a discussion of these differences.)

One distinguishing characteristic of promotion in Canada that is impossible to ignore is the necessity for any national advertiser to communicate in at least the two official languages, namely, English and French. While this fact has long been recognized and is well known, it has taken most Canadian advertisers many years to learn the techniques of advertising in two languages.

As indicated above, advertising in Canada has been greatly influenced by the practices of advertisers in the United States. Similarly, advertising in French Canada has long been dominated and influenced by that of English Canada. Nor is such dominance due entirely to the fact that English Canada is numerically larger. It is at least partly a result of the manner in which the English and French cultures have historically accomodated themselves each to the other. The English community with its access to capital, its Protestant ethic, and its easy means of communicating with the dynamic, industrialized economies of the United States and Britain tended to produce Canada's men of commerce and the young nation's captains of industry. It was, therefore, the well-established English-Canadian and U.S. firms which most felt the need for national advertising and which were best able to take advantage of advertising opportunities. Of these early national advertisers Elkin has written:

> Thus the English-Canadian and American advertisers had a relatively free hand in introducing advertising into Quebec. Their only concern was with the language, since the advertising had to be in French. They saw no reason why advertising carefully prepared and effective for the English should not be equally effective in another language. Therefore, they followed the simplest and cheapest policy: they used the same illustrations and hired translators. Translation was assumed to be a relatively simple task which any French speaking person could handle.[5]

While the technique of translation has undoubtedly served many advertisers well in the past, and even though it is still used extensively, it is no longer the favoured technique it once was. Some slang expressions have no equivalent in French. Some themes such as "Fit for a King" do not hold the same sort of appeal for the French Canadians as

---

[5] Frederick Elkin, "Advertising in French Canada: Innovations and Deviations in the Context of a Changing Society," in G. K. Zollschan and W. Hirsch, eds., *Explorations in Social Change* (Boston: Houghton Mifflin Company, 1963) .

they do for the English Canadian. For these and other reasons, Canadian advertisers have slowly come to recognize that translating English advertisements into French (especially when done literally) may do more to prejudice their image in the French-Canadian market place than if they didn't bother at all.

Fortunately for the Canadian advertiser there are other means of advertising in French Canada. Advertisers can choose, instead of simply translating English advertisements into French advertisements, to adapt their advertisements or to develop a completely separate campaign for the French-Canadian market. According to Elkin,

> The line between translation and adaptation is blurred but, in general adapted advertisements are derived from the English, but have additions or are significantly different in design or meaning. These changes, for any particular advertising campaign, may occur in one or more medium and may vary in their degree of importance. Adaptations may occur in the illustrations, the ideas of the copy or both.[6]

While the technique of adaptation may tend to insure that the advertiser does not commit a faux pas (as so often occurs in the simply translated advertisements) it provides no guarantee that communication will take place; that the advertisement will be relevant to the French-Canadian consumer.

Effectiveness, which in the world of advertising is always difficult to predict, is nevertheless most likely to occur when the advertiser decides to build a separate campaign for the French-Canadian market. Such a decision is of course costly, but it does enable the advertiser to capitalize on our ever increasing knowledge of the unique characteristics of the French market (see Chapter 3). Because in a separate campaign the advertiser is free to choose themes, language and symbols that are particularly appropriate to French Canadians, he is more likely than he otherwise would be, to create advertisements that are unified and consequently synergetically powerful.

However, even though the separate campaign approach may be in general the most effective, it is not necessarily the most efficient choice of an advertiser in every instance. A decision maker should always consider such factors as cost and risk which may justifiably lead him to choose one of the less effective methods.

PERSONAL SELLING

As in most other western industrialized countries, the Canadian businessman can communicate with his customers (and potential customers) in a multitude of ways. For purposes of this discussion, the

---

[6] *Ibid.*

TABLE 11-1 Remuneration of Commercial Travellers

	Executives	Salesmen	Agents	Others
How are you paid?				
Salary only	43.1%	24.8%	3.3%	35.7%
Salary + Bonus	37.6%	34.9%	3.4%	42.9%
Salary + Commission	10.0%	13.2%		14.3%
Salary + Bonus + Commission	4.5%	3.9%		
Commission only	2.8%	17.0%	90.0%	
Commission with Draw	1.0%	5.4%	3.3%	
Commission + Bonus	1.0%	.8%		
Salary + Commission + Draw				
Draw				7.1%
	100.0%	100.0%	100.0%	100.0%
If commission, what percentage?				
Straight Commission:	Range 3–7½%. Average 5%.	Range 2%–50% with many sliding scales; ex: 2–8%; 15–25%. Average 8%.	Range 3–30% sliding scales for different products (1–7%; 3–10%).	(NA)
Commission above Salary (1)	Range .15% to 3–10%. Average 1% for all sales exs. Many overrides of .15%–5%.	Range .15%–5%. Many depend upon quotas; ex: 5% over quotas. Average 2% of sales.	(NA)	Range 2.3%–21%. 6.8% gross profits.
Bonus arrangement (2)	Range of 5% of salary to the discretion of president. Average is based on (a) Company profits, (b) % over quota.	Range 1–5% over quota to discretion of President. Usually tied into sales quotas and company profit.	Range on increase in sales to 15–20% at year end.	Range 1% of this year's sales over average of past 5 years up to 10% of salary, according to performance.
What was your income in 1969? (3)	Range $7,500–55,000. Average: $15,500.	Range $5,300–$40,000. Average: $12,800.	Range $7,500–$82,000. Average $24,400.	Range $5,600–$20,000. Average $12,170.

What type of selling are you engaged in?				
Trade	53.1%	55.0%	70.0%	42.9%
Missionary	19.5%	14.0%	20.0%	42.8%
Technical	45.8%	47.2%	13.3%	57.1%
New Business	22.0%	20.2%	50.0%	28.6%

What fringe benefits do you receive?				
Paid annual vacation	93.6%	69.8%	10.0%	92.8%
Group Life	87.2%	79.1%	23.3%	78.6%
Hospital Ins.	87.2%	77.5%	26.7%	78.7%
Major Medical	81.7%	74.4%	23.3%	71.4%
Entertainment Expenses	86.2%	69.0%	13.3%	78.6%
Out-of-town Expenses	91.7%	74.4%	16.7%	92.9%
Paid phone calls	82.6%	76.7%	23.3%	85.7%
Pension Plan	79.8%	67.4%	16.7%	64.3%
Car or car use compensation	85.3%	76.7%	13.3%	92.9%
Sales samples provided	61.5%	69.8%	56.7%	49.9%

What sales incentives does your firm use?				
Cash	29.4%	20.2%	10.0%	28.5%
Gifts	28.4%	15.5%	16.7%	14.3%
Travel	13.8%	3.1%	6.7%	7.1%
Other		.7%		
	71.5%	39.5%	33.4%	49.9%

SOURCE: Canadian Salesman 21:4(July 1970), p. 3.

[1] The average varies greatly — probably because of the different types of products and services and types of customers. For example, heavy machinery vs. groceries; small stores vs. institutions.

[2] Bonus systems vary widely and it is impossible to give averages.

[3] It is difficult to find a real average because some (especially commission men) reported gross earnings, while others reported net. For example, one reported a gross of $55,000 and a net of $10,000. Lack of benefits cause commiss on incomes to distort picture.

forms of promotion are broken down into two broad categories — personal selling and advertising. Since personal selling is the oldest and most flexible form of promotion, it will be examined first.

Personal selling is a potent and rapidly growing element in Canadian marketing. As of the 1961 census, sales occupations totaled just over 410,000* and involved 6.35 percent of the labour force. This represented an increase of 43 percent over the previous ten years, a rate that was considerably higher than the average rate of increase (22.4 percent) for all occupations.[7]

While there is no evidence to suggest that the techniques of personal selling, as practiced in Canada, differ from those of other economically advanced countries, there are differences in the environment. The average travelling salesman in Canada for example is likely to have a much larger territory to cover than does his counterpart in the United States or in Europe. If his territory is based in, or includes, the province of Quebec, or even particular areas of Ontario or the maritime provinces, he will probably be required to be fluent in French, if not bilingual.[8] If his territory is at all large, he must be aware of, and develop a healthy respect for, the many significant inter-regional differences in language, custom, culture and business methods that he will encounter. In short, he must recognize that Canada is not a mass market, but "a string of regional markets strung along the U.S. border."[9]

For his efforts, the professional salesman in Canada can expect to be well paid although his earnings are likely to be twenty to thirty percent lower than in the United States.[10] In 1968, the starting base for new men was $5,881 (vs. $6,600 for the U.S.).[11] Although the average earnings are lower than in the United States, there is a greater tendency for Canadian firms to make use of "straight salary" and "salary and commission" plans. Thus, the Canadian salesman is likely to receive more fringe benefits. For example, 90 percent of Canadian firms reported that they pay for all their salesmens' vacations, compared with 79 percent in the U.S.[12]

While averages are meaningful, it would be erroneous to conclude that the opportunities for the professional salesman in Canada are very much different from that of his U.S. counterpart. A recent study of its members by the Commercial Travellers Association, one of the oldest and largest organizations of professional salesmen, indicates a very wide range of incomes and terms of employment (see Table 11-1).

* It should be noted that this figure represents a very broad definition. It includes such occupations as service station attendants, sales clerks and auctioneers, but excludes driver salesmen and sales managers.

[7] Sylvia Ostry, *The Occupational Composition of The Canadian Labour Force* (Ottawa: Queen's Printer, 1967), pp. 56-73.

[8] See J. Pierre Jasmin, "How to Hire Salesmen in Quebec," *Sales Promotion*, February-March 1964, p. 28.

[9] G. Robert McGoldrick, "The Case for Market Segmentation in Canada," *The Marketer* 1 (Spring 1965), p. 3.

[10] "Memo," *Canadian Business* 42 (June 1969), p. 72.

[11] *Ibid.*

[12] *Ibid.*

ADVERTISING

Mass Media

The advertiser in Canada can choose from among 395 radio stations, 77 primary television stations (i.e., exclusive of satellite stations), 116 daily newspapers, not to mention over 1600 other assorted publications ranging from the *Georgia Straight* (one of several underground newspapers) to the *United Church Observer*.[13]

These organizations, together with those who publish directories, catalogues and various other forms of print media, and those who handle outdoor advertising receive about a billion dollars annually in advertising revenues, as shown in Table 11-2.

TABLE 11-2 Estimated Net Advertising Revenue by Medium, 1972

	(thousands of dollars)	
Broadcast		
Radio	$124,000	
Television	136,000	$ 260,000
Newspapers		
Dailies	$335,000	
Weekend supplements	22,000	
Weeklies (incl. semi. and tri.)	55,000	412,000
Periodicals		
General magazines	$ 30,000	
Business papers	28,000	
Farm papers	5,000	
Directories (phone, city)	55,000	
Religious, school and other	3,000	121,000
Other Print (Catalogues, direct mail, etc.)		244,000
Outdoor		108,000
Total		$1,145,000*

SOURCE: *Adapted from Maclean-Hunter Research Bureau,* A Report on Advertising Revenues in Canada *(Toronto: Maclean-Hunter Limited, 1971) pp. 1-5.*

* It should be noted that this figure does not represent total advertising expenditures in Canada. It does not include internal advertising costs (estimated by DBS at $3 million for 1965), agency billings and several other items such as imported signs and certain direct mail costs.

While advertising revenue for all media has more than tripled since 1954, some media appear to have grown much more than others, as Table 11-3 shows. The most impressive growth has, of course, been achieved by television followed by that of outdoor advertising. Weekly newspapers have almost managed to hold their own, while radio and directories have experienced only modest relative growth. Daily newspapers have lost some of their influence, but still receive the largest

[13] Honourable Keith Davey (Chairman), *The Report of the Special Senate Committee on Mass Media* (Ottawa: Queen's Printer, 1970).

TABLE 11-3 Net Advertising Revenues, Share of each Medium, 1954-1971

| | Broadcast | | Newspapers | | | Periodicals | | | | | Other Print | Outdoor |
	Radio	TV	Daily	Weekend Supplements	Weekly Semi- and Tri	General Maga-zines	Business Papers	Farm Papers	Direct. Phone, City	Relig., School and Other	Catalogues, Direct Mail	Billboards, Car Cards Signs, etc.
1954	9.3%	2.5%	34.2%	3.4%	5.3%	4.2%	4.9%	1.4%	3.6%	0.7%	25.2%	5.2%
1955	8.7	3.6	33.9	3.4	5.1	4.2	4.9	1.3	3.7	0.7	24.9	5.8
1956	9.0	6.3	32.9	3.4	4.5	4.1	4.8	1.5	3.7	0.6	23.4	5.8
1957	8.9	7.0	31.9	3.3	4.2	3.9	5.0	1.4	4.1	0.6	24.0	5.7
1958	9.0	7.8	31.4	3.2	4.2	3.7	4.8	1.3	4.6	0.6	23.3	6.1
1959	9.2	9.1	31.8	2.9	4.2	3.5	4.8	1.3	4.9	0.6	21.2	6.4
1960	9.2	9.1	30.9	3.1	4.3	3.8	4.7	1.2	5.2	0.4	21.4	6.7
1961	8.8	9.6	30.8	3.0	4.3	3.5	4.5	1.0	5.4	0.4	21.9	6.9
1962	9.0	10.3	30.8	2.8	4.3	3.0	4.1	0.9	5.4	0.4	21.7	7.2
1963	9.4	11.2	29.9	2.7	4.1	2.8	4.0	0.9	5.2	0.4	22.7	6.7
1964	9.7	12.0	29.0	2.7	4.0	2.6	3.9	0.8	5.1	0.3	22.2	7.7
1965	9.5	12.3	29.8	2.3	4.2	2.6	4.0	0.6	4.7	0.4	21.3	8.2
1966	9.9	12.4	28.9	2.1	4.2	2.7	3.6	0.7	4.6	0.4	21.3	9.1
1967	10.1	12.7	27.4	1.8	5.1	2.6	3.7	0.7	4.6	0.4	21.0	9.7
1968	10.4	12.6	28.4	1.9	5.5	2.6	3.1	0.6	4.7	0.4	20.4	9.4
1969	10.7	12.3	29.4	1.9	5.0	2.6	3.0	0.6	4.8	0.3	20.0	9.3
1970*	10.7	12.3	28.5	1.8	4.8	2.7	2.8	0.5	4.7	0.3	21.4	9.4
1971*	10.8	11.8	29.1	1.9	4.8	2.6	2.6	0.5	4.8	0.3	21.4	9.4
1972*	10.8	11.9	29.3	1.9	4.8	2.6	2.4	0.4	4.8	0.3	21.3	9.4

SOURCE: *Maclean-Hunter Research Bureau, A Report on Advertising Revenues in Canada, p. 8.*

* M-H Research Bureau estimates.

single portion of the advertiser's dollar. Similarly, catalogues and direct mail would appear to be firmly entrenched on the scene even though they have not grown as rapidly as the other media. Those media that appear to have been significantly hurt by the changing times are the periodicals and the weekend supplements.

RADIO

As of the beginning of 1970, there were 395 AM and FM radio stations broadcasting in Canada. Slightly less than half, or 164, were owned by, or affiliated with the CBC (the Canadian Broadcasting Corporation), a Crown Corporation owned by the federal government, but in part supported by advertising. The geographical distribution of these stations is shown in Table 11-4. Even though about 80 percent of the French-language stations are found in Quebec, 80 percent of the Canadian population have access to one or more French-language stations.[14]

TABLE 11-4 Canadian Radio Stations as of February, 1970

Province	Number of Stations	CBC Owned	CBC Affiliate	French Language
CANADA	395	45	119	84
British Columbia	58	4	27	1
Alberta	29	2	4	1
Saskatchewan	22	2	3	3
Manitoba	19	3	5	1
Ontario	125	7	37	8
Quebec	79	8	31	69*
New Brunswick	15	5	5	3
Nova Scotia	21	2	6	0
Prince Edward Island	3	1	1	0
Newfoundland	18	7	0	0
Yukon	2	1	0	0
Northwest Territories	4	3	0	0

SOURCE: *Canadian Radio-Television Commission*, Annual Report, 1969-70.

* Two of these stations are bilingual.

Since the advent of television in Canada in the early fifties, radio has had to make some considerable adjustments in order to hold its own. In general, radio station have successfully adjusted by catering to their local community and often to some particular segment of their community. The result is that radio has become an important voice for local advertisers, who provide about 60 percent of the revenue for radio stations compared to only 20 percent for television stations.[15]

Two other factors that contribute towards making radio an efficient and effective medium are the relatively small number of radio

[14] Davey, *Report of the Committee*, vol. II, p. 273.
[15] Dominion Bureau of Statistics, *Advertising Expenditures in Canada, 1967* (Ottawa: Queen's Printer, June 1970), p. 10.

stations and the fact that Canadians do tend to listen to radio. On the first point, R. M. McClelland has noted that Canada has considerably fewer stations per capita than the U.S. He points out that in 1966 there were only eight stations in Toronto, while Washington, D.C., a city of similar size, had twenty-six stations.[16] McClelland also cites evidence to suggest that Canadians tend to spend a significantly greater number of hours listening to radio than do their American neighbours.[17]

TELEVISION

Like radio, television in Canada is a mixture of private and public ownership. There are two major network systems, the aforementioned CBC (publicly owned) and CTV (privately owned). (At the time of writing, the formation of a new privately-owned television network was announced.) Also, like radio, the CBC television networks

TABLE 11-5 Canadian Basic Television Stations as of March, 1970

| Province | Total | Network Affiliation | | | French |
		CBC	CTV	Independent	
CANADA	77	61	12	4	15
British Columbia	8	7	1	0	
Yukon	1	1	0	0	
Alberta	7	5	2	0	1
Saskatchewan	7	6	1	0	0
Manitoba	5	4	1	0	1
Ontario	19	15	3	1	1
Quebec	17	13	1	3	11
New Brunswick	4	3	1	0	1
Nova Scotia	3	2	1	0	0
Prince Edward Island	1	1	0	0	0
Newfoundland	5	4	1	0	0

SOURCE: Adapted from Keith Davey (Chairman), The Report of the Special Senate Committee on Mass Media, vol. II (Ottawa: Queen's Printer, 1970), p. 274.

(English and French) are dependent in part upon commercials for revenue.[18] Although the CTV network has only twelve stations compared to the CBC's sixty-one (see Table 11-5), CTV's stations are located in the largest urban markets enabling it to provide relatively complete and competitive national coverage. While French-language TV does not have

---

[16] R. M. McClelland, "Advertising in a Foreign Country — Canada," in Bruce E. Mallen and Isaiah A. Litvak, eds., Marketing: Canada, 2nd ed. (Toronto: McGraw-Hill Book Company of Canada Limited, 1968), p. 290.

[17] Ibid.

[18] In 1969 the CBC as a whole (Radio and TV) received about $40 million or about 20 percent of its income from advertising. The major portion of its income was in the form of government grants totalling some $148 million. See Davey, Report of the Committee, vol. II, p. 548.

as large a penetration as French-language radio, it is important to note that nearly a third of the French-language stations are located outside the province of Quebec.

One important fact about TV in Canada that is not revealed by analyzing Canadian television statistics is the extent to which Canadians watch American television. In a recent study, 54 percent of Canadians stated that they preferred American TV (compared to only 4 percent preferring American radio and only 2 percent American newspapers).[19] And most Canadians have the opportunity to exercise this preference. It has been estimated that about 70 percent of the population have access to American TV, either directly or via a cable system.[20] In the Vancouver area, one study found that in cable homes, 40 percent of the viewing hours were on U.S. channels.[21] While it is difficult to predict the future, there is little doubt that cable television will revolutionize TV broadcasting in Canada and will do so fairly soon. At present it is estimated that 17 percent of all Canadian homes have cable TV (compared to only 6.29 percent in the U.S.) and that this figure is growing at an annual rate of as much as 48 percent![22] At this rate, virtually all homes in Canada may be serviced with cable TV by 1975. What effect such a development will have upon television's status as the medium of national advertisers (80 percent of TV revenue came from national advertisers in 1967[23]) is uncertain.

NEWSPAPERS

There are in Canada 116 daily newspapers, about one for every 200,000 people. In the U.S. there is one daily newspaper for about every 100,000 people.[24] Thus an advertiser in Canada can cover a larger proportion of the population with fewer papers. The task is also made somewhat simpler by the fact that only ten Canadian cities have more than one daily newspaper.[25] When one considers this, together with the facts that (a) about 80 percent of the population claim to read a daily newspaper on a daily basis,[26] and (b) more than half of Canadians consider newspaper advertising to be "news,"[27] it is little wonder that advertisers have continued to invest heavily in newspaper advertising. The bulk of the growth, however, has come from local rather than national advertisers. Like radio, the role of the newspaper appears to be shifting from that of a national medium to more and more of a local medium (see Table 11-6).

[19] Davey, *Report of the Committee*, vol. III, p. 131.
[20] Davey, *Report of the Committee*, vol. II, p. 359.
[21] *Ibid.*, p. 387.
[22] *Ibid.*, p. 357.
[23] DBS, *Advertising Expenditures in Canada, 1967*, p. 10.
[24] McClelland, "Advertising," p. 289.
[25] Davey, *Report of the Committee*, vol. I, p. 19.
[26] *Ibid.*, vol. III, pp. 47-48.
[27] *Ibid.*, p. 99.

TABLE 11-6 Components of Net Advertising Revenues of Newspapers 1966–1971 ($000)

	1966	1967	1968	1969	1970 (est.)	1971 (est.)
Dailies						
National	59,761	58,972	56,411	66,236	65,700	75,000
Local	121,906	126,705	142,056	156,459	164,300	176,000
Classified	53,248	54,133	61,605	73,464	72,000	71,000
Total	234,915	239,810	260,072	269,159	302,000	322,000
Weekend Supplements						
National	16,131	15,506	15,815	17,263	17,400	19,000
Local	1,259	412	1,412	2,132	2,000	2,200
Total	17,391	15,918	17,227	19,395	19,400	21,200
Weeklies (incl. semi. tri., etc).						
National	7,395	8,612	11,002	10,453	10,000	10,500
Local	27,062	36,140	38,901	39,934	41,000	43,000
Total	34,457	44,752	49,903	50,387	51,000	53,500

SOURCE: *Adapted from Maclean-Hunter Research Bureau,* A Report on Advertising Revenues in Canada, *p. 6.*

While daily newspapers appear to have become more of a medium for the local advertiser, Canada's 900 or so weeklies (including semi-weeklies, tri-weeklies, etc.) have been fairly successful in garnering both national and local advertising although, of course, their real source of support is local advertising.

PERIODICALS

For purposes of this section, the term periodicals includes general magazines, business trade and agricultural publications, religious and school publications, as well as assorted other journals not included under the heading of newspapers. Since space precludes dealing with each of these types of periodical in detail, the discussion here will be confined mainly to that of the most important category — general circulation magazines.

While the advertiser in Canada still has considerable choice among magazines, as shown in Table 11-7, he has tended in the last few years to rely relatively less upon this medium than upon most others. As was seen in Table 11-3, the share of the advertiser's media dollars for virtually all categories of periodicals has declined steadily.

The primary reason for the decline of magazines as an advertising medium in Canada is, of course, the lack of circulation or conversely the relatively high cost to the advertiser. For example, the advertising cost-per-thousand of *Time* (Canadian edition) is $9.14 compared to only $5.45 for its American edition.[28]

The lack of circulation of Canadian magazines appears to be a

[28] *Ibid.,* p. 218.

TABLE 11-7 Canadian Magazines by Per Issue Circulation

Magazine	Per Issue Circulation	Magazine	Per Issue Circulation
Weekend Magazine (E)	2,017,000	Co-operative Consumer (E)	209,000
The Canadian (E)	2,000,000	The Saskatchewan Motorist (E)	188,000
Homemakers Digest (E)	1,100,000	Allo Police (F)	174,000
Madame Au Foyer (F)		Canadian Motorist (E)	167,000
Reader's Digest (E)	1,085,000	Canadian High News (E)	159,000
Key Map Digest (E)	1,005,000	TV Hebdo (F)	142,000
Chatelaine (E&F)	944,000	La Patrie (F)	138,000
Maclean's (E&F)	885,000	The Alberta Motorist (E)	131,000
TV Guide (E)	759,000	Photo Journal (F)	131,000
Perspectives (F)	473,000	Almanach du Peuple (F)	123,000
Time Canada (E)	410,000	Miss Chatelaine (E)	120,000
The United Church Observer (E)	323,000	Saturday Night (E)	102,000
Canadian Boy (E)	306,000	B.C. Motorist (E)	112,000
Dimanche Matin (F)	289,000	Sports Famille (F)	110,000
Legion (E)	286,000	Actualité (F)	110,000
Globe Magazine (E)	258,625	Echos Vedettes (F)	110,000
Sélection du Reader's Digest (F)	265,000	Quest (E)	107,000
Canadian Churchman (E)	266,000	Nouvelles Illustrées (F)	104,000
Le Petit Journal (F)	225,000	Toronto Calendar (E)	120,000

Magazines with circulations between 20,000 and 100,000: Passport, Best Wishes (E), Hockey News (E), Le Nouveau Samedi (F), Téléradiomonde (F), Sunday Sun (E), Dernière Heure (F), Le Journal Des Vedettes (F), Autoclub (Bi), Rod & Gun in Canada (E), Hockey Pictorial (E), La Semaine (F), Canadian Football News (E), Photo Vedettes (F), Vie et Carrière (F), Toronto Life (E), What's On in Ottawa (E), Know Canada (E), Current Events à Montréal (E), Golf Canada (Bi), Wildlife Crusader (E), Country Guide (E), Echoes (E), The Scout Leader (E), B.C. Outdoors (E), Blue Water Circle Drives (E), Canadian Geographic Journal (E), The Atlantic Advocate (E), Au Grand Air (F), The Cadet Traveller (E), Key to Toronto (E).

SOURCE: Davey, Report of the Committee, vol. III (Ottawa: Queen's Printer, 1970), p. 240.

CODE: English (E), French (F).

function of three basic factors. First of all, Canadians do not buy many magazines. Americans buy 60 percent more magazines per capita than do Canadians.[29] At the same time, there is some evidence that the magazines that Canadians do buy are better read.[30] Second, as in the U.S. the growth of television seems to have had a more adverse effect upon magazines than upon other competing media. Third, Canadians have a far greater propensity to buy American magazines than their own. And while the magazines of both countries are losing circulation in Canada, the Canadian magazines are losing more rapidly, as Table 11-8 shows. The implications of the Canadian scene for the multinational advertiser are obvious. He can, for example, reach more Canadians by advertising in *Life* than he can by advertising in *Chatelaine,* even though *Chatelaine* has one of the highest per capita penetrations of its available audience

[29] *Ibid.,* vol. I, p. 156.
[30] McClelland, "Advertising," p. 293.

in the world.[31] And he'll reach more young Canadian men with one advertisement in *Playboy* than he will by advertising in any number of Canadian magazines.

TABLE 11-8 Magazine Circulation in Canada

| | Thousands of Copies | | Percentage |
	1959	1969	Decrease
American magazines	147,000	130,000	11.2%
Canadian magazines	45,000	33,800	24.9%
Total	192,000	164,300	

SOURCE: *Adapted from Davey,* Report of the Committee, vol. I *(Ottawa: Queen's Printer, 1970), p. 156.*

Advertising Agencies

As in the United States, advertising agencies in Canada were preceded by independent agents who solicited advertising from businessmen on behalf of one or a few newspapers. It is generally conceded that the first real advertising agency in Canada was that formed by Anson McKim who previously had solicited advertising in Montreal on behalf of *The Mail,* a Toronto newspaper. He founded A. McKim and Company in January 1889 on St. James Street in Montreal.[32] This was about twenty years after N. W. Ayer and Son Inc. was founded in the U.S.

The practices developed by Anson McKim and succeeding advertising agencies appear to have closely paralleled those of the U.S. agencies. In particular, the practice of remunerating the agencies by way of a 15 percent commission paid by the media has dominated in both countries. Only today is this practice being actively questioned, although most people have long recognized that the real clients of the advertising agencies are the advertisers not the media.

While advertising agencies in Canada have grown to the extent that their role in the promotional process is no longer questioned (see Table 11-9) it has not been without considerable difficulty. Even today much advertising (especially local advertising) is placed not by agencies but directly by the advertiser, as detailed in Table 11-10.

Advertising agencies in Canada, relative to their U.S. counterparts, must also contend with the problem of a higher relative cost of doing business. For example, the cost of preparing a television storyboard is not likely to be much less in Toronto than it is in New York.[33] Yet the size of the account, in terms of commissionable billings, is likely to be much less in Canada. One way to minimize these costs for both the agency

[31] Davey, *Report of the Committee,* vol. I, p. 156.
[32] Stephenson and McNaught, *Story of Advertising,* pp. 18-30.
[33] In many cases, two storyboards might be required — one French and one English.

TABLE 11-9 Advertising Agencies in Canada, 1966-1969

Year	Amount of Billings				Gross Revenue on						Net Profit (before deduction for income taxes)
	Number of Firms	Advertising Billings (1)	Market Surveys, Research and Other Fees	Total	Advertising Billings (1) Amount	Per cent of Billings	Market Surveys, Research and Other Fees (2)	Other Gross Operating Revenue (retainers, fees where commission is not applicable or was rebatable to the client)	Total Amount	Per cent of Billings	
		dollars						dollars			dollars
1964	149	314,354,627	3,785,712	318,140,339	49,619,164	15.8	3,785,712	187,056	53,591,932	16.8	4,081,379
1965	159	358,264,704	4,294,643	362,559,347	56,497,703	15.8	4,294,643	202,368	60,994,714	16.8	5,712,001
1966	165	396,687,409	5,488,460	402,175,869	61,227,597	15.4	5,488,460	199,128	66,915,185	16.6	6,578,493
1967	176	424,845,770	4,749,467	429,595,237	67,871,692	16.0	4,749,467	213,445	72,834,604	17.0	6,019,603
1968	171	421,812,807	4,332,114	426,144,921	67,833,415	16.1	4,332,114	310,745	72,476,274	17.0	4,744,010
1969	163	450,332,349	5,810,461	455,142,810	73,225,447	16.3	3,964,017	1,684,711	78,874,175	17.3	9,388,551

SOURCE: Dominion Bureau of Statistics, Advertising Agencies (Ottawa: Queen's Printer, 1971), p. 5.

1 Includes production work done by agency staff.
2 The 1969 data is not comparable to prior years

TABLE 11-10 Proportion of Advertising Placed by Agencies

Medium	Estimated Gross Expenditure by Medium ($)	Proportion of Total Gross Advertising Handled through Agency Accounts (%)	Proportion of Total Gross Advertising for Each Medium made up of National Advertising (%)
Publications	429,176,000	35.6	38.8
Television	129,589,000	94.3	80.0
Radio	95,678,000	49.6	44.0

SOURCE: *Davey*, Report of the Committee, *vol. II, p. 144.*

and the advertiser, is to import or borrow campaigns and commercials from a U.S. parent or affiliate whenever possible. This, of course, encourages those companies that operate in both countries to choose an agency that also operates in both countries. Consequently, the number of American firms who are members of the Institute of Canadian Advertisers (formerly the Canadian Association of Advertising Agencies) has grown from three in 1950 to thirteen in 1968. These thirteen American-owned agencies in 1968 represented 26 percent of ICA membership and accounted for 36 percent of the volume of business done by member agencies.[34]

"The Advertising Gap"

One of the curious facts about advertising in Canada which has become generally acknowledged, is that considerably less advertising is done in Canada than in the United States. In absolute terms, most of the difference is, of course, accounted for by virtue of the fact that the United States has approximately ten times the population of Canada. But even after acknowledging this fact, it remains that about twice as many dollars per capita are spent in the United States as are spent in Canada. Part of this remaining difference can be explained in terms of the lower per capita income of Canadians. And part can be explained by American businesses advertising to Canadians through American magazines and television (the cost of which will not be reflected in Canadian data unless the American firm pro-rates the cost to a Canadian subsidiary). These differences of course are at least partially, if not completely, offset by the higher cost of advertising in two languages in Canada.

Not only does this differential between levels of advertising exist for two countries so close together geographically, but it has existed at least since the end of World War II.[35] And furthermore, it does

[34] Davey, *Report of the Committee,* vol. II, pp. 136-137.
[35] O. J. Firestone, *The Economic Implications of Advertising* (Toronto: Methuen Publications, 1967), p. 49.

not appear that the gap will get any narrower in the near future. In fact, the Economic Council of Canada predicts that while advertising expenditures will continue to rise in an absolute sense, as a percentage of Gross National Product they will fall from 1.41 percent in 1969 to 1.37 percent in 1975.[36]

Probably the most complete analysis of "the advertising gap" is that of O. J. Firestone, who has concluded that the underlying reasons are:

1. *Innovation lag.* Since new products are most often the work of American entrepreneurs they are usually introduced to the American market first. If a new product fails in the U.S. it is not likely to be introduced in Canada. Thus, much of the advertising for product failures never takes place in Canada. If a new product is successful in the U.S. it is likely to have already become somewhat known by the time it is introduced in Canada, due to the spillover effect of U.S. advertising and publicity. Thus, the amount of new product advertising in Cnaada is likely to be proportionately less than in the United States.

2. *Psychological lag.* The American businessman, existing in a more affluent society, may tend to have a set of attitudes and values (e.g. optimism, venturesomeness) that leads him to be more experimental than his Canadian counterpart when it comes to satisfying consumers' needs — both material and non-material.

3. *Expenditure lag.* Given the innovation lag and the psychological lag, it follows that there would be differences in the rates and types of business investment which would in turn affect the rates of advertising expenditure.[37]

Promotion and Canadian Society

Promotion, by its simplest definition, is no more and no less than communication; a particular form of communication — from expectant seller to prospective buyer — but communication nonetheless. As John Dewey once said, "the community exists in communication." One cannot and should not therefore ignore the fact that promotion is inextricably a part of the community within which it is presented. If a firm's promotion is to have any value, it must have some effect upon the community; yet to be accepted by the community the promotion must be a function of the mores, values and attitudes prevalent in the community at that time. It is this dual realization — that promotion is both a cause and an effect — combined with the fact that promotion is highly visible and obvious, that makes it, more than any other business activity, a matter of public examination.

In recent years, promotion in Canada has received a good deal of public attention and is likely in the future to receive much more.

[36] Economic Council of Canada, *Sixth Annual Review* (Ottawa: Queen's Printer, September 1969) .

[37] Firestone, *Economic Implications of Advertising*, pp. 54-57.

Many provinces, for example, have passed "second thought" legislation which permits a consumer, under certain circumstances, to break a sales contract with a salesman within a specified period of time. Advertising has been subjected to critical examination in several investigations by such public bodies as the Economic Council of Canada, the Prairie Provinces' Royal Commission on Consumer Problems & Inflation, and the Special Senate Committee on Mass Media. In addition, the Consumers Association of Canada and the federal government's Department of Consumer and Corporate Affairs are continuously and actively concerned with the matter of promotion (see Chapter 6 for elaboration of this point). While most of these studies have suggested that particular promotional practices are not what they should be, they have also in general affirmed the need for consumers to have information and the right of businessmen to promote their products and services.

Perhaps most revealing of the public's attitudes towards promotion are the findings of a recent study by Martin Goldfarb, commissioned by the Special Senate Committee on Mass Media.[38] Goldfarb found that 84 percent of Canadians believe that advertising has a positive role to play, although 35 percent believe they are not at all influenced by advertising. An astonishingly high 42 percent believe that advertising influences society more than the Canadian school system. Canadians appear

TABLE 11-11 Attitudes of Canadians Toward Advertisement of Certain Products

Articles	Percent of Individuals Stating Product should be Banned in Advertising
Sleeping pills	66
Cigarettes	60
Liquor	55
Glue	52
Beer	39
Wine	35
Soft drinks	16
Gasoline	11

SOURCE: *Davey*, Report of the Committee, *vol. III, p. 33*

as well to consider advertising to be much more than a purely business activity. Thirty-three percent stated that they find television advertisements sometimes more interesting than the programmes, 51 percent consider newspaper advertisements can be called news, and fully 72 percent think advertising is an art form. Such positive attitudes to advertising notwithstanding, Canadians feel that a number of products should not be advertised at all (see Table 11-11).

While such findings would seem to indicate that the notion of promotion is one that is generally accepted and supported within the Canadian community, one must be aware, as John A. Irving has argued,

[38] Davey, *Report of the Committee,* vol. III.

that Canadians have not yet developed a genuine community.[39] Until Canada can overcome (or compensate for) the problems of vast distances between cities, the closeness to the U.S. and the solitude of two major cultural groups, promotion in general and advertising in particular is likely to remain a subject of much mixed opinion and an object of continuing public scrutiny.

APPENDIX: Associations Basically Concerned with Advertising[40]

*Association of Canadian Advertisers,** 159 Bay Street, Toronto 116, represents 200 Canadian national advertisers whose combined budgets represent approximately 75 per cent of the total amount spent on national advertising. The primary object of the A.C.A. is to promote the highest standards of advertising so that it may be a more effective tool of business and management.

Association Canadienne de la Radio et de la Télévision de Langue Française Inc., 1454 Mountain Street, Montreal 25, represents the majority of French radio and television stations in promoting, encouraging and developing interest towards French radio and television broadcasting.

*Association of Industrial Advertisers,** 255 Davenport Road, Toronto 180, promotes better communication in the industrial advertising field. Membership 310, representing major industrial advertisers. The Canadian A.I.A. is Region Six of the U.S.-based Association of Industrial Advertisers, with chapters in Montreal and Toronto. Canadian Industrial Advertisers, on the other hand, is a wholly Canadian organization.

Audit Bureau of Circulations, 335 Bay Street, Toronto 105, reports figures and facts relating to the quantity and quality of member publishers' circulations, verifies the data through regular audit, then disseminates the data to its advertiser, advertising agency and publisher members. Membership 4,070.

BBM Bureau of Measurement, 120 Eglinton Avenue East, Toronto 310, conducts measurements of radio and television station audiences for the use of its members. Membership 530.

Canadian Advertising Advisory Board, 159 Bay Street, Toronto 116, advances the interests of the advertising industry as a whole and handles consumer complaints. Its membership, totalling 125, consists of the main media organizations and associations, individual advertisers and advertising agencies.

Canadian Advertising & Marketing Personnel Bureau, 67 Yonge Street, Toronto 215, services advertising agencies and marketing companies

---

[39] John A. Irving, *Mass Media in Canada* (Toronto: Ryerson Press, 1962), p. 223.

[40] Most of the information in this section has been adapted from *Report of the Committee,* vol. II, chapter 2.

* Denotes an association that is in turn a member of the Canadian Advertising Advisory Board.

in personnel matters and staff recruitment. Most agencies operating in Canada are members.

Canadian Advertising Research Foundation Inc., 159 Bay Street, Toronto 116, conducts research into advertising and marketing techniques. Membership 12, representing industry organizations.

Canadian Association of Broadcasters* (L'Association Canadienne des Radio-diffusers), 85 Sparks Street, Ottawa 4, represents 286 radio, 54 television stations, and the CTV network, or nearly all the private sector of broadcasting in Canada. Established in 1926, as a voluntary trade association, the C.A.B.'s aims and objectives are to foster and develop, protect and serve the interests of broadcasting. C.A.B.'s head office is in Ottawa, with branches in Montreal and Toronto.

The C.A.B. controls the franchise and commission system in radio and television.

Canadian Daily Newspaper Publishers Association,* 250 Bloor Street East, Toronto 285, represents almost all daily newspapers in Canada. Its purpose is to elevate the standard of newspaper publishing in Canada, to foster business and business interests of its members. The C.D.N.P.A. formerly controlled the franchises of advertising agencies and the commission system through which advertising agencies are paid for their services. Since April, 1970, they have restricted themselves to providing a credit listing service to member newspapers, which decide themselves whether or not to do business with agencies.

Canadian Direct Mail Association, 4102 Hingston Avenue, Montreal 28, promotes the use of direct mail as an effective means of advertising. Membership 100.

Canadian Industrial Advertisers, 53 Gibson Avenue, Hamilton, promotes industrial advertising. Membership 70, representing major industrial advertisers.

Canadian Weekly Newspapers Association,* 2 Bloor Street East, Toronto 285, represents 454 member newspapers across Canada. Its purpose is to maintain high standards of newspaper writing and publishing, and to promote the business and business interest of members.

Federation of Canadian Advertising & Sales Clubs,* Suite 369, Queen Elizabeth Hotel, Montreal, promotes the use of sound advertising and sales in Canada and acts as a clearing house of information for mem-clubs. Membership 33 clubs representing 6,500 members.

French Weeklies Association of Canada (Hebdos du Canada), Saint-Jean, Quebec, represents 100 French-language newspapers. The association provides services to help develop information and culture in French-speaking Canada.

Graphic Arts Industries Association, 75 Albert Street, Ottawa, advances the interest of printing and allied industries. Membership 553.

Institute of Canadian Advertising,* 8 King Street East, Toronto 210, promotes and protects the interests of advertising agencies and the advancement of the profession. Membership 48; about 40 per cent of agencies in Canada. Member agencies placed about 85 to 90 per cent of all national advertising in 1969.

Magazine Advertising Bureau of Canada,* 11 King Street West, Toronto 105, promotes magazines as an effective advertising medium. Membership 10, representing consumer magazines.

Outdoor Advertising Association of Canada, 250 Bloor Street East, Toronto 285, represents 50 members operating in 181 market areas in Canada. The OAAC awards franchises to companies on a regional basis. Regional sales representatives, or "solicitors," sell national advertising in their franchise areas.

Packaging Association of Canada (Association Canadienne de l'Emballage), 45 Charles Street East, Toronto 189, promotes the study, knowledge and understanding of improved techniques for packaging, packing, shipping and storing of merchandise, and the use and development of graphic arts in the packaging industry. Membership 1,200.

*Periodical Press Association,** 100 University Avenue, Toronto 116, represents three sectors of the print media: Agricultural Press Association of Canada, Canadian Business Press, and the Magazine Publishers Association of Canada. The Periodical Press Association stipulates no capital requirements for agencies seeking franchises to place national advertising in member publications. The disappearance of agricultural magazines over the years has reduced membership in the Agricultural Press Association to two: the *Country Guide* and *Le Bulletin des Agriculteurs. The Magazine Publishers Association of Canada* also has a membership of two: Chatelaine (English and French) and Maclean's (English and French). Although some 400-500 business publications exist in Canada, the circulations of only 50 per cent are audited. Publications audited by the Canadian Circulations Audit Board are eligible for membership in the Canadian Business Press Association. The greater number of publications represented in the C.B.P.A. are produced by Maclean-Hunter Ltd., Southam Business Publications Ltd., and National Business Publications Ltd. To prevent domination of the Association by member publications from these groups, each group is allowed a maximum of five votes at the annual meetings of the C.B.P.A. C.B.P.A. publications come under direct competition from American business publications in seeking advertising dollars, particularly in such specialized fields as oil and mining.

Professional Marketing Research Society, 369 Olivewood Road, Toronto 570, provides a forum for the development and advancement of marketing research and encourages the highest ethical practices. Membership 64.

Radio Sales Bureau, 321 Bloor Street East, Toronto 285, created by the Canadian Association of Broadcasters in 1961, operates independently in the promotion of radio as an effective advertising medium. The Bureau is concerned only with the promotion of national advertising. It represents 114 stations, of which 12 are outside the C.A.B.

Television Bureau of Advertising of Canada, 500 University Avenue, Toronto 101, created by the C.A.B. in 1961 as well, promotes television as an effective advertising medium on a local, regional and national scale. Membership 45 stations.

*Transit Advertising—Trans-Ad Division, Warnock Hersey International Ltd.,** 1220 Yonge Street, Toronto 290, represents 40 member companies in providing advertisers and advertising agencies with research data on transit advertising.

12

Marketing Research and Information in Canada

This chapter is divided into seven sections. The first deals with the history and use of marketing research, and the second with the problems of marketing research peculiar to Canada. This section emphasizes the high cost of such research due to the limitations imposed by relatively small markets in Canada, and the problems caused by bilingualism and by the shortages of skilled research. It also comments on various facets and difficulties connected with industrial marketing research. The third and fourth sections are concerned with data sources and test markets respectively. The fifth comments on the various marketing research agencies and the services they offer. The sixth is concerned with the marketing research department's position in the firm's organization. The last section discusses the future growth of marketing research.

THE HISTORY AND USE OF MARKETING RESEARCH

As in the United States, the need of the advertising world for more and better information about markets led to the start of organized marketing research. In the U.S., the Curtis Publishing Company was the innovator, around 1910.[1] In Canada, marketing research was initiated in 1929 by Cockfield Brown & Co. Ltd., an advertising house formed by the merger of Cockfield Advertising Services and Brown's National Publicity Company. Henry King, their employee, became the first full-time marketing researcher in Canada and William Goforth was later appointed their Director of Research. They had the field to themselves until 1932 when the first independent marketing research agency, Canadian Facts Co. Ltd., began operations.[2]

However, even in 1944 there were only five "research houses" in Canada and less than 2 percent of Canadian companies had research

---

[1] Ralph Star Butler, address quoted in Donald M. Hobart, *Marketing Research Practice* (New York: Ronald Press, 1949) , pp. 3-4.
[2] Henry King, "The Beginning of Marketing Research in Canada," *The Marketer* 2 (Spring/Summer 1966) , pp. 4-5.

units.[3] Since World War II, marketing research has grown very rapidly. By 1967, the number of research houses approached 100,[4] and, as indicated in Table 12-1, 45 percent of Canadian companies had access to marketing research through a formal research unit. This percentage had risen to 57 percent by 1969.

TABLE 12-1 Marketing Research Units in Canadian Companies, 1966 and 1969

		1966		1969
	Total* (%)	Industrial Good Manu- facturers (%)	Consumer Good Manu- facturers (%)	Total (%)
Formal Canadian research departments	12	10	15	12
No formal department, but at least one person assigned to research function	25	18	34	25
Research department in foreign country doing work for Canadian operation	8	11	6	12
No formal marketing research department in foreign country, but at least one person assigned to marketing research for Canada	—	—	—	8
Sub-total	45	39	55	57
No person formally engaged in research	55	61	45	43
	100	100	100	100

SOURCES. Winston H. Mahatoo, "Marketing," Executive 10:4(April 1968), p. 35. Results of a survey sample of 302 companies. Also, Winston H. Mahatoo and A. B. Blakenship, "The Status of Marketing Research in Canada," Canadian Marketer, Winter, 1971, p. 26.

* Total includes other small categories such as retailers and wholesalers, advertising agencies, publishing and broadcasting and others apart from industrial and consumer goods manufacturers.

The comparable figures for the U.S. are much higher: approximately 53 percent of U.S. companies had formal departments in 1963, and if one included the category of "No formal department, but at least one person assigned to research function," then the figure rose to 76 percent.[5] These percentages would almost certainly be higher now.

[3] The research agencies, by their present names, were Canadian Facts Ltd., Elliot Research Corp. Ltd., The Canadian Institute of Public Opinion, A. C. Nielsen Co., and International Surveys Ltd. See Dr. Winston H. Mahatoo, "Marketing Research in Canada," The Analyst, June 1969, p. 47.

[4] Ibid.

[5] D. W. Twedt, A Survey of Marketing Research (Chicago: American Marketing Association, November 1963), p. 13.

The total national marketing research budgets of Canada and the U.S. were both approximately .07 percent of their respective Gross National Products in 1966.[6] Total national Canadian research expenditures, excluding "direct costs" such as personnel and overhead within buyer/user firms, were approximately $41 million in that year. If one includes "direct costs," the Canadian total rises to over $60 million which exceeds 0.1 percent of GNP. By 1969 this figure had risen to $74 million. In 1966 over half of the $41 million was channelled through research houses, syndicated services and advertising agencies. By 1969, the proportion spent on such "outside research" had risen. Of the $74 million some $40 million was "outside spending." Moreover, the share taken by research houses and syndicated services had grown from 66 percent in 1966 to 92 percent in 1969, with a corresponding fall in the share of advertising agencies from 21 to 4 percent respectively in these years.[7] Since a much smaller percentage of Canadian companies do their own research, one could infer that existing Canadian company research departments do a great deal more research on average. In fact, the above inference should be qualified.

It is likely that a large segment of the 76 percent of U.S. companies who have marketing research budgets are smaller companies carrying out small studies, accounting for a relatively small part of the national research budget. Thus the larger U.S. companies doing research would be spending amounts much greater than their Canadian counterparts. Moreover, these U.S. companies also would tend to do more studies which are sophisticated and/or large-scale. In addition, the types of research done in Canada are not as extensive as that done in the U.S. Table 12-2 outlines a comparative picture for selected categories in which a relatively large number of Canadian companies participate. Probably Canadian consumer-goods companies predominate, since a recent study reveals that market assessment activities enjoy a relatively minor role in the operations of Canadian industrial-goods manufacturers. Of 152 companies of the latter type only 34 had at least one person actively involved full-time in market analysis and assessment.[8]

As can be seen, even in 1962 very many more U.S. companies were doing research in important categories than were Canadian companies in 1966. The differences seem especially marked in research on new products. The Canadian figures probably underestimate the extent to which studies on new products, advertising effectiveness and motiva-

---

[6] For Canada — total includes research expenditures by other small categories such as retailers and wholesalers, advertising agencies, publishing and broadcasting and others. For U.S. — projection from A. Blankenship & J. Doule, *Marketing Research Management* (New York: American Management Association, Inc., 1964), pp. 12-13.

[7] Winston H. Mahatoo and A. B. Blankenship, "The Status of Marketing Research in Canada," *The Canadian Marketer*, Winter 1971, p. 26.

[8] Blair Little, Robert G. Cooper and Roger A. More, "Putting the Market into Technology to get Technology into the Market," *Business Quarterly* 37 (Summer 1972), pp. 62-69.

TABLE 12-2 Selected Types of Marketing Research

Per Cent of Companies Doing:	In Canada	In U.S.
	1966	1962
Market share analysis	19	67
Determination of market size and characteristics	18	67
Determination of market potential for new products	17	68
Sales analysis (quotes, territories, etc.)	15	57
New product acceptance and potential	11	63
Business trend studies	9	58
Advertising effectiveness	8	48
Motivation research (opinions, attitudes)	8	30

SOURCES: *For Canada, Mahatoo, "Marketing," p. 3; for U.S., reprinted from D. W. Twedt,* A Survey of Marketing Research *(Chicago: American Marketing Association, November 1963) p. 41.*

tion research are utilized by Canadian companies. Certainly those companies which are U.S. subsidiaries have available to them the benefits of research conducted in the U.S. by their parent corporations.

The increasing use of marketing research is a function of the attitude of business and government administration towards marketing. If the supply of goods and services available in the economy is much below demand and marketing is viewed largely as a matter of transportation, storage and exchange, then the use of research tends to be limited, although some research surely would help in all cases. Even under the perpetual scarcities that exist in the U.S.S.R. and other socialist nations, demand cannot be assumed. For instance, Moscow's Red Giant Shoe Factory "burned as fuel thousands of pairs of rubber boots and shoes that couldn't be sold for lack of demand" in 1962.[9]

However, if the economy is affluent, and the new marketing concept with its emphasis on consumer satisfaction has taken hold, then the volume of marketing research tends to rise. In Canada, the latter set of conditions has existed increasingly in the postwar period, and it has been estimated that total dollar volume of Canadian marketing research has more than tripled from 1962 to 1969.[10]

PROBLEMS OF MARKETING RESEARCH PECULIAR TO CANADA

Some very basic problems impede marketing research in most parts of the world. Examples are illiteracy and the scarcity of appropriate

[9] "Russians Get More Pie," *Business Week*, 20 July 1963, p. 50.
[10] A. B. Blankenship "Canadian Marketing Research has Come of Age," *Canadian Marketer*, Fall 1970, p. 19.

data. Illiteracy tends to breed suspicion and fear of authority. It is difficult to conduct surveys under such circumstances. Lack of appropriate data makes it exceedingly difficult to do realistic forecasting and market planning, or, to give another example, to draw up a probability sample.[11]

Fortunately, Canada has very high levels of literacy and rather good statistical data. Moreover, it has an affluent, high consumption economy. Thus, marketing research here is not stymied by the kind of problems outlined above, which affect such research in most parts of the world. Nevertheless, research in Canada suffers from a number of problems peculiar to its economic, geographic and cultural environment.

High Cost — Market Size

Marketing research is a far more expensive activity in Canada than in the U.S. when measured as a ratio of the cost of research to gross sales. Such gross sales depend, to a major extent, on the size of market segments. Three main factors limit market segments in Canada — small population, wide dispersion of the population and ethnic diversification.

Unfortunately, the sizes of samples required for research surveys (and hence the cost of research) are not a function of the size of the population, but are dependent on the level of statistical efficiency required. Thus, a given level of efficiency dictates the same sample size in Canada and in the U.S. So, one has to have comparable minimum sample sizes in both countries, but gross sales in Canada are much smaller.

Statistics describing Canada's limited market size may be found in Chapter 2 of this book. In brief, the population numbers approximately 22 million people of which some 44 percent are of English origin, 30 percent of French, 6 percent of German, 5 percent of Ukranian, 4 percent of Italian and the rest, numerous smaller groups of diverse nationalities. With the above picture in mind, one can see how costly it can become to research the Canadian market effectively.

Bilingualism

The problems raised by the English-French language segments in particular and other language segments in general, contribute to the high cost of marketing research in Canada.

An operational definition of the French-Canadian market segment for marketing research purposes should result in a segment as homogeneous as possible from a cultural as well as language point of view. With this in mind, a French Canadian can best be defined as a person whose mother tongue is French or whose language of adoption is likely

---

[11] A. Graeme Cranch, "Marketing Research: The Uncommon Thread," *The International Advertiser* 9:2 (April/May, 1968), pp. 11-18.

to be French in the case of those having a mother tongue other than French or English. However, geographical concentration must be taken into account in elaborating marketing policies for specific segments. Thus, the firm which is marketing its products across the country would possibly not treat the small number of French Canadians living in Newfoundland, P.E.I., Nova Scotia, the Prairies and B.C. as separate segments.

However, our definition of French-Canadian market segments would include the northern part of New Brunswick and the eastern and northeastern parts of Ontario which are contiguous to Quebec. In these areas, the number of those whose mother tongue is French exceeded 25 percent of the total population in 1966.

Moreover, of this French-Canadian population, in New Brunswick 51 percent of the males and 56 percent of the females spoke French only, and in Ontario the proportions were 21 percent of the males and 24 percent of the females. In Quebec itself, of the French-Canadian population, 72 percent of the males and 81 percent of the females were unilingual.[12]

Language market segments add to marketing research costs in Canada in three significant ways. For example, as mentioned before, sample size is not related to population size; thus for a given level of accuracy the same size of sample would be required in each language marketing segment as would be required for the whole country if there were no such segments. Hence, comparable surveys cost far more in each segment (in relation to gross sales) than they would for the whole country. In any event, sampling costs are higher in Canada than in the U.S. because of Canada's small markets. (For example, Starch uses the same sample size in Canada and the U.S.) Such cost disadvantages are heightened by Canada's mosaic of different cultures, which often require relatively large sub-samples for specific marketing research, as opposed to the U.S. melting pot[13] which tends to be more homogeneous from the marketing research viewpoint.

The second way that language market segments add to marketing research costs is by making advertising and media research more complicated and expensive. Such research consists mainly of discovering and determining what should and will be said; and then deciding upon and developing the best way or form for communicating these messages. For national Canadian advertisers it is often necessary to build parallel research programmes in both English- and French-speaking Canada.

However, faced with the inevitability of spending money on the development of French advertising and the high cost yet small market inefficiency of English advertising, a decision to produce uniquely Canadian material cannot be taken lightly. The costs of the English-Canadian

[12] Isaiah A. Litvak and Raymond A. Young, "Researching the Canadian Consumer," *The Marketer* 2 (Spring/Summer, 1966) , pp. 6-8.
[13] Bruce Mallen, "How Different is the French Canadian Market," *Business Quarterly* 32 (Autumn 1967) , pp. 59-66.

commercial must be amortized in a market of roughly 15 million people, two-thirds of the Canadian population, compared to the U.S. market of over 200 million people. In fact, cost considerations often lead the advertiser to use U.S. advertising for the English market (making appropriate changes where necessary) and to accept only the cost of French research, adaptation and production.

Third, language market segments add to costs by requiring field interviews to be bilingual, since while interviewing in the English-language segment it is possible to run across a French-speaking respondent, and vice versa. Also, for instance, there are a large number of Italians in Toronto, many of whom speak no English at all.[14] Furthermore, interviewer-briefing sessions must be conducted by individuals who speak all relevant languages well so that all instruction and anticipated problems will be communicated properly to the interviewers. Costs also mount because of the necessity that individuals translating questionnaires into the other language, and coding, classifying and translating responses should not only be completely bilingual, but also conversant with the language of marketing and research.

Skills Available

Marketing research is the tool which the marketer uses in his attempts to identify precisely the physiological and psychological needs which find expression in customer wants; to inspire the conception of those goods or services which will best satisfy these wants; to measure the success of these attempts; and to determine the optimal marketing strategies that can be utilized to attain a high level of customer satisfaction within the constraints set by the objectives of the marketer.

The four main fields in which marketing research expertise is required are measurement, surveys, experiments, and marketing models of both the descriptive and decision-making kind. In all four fields, but particularly in the latter three, Canada is short of available qualified personnel.[15] This is reflected in the lack of specialization and of highly developed marketing research technology compared to the level available in the U.S. Again, this situation is caused by the small, dispersed and diverse Canadian market.

For example, skills such as the practical use of modern decision theory utilizing the Bayesian approach, cluster analysis for market segmentation, advanced multiple regression theory and motivation research techniques are relatively little-used in Canada except by some of the largest companies, most of which are U.S. subsidiaries.

However, the picture is currently improving. There were only five marketing research companies in Canada in 1945; by 1966 there were

[14] Winston H. Mahatoo, *Marketing Research in Canada* (Toronto: Thomas Nelson & Sons [Canada] Ltd., 1968), p. 52.
[15] *Ibid.,* p. 363.

eighty-five such companies. The majority of these companies are Toronto-based: some 82 percent have their head office in Toronto and 9 percent in Montreal. Quite a few have annual billings of at least half a million dollars — for example, Canadian Facts Ltd., Market Facts Canada Ltd., A. C. Nielsen of Canada Ltd. and Daniel Starch Canada Ltd.[16] In addition, there are a number of U.S. research companies which, from time to time, conduct studies in Canada for Canadian manufacturers.[17]

Marketing research companies in Canada currently provide a wide range of services and there are very few companies which can be described as providing specialities in a particular field. Neither is such a development likely to occur in the foreseeable future, particularly because the small size of the population could not support such specialization. Thus, although the number of independent research companies may increase, the generalized nature of their service is not likely to change.

The relatively smaller size of many Canadian manufacturing and service companies means that many cannot afford adequate research. Moreover, when this is combined with the lack of skilled marketing research personnel available, there are two results. First, only 46 percent of Canadian companies reported any marketing research expenditures in 1966. Further, almost three-quarters of these reported using outside marketing research facilities. The three-quarters is a weighted average of the 93 percent of consumer-goods companies and 46 percent of industrial-goods companies incurring market research expenditures.[18]

A second phenomenon caused by the general lack of skilled company personnel is that almost 21 percent of the marketing research dollar volume went through established advertising agencies in 1966. In the U.S., by comparison, reliance on advertising agencies for marketing research had almost disappeared by that time. However, it should be noted that the advertising agencies' percentage share in Canada is dropping rapidly.[19]

The small Canadian market also affects the area of field interviewing. In general, part-time interviewer staffs are employed. In Canada, the concept of permanent interviewers, working out of major centres or regional offices is impractical. The research companies would find the higher fixed overhead expensive and the research buyers are not likely to consider the improved facilities worthwhile in light of the additional cost. In the U.S., numerous independent interviewing companies operate on a regional basis to service the national research organization, thus providing greater specialization and less control and communication problems than in Canada.

[16] Taken from lists prepared by J. N. Milne, formerly Vice-President of Research, Maclaren Advertising Ltd. and by Batten, Barton, Durstine & Osborn, Inc., Toronto, 1966.

[17] See *Financial Post Survey of Markets, 1970* (Toronto: Maclean-Hunter Ltd., 1970), pp. 29-31, for a listing of well-known marketing research houses in Canada and the services they provide.

[18] Mahatoo, *Marketing Research in Canada*, pp. 15-16.

[19] *Ibid.*, p. 16 and source note 2, Table 12-1.

SECONDARY DATA SOURCES

Secondary data sources can be of great use to the marketing researcher. A search of such sources is almost always helpful in assisting the researcher to formulate his own research plans, and in some cases, may make primary research unnecessary. Government data sources are very important; these are detailed in Chapter 6.

Media

There are a number of Canadian periodicals which deal specifically with marketing topics. Some are devoted entirely to such subjects. The list given in Table 12-3 below is not exhaustive, but covers the principal publications. Also, the Maclean Hunter Publishing Company produces a number of publications covering a range of industries.

TABLE 12-3 Selected List of Canadian Periodicals Dealing Wholly or Partly with Marketing Topics

The Business Quarterly
Canadian Business
Canadian Journal of Economics
Canadian Journal of Farm Economics
Canadian Journal of Political Science
Canadian Journal of Sociology and Anthropology
Canadian Grocer
Executive
Financial Times
Financial Post
Financial Post Survey of Markets
Industrial Canada
The Marketer
Marketing Magazine
Monthly Bank Newsletter published by
    various chartered banks
Sales Promotion
Western Business and Industry

Associations

A number of trade associations issue publications. Some of the important ones concerning marketing research are given in Table 12-4. In addition, a number of industry associations — for instance, the Canadian Textile Institute — publish industry data for their members.

Other

There are a number of other sources of useful secondary data. First and foremost for locating such data are the indexing services. In particular, the Canadian Periodicals Index and the Maclean-Hunter

TABLE 12-4 Selected List of Associations and their Reports of Use to Marketing Researchers

Audit Bureau of Circulations	Measures newspaper circulation by city and retail trading zone.
B.B.M. Bureau of Measurement	Television and radio stations and area circulation and audience reports.
Canadian Advertising Research Foundation	On member request, will evaluate, assess and plan research projects and analyze findings.
Canadian Advertising Media Rates and Data	Monthly publication of Maclean Hunter Publishing Company.
The Canadian Daily Newspaper Publishers Association	Issues Annual Consumer Survey of consumer buying habits and brand preferences based on sample of 40,000 respondents. Also issues market data manual covering towns where daily newspapers are published.
The Canadian Export Association	Various publications.
The Canadian Import Association	Various publications.
The Canadian Manufacturers Association	Various publications.

Bibliography of marketing research studies, companies and consultants are useful. More selective sources are listed in *A Basic Bibliography on Marketing in Canada*, by Mallen and Litvak[20], and a readings book of articles compiled by these two authors.[21]

TEST MARKETS

There is an insufficient number of suitable test cities in Canada. This stems from the fact that in many provinces there are only one or two major cities and a hinterland dotted with rather small towns. This is the pattern throughout British Columbia and the Prairie provinces although it is less true of eastern Canada. Furthermore, as pointed out earlier, the Canadian market is relatively small and has wide regional and cultural differences. Such differences are not combined in any comparatively small test cities.

The cities which are probably most used for testing are London, Peterborough and Sherbrooke, the first two being representative of much of Ontario, and the latter of Quebec.[22] Other cities used less

[20] Bruce E. Mallen and Isaiah A. Litvak, *A Basic Bibliography on Marketing in Canada* (U.S.A.: American Marketing Association Bibliography Series No. 13, 1967).

[21] Bruce E. Mallen and Isaiah A. Litvak, *Marketing: Canada* 2nd ed. (Toronto: McGraw-Hill Book Company of Canada Limited, 1968).

[22] Dominion Bureau of Statistics, *Census*, Nos. 92-601ff, 93-601ff, 99-601ff, (Ottawa: Queen's Printer).

extensively are Calgary, Kingston, Kitchener-Waterloo, North Bay, St. Catharines, Regina and Sudbury.

Because of their limited number, there is the danger of the overextensive use of the same test cities, which creates the possibility that the consumer environment in those cities is comparatively insensitized by exposure to heavy promotional expenditures and frequent new product innovations. Consequently, the danger exists of test results being somewhat biased. Also as a result of the limited number of good test cities, a manufacturer may find that a test of a different brand of a similar product is in progress at the same time. Under such circumstances, it is probably best to test coincidentally in the same city plus conducting a test in "less suitable cities." This would yield a "control group" result as a check on the unknown bias in the results of the coincidental testing programme.

Costs of market tests do not vary with market size, but tend to vary with market diversity. Thus, for the same standard of validity and precision in market tests, Canada's heterogeneous market necessitates relatively high test expenditures compared to those in the U.S. All too often the consequence of this is that Canadian marketers try to reduce test costs.[23] Since tests are at best a rather crude process, such cost cutting is usually a false economy.

In conclusion, one can only say that an explicit weighing of rewards against test costs is particularly important in Canada where a small and heterogeneous market gives rise to marginal justification for many test applications.

MARKETING RESEARCH AGENCIES

A listing of well known marketing research companies and the main services they provide is prepared annually by the Financial Post.[24] Some of the largest such companies are Canadian Facts Co. Ltd., Daniel Starch Canada Ltd., International Surveys Ltd., Market Facts Canada Ltd., and A. C. Nielsen of Canada Ltd.

There are also several marketing consulting firms in Canada. Some of the better-known ones are P. S. Ross and Partners, Stevenson and Kellogg Ltd., The Thorne Group Ltd., Urwick Currie Ltd., Woods Gordon and Co., Kates, Peat, Marwick & Co. and Bruce Mallen and Associates Inc.

Moreover, certain special services are offered by specific groups. For instance, the Broadcast division of A. C. Nielson Co. of Canada issues a Broadcast Index, a Television Index and a Coverage Service. All of these report radio and television coverage.

Further, there are a number of syndicated market services. This refers to those companies which collect data about brand share, buying

[23] Joseph N. Fry, "Market Testing in Canada," *Business Quarterly* 27 (Spring 1962) , pp. 53-56.
[24] See footnote 17.

habits, sizes purchased and general product movement for sale to inter-ested buyers. These companies usually employ panels (fixed samples) which provide the relevant information at regular intervals. Some of the leading houses run such "panels." For example, the Nielsen Retail Index services are store audit services obtained from panels whose members are dealers (retail outlets). Consumer Panel of Canada maintains a relatively large consumer purchase panel, and Market Facts Ltd. runs a consumer mails panel division which is a sizable national sample of households that have agreed to respond to mail questionnaires and product tests. More-over, the School of Business Administration, at the University of Western Ontario has recently established a Consumer Research Laboratory which is initially utilizing a panel of 600 households from London, Ontario The panel is available to government and business organizations who wish to initiate their own research or to participate jointly with the business school.[25]

Other institutions and their services of importance to marketing researchers were named in Table 12-4 above in connection with detailing sources of secondary data. In addition, the Consumer Association of Can-ada (CAC) can be of help to marketing researchers. The CAC has 22,-000 members,[26] and receives and prints a significant amount of consumer information in its by-monthly magazine the *Canadian Consumer* and *Le Consommateur Canadienne*. Further, it conducts special studies and na-tional surveys on consumers and goods from time to time.

A new environmental force on the marketing research scene in Canada is the federal government's Department of Consumer and Cor-porate Affairs (CCA) headed by the Right Honourable Herbert Gray.[27]

ORGANIZATION OF THE MARKETING RESEARCH FUNCTION

Marketing research is problem and information-oriented re-search. Because of the economic costs and the lack of skilled personnel, most Canadian business organizations, as mentioned before, have not found it feasible to maintain sizable marketing research units and have relied heavily on the research facilities of their advertising agencies and/or on outside research companies. Nevertheless, as was shown in Table 12-1, 12 percent of Canadian companies had formal marketing research departments and another 25 percent had no formal department, but at least one person assigned to this research function. In addition, a further 20 percent had marketing research personnel in a foreign country doing work for the Canadian operation. One estimate is that there are 1,357 people employed in marketing research in buyer/user firms and another 1,300 such people employed by research firms and consultants, plus an additional 1,500 field workers.[28]

[25] *Business Quarterly* 34 (Autumn 1969), p. 71.
[26] *Canadian Consumer* 6:6 (May/June 1969), p. 220.
[27] See pp. 129-138.
[28] See Table 12-1.

An index of company policy and attitude to marketing research is found in the title assigned to the person in charge of marketing research activities and the person to whom he reports. Among the companies doing some kind of research in 1966, slightly more than one fourth assigned specific research titles such as Marketing Research Director, Manager, Supervisor or Analyst to these personnel. Approximately another quarter of the marketing research heads carried marketing titles, yet another quarter had sales or advertising titles and the remainder were senior management executives. By 1969, about 40 percent were assigned specific research titles while only 11 percent carried sales or advertising titles.

Further, in over 50 percent of the cases, the marketing research head reported to the President, Vice-President or General Manager,[29] which gives some indication of the acceptance that marketing research has won.

The 1969 and 1967 survey results mentioned above broadly validated an earlier study done in 1964.[30] Another more recent study, but with a smaller sample, indicated that there has been a shift from smaller to larger formal marketing research departments and an extension of the areas in which more sophisticated work is being performed. Thus the importance of the marketing research function in the organization would appear to be rising.[31]

The actual organization within the marketing research department can basically be developed in three ways: by brand/product orientation, by specialist orientation, or by a mix of these two. Brand/product orientation tends to make the market researcher part of that brand/product's marketing team and his work tends to have greater "actionability." The advantage of the specialist orientation is that it enables the department to develop a staff of experts in many different areas of research. This latter type of department involves a higher cost and can only be afforded by large multi-product companies.

THE FUTURE OF MARKETING RESEARCH IN CANADA

"Consumerism" has been launched and is being energetically supported by the activities of the Department of Corporate and Consumer Affairs and its affiliated organizations like the Canadian Consumer

---

[29] Mahatoo, *Marketing Research in Canada,* pp. 17-19. See also Table 12-1, source 2.

[30] Isaiah A. Litvak and Raymond A. Young, "Researching the Canadian Consumer," *The Marketer* 2 (Spring/Summer 1966) , pp. 8-9, and the same authors, "Marketing Research by U.S. subsidiaries — Domestic or Imported," *Business Quarterly* 30 (Summer 1965) , pp. 62-69.

[31] Earl Fixman, *The Marketing Research Function — A Model Measuring Importance,* Unpublished M.B.A. research paper (Montreal: Sir George Williams University, 1 March 1971) .

Council, by independent bodies such as the Consumer Association of Canada and by the response of manufacturers and advertisers to CCA's "information releases."[32] Certainly the growth in "consumerism" is going to increase the total flow of market information and this in turn is very likely to increase the quantity and quality of marketing research done in Canada in the future.

Moreover, acceptance and practical use of the new marketing concept is growing in Canada. This has brought about more forward planning of market operations, more extended use of the product or brand manager system of organization, the "marketing mix" concept, product planning and development, and increasing use of marketing research. All these developments, often seemingly isolated, are in fact integrally related; they flow from acceptance of the marketing point of view which starts with consumer needs and works back to the development of products, services, distribution channels, prices and promotional programmes designed to meet those needs.

Sound planning procedures require an adequate information base This has come to be realized in the U.S. and in Canada. Concomitantly, the concept of marketing research is broadening to include the provision of all information for decision-making by the marketing manager. This concept has already invaded Canadian university curriculums.[33] The marketing man, then, must be skilled in the use of marketing research as an inherently important part of his job; and in marketing research and information-gathering "pay-offs" which are reflected in better decisions, fewer mistakes and reduced risk.

Canada is already very much in the computer age. This is acting as a further impetus to the growth of marketing research. Certainly much of the statistical work connected with sales and market forecasting is even now computerized in many of the larger Canadian companies. Also, some interesting market model building has started to take place.

Most Canadian companies are relatively small, and to maintain "in company" fully-staffed marketing research units is a fairly expensive proposition. The most probable development is likely to be a continuation of the existing trend whereby the Canadian user has a small company marketing research unit, which farms out its bigger and more complex projects to outside research firms or advertising agencies who have in-house research facilities.[34] Two-thirds of the existing marketing research agencies and units in Canada have been established in the 1960's.[35] There is every possibility that more such units will come into

---

[32] Courtney Tower, "Q: Who needs Ralph Nader?, A: Canada," *Maclean's*, 83:4 (April 1970) , p. 1.

[33] For instance, the course description of the M.B.A. seminar on "Marketing Research and Information Systems" at Sir George Williams University, Montreal, explicitly states this concept.

[34] See footnote 17.

[35] Ralph Star Butler, address quoted in Donald M. Hobart, *Marketing Research Practice* (New York: Ronald Press, 1949) pp. 3-4.

operation in the near future; and that the quality and size of the units will grow. In the past it appears that most marketing research consisted of sales and market studies. One can expect that in the future, as Canadian expertise in the profession grows, more qualitative types of studies, such as opinion and attitude surveys, image studies, advertising pre- and post-tests and concept testing, will increase. Such changes in emphasis will result, for example, in more product, attitude and advertising research.

It may be mentioned that the major Canadian chartered banks whose asset sizes compare favourably with most of the largest companies in the U.S., have commenced in 1968–70 to build very sizable marketing and marketing research departments. Some of the bigger industrial companies are also trying to build expertise in the field. This should tend to augment the quantity and improve the quality of marketing research in Canada.

In conclusion, however, it must be restated that although rapid growth of the Canadian marketing research industry is strongly indicated, it should not be expected that the industry will reach the level attained in the U.S., mainly because of the limitations imposed by the size of the Canadian market and, on average, the smaller size of company. The major constraint in the past and in the future will always be the cost of research in Canada as compared to the possible sales benefits in a basically small and fractured market.

Epilogue

Canada — one of the world's ten largest national economies with its GNP of over $100 billion and with (usually) the world's second highest living standard — possesses certain indigenous characteristics — physical, economic, legal, ethical, political, social, and psychological — which distinguish it from other countries. These differences are reflected by the Canadian market.

The Canadian consumer and industrial markets have their own unique socio-economic characteristics. Population, income, expenditure, occupational and sales profiles differ markedly from region to region. Canada has never been a "melting pot" to the same degree as the United States. Ethnic groups, particularly the French, have resisted integration with other Canadians and, if present social dynamics are a good indication of the future, will continue to do so with increasing vigour.

There is a rising sense of nationhood in this country which is taking two forms simultaneously: Canadians in general are becoming aware of themselves as citizens of a distinct nation, separate and different from the United States. There is definite uneasiness about American ownership of a large segment of Canadian industry, an uneasiness which is beginning to express itself in new attitudes, opinions and even legislation with regard to American companies, products, promotion and media.

At the same time that Canadians are reacting to what many feel is American domination of their culture, French-Canadians are reacting in a similar fashion to a perceived domination of their culture by English-Canadians. The province of Quebec is spearheading this movement. French-Canadians seek to become more directly involved in commerce and industry: there is a modern industrial revolution in Quebec. This growing commercial-mindedness is also beginning to express itself in new attitudes, opinions and legislation not only with regard to American institutions, but towards English-Canadian institutions as well.

These patterns of socio-economic development have profound implications for Canadian marketing. Selling and promotional appeals, for example, must be specially adapted for useful results; and

This epilogue is adapted from Isaiah A. Litvak and Bruce E. Mallen, *Marketing: Canada* (Toronto: McGraw-Hill Book Company of Canada, 1964), pp. xi-xii.

compensation of the sales force is made more difficult because of the great differences in potential between areas.

The population is highly concentrated along a thin line close to the U.S. border, some 4,000 miles in length and 100 miles in width. Seven hundred miles of this "life-line" from Windsor, Ontario, to Quebec City, Quebec, includes a tremendous share of the country's population, and an even greater share of its income.

The geographical distribution of the market intensifies the already complex problems created by the cultural differences. Marketing costs, accounting for half of the value of the goods economy, are in general higher than those in the United States; the field force is harder to control and communicate with; travelling costs are greater; more physical distribution problems are involved, and middlemen take on a greater importance, particularly in the more isolated areas; there is a tendency for less price uniformity; and marketing research, advertising and promotion are relatively more expensive.

There are other problems which Canadian conditions present to the marketing man. For example, the colder weather affects product specifications and packaging considerations.

All these cultural, economic and physical patterns have tended to divide the country into five major regions – the lower-income and less populated Atlantic provinces of Newfoundland, Nova Scotia, New Brunswick, and Prince Edward Island; the French province of Quebec; the highest-income, most industrialized and most populated province of Ontario; the agricultural prairie provinces of Manitoba, Saskatchewan and Alberta; and the Pacific province of British Columbia.

The Canadian legal environment also contributes to the unique framework for marketing in this country. Legislation relating to patents, industrial design, pricing and discounts, product specifications, advertising and selling appeal, media, retailing, wholesaling, etc, all plays a role.

Retailing in this country as in the United States, is in a constant state of ferment. Private brands, discounters, shopping hours, vending, and growth of mass retailers, superimposed upon the unique background of a very strong department store system, can complicate marketing channel decisions.

International marketing is relatively much more important in Canada than in the United States. Exports account for approximately 20 percent of the Canadian GNP, and many industries are almost completely dependent upon foreign markets for their survival.

Canada *is* different. In all aspects of marketing this book has pointed out the differences. Peculiar Canadian marketing phenomena were seen in the consumer market, the industrial market, marketing research, product development, pricing legislation, retailing, personal selling, advertising and sales promotion, and international marketing. It is hoped that this book has provided the student and businessman with an appreciation of these Canadian marketing differences and the need to adjust marketing strategy to this environment.

INDEX